Pseudo-Skylax's

PERIPLOUS

The *Periplous* or 'circumnavigation' preserved under the name of Skylax of Karyanda is in fact the work of an unknown author of the fourth century BC.

This is the first full edition of the *Periplous* for over 150 years, and includes a newly revised Greek text and specially produced maps. The text is made accessible to an English-speaking audience for the first time through a complete translation. With its relatively limited vocabulary and simple, yet varied, syntax, the *Periplous* will also provide a useful text for those moving beyond the elementary study of ancient Greek.

Graham Shipley is Professor of Ancient History at the University of Leicester. He is a Fellow of the Society of Antiquaries of London, the Royal Historical Society, and the Royal Geographical Society and a former chair of the Council of University Classical Departments.

Pseudo-Skylax's

PERIPLOUS

The Circumnavigation of the Inhabited World

Text, Translation and Commentary

Graham Shipley

BRISTOL
PHOENIX
PRESS

Cover image: map of Greece by Benedetto Bordone, *Isolario* (1528).
Reproduced with the kind permission of the Map Collection, The
University of Melbourne Library

First published in 2011 by
Bristol Phoenix Press
an imprint of The Exeter Press
Reed Hall, Streatham Drive
Exeter, Devon, EX4 4QR

www.exeterpress.co.uk

Arts & Humanities
Research Council

British Library Cataloguing in Publication Data
A catalogue record for this book is available
from the British Library.

Paperback ISBN: 978 1 904675 83 9
Hardback ISBN: 978 1 904675 82 2

Printed in Great Britain by CPI Antony Rowe

CONTENTS

ILLUSTRATIONS

PREFACE

THIS study of Pseudo-Skylax offers the first full revision of the complete Greek text since 1878 and the only complete English translation published to date.* It reinterprets this intriguing but neglected fourth-century BC text in the light of recent work on Greek history, archaeology, and geographical writings, and aims to make it more widely available not only to classicists and ancient historians but also to readers in fields such as geography, archaeology, and modern history, as well as non-specialists with an interest in ancient geography or maritime history. The text, with its limited vocabulary and uncomplicated syntax, should also prove stimulating to those learning Greek, especially if studying ancient history.

In mapping out a new interpretation of a text about the whole of the Greek world that has not been synoptically treated since the nineteenth century, an editor often finds himself led by the evidence and by the availability or otherwise of recent research on particular regions. I ask the reader's indulgence if she finds that the nature of the Commentary varies unduly, for example where topographical problems remain unresolved (as in NW Africa) or where a passage has a particular bearing on fundamental questions about the nature of the work (as in the western Mediterranean). Within the confines of a modest volume, it is impossible to explore fully all the problems of the text and its historical background.

For this edition, subsections have been created within Müller's now standard numeration. In the Commentary, modern locations are often taken silently from the *Barrington Atlas* (Talbert 2000). Foundation dates, for the most part, are noted only if they are later than c.520 BC, the date of the journey of Skylax of Karyanda, to whom the *periplous* is falsely attributed, or have an Athenian connection. In the translation and in the lemmata of the commentary, ancient Greek place-names are transliterated in a form close to the original (e.g. Athenai); elsewhere conventional forms are sometimes used (e.g. Athens). In names and words transliterated from Greek, macrons are used only on the rare occasions when it seemed necessary to indicate eta and omega (e.g. Pontiōn).

---

* Though cf. Warmington 1934, 134–41 (extracts); Allain 1977, 89–132 (unpublished).

The volume is dedicated to my mother and to the memory of my father, who first inspired in me a love of maps.

Acknowledgements

This research could not have been completed without generous grants from the Loeb Classical Library Foundation (2006) and from the Arts and Humanities Research Council under its Research Leave Scheme (2009). These allowed me to extend two periods of study leave granted by the University of Leicester (I thank colleagues in the School of Archaeology and Ancient History for shouldering additional burdens during my absences). Simultaneous paperback publication was made possible by a Publication Grant from the M. Aylwin Cotton Foundation (2007).

The original commission for Bristol Phoenix Press was due to the late John Betts, who is greatly missed. Production of the volume owes much to his colleagues Simon Baker and Anna Henderson. I thank the Press's anonymous readers for their positive reports, and Sara Bryant for her eagle-eyed copy-editing.

The Introduction records my debts to both predecessors and colleagues. It would be invidious to distinguish among the remaining acknowledgements. Space forbids a detailed account of the ways in which colleagues, students (both present and former), and others helped with expert advice, feedback on drafts, suggestions about translation, questions, guidance on modern languages, comments on presentation, responses to seminar papers, references, copies of publications, support, and hospitality—many at a level of generosity I am unable to describe adequately here. On that basis, nevertheless, I take this opportunity to thank Colin Adams, Michael Allain, Zosia Archibald, Alexander Arenz, Kalliopi Baika, Dominic Berry, James Bide-Thomas, David Blackman, Kai Brodersen, Veronica Bucciantini, Duncan Campbell, Gordon R. Campbell, Carlos Cañete, Chris Carey, Arnold Cassola, Paola Ceccarelli, Katherine Clarke, Christy Constantakopoulou, Patrick Counillon, Elly Cowan, Enrico Dal Lago, Mike Edwards, James Ermatinger, Pernille Flensted-Jensen, Lin Foxhall, Hans-Joachim Gehrke, Olivier Gengler, Klaus Geus, Guðmundur Halldórsson, Mogens Herman Hansen, Kim Harman, Rod Heikell, Terry Hopkinson, Simon Hornblower, Richard Hunter, Lindsay Judson, Philip Kay, Konrad Kinzl, Bertil Koch, Anna Leone, Morgane L'Homme, Benedict Lowe, Marcello Lupi, Céline Marquaille-Telliez, David Mattingly, Andy Merrills, Fergus Millar, Paul Millett, Lynette Mitchell, Stephen Mitchell, Astrid Möller, Marie-Victoire Népote,

Reviel Netz, Oliver Nicholson, Thomas Heine Nielsen, Julia Nikolaus, Graham Oliver, Robin Osborne, Jordan Page, Grant Parker, John Patterson, Christopher Pelling, Dominic Perry, Thomas Porathe, Jonathan Prag, Philomen Probert, Marcella Raiconi, Michael Rathmann, Michael Reeve, Gary Reger, Peter Rhodes, Amy Richardson, Duane W. Roller, James Romm, Anne Sackett, Francesca Sardi, Bärbel Schäfer, Dirk Schnurbusch, Sarah Scott, Michaela Šenková, Alan Shapiro, Mrs K. V. Shipley, Richard Talbert, Gocha Tsetskhladze, Jaime Vives-Ferrándiz, James Whitley, Roger and Deborah Whittaker, Nick Wilshere, Nigel Wilson, Roger Wilson, and Mark Woolmer. I apologize for any omissions. None of the above is responsible for the views advanced in the book; I hope none need feel debarred from reviewing it.

Research, editing, and typography were facilitated in no small measure by Victor Gaultney and Ralph Hancock (fonts); John Waś (editing queries); the staffs of AVS Print, Bookshop, IT Services, the Library, and the Research Office (especially Juliet Bailey) at the University of Leicester, and the administrative staff of the School of Archaeology and Ancient History (especially Rachel Bown, Sharon North); and the library staffs of the Institute of Classical Studies (Sue Willetts and colleagues), Bibliothèque Nationale de France (Christian Förstel, Marie-Pierre Laffitte), and British School at Athens (Penny Wilson-Zarganis, Sandra Pepelasi). Google Earth proved an invaluable resource in the later stages of research.

The maps were drawn by Duncan Campbell; some are based on originals by Mark Collins and Deborah Miles-Williams.

The inspiration of the HCC, JRRT, LT, and QG is acknowledged.

My greatest debt is to my family for their love and support.

University of Leicester, April 2011   D.G.J.S.

SYMBOLS AND SPECIAL ABBREVIATIONS

Unless listed here, abbreviations of ancient authors and works follow *OCD*³.
Details of works cited here by author and date are in the Bibliography.

§, §§	section(s) of Pseudo-Skylax, when necessary for clarity
⟨ ⟩	text added by a modern editor
[ ]	(in §§104–6 only) text restored where MS is damaged; (elsewhere) MS text that is deemed to be misplaced or erroneous
[—]	lacuna (text omitted in MS and not reconstructed here)
{ }	MS text deemed to be an addition to the original work
†	corrupt word († . . . † encloses two or more words)

2nd Messenian Congress	Πρακτικὰ τοῦ Βʹ τοπικοῦ συνεδρίου μεσσηνιακῶν σπουδῶν (Athinai)
A./Allain	Allain 1977
anc.	ancient
Ar	archaic
Barr.	*Barrington Atlas* (Talbert 2000)
Barr. Dir.	*Map-by-map Directory* (to *Barr.*)
C.	(*a*) Cape
	(*b*) Counillon 2004, with page no. (e.g. 'C. 123'), in commentary on §§67–92
	(*c*) Counillon (in *apparatus criticus*), without page no.; specifically, for §§17–26, Counillon 2007b; for §47, Counillon 2001a; for §48, Counillon 2001b; for §§67–92, Counillon 2004
C1, C2, . . .	centuries (ʙᴄ unless 'ᴀᴅ' specified); suffixes 'f/s' = 1st/2nd halves (e.g. C5s), 'e/m/l' = early/middle/late (e.g. C3e), 'a/b/c/d' = quarter-centuries (e.g. C3a)
Cary	Cary 1949
Cl	Classical
Cluv.	Cluverius 1624
Comm.	commentary in this volume
D	manuscript Parisinus Supplément grec 443
del.	deleted by (*delevit*)
Desanges	Desanges 1978
Diod.	Diodoros of Sicily
Dion. Kall.	Dionysios son of Kalliphon
Dion. Peri.	Dionysios Periegetes
Eux.	see Ps.-Arr. *Eux.*, below
f.	formerly
F, FF	(no full point) fragment(s) in *FGrH*

F.	Fabricius 1878
F.¹	Fabricius 1848
FGrH	Jacoby 1923–58
FHG	C. W. L. Müller 1841–70
fr., frs	fragment; fragments (but 'F' in *FGrH* citations)
G.	Gronovius 1700
GGM	C. W. L. Müller 1855–61
Hekat.	Hekataios
Hl	hellenistic
I.	island
IG	*Inscriptiones Graecae*
Is.	islands
Inv.	M. H. Hansen and Nielsen 2004 (*Inv.* 234 = page no.; *Inv.* 123 = *polis* number)
K./Klausen	Klausen 1831
l.	left
L.	(*a*) Lake (*b*) in commentary on §§104–12 and in *apparatus criticus,* Lipiński 2003
Lat.	Latin
LSJ	Liddell and Scott 1968
m	codex Monacensis Graecus 566
M./Müller	*GGM* i (1855); M.ᶜ = commentary; M.ᵗ = Greek text; M.ᵗʳ = translation)
mod.	modern
om.	omitted by (*omisit*)
P.	Peretti
Pliny	Pliny the Elder, *Natural History*
PS	Pseudo-Skylax
Ps.-Arr. *Eux.*	anonymous (pseudo-Arrianic) *Periplous of the Black Sea* (*Periplus Ponti Euxini*) (*GGM* vol. i, pp. cxv–cxxii, cxliv–cxlv, 402–23; *FHG* vol. v, pp. xix–xxii)
r.	(*a*) right (*b*) before a date: reigned, ruled
R	(no full point) Roman
R.	River
S.	(in *apparatus criticus*) Shipley
Salm.	Salmasius (Saumaise)
SK	Skylax of Karyanda (*FGrH* 709 and 1000)
st.	*stadia* (Gr. *stadia* or *stadioi*)
Stad.	anonymous *Stadiasmos* or *Periplous of the Great Sea* ('Periplus Maris Magni' in Thesaurus Linguae Graecae), Roman period (*GGM* vol. i, cxxiii–cxxviii, cxlv, 427–514)
*Syll.*³	Dittenberger 1915–24
trad.	traditional(ly)
V.	Vossius 1639

Greek numerals

α	1	ι	10	ρ	100
β	2	κ	20	σ	200
γ	3	λ	30	τ	300
δ	4	μ	40	υ	400
ε	5	ν	50	φ	500
ϝ	6	ξ	60	χ	600
ζ	7	ο	70	ψ	700
η	8	π	80	ω	800
θ	9	ϙ	90	ϡ	900

There is no zero. Numbers from 1 to 999 are followed by ´ (ε´ = 5). Larger ones are preceded by ͵ (͵ε = 5,000). Symbols are combined thus: ρια´ = 111; ͵βτ´ = 2,300.

Digamma (ϝ), qoppa (ϙ), and sampi (ϡ) were obsolete in some regional Greek scripts, including Attic, by the late classical period, but remained in use as numerals.

INTRODUCTION[1]

I. The text

The treatise known as the *Periplous* of Pseudo-Skylax (hereinafter Ps.-Skylax or PS)—of which this is the first English edition—survives on 44 pages of a 700-year-old codex (a manuscript bound in book form) in the Bibliothèque Nationale in Paris. The manuscript as a whole comprises a set of geographical texts assembled by Markianos of Herakleia, probably in the sixth century AD (Marcotte 2000, xix–xx),[2] and is cited as **D** in recent scholarship on the ancient Greek geographers. (Three later copies of D, one of which omits the *Periplous*, have no independent authority.)[3] D is thought to have been made in southern Italy.

The work describes the coasts of the Mediterranean and Black Sea, beginning at Gibraltar and proceeding clockwise to return to the same place (and a little way into the Atlantic). An introductory note calls the work Σκύλακος Καρυανδέως περίπλους τῆς οἰκουμένης, 'Skylax of Karyanda's circumnavigation of the inhabited world'. A few lines later we find the same information in a fuller form:

> Σκύλακος Καρυανδέως περίπλους τῆς θαλάσσης τῆς οἰκουμένης Εὐρώπης καὶ Ἀσίας καὶ Λιβύης, καὶ ὅσα καὶ ὁποῖα ἔθνη ἕκαστα, ἑξῆς καὶ χῶραι καὶ λιμένες καὶ ποταμοὶ καὶ ὅσα μήκη τῶν πλῶν, καὶ αἱ νῆσοι αἱ ἑπτὰ αἱ οἰκούμεναι, καθότι ἑκάστη κεῖται τῆς ἠπείρου.

> Skylax of Karyanda's circumnavigation of the sea of the *oikoumenē* (inhabited part) of Europe and Asia and Libyē, and the number and nature of each of the *ethnē* (communities), and successively the lands and harbours and rivers and how great (are) the lengths of the voyages, and the seven islands that are inhabited, according as each lies in relation to the mainland.

The sense of the words immediately after the opening depends

---

[1] These pages partly draw on papers given at San Diego, Freiburg im Breisgau (2007); Chicago, Leicester, Durham (2008); Manchester (2009); and Cardiff and Berlin (2010). Some ideas are also explored in Shipley 2008; 2010; under review.

[2] Parisinus supplément grec 443 (late 13th cent.).

[3] These are (1) *m* (c.1481–1508), now in Munich (Monacensis gr. 566), downloadable from the Bayerische Staatsbibliothek website; (2) *v*, of similar date and provenance, copied from D and *m*, now in Rome (Palatinus Vaticanus gr. 142); (3) *Scal.*, a selection from D made by Joseph Scaliger in c.1570, now in Leiden (Leidensis Scaligeranus 32), which omits PS. See Marcotte lxxxiv–lxxxvii.

Facsimile of part of p. 92 of the MS (after Poulain de Bossay). Scale c.5 : 6.

crucially on how they are punctuated. They could mean 'of the sea, the *oikoumenē*, Europe, Asia, and Libyē'; or 'of the inhabited sea, Europe, Asia, and Libyē'; or 'of the inhabited sea of Europe and Asia and Libyē'. The final twelve words are partly nonsense (there are many more inhabited islands than seven), and they contradict the ending of the work, where twenty islands are listed (in a passage that is certainly a later addition). The whole extract above must be later than the original work; the shorter title may be a summary of this note. So we do not know the original name of the work.

Notoriously one of the most corrupt classical texts, the *periplous* contains errors of three main kinds.

(*a*) Errors due to miscopying. These include spellings that represent post-classical forms of names (e.g. Mitylene, 97), late pronunciation (e.g. Aichinades for Echinades, 34. 3), or late medieval copyists' habits (e.g. innumerable superfluous iota subscripts). At some stage the text must have been copied by someone insufficiently skilled to rectify the mistakes; the possibility should be borne in mind that the copy from which they were working was badly damaged or worn. Some mistakes are plausibly attributed to confusion between the uncial forms of Greek letters used in the early medieval period; e.g. ΘΥΡΡΕΙΟΝ (Thyrrheion) became ΟΥΡΙΤΟΝ (Ouriton) at 34. 1 (Marcotte 1985, 255). It would therefore be wrong to assume that many of this class of errors are the fault of the copyist of the surviving MS. Photocopies or half-tones (e.g. Diller 1952, pl. before p. 33) do not convey how careful a worker he was (assuming he was male); only personal inspection of the codex reveals it, though one can gain a fair impression from the accurate facsimile in Poulain de Bossay 1864, following his p. 596 (see illustration, p. 2 above). The copyist, however, was clearly unqualified to correct all, if any, of the errors he encountered.

(b) 'Improvements' by ancient and modern editors, such as the headings at the start of sections, where were certainly added to the original text (see e.g. Counillon 2004, 38–9). (Some of these are inept, e.g. 26. 1 'Illyrioi' instead of 'Taulantioi'.)

(c) Errors that may have been in the original, such as the misplacing of the description of the Lesser Syrtis at 110. 8–9 (instead of before 110. 6) and the account of the area between *Ceuta* and *Tangier* at 112. 4 (instead of 111. 6). Some 'errors' of this kind seem trivial, such as the occasional departure from correct coastal sequence within a locality (e.g. at Corinth).[4] Others exist largely in the minds of editors.

Clearly there will often be room for debate about whether a passage has been transmitted correctly and, if not, in which category the error belongs and how it is to be dealt with. Errors of type (c) may be detected but should not be corrected. Some editors are overly interventionist: Müller, for example, moves several short passages to new locations (e.g. from §2 to §1) or deletes words as 'glosses' deriving from marginal notes (e.g. at 111. 6), without considering alternative explanations. The present edition broadly follows Counillon's principle of adhering as closely as possible to the manuscript, though on occasion I have emended where he might not.

The Greek text printed here deliberately follows, in many respects, the inconsistencies of the manuscript: variation between Attic and non-Attic spelling, presence or absence of elision (e.g. δέ/δ'), use or omission of paragogic nu (ἐστί/ἐστίν), and so on. To standardize these would involve assumptions about the original text that are unwarranted in the absence of alternative, independent manuscripts. In particular, the rendering of numerals—which in D are sometimes spelled out and sometimes appear as single letters (see table on p. ix)—has been left inconsistent (in the text and translation) for the same reason.

Some features of the text, however, have been standardized, usually silently. Superfluous iota subscripts are rarely noted. Abbreviations and ligatures, used inconsistently and in different forms, are expanded (e.g. δέ, καί, πόλις, στάδια, στάδιοι, σταδίων, ἐστί(ν), and many terminations). Accents and other diacritics are regularized.

Of the hundreds of names in the text, only a minority are correct,

---

[4] See nn. on 13. 3 Symaithos; 63 Larissa; 65. 1 Amyros; 66. 3 Skione; 67. 3 Kypasis; 96 Neandreia; 98. 2 Adramyttion, Atarneus, Aigai; 101. 1 Sylleion; 110. 10 Hermaia.

but in many cases the right form is not in doubt and the *apparatus criticus* is therefore silent. Where, however, the reading of a name or other word is especially uncertain, it is printed in *italics* (even if it matches the MS text) so that the reader is not misled by the apparent certainty of a printed text.

The original contains no paragraphing, but the rubricator (a second scribe using red ink) has put in the first letters of the (added) headings (except when he has omitted to do so, e.g. at 35; 64. 1). He also indicates many place-names by a red bar above them. My paragraphing attempts to show the patterning of the text: for example, after a coastal measurement (*paraplous*), or a series of them, I normally begin a new paragraph. Müller's section numbers are retained as standard; but subsections are created to aid navigation.

The translation aspires to the late Raymond Dawson's principle that 'one should get as close to the original as possible, even if the result is sometimes a little outlandish' (Dawson 1993, 6). Thus it aims to convey the variations in word order that PS seems to favour; and where he is compressed, awkward, or unclear it attempts to reflect his irregularity rather than smooth it away. Conversely, as far as possible a word is always translated in the same way, though this is not attainable with (for example) some prepositions. Conjunctions and particles are not neglected; the reader may tire of the repetitious introductory 'And' for δέ (*de*), but may be helped thereby to notice when it is absent. According to context, however, καί (*kai*) as a copula may become 'and' or 'with'; ἐν (*en*) may be 'in', 'on', or 'among'; and so on. Place-names usually follow Greek forms (note that 'Cherronesos', the name of several places, is translated as 'Chersonesos', its usual form in scholarship).

II. *Prima facie* evidence of authorship

The introductory note, probably by the late antique editor Markianos, names the author as Skylax of Karyanda and says he dedicated the work to Dareios, presumably one of the Persian kings of that name; but no Dareios appears in the text. Markianos probably has in mind Herodotos's report (4. 44)[5] that Dareios I sent Skylax of Karyanda and others to explore the river Indus. The date was perhaps 518 BC (Panchenko 2002, 11), and Skylax may be the Skylax of Myndos (another Karian city) mistreated by Megabates during the Ionian revolt of the 490s (Hdt. 5. 33; Panchenko 2002, 7 n. 10). But many statements in the text are inconsistent with so early a date, and the work clearly belongs to the fourth century. Accordingly it and its

---

[5] Skylax of Karyanda, T 3a Jacoby.

author are known as Pseudo-Skylax.

A relevant entry (σ 510) in the Suda, a tenth-century Byzantine encyclopaedia, runs as follows (omitting a comment about the city of Karyanda, and with item numbers added by the present editor):

Σκύλαξ Καρυανδεὺς: . . . μαθηματικὸς καὶ μουσικός. ἔγραψε (1) Περί-πλουν τῶν ἐκτὸς τῶν Ἡρακλέος στηλῶν· (2) Τὰ κατὰ τὸν Ἡρακλείδην τὸν Μυλασσῶν βασιλέα· (3) Γῆς περίοδον· (4) Ἀντιγραφὴν πρὸς τὴν Πολυβίου ἱστορίαν.

(FGrH 709 T 1 = 1000 T 1)

ἐκτὸς ms. A: ⟨ἐντὸς καὶ⟩ ἐ. G. J. Vossius: ἐντὸς Müller, Bernhardy

Skylax of Karyanda. . . . Mathematician and man of letters. (Wrote) (1) *Circumnavigation* (Periplous*) of Places Outside the Pillars of Herakles*; (2) *The Story of Herakleides King of the Mylasians*; (3) *Circuit of the Earth*; (4) *Response to the History of Polybios.*[6]

Item (4) must be by the later Skylax of Karyanda whom Cicero (*On Divination*, 2. 42) names as a contemporary of Panaitios. Of item (2) nothing else is known; its nature is disputed, but a recent view is that it is a historical work by Darius's Skylax (Schepens 1998, 4). Our interest is chiefly in items (1) and (3).

Either 'Skylax of Karyanda' or simply 'Skylax' is cited by Aristotle (*Politics*, 7. 13. 1332b24) and a small number of later authors[7] for facts about India. Others (see below) cite him for information about Greek lands. There has been debate about which of the works listed by Suda dealt with Skylax's Indian voyage. The title of (1), referring to 'outside the Pillars', seems to point to the far West; some editors change 'outside' to 'inside and outside', or to 'inside', to make it refer to our *periplous*. But 'outside' need not point to the West: it is consist-ent with a voyage to the Indian Ocean, given the ancient debate about whether East or even West Africa was joined by land to India and whether one could sail around it (Panchenko 2003, 281–3). In itself, this title in Suda cannot be used as evidence that Skylax of Karyanda wrote our *periplous*.

We have no continuous extracts from Skylax's Indian voyage, only a few 'fragments'—that is, quotations or citations by later authors (gathered by Jacoby at *FGrH* 709). In our *Periplous* there is no mention of the Indian Ocean, though in a passage where the MS page is incomplete the author may have mentioned it (105. 1). It is important, then, to keep (1) and (3) distinct. *Circuit of the Earth* (*Gēs periodos*) could describe our work; but we know that, at least in its

---

[6] My trans. at Suda On Line (www.stoa.org/sol/).

[7] Harpocration (C2 AD), *Lexikon*, s.v. ὑπὸ γῆν οἰκοῦντες ('living underground'), on Troglodytes, may refer to India; Athenaeus, 2. 82/70 a–d, citing 'Skylax or Polemon' for Indian artichokes; Philostratos, *Life of Apollonios of Tyana*, discussed below.

present form, it is not by Herodotos's Skylax. Nevertheless the evidence of the Suda and other considerations have led some, notably Peretti, to suppose that our work is a much-modified version of a work by the 'real' Skylax of Karyanda. As we shall see, the arguments for this view are unconvincing (see V below).

Skylax of Karyanda was probably known chiefly for his eastern voyage, which probably took him down the Ganges (rather than, or as well as, the Indus) and to Sri Lanka (Panchenko 1998, 225–30). He is drawn upon most often in Philostratos's semi-fictionalized account (third century AD) of the life of Apollonios of Tyana, a travelling philosopher of the first century AD. Recent studies have revealed many more borrowings by Philostratos from Skylax than were hitherto known (Panchenko 2002; 2003). There is no good evidence that Skylax ever travelled round the Mediterranean and Black Sea, though in the identified fragments he sometimes compares things he saw in the East with places well known to his readers, usually in western Asia Minor though occasionally in the Black Sea or Italy (Panchenko 2002, 6).

Skylax was from Karia in Asia Minor; but the unnamed person (presumably male) who wrote our *Periplous* in the fourth century BC views the world from Athens or the region around it. He refers, for example, to 'the sea on our side' (40), clearly the Saronic gulf of the Aegean, and to 'this sea' (59), clearly the Aegean. Some scholars assume he was an Athenian (Marcotte 1986, 168 with 169, 176; Counillon 1998b, 124; Counillon 2004, 11). It is safer to say that, whatever his origin, he wrote in or near Athens and that this city, with its lively intellectual culture, is his most likely place of residence. Müller (page l) speculates that he might be the known geographical writer Phileas of Athens (see VII below);[8] but he is now dated to the fifth century (Marcotte 1986, 169–70, also rejects the identification).

We shall return to the author's possible identity when we discuss the purpose and context of the work (see V–VII below).

III. Date

It is easy to show that the bulk of the work postdates Darius's Skylax. Many references within it give a *terminus post quem* ('limit after which', or earliest possible date) in the fifth or fourth century BC. The latest of these is the inclusion of Naupaktos under Aitolia (35). Philip II of Macedonia had promised the city to the Aitolians by c.340

---

[8] He does not urge the suggestion as strongly as Baschmakoff 1948, 23, and Counillon 2004, 28, assume.

(Demosthenes, *3rd Philippic*, 34), a promise he fulfilled (Strabo 9. 4. 7) presumably soon after defeating the southern Greek allies at Chaironeia in 338.[9] (The reference to Latmos as 'Herakleia', and the placing of Lykian Telmessos in Karia, do not require a date in Alexander's reign: see Commentary on 99. 1, 100. 1.)

As Markianos observed in his introductory note, nothing in the text indicates that the author knew of Alexander or his eastern conquests. Even his new capital of Egypt, Alexandria, is absent. This silence provides a general *terminus ante quem* ('limit before which', latest possible date), while the inclusion of the coastal cities of southern Messenia within Lakedaimon (46. 1) points to a time before Philip removed them from Spartan power after Chaironeia, perhaps as late as 337 if the reorganization did not happen at once. The mention of Boiotian Thebes as if extant (59), even though Alexander destroyed it in 335, points to the same period.

This lower limit, however, cannot be as impermeable as the upper limit of 338. An author writing later may have deliberately ignored the Macedonian conquest of Greece from political motives, or may have adopted a retrospective stance for a literary reason, portraying how things were at some date before his own time (Counillon 2007c, 38–9, 42).[10] He could also have taken some years to compose his work, leaving parts of it out of date; or perhaps he relied on out-of-date sources which he did not correct, though it would be odd if he forgot that Thebes no longer existed. But the further we go past Alexander's accession in 336, the more surprising—and impressive—becomes the concealment of, or failure to exclude, anything contemporary.

A strict date of 338–335, which we can now refine to 338–337, was established by Müller xliv, but he argued, on the basis of later alterations, additions, and omissions that can be detected, that we have only a précis of the work made by schoolmasters in the Byzantine period (for similar views see Fabricius 1878, v–vi; Peretti 1961, 6). But, as argued in part I above, demonstrable alterations concern mostly linguistic points, the additions are easily spotted, and the few glaring omissions—the cities of Megalopolis, Byzantion, Olbia (in the Black Sea), and Istros—can be explained in other ways.[11]

Some editors take the view that the summative *paraploi* (69, 106. 4, 111. 8), including the formula by which stades are converted

---

[9] The *terminus post quem* of 338 for the Aitolian presence in Naupaktos is accepted by Merker 1989, 307.

[10] Earlier, Counillon dated the *periplous* to the early part of Philip II's reign, e.g. Counillon 2001b, 13.

[11] See Commentary on 44 Megale Polis, 67. 8 Hieron, 67. 9 Istros, 68. 1 Ophiousa.

to days of sailing (69), are later additions; but PS is not the first author to offer such a formula (see Hdt. 4. 85–6). Nothing in their content or style seems at odds with the rest of the work (see IV and VII below), and they are consistently designed, each ending with a supplementary piece of information.

Paradoxically, some *terminus ante quem* dates are earlier than the *terminus post quem* of 338. For example, some *poleis*, such as Sicilian Naxos (13. 3) and Olynthos (66. 4), are mentioned as if they still exist even though other sources say they were destroyed earlier. Archaeological evidence shows that some of these places endured as settlements; but occupation does not prove *polis* status, and the more one explains away such instances the more it may look like special pleading. A better general explanation must be found.

IV. Measurements

One of the most striking inconsistencies in the text is that some distances are expressed in days (or days and nights) of sailing—occasionally in fractions of days—while others are in *stadia*, the plural of *stadion* (a term Englished as 'stade').[12] The *stadion* is a conventional measure in Greek texts and inscriptions; notionally it is the length of a *stadion* (race-track), but it was not standardized before the Ptolemaic and Roman periods, and then differently in different regions. We cannot always identify which stade an author is using. The present work adopts for convenience the common value of *c.*185 m (*c.*607 feet), corresponding to the Roman definition of one-eighth of a mile; the Ptolemaic stade was 15 per cent shorter at *c.*157.5 m. PS may operate with different values in different passages, for reasons given below.

The reader might suppose that distances in stades are inherently more accurate than those in days and nights, and, further, that they represent a more advanced, 'scientific' class of data. It is true that some of the short distances transmitted by PS (e.g. the distance of a town from the sea, the width of a strait, a journey up-river, the length of a small island, or the coast of a small region) are broadly accurate and may originally have literally been measured (though not by him, as we shall see)—perhaps on land by pacing (there were professional 'bematists' in fourth-century Greece) or, in some cases, at sea using ropes, chains, or even triangulation. Some of PS's longer coastal transects in central Greece, expressed to the nearest 10 stades, such as in Attica (57), may have been arrived at by adding up relatively accurate shorter distances (probably reckoned at sea, not

---

[12] Occasionally *stadioi*, probably because of inconsistent transmission of the MS.

on land: Shipley 2010, 106; but cf. 31 n. for a possible land-based measurement of a gulf).

About one in three of PS's stade measurements, however, are very round numbers (e.g. 200 or 500 stades). Since sailors had no instruments with which to measure location or speed at sea, and could report distances travelled only in terms of duration, it is a moot point whether 'so many hundred stades' means more than 'such-and-such a part of a day'. Arnaud argues that many such figures in ancient texts may be simple fractions of a day's sailing (rated at 500, 600, or 700 stades), or totals of such fractions, or daily distances reduced by a round figure (Arnaud 1993; at 236 he notes that PS's half-days have no parallel in other literature; see also Arnaud 2005, 61–96). In making such statements an author would probably assume that a ship is under sail, not oar, and that there is a 'fair wind', meaning not too strong (Arnaud 2005, 21–3), otherwise voyages would not take place at all.

PS is not the first Greek author to measure distances more than one way. Herodotos, in his passage on the Black Sea already cited (4. 85–6), reckons a ship's progress as 70,000 *orguiai* (fathoms) by day and 60,000 by night (equivalent to 700 and 600 stades respectively). He calculates that 'to the (river) Phasis from the mouth (of the Black Sea) is a voyage of nine days and nights, eight; these make 111 myriads of fathoms' (that is, 111,000), 'and from these fathoms are made a myriad, a thousand, and a hundred stades' (that is, 11,100). He seems to reserve statements involving conversion between units for overviews of wide regions (e.g. 2. 6–9, Egypt; 4. 41, Libyē; 4. 101, Skythia; 5. 53–4, the Persian royal road).[13] Elsewhere Herodotos gives many individual distances in stades, parasangs (Persian leagues), or days' sailing; he does not standardize, but stades are most common. So when PS switches, somewhat indiscriminately it seems, between stades and days–nights, he is not departing from literary precedent. In the case of both authors, however, what is the reason for the variation?

We shall return to this. Whatever the explanation, the fact that PS's summative *paraploi* (69, 106. 4, 111. 8) convert stades into days, not days into stades as Herodotos does, may tell us something about his purpose in writing.

V. Purpose

The *periplous* is patently not the record of what would have been an astonishing voyage or series of voyages. PS never says he has seen

[13] Note the inversion 'nights, eight', which PS may imitate at various junctures.

anything or been anywhere, and the nature of the description varies so greatly that it cannot be a report by one eye-witness. He makes none of the first-person statements we see in the brief text preserved under the name of Hanno the Carthaginian (see VII below): 'And then setting off westwards we arrived at Soloëis ... After setting up an altar of Poseidon we went on again for half a day towards the rising sun' (3–4). Neither does PS offer a fictional travelogue, adopting novelistic conventions we are expected to read knowingly. When he does use the first person, his very choice of words, and his use of the future or present tense, may show that he is *not* recounting a journey, as in the introductory 'I shall begin from' or the recurrent formula 'I return to the mainland from which I turned aside'. Had he been narrating, or pretending to narrate, a journey, he could have used the aorist, 'I returned'. Instead, these statements are the self-describing call signs of one who is 'taking us through' a body of knowledge or data, like a lecturer.

This knowledge was not embodied in a map. The text was not an appendix to a map, or *vice versa*. Though maps existed as display pieces (like that of Aristagoras, Hdt. 5. 49), there is no evidence that they were everyday items or that seafarers used them (Talbert 1987; Talbert 1989; Janni 1998). Neither did writers use maps or conceive of geographical areas using the two-dimensional 'bird's eye view'; it was a non-cartographic culture in which verbal or mental maps (usually describing what are now called 'hodological' or route-governed spaces) were what delighted readers of ethnographic or geographical writings (Janni 1982, 605–6; Janni 1984, 15–47; Arnaud 1989; Sundwall 1996, 641). Only twice does PS use a topological description that would be consistent with cartography: Sicily is triangular (13. 4) and Egypt is oddly compared to a double axe (106. 3).[14] But these are very simple observations that any traveller could make from personal experience; Thucydides (6. 2. 2) even says Sicily was once called Trinakria ('Three Capes Island'). They could also be learned from display-piece maps.

A few moments' reflection on the text of the *periplous* makes it clear that it is not a seafarer's guide—an ancient counterpart of the *Mediterranean Pilot* or (as in Peretti's optimistic subtitle) 'the first Mediterranean portulan'. (This was noted even before Müller, e.g. by Letronne 1840, 172.) Even though navigational details do occur (harbours, river mouths, capes, a few mountains), they are not

---

[14] Müller deletes the note about Sicily as a gloss, but only because it uses stades in contrast to the surrounding material; deletion is, however, unnecessary. Note also the unnamed island at 22. 3, where Müller's conjecture would liken it to 'a straight band' but other restorations do not introduce such a comparison.

systematic, the distances between them are rarely short, and too many are omitted for the text to be useful to sailors unfamiliar with a region. PS even fails to note the notorious dangers of the strait of Messina (13. 1) or C. Malea (46. 1). A captain did not need a book; if he was setting off for an unfamiliar destination, he went down to the harbour and asked people what they knew. Sea distances, in particular, while they may appear precise and helpful, are literally *less useful* than sailing times to a navigator with no instruments.[15] One may justly doubt whether a statement of the length of a region, particularly a small *polis* territory, has any navigational value; land frontiers, even supposing they were clearly marked, meant nothing to ships, for 'national waters' were not defined as they are today. Again, what is the place of the width of Asia Minor (102. 2) in a seafarers' manual?

Neither is the work likely to be intended for a financier of voyages, since their homeland (wherever it is) is covered in the same way as any other region, and distances are not standardized. It remains the case, however, that PS logically must at some level preserve sailors' first-hand experience—just as, despite the paucity of his references to trade, he incidentally preserves evidence of a network of trade routes. Although trade is not to the fore in his account, it is always present as a frame of reference; the lack of explicit discussion does not preclude a trade-related context for some of his primary data. His use of distances expressed in days and nights also supports the idea that mid-length voyages of up to a few days were normal (Arnaud 1993, 233–8; Arnaud 2005, 107–26). The occurrence of nights as well as days, furthermore, shows that there was a notion of sailing continuously for 24 hours or more. Not all these need be direct crossings; their occurrence in PS's coastal measurements suggests that at least some ships when coasting did not have to put in at night.

Whatever its purpose, the work is clearly much more than a compendium of oral information, and though it is true that, at *some* level, sailors' first-hand experience must underlie the coastal descriptions (at least outside Attica), that tells us nothing about the work we have. Neither can Peretti's case be accepted, that some passages can be assigned to an 'ancient nucleus' (*nucleo antico*) of material going back to the real Skylax of Karyanda. A far more economical hypothesis is that PS is simply using multifarious written (and perhaps some oral) sources, some of which were older than others (the idea of a compilation goes back at least to Letronne 1840,

---

[15] This would be untrue if the Greeks classified ships by their different daily rates, which is theoretically possible.

243). This explains why his information is often more up to date for the Greek heartland, less so in, for example, Italy and the Black Sea (cf. Counillon 2004, 26 on the latter).

For this reason it seems unlikely that PS consulted sailors or financiers of trade voyages, who surely would have had nothing but the most up-to-date information. He may have used documents, perhaps including old lists of destinations (and sailing times?) archived in the houses of merchants or moneylenders, which would explain why they are otherwise invisible to us. Several speeches for the prosecution in lawsuits at Athens show that financiers sometimes required shippers to sail only to agreed destinations (Ps.-Dem. 56. 3–8), took an interest in seasonal sailing conditions (Ps.-Dem. 35. 10), and knew the dangers of certain waters (Lys. 32. 25)—but not in such detail as to suggest that they kept records of maritime itineraries organized by daily stages with sailing times and distances included. Neither, of course, does the evidence disprove the existence of such records. If PS did consult documents of this kind, he surely blended them with literary and historical works, which would explain why some of his information is out of date. Only in the case of the Carthaginian far west, for which literary sources may have been hard to obtain, may we suppose that he consulted Phoenicians or Carthaginians resident at Piraeus or Athens.[16]

If the book is an intelligent compilation from a range of sources, we may more straightforwardly regard it as a work of library-based research. What kind of writer would want to write such a work in the third quarter of the fourth century? (*a*) A historian or philosopher might wish to gather data on city-states from navigational sources, but why would he leave in nautical landmarks, distances, and so on? He might wish to catalogue the *ethnē* of the world, but why would he leave out major inland peoples? (*b*) A work commissioned by military or political authorities in, say, Athens or Macedonia for purposes of diplomacy, defence, or imperial aspirations, is conceivable; but NW Africa was no threat to anyone in Old Greece and hardly a realistic goal of conquest, other than for Alexander. Why include the author or patron's homeland (Attica, Macedonia)? Why limit the scope to coasts, and why omit the bulk of the Persian empire? (*c*) If the work was meant to aid the management of trade relations, why does it cover the patron's homeland? Why does it omit the majority of significant direct sea crossings (e.g. from Karambis to the Crimea, see 90 n.) and such obvious matters as Athens's grain trade route to the Black Sea via Skyros, Lemnos, and

---

[16] I am grateful to Mark Woolmer for discussion of this point.

Imbros? It is hard to see much emphasis on trade routes or Mediter-ranean 'networks' (for this concept see e.g. Malkin *et al.* 2007 = Malkin *et al.* 2009)? (On PS's lack of interest in trade, cf. Counillon 1998b, 57, 64–5.)

The work is not intended to convey an over-arching concept of 'the Mediterranean' as such; it gives the sea no name,[17] and addition-ally covers the Black Sea and part of Atlantic Morocco. It is not simply a picture of the world where Greeks have settled, for it covers NW Africa to the west of Cyrenaica, where there were no Greek cities, and includes 'barbarian' regions such as Phoenicia. Since, however, it repeatedly expresses a distinction between Hellenic and barbarian communities, the author may be trying, consciously or subconsciously, to define the extent of the world, and the relation-ships between its parts, in terms of its potential to be visited, exploited, or ultimately controlled by Greeks. Perhaps he intended to bring into a single frame the whole of 'the world that we can access'. This would explain the absence of the Persians and their empire, and the omission of India and the Indian Ocean, famously explored by Skylax of Karyanda nearly two centuries before but perhaps almost unknown to Greeks by the mid-fourth century.[18]

What appears to be a dry enumeration turns out, on this view, to possess potent ideological value, written as it was at a time when colonialism seemed natural. On a very small scale, it prefigures the *Geography* of Strabo, written under Augustus and Tiberius, which presents the world to readers who are inclined to see themselves as masters of it (cf. Nicolet 1991; Clarke 1999).

Besides this possibly unconscious ideological aspect, PS seems to be attempting to assemble a systematic reckoning of the scale of the world accessible to Greeks, and an enumeration of its constituent parts. His work is, in short, a work of geography. A number of agendas compete for attention—earth measurement, the cataloguing of the ethnic territories and towns that make up the world, with an occasional emphasis on history, geography, ethnography, and mili-tary strongpoints (as in Cyprus, 103). The author did not focus his work adequately on one main 'research question', but there can be little doubt that his agenda was an academic one.

---

[17] The same is true e.g. of Strabo, who calls it 'the sea', 'the inner sea' (e.g. 1. 1. 10, 1. 3. 4), or *hē kath' hēmas thalassa*, literally 'the sea by us' or 'our sea' (e.g. 2. 1. 1, 2. 5. 25).

[18] Though SK's work was known to e.g. Aristotle, see *Politics*, 7. 14. 1332 b 24.

VI. Pseudo-Skylax's geography

As such, the periplous is the earliest surviving Greek work entirely devoted to what we now call geography, though extant histories of earlier date (notably Herodotos's *Histories*) deal extensively with such matters, while earlier works surviving only as 'fragments' or quotations were certainly geographical in framing and content (e.g. Hekataios, Phileas). So what kind of geography does PS offer us?

First, his choice to focus on coasts known to Hellenes may have been intended to allow him to present, from the sources at his disposal, a figure for the total length of the world, in the sense in which he defines that world (implicitly, unless we retain the disorderly summary at the top of the text). Depending on whether we accept the summations of distances (at 69; 106. 4; 111. 8) as original, the text offers an implicit or explicit assessment of the dimensions of the world as defined. The variation between the 'practical' day–night measurements and the 'scientific' distances in stades must reflect the variety of his sources. Since he does not standardize them, he is not using stade measurements to pose as an authority—especially if the summations are genuine, for they are in days, not stades.

Second, within his artificial coastal purview PS composes his world out of building blocks that he defines as *ethnē*, which is here translated by the semantically neutral 'communities'[19] but could more accurately be rendered 'ethnically defined political units'. (This remains the case even if we discard—as in the present edition—the headings above successive passages as later additions: e.g. 5 Tyrrhenoi, 6 Kyrnos.) Every named place lies within an *ethnos*, though the scheme works more loosely after Egypt. That some of these blocs are topographical, not truly ethnic, is shown by statements of the sort 'in this *ethnos* are these Greek *poleis*' (e.g. 4, 10, 12). At times he creates or follows purely topographical unities, such as when summing up the coast from Gibraltar to Liguria (4) or the Adriatic (27. 2), inserting Crete (47) into his description of the Peloponnese, and organizing the account of Crete from end to end rather than around the coast.

Further evidence of the limited degree to which PS develops his scientific persona may lie, perhaps, in the absence of any indications of latitude (the *diaphragmata*, 'partitions' rather than 'parallels', at 113 are probably not original). Yet by this period Eudoxos of Knidos had invented zones of latitude, putting Knidos, Rhodes, and Gadeira on the same *klima* or 'inclination' (fr. 75a Lasserre).

---

[19] I owe this suggestion to Enrico Dal Lago.

VII. Intellectual context

PS has a limited relationship with his literary predecessors. He takes little from Theopompos (Peretti 1963) or Ephoros (Peretti 1961), though he may have got from Ephoros (who published his major work in the 330s) the idea of organizing material by area and people (Drews 1963, 250–1).

It is often claimed that his account of NW Africa draws on the brief *periplous* preserved under the name of Hanno the Carthaginian (translated at Lipiński 2003, 438–43; Roller 2006, 129–32). This is usually thought to be a Greek version of a late archaic Punic text (Roller 2006, 31–2, accepts an early date), but some recent studies date it early hellenistic (Desanges 39–85, esp. 78–85; Euzennat 1994, 78). We can only be sure that it precedes Pseudo-Aristotle, *On Wondrous Things Heard* (*Mir. ausc.*; probably 3rd-century), 37, which cites it. It could still, of course, be describing an early voyage. As noted in the Commentary (introductory n. to 112), however, careful comparison of PS and Hanno reveals important differences. If Hanno's *periplous* existed in PS's day, he used it indirectly at best (Roller 2006, 19).

Though PS often recalls Herodotos—e.g. in noting the narrow waist of Asia Minor (see 102. 2) and the largest rivers (69), and in relating the Istros to the Nile (20)—he also differs from him or adds important information (e.g. on the peoples of the NE Black Sea: Counillon 2004, 83 = Counillon 2007a, 39). PS appears not to draw much from Hekataios, from whom he often differs about details (e.g. the boundary between Europe and Asia lies probably at the R. Phasis, Hekat. F 18 a–b; Counillon 2004, 99). Although he follows Hekataios in starting in the west and moving clockwise, he does not cover inland Europe, India, or Nubia as his Milesian predecessor did.

One writer upon whom PS does appears to draw is Phileas of Athens, currently dated to the fifth century BC (González Ponce 2011a). Phileas may, for example, have invented the label 'continuous Hellas', though it is suggested below (introductory n. to 33. 2–65) that PS is more likely to have done so. If the date is right, however, he cannot be PS's source for fourth-century information. (See also 47. 1 n.)

If there is no sustained resemblance between PS and any other known literary author, we must postulate the existence of sources of which we have no surviving examples and about whose nature we can only speculate. Some will have been ethnographic or rhetorical; Counillon 2007a, 39, pertinently comments that Hekataios and Herodotos are no longer seen as the sole sources of fifth-century ethnography (citing among other studies Thomas 2000, chs 2–3). For sailing times, landmarks, and distances PS surely had access to non-literary sources, possibly administrative or mercantile (part V above) and in some cases perhaps oral. They may have included other *periploi*, as has been argued persuasively for the Black Sea (Counillon 2004, 42–3). Their traces can be seen in the possible instances of 'reverse' progress in the *periplous*.[20]

If PS uses mainly non-literary sources of information, he also infuses them with material reflecting the literary-philosophical world of mid-fourth-century Athens. He twice mentions geological phenomena: one involving change (alluviation by a river, 34. 3), one unchanging (natural methane flames, 100. 1).

More often he includes historical information, most commonly about the parentage of colonies[21] and about Homeric and other legends connected with specific places.[22] Among historical events, he notes the Celts 'left behind' in North Italy (18), the renaming of Epileukadioi (34. 1), Daton's foundation by Kallistratos of Athens (67. 2), the birthplace of the astronomer Kleostratos (95), and the Mysians' migration (98. 1). Kallistratos and Kleostratos are the only historical figures he names. Perhaps the oddest excursion into history is the one about the war between Akarnania and Corinth which accompanies the renaming of Epileukadioi (34. 1); perhaps he views it as a helpful prelude to the dredging of the Leukas channel. None of this, however, amounts to a systematic attempt to give historical depth and identity to places.[23]

Likewise the occasional forays into ethnography, such as the two matriarchies (21. 1 and 70) or the pastoralism of the Makai (109. 3), give little sense of place. Only the account of the western Ethiopians starts to build a more detailed picture of economy and customs (112. 7–11); but it embodies stereotypical notions of barbarian trading customs that other authors variously locate in India (Mela 3. 60; Pliny 6. 88), Ethiopia (Philostratos 6. 2), and Libyē (Hdt. 4. 196). (See Panchenko 2003, 277, on the interchangeability of these locales.)

These nuggets of natural and human history are too consistent in

[20] See commentary on 23. 3 Kerkyra Melaina; 46. 1 Asine and Achilleios; 100. 2 'that beside land'; 109. 4 'from Neapolis'; 109. 5 'days, four'.
[21] 2 Emporion, 3 Olbia etc., 12 Laos, 34. 1 Leukas, 101. 1 Side, plus Cretans generally at 47. 2.
[22] 8 Elpenor and implicitly Kirke, 13. 5 Laos, 16 Diomedes, 22. 2 Hyllos, 58. 2 Homer's burial-place, 81 Medea's home, 95 Chryses, 104. 3 Andromeda, 106. 5 Kanopos, and several times at 98. 2.
[23] On geographers using history to enrich an account of space, see Clarke 1999, esp. chs 5–6. Cf. Tuan's distinction (Tuan 1977) between mere 'spaces' and 'places' that are also 'fields of care' (for the latter see Tuan 1974, 236–7, 241–5).

their general emphasis to have been found by PS in the sources he consulted on different parts of the *oikoumenē*. He surely took them in, albeit sporadically, from non-maritime sources or his own general knowledge. Their tone and range, in fact, conform to the intellectual climate of Athenian philosophical circles of the third quarter of the fourth century (as argued more fully in Shipley, under review).

On Plato's death in 347 his successor as head of the Academy, Speusippos, inaugurated a programme of data collection and classification (notably in his *Homoia*, 'similar things'; Athenaeus, 2. 58/61c, etc.) prefiguring that more commonly associated with the Peripatos (Lyceum) founded by Aristotle after his return to Athens in autumn 335. Indeed, like members of the Academy, Aristotle and Theophrastos in the late 340s were engaged in intensive data-gathering on Lesbos, and their progress must have been watched closely from Athens. Though space does not permit a full examination here of the intellectual context of PS (see Shipley forthcoming; Shipley, under review), the correspondence between his scientific interests and those of his contemporaries shows that he was aware of philosophical trends.

We cannot make a close link between the *Periplous* (written by 335 or very shortly afterwards) and another work that mentions a wide range of *poleis* all over the Mediterranean and Black Sea, Aristotle's *Politics* (written after 335). But it is hardly coincidental that geographers like Pytheas of Massalia and Dikaiarchos of Messana became active in the years after PS. In about the 320s (Roller 2006, 57–91), Pytheas observed the astronomical effects of latitude in NW Europe. PS's calculation of the sailing lengths of continents prefigures Aristotle's distance from Gibraltar to Asia Minor (*Mete.* 2. 5. 362b19–25), which he specifically says he worked out by adding up the lengths of sea and land journeys—just as PS does. Aristotle's estimate directly led to the devising by Dikaiarchos of Messana (active in the Peripatos c.330–300) of a baseline of latitude stretching from the straits of Gibraltar to the Himalayas.[24]

Among the few classical authors to show an awareness of tides (like PS 1, 110. 8, cf. 112. 2) are Ephoros (FF 65, 132), Herakleides Pontikos (fr. 117 Wehrli), Aristotle (*Mete.* 2. 8. 366a18–20), Theophrastos (*HP* 4. 6. 3; 4. 7. 4–7, etc.), Dikaiarchos (fr. 127 Mirhady), and Pytheas (fr. 2. 8 Mette). PS shares an interest in the Nile with Dikaiarchos (fr. 126 Mirhady) and an interest in alluviation with Theophrastos (*HP* 5. 8. 3). PS and Dikaiarchos both refer to Arkadia having a coastline (see

---

[24] Longitude is harder to describe empirically and to explain. Coordinates using longitude and latitude were not used regularly until the time of Ptolemy (2nd centuy AD).

n. on 44 Lepreon). His reference to Celts in Italy recalls Herakleides Pontikos's mention of their attack on Rome (fr. 102 Wehrli). PS and Theophrastos (*HP* 4. 5. 6) are among the earliest authors to mention the cult of Diomedes in the Adriatic. Many of the botanical species named by PS turn up in Theophrastos (see Commentary). These, and other parallels which there is no space to set out here, make clear that PS's interests reflect not only those of the Peripatos after 335, but also those of the Academy in the preceding years. His intellectual formation is likely to have taken place before the foundation of the Peripatos; and it would be a mistake to draw a hard and fast line between the interests of the two philosophical schools.

Quite why the author chose to seed such disconnected nuggets of knowledge into a geographical work in which they hardly fit is an interesting question that awaits a definite answer. Perhaps his difficulty was that he was mapping out (sometimes) a new field of discourse with little to guide him; or perhaps he was a relatively junior colleague among older scholars and needed to establish his credentials.

It is even theoretically possible that the *periplous* is an early work by Dikaiarchos or Pytheas; but there is no positive evidence for this, and one would have to ask how it came to be detached from the *oeuvre* of a famous writer. We remain on firmer ground if we merely place PS in the same intellectual milieu as these and other innovators.[25] A detailed exploration of the intellectual context of his work is something we await from future researches.

VIII. Literary features

Although the work can be called a compilation, Pseudo-Skylax has a consistent method of presenting his data, and his text has a unified linguistic character. This recent insight (Marcotte 1986, 167–8) invites the question whether the author also has literary aspirations.

Even unsophisticated geographical texts can have their own *poétique* (Marcotte 2000, lxx). Certainly Pseudo-Skylax's text has, at times, a formulaic quality: after *ethnos* X is *ethnos* Y; in it are the following *poleis*; perhaps a river and a mountain; the coastal sailing is this long. But he subtly varies his phraseology and word order, perhaps to maintain the reader's interest or to demonstrate his own literary skill. This *variatio* may be seen within a phrase ('the river

---

[25] Peretti 417 n. 449 briefly notes Peripatetic echoes in PS but does not go further. On the Peripatos under Aristotle, see Zhmud 2006, esp. 117–65; on Dikaiarchos's geography, Wehrli 1967, 34–6, 75–80, and Keyser 2000; on Pytheas, Roller 57–91; Roseman 1994.

Pordanis, and the Arabis river', 83) or between the beginnings of
sections ('After Tyrrhenia there follow the Latinoi', 8; 'And after
Leukania are the Iapyges', 14; 'And after the Daunitai is the *ethnos* of
the Ombrikoi', 16; etc.) or between the *paraploi* at the ends of
sections ('The Latinoi, coastal voyage: a day and a night', 8; 'And the
Olsoi, coastal voyage: days, one', 9; 'And the coastal voyage of Kampania is of days, one', 10; 'And the coastal voyage is, of the Saunitai, a
day's half', 11; etc.). These variations are likely to be original; an
ignorant copyist would probably repeat the word-patterns with
which he was most comfortable, flattening out any variation, while
one can more easily imagine a post-classical editor standardizing the
text than introducing *variatio*.

PS uses what we may call architectural devices to keep the reader
interested.[26] Thus at the beginning our expectation is raised by the
promise to return to the Pillars of Herakles and then go further, and
as we approach Gibraltar for the second time we may feel anticipa-
tion or suspense, wondering when we will reach and pass through
the Straits. He opens loops and closes them later, interrupting the
north shore of the Mediterranean by inserting the distances from
Sardinia to Libyē and to Sicily (7) and, in the description of Libyē,
giving the distance back to Sicily (11).[27] The transit from Sardinia to
Sicily is particularly interesting for his view of written navigational
space, giving an alternative 'short cut' to a place we will reach later
and demonstrating his geographical expertise. Similarly, the transit
to Libyē has narratological force, whetting the appetite of the
reader, who already knows that we will eventually reach it but does
not know what lies between us and it. He marks the beginnings of
Europe, of continuous Hellas, and of the Peloponnese, and in each
case marks the endpoint.

He makes implicit rather than explicit claims to authority, as
when he says (47) that 'of all Europe' Lakedaimon lies closest to
Crete but does not explain how he knows this.[28] He hints at knowing
more than he chooses to reveal, with tantalizing statements like
'there are many cities' and 'there are many other islands'. He implies
he is capable of informed judgement when he describes certain
places as large or small. Even his occasional presentations of distances as inexact (with μάλιστα, *malista*, 'approximately', 13. 4, 108.
2, 109. 1; ὡς, *hōs*, or ὡσεί, *hōsei*, 'about', 17, 27. 2, 110. 4 and 8; ὅσον,

---

[26] '[T]he whole structure shows a quite self-conscious manipulation of narrative ex-
pectations.' Clarke 1999, 39.

[27] Also from Crete to Libya and Cyrenaica, 47; from the Argolic Akte to Sounion, 51.

[28] Cf. 22. 2, Illyria smaller than the Peloponnese; 27. 2, Adriatic same as Ionios; 29,
Kerkyra belongs more to Thesprotia than to Chaonia.

hoson, 'roughly', 104. 2) may perhaps express expertise, though it may be more relevant that they all refer to the West, the Adriatic, the Levant, and Africa—areas where Greek knowledge may have been less detailed. As we have seen, he occasionally parades his knowledge of the natural and physical world, and of history.

The relatively frequent use of the first person (1, 'I shall begin'; 21. 2, 'of which I have the names to tell'; 111. 9, 'of whom we know') may be a device to engage the reader and enhance his credibility (cf. V above), though the frequent statement 'I return again onto the mainland from where I departed' may be a framing device rather than a rhetorical claim to authority. He repeatedly uses a dative present participle (63, 68. 5, 69 twice, 93, and seven times at 106–12), and twice the second person subjunctive (67. 8, 100. 2), to personalize hypothetical movement; the concentration of these features in the second half of the work may reflect a characteristic of his sources.

On the other hand, it is rare that he expresses a clear narrative point of view. Phrases such as 'the sea on our side' (40, probably the Saronic gulf) and 'this sea' (59 and 61, meaning the Aegean) are all the more striking for their scarcity.

Though hardly the height of sophistication, these features give authorial unity and enhanced authority. They may be scattered and unsystematic, and the authorial voice cannot by any means be said to have the strength of Thucydides, but Pseudo-Skylax is not an unthinking replicator of what he reads.

One more point deserves emphasis. Historians of Greek geography often refer to a 'periplographic genre'.[29] It must be questionable whether 'genre' appropriately describes works of such varied character (all in Greek) as Hanno,[30] Arrian's *Periplous of the Euxine*,[31] the Pseudo-Arrianic work of the same title (known as *Eux.*),[32] the *Periplus maris Erythraei* (*PME*),[33] all in prose; the iambics of 'Ps.-Skymnos' (late 2nd century)[34] and Dionysios the son of Kalliphon;[35] and so on. They seem to have no shared rules of composition (other than coastwise progression), no conscious imitation of one another (apart from quotations, usually unattributed), and no common

---

[29] e.g. González Ponce 1991, and later articles; Counillon 2001b, 16; Marcotte 2000, lv–lxxii, esp. lxiv–lxvi.

[30] Text: Oikonomides and Miller 1995; González Ponce 2011b. Analysis: Euzennat 1994.

[31] Liddle 2003.

[32] Diller 1952, 102–46.

[33] Casson 1989.

[34] Marcotte 2000, 1–307.

[35] Marcotte 1990.

rhetorical structure (proem, exposition, conclusion, or whatever). Even if these represent a genre, PS is earlier than them all (with the possible exception of Hanno, an extremely short and laconic work), so we know of no work that he could have used as a model. It is even doubtful whether 'genre' is an appropriate term for prose works before the hellenistic period (Pelling 2007, esp. 77–81).

PS surely intended his work—whether or not he intended it to be published—as an addition to the body of philosophical work that dealt with the structure of the earth. He did not see it as part of a tradition that made coastal exposition into a coherent and defined subset of literature; for there was no such literary tradition.

IX. Legacy

Despite his contribution to the innovations in late fourth-century geography, Ps.-Skylax's is almost invisible in subsequent developments. The work was rarely used or cited, and was sometimes confused with that of Skylax of Karyanda. While Aristotle[36] and later authors (notably Philostratos, see II above) draw information about India from the 'real' Skylax of Karyanda,[37] only a small number of sources appear to use our *periplous*. The *Periplous* was probably known to Ps.-Lykophron (see n. on 15 Daunitai; cf. also perhaps n. on 108. 2 'fields'). Two scholia (of uncertain date) to the third-century poet Apollonios Rhodios (on *Argonautika*, 1. 1177–1178a and 4. 1215; see *FGrH* 709 FF 9–10) appear to misquote PS slightly on the Adriatic and on Mysia, using the name Skylax of Karyanda. There appears to be no use of PS in 'Ps.-Skymnos' (more correctly called the anonymous *Iambics to King Nikomedes*; late 2nd century BC; possibly by Apollodoros, see Marcotte 2000, 35–46). The next source to use our *periplous* may be Dionysios son of Kalliphon (first century BC), who consults both PS and Phileas (Müller l; Marcotte 1990, 29–33, 172–85; González Ponce 1997, 50; Counillon 2001a, 384, 391). Strabo (13. 1. 4 = Skylax F 12) reports that Skylax begins the Troad at Abydos, which is true for PS (93–4) though it may have also been in Skylax; if it is from PS, it implies that the *periplous* was circulating under Skylax's name by the time of Augustus or Tiberius. The principal repository of quotations (all unattributed) is the Roman-period *Eux.*, already mentioned (see nn. on 68. 5 Maiotis; 81 Aia; 83 Ekecheirieis), who is

[36] Arist. *Politics*, 7. 13. 1. 1332b12 = Skylax F 5, on Indian kings.
[37] They include Strabo 12. 4. 8 = Skylax F 11, citing Skylax of Karyanda for Phryges and Mysoi living around L. Askania'; PS 93 ff. does not mention the lake or the Phrygians, only Phrygia, so this probably came from SK. Other sources: Harpocration and Athenaeus (n. 7 above).

therefore justifiably used to fill a lacuna at 73. While there are similarities between PS, Pomponius Mela, and Pliny the Elder (e.g. regarding the Black Sea; Counillon 2004, 28), there is no evidence that these writers used the *periplous* directly (cf. e.g. Vandermersch 1994, 244–6). Only the late poet Avienus among Latin authors appears to have done so (see n. on '7 stades' at 67. 8). After Markianos (see II above) in about the sixth century AD, the next explicit reference is by the emperor Constantine Porphyrogenitus in the tenth (*De thematibus*, 1. 2), who notes that the work does not mention Armenia (though it is theoretically possible that he is using Skylax of Karyanda, who we know compares things seen in India with things in Asia Minor). The Suda, of similar date, probably knows of our *periplous* under the name of Skylax of Karyanda (see, again, II above).

It is not much of a legacy, but we must remember that authors whom we regard as of the first importance, such as Strabo and Pausanias, are rarely cited by later authors.

The short-term impact may have been greater. If researchers like Aristotle and Theophrastos motivated PS, his own work may have inspired Pytheas (who effectively filled the gap PS left in the North Atlantic) and Dikaiarchos (if he is not himself Dikaiarchos) to go further, both metaphorically and, in Pytheas's case, literally. The advances in geography in the late fourth century paved the way for Eratosthenes (*c.*275–194) to compute the circumference of the Earth (or to refine Dikaiarchos's calculation and to re-calculate the dimensions of the seas (see e.g. Strabo 2. 5. 19).[38]

X. The *Periplous* today

A dull though valuable work bristling with philological difficulties, it has been studied vigorously in the past but is apparently being shirked at the moment (Diller 1952, 101)

Diller's damning epithet 'dull' entirely misses the importance of PS for the history of geography; otherwise he is on the mark. The *periplous* was actively researched in the early modern period, though from the first edition (Hoeschelius 1600) to that of Klausen (1831) all editors were reliant on copies of D, as the MS itself disappeared from public view for over 200 years.[39] The *periplous* has largely been neglected since its inclusion in GGM, and Müller's text has become

[38] On the geographical legacy of the early Peripatos or Lyceum under Aristotle, see Zhmud 2006, 278–9.
[39] The other editions before Müller's are Vossius 1639; Gronovius 1697; Hudson 1698; Gail 1826, 235–326; Klausen 1831. E. Miller 1839, 195–244, lists readings from the newly rediscovered D (without a complete text). Fabricius 1848 was the first modern edition to take account of D. All are available on line.

standard even though that of Fabricius 1878 is more cautious in its editorial interventions.[40] Since then there has been no complete publication. Happily, the pace of progress has increased in recent decades with important publications by, among others, Peretti, Marcotte, Desanges, Lipiński, González Ponce, Flensted-Jensen and Hansen, and above all Counillon, chiefly his magisterial edition of the Black Sea passage.[41] Marcotte's Budé edition is eagerly awaited.[42]

The editor's hope is that by making Pseudo-Skylax available to a wider English-speaking audience he will stimulate renewed debate among scholars, students, and general readers, in which the topographical problems of the text can be tackled afresh in the light of a new appreciation of its place in the development of Greek science.

[40] This was the 2nd edition by 'B. Fabricius' (real name H. T. Dittrich); he had published his commentary piecemeal before the appearance of Müller; see Fabricius 1841; 1844; 1846; and an earlier edition of the Greek text, Fabricius 1848.

[41] See review by Shipley 2007. Also an unpublished Ph.D. thesis (Allain 1977) and an annotated Spanish translation (Garzón Díaz 2008).

[42] The present editor is preparing a shorter study of the work's antecedents and context for *FGrH* V (Shipley forthcoming).

TEXT

1. {Εὐρώπη.} ἄρξομαι δὲ ἀπὸ Ἡρακλείων στηλῶν τῶν ἐν τῇ Εὐρώπῃ μέχρι Ἡρακλείων στηλῶν τῶν ἐν τῇ Λιβύῃ, καὶ μέχρι Αἰθιόπων τῶν μεγάλων. εἰσὶ δὲ ἀλλήλων καταντικρὺ αἱ Ἡράκλειαι στῆλαι καὶ ἀπέχουσιν ἀλλήλων πλοῦν ἡμέρας.

ἀπὸ Ἡρακλείων στηλῶν τῶν ἐν τῇ Εὐρώπῃ ἐμπόρια πολλὰ Καρχηδονίων καὶ πηλὸς καὶ πλημμυρίδες καὶ τενάγη.

2. {Ἴβηρες.} τῆς Εὐρώπης εἰσὶ πρῶτοι Ἴβηρες, Ἰβηρίας ἔθνος, καὶ ποταμὸς Ἴβηρ. καὶ νῆσοι ἐνταῦθα ἔπεισι δύο αἷς ὄνομα Γάδειρα. τούτων ἡ ἑτέρα πόλιν ἔχει ἀπέχουσαν ἡμέρας πλοῦν ἀπὸ Ἡρακλείων στηλῶν. εἶτα ἐμπόριον ⟨καὶ⟩ πόλις Ἑλληνὶς ἦ ὄνομα Ἐμπόριον· εἰσὶ δὲ οὗτοι Μασσαλιωτῶν ἄποικοι.

παράπλους τῆς Ἰβηρίας ἑπτὰ ἡμερῶν καὶ ἑπτὰ νυκτῶν.

3. {Λίγυες καὶ Ἴβηρες.} ἀπὸ δὲ Ἰβήρων ἔχονται Λίγυες καὶ Ἴβηρες μιγάδες μέχρι ποταμοῦ Ῥοδανοῦ.

παράπλους Λιγύων ἀπὸ Ἐμπορίου μέχρι Ῥοδανοῦ ποταμοῦ δύο ἡμερῶν καὶ μιᾶς νυκτός.

4. {Λίγυες.} ἀπὸ Ῥοδανοῦ ποταμοῦ ἔχονται Λίγυες μέχρι Ἀντίου. ἐν ταύτῃ τῇ χώρᾳ πόλις ἐστὶν Ἑλληνίς, Μασσαλία, καὶ λιμήν, ⟨καὶ Ὀλβία καὶ Ἄντιον καὶ λιμήν⟩. ἄποικοι αὗται Μασσαλίας εἰσίν.

παράπλους δ' ἐστὶ ταύτης ἀπὸ Ῥοδανοῦ ποταμοῦ μέχρι Ἀντίου ἡμερῶν δύο καὶ νυκτῶν δύο.

ἀπὸ δὲ Ἡρακλείων στηλῶν μέχρι Ἀντίου ἡ χώρα πᾶσα αὕτη εὐλίμενος.

5. {Τυρρηνοί.} ἀπὸ δὲ Ἀντίου Τυρρηνοὶ ἔθνος μέχρι Ῥώμης πόλεως.

παράπλους ἡμερῶν τεσσάρων καὶ νυκτῶν τεσσάρων.

6. {Κύρνος.} κατὰ δὲ Τυρρηνίαν κεῖται νῆσος Κύρνος. ἔστι δὲ ἀπὸ Τυρρηνίας ὁ πλοῦς εἰς Κύρνον ἡμέρας καὶ ἡμίσεως. καὶ νῆσος ἐν μέσῳ τῷ πλῷ τούτῳ οἰκουμένη ἦ ὄνομα Αἰθαλία, καὶ ἄλλαι πολλαὶ ἔρημοι νῆσοι.

7. {Σαρδώ.} ἀπὸ δὲ Κύρνου νήσου εἰς Σαρδὼ νῆσον πλοῦς ἡμέρας τρίτον μέρος, καὶ νῆσος ἐρήμη ἐν τῷ μεταξύ.

ἀπὸ Σαρδοῦς δὲ εἰς Λιβύην πλοῦς ἡμέρας καὶ νυκτός. εἰς δὲ Σικελίαν ἀπὸ Σαρδοῦς πλοῦς ἡμερῶν δύο καὶ νυκτός.

ἐπάνειμι δὲ πάλιν ἐπὶ τὴν ἤπειρον, ὅθεν εἰς τὴν Κύρνον ἐξετραπόμην.

8. {Λατῖνοι.} Τυρρηνίας ἔχονται Λατῖνοι μέχρι τοῦ Κιρκαίου. καὶ τὸ τοῦ Ἐλπήνορος μνῆμά ἐστι Λατίνων.

Λατίνων παράπλους ἡμέρας καὶ νυκτός.

9. {Ὀλσοί.} Λατίνων δὲ ἔχονται Ὀλσοί.

Ὀλσῶν δὲ παράπλους ἡμέρας μιᾶς.

10. {Καμπανοί.} Ὀλσῶν δὲ ἔχονται Καμπανοί. καὶ εἰσὶ πόλεις Ἑλληνίδες αὗται ἐν τῇ Καμπανίᾳ· Κύμη, Νεάπολις. κατὰ ταῦτά ἐστι Πιθηκοῦσσα νῆσος καὶ πόλις Ἑλληνίς.

παράπλους δὲ τῆς Καμπανίας ἐστὶν ἡμέρας μιᾶς.

11. {Σαυνῖται.} Καμπανῶν δὲ ἔχονται Σαυνῖται.

καὶ παράπλους ἐστὶ Σαυνιτῶν ἡμέρας ἥμισυ.

12. {Λευκανοί.} Σαυνιτῶν δὲ ἔχονται Λευκανοὶ μέχρι Θουρίας.

ὁ πλοῦς δέ ἐστι παρὰ Λευκανίαν ἡμερῶν Ϝ´ καὶ νυκτῶν Ϝ´.

ἡ δὲ Λευκανία ἐστὶν ἀκτή. ἐν ταύτῃ πόλεις εἰσὶν Ἑλληνίδες αἵδε· Ποσειδωνία καὶ Ἐλέα, ⟨Λᾶος⟩ Θουρίων ἀποικία, Πανδοσία, Κλαμπέτεια, Τερίνα, Ἱππώνιον, Μέσμα, Ῥήγιον ἀκρωτήριον καὶ πόλις.

13. 1. {Σικελία.} κατὰ δὲ Ῥήγιόν ἐστι Σικελία νῆσος, ἀπὸ τῆς Εὐρώπης ἀπέχουσα στάδια ιβ´ ἐπὶ Πελωριάδα ἀπὸ Ῥηγίου.

2. ἐν δὲ Σικελίᾳ ἔθνη βάρβαρα τάδε ἐστίν· Ἔλυμοι, Σικανοί, Σικελοί, Φοίνικες, Τρῶες. οὗτοι μὲν βάρβαροι, οἰκοῦσι δὲ καὶ Ἕλληνες. ἀκρωτήριον δὲ Σικελίας Πελωριάς.

3. πόλεις δ᾽ εἰσὶν ἀπὸ Πελωριάδος Ἑλληνίδες αἵδε· Μεσσήνη καὶ λιμήν, Ταυρομένιον, Νάξος, Κατάνη, Λεοντῖνοι· εἰς τοὺς Λεοντίνους δὲ κατὰ Τηρίαν ποταμὸν ἀνάπλους κ´ σταδίων. Σύμαιθος ποταμὸς καὶ πόλις Μεγαρὶς καὶ λιμὴν Ξιφώνειος. ἐχομένη δὲ Μεγαρίδος πόλις ἐστὶ Συράκουσαι, καὶ λιμένες ἐν αὐτῇ δύο· τούτων ὁ ἕτερος ἐντὸς τείχους, ὁ δ᾽ ἄλλος ἔξω. μετὰ δὲ ταύτην πόλις Ἔλωρον καὶ Πάχυνος ἀκρωτήριον. ἀπὸ Παχύνου δὲ πόλεις Ἑλληνίδες αἵδε· Καμάρινα, Γέλα, Ἀκράγας, Σελινοῦς, Λιλύβαιον ἀκρωτήριον. ἀπὸ δὲ Λιλυβαίου πόλις ἐστὶν Ἑλληνὶς

Ἰμέρα.

4. ἔστι δὲ ἡ Σικελία τρίγωνος· τὸ δὲ κῶλον ἕκαστον αὐτῆς ἐστι μάλιστα σταδίων ͵αφ´.

μετὰ δὲ Ἰμέραν πόλιν Λιπάρα νῆσός ἐστι, καὶ πόλις Ἑλληνὶς Μύλαι καὶ λιμήν. ἔστι δὲ ἀπὸ Μυλῶν ἐπὶ Λιπάραν νῆσον πλοῦς ἡμέρας ἥμισυ.

5. ἐπάνειμι δὲ πάλιν ἐπὶ τὴν ἤπειρον, ὅθεν ἐξετραπόμην. ἀπὸ γὰρ Ῥηγίου πόλεις εἰσὶν αἵδε· Λοκροί, Καυλωνία, Κρότων, Λακίνιον ἱερὸν Ἥρας καὶ νῆσος Καλυψοῦς, ἐν ᾗ Ὀδυσσεὺς ᾤκει παρὰ Καλυψοῖ, καὶ ποταμὸς Κρᾶθις, καὶ Σύβαρις καὶ Θουρία πόλις. οὗτοι ἐν τῇ Λευκανίᾳ Ἕλληνες.

14. {Ἰαπυγία.} μετὰ δὲ τὴν Λευκανίαν Ἰάπυγές εἰσιν ἔθνος μέχρι Ὑρίωνος ὄρους τοῦ ἐν τῷ κόλπῳ τῷ Ἀδρίᾳ.

παράπλους παρὰ τὴν Ἰαπυγίαν ἓξ ἡμερῶν καὶ ἓξ νυκτῶν.

ἐν δὲ τῇ Ἰαπυγίᾳ οἰκοῦσιν Ἕλληνες, καὶ πόλεις εἰσὶν αἵδε· Ἡράκλειον, Μεταπόντιον, Τάρας καὶ λιμήν, Ὑδροῦς ἐπὶ τῷ τοῦ Ἀδρίου ἢ τῷ τοῦ Ἰονίου κόλπου στόματι.

15. {Δαυνῖται.} μετὰ δὲ Ἰάπυγας ἀπὸ Ὑριῶνος Δαυνῖται ἔθνος ἐστίν. ἐν δὲ τούτῳ τῷ ἔθνει γλῶσσαι {ἤτοι στόματα} αἵδε· Ἀλφατέρνιοι, Ὀπικοί, Καρακῶνες, Βορεοντῖνοι, Πευκετιεῖς διήκοντες ἀπὸ [δὲ] τοῦ Τυρσηνικοῦ πελάγους εἰς τὸν Ἀδρίαν.

παράπλους τῆς Δαυνίτιδος χώρας ἡμερῶν δύο καὶ νυκτός.

16. {Ὀμβρικοί.} μετὰ δὲ Δαυνίτας ἔθνος ἐστὶν Ὀμβρικοί, καὶ πόλις ἐν αὐτοῖς Ἀγκών ἐστι. τοῦτο δὲ τὸ ἔθνος τιμᾷ Διομήδην, εὐεργετηθὲν ὑπ᾽ αὐτοῦ· καὶ ἱερόν ἐστιν αὐτοῦ.

παράπλους δὲ τῆς Ὀμβρικῆς ἐστιν ἡμερῶν δύο καὶ νυκτός.

17. {Τυρρηνοί.} μετὰ δὲ τὸ Ὀμβρικὸν Τυρρηνοί. διήκουσι δὲ καὶ οὗτοι ἀπὸ τοῦ Τυρρηνικοῦ πελάγους [ἔξωθεν] εἰς τὸν Ἀδρίαν κόλπον. καὶ πόλις ἐν αὐτοῖς Ἑλληνὶς ⟨Σπίνα⟩ καὶ ποταμός· καὶ ἀνάπλους εἰς τὴν πόλιν κατὰ ποταμὸν ὡς εἴκοσι σταδίων. [καὶ Τυρρηνία ἐστὶν διήκουσα ἀπὸ τῆς ἔξωθεν θαλάττης ἕως εἰς τὸν Ἀδρίαν κόλπον.]

⟨Τυρρηνῶν δὲ παράπλους ἡμέρας μιᾶς⟩ ἀπὸ †πόλεων πόλεως· καὶ ἔστιν ὁδὸς ἡμερῶν τριῶν.

18. {Κελτοί.} μετὰ δὲ Τυρρηνούς εἰσι Κελτοὶ ἔθνος, ἀπολειφθέντες τῆς στρατείας, ἐπὶ στενῶν μέχρι Ἀδρίου, ⟨διήκοντες ἀπὸ τῆς ἔξωθεν θαλάττης ἕως εἰς τὸν Ἀδρίαν κόλπον⟩. ἐνταῦθα δέ ἐστιν ὁ μυχὸς τοῦ Ἀδρίου κόλπου.

19. {Ἑνετοί.} μετὰ δὲ Κελτοὺς Ἐνετοί εἰσιν ἔθνος, καὶ ποταμὸς Ἠριδανὸς ἐν αὐτοῖς.

Ἐνετῶν δὲ παράπλους ἐστὶν ἐπ' εὐθείας [ἀπὸ Πίσης πόλεως] ἡμέρας μιᾶς.

20. {Ἴστροι.} μετὰ δὲ Ἐνέτους εἰσὶν ἔθνος Ἴστροι, καὶ ποταμὸς Ἴστρος. οὗτος ὁ ποταμὸς καὶ εἰς τὸν Πόντον ἐκβάλλει ἐν διε-σκεδασμένῃ εὐνῇ, ὡς ⟨ὁ Νεῖλος⟩ εἰς Αἴγυπτον.

παράπλους δὲ τῆς Ἴστρων χώρας ἡμέρας καὶ νυκτός.

21. 1. {Λιβυρνοί.} μετὰ δὲ Ἴστρους Λιβυρνοί εἰσιν ἔθνος. ἐν δὲ τούτῳ τῷ ἔθνει πόλεις εἰσὶ παρὰ θάλατταν Ἀρσίας, Δασσάτικα, Σενίτης, Ἀψύρτα, Λουψοί, Ὀρτοπελῆται, Ἡγῖνοι. οὗτοι γυναικο-κρατοῦνται, καὶ εἰσὶν αἱ γυναῖκες ἀνδρῶν ἐλευθέρων, μίσγον-ται δὲ τοῖς ἑαυτῶν δούλοις καὶ τοῖς πλησιοχώροις ἀνδράσι. **2.** κατὰ ταύτην τὴν χώραν αἵδε νῆσοί εἰσιν, ὧν ἔχω εἰπεῖν τὰ ὀνόματα, εἰσὶ δὲ καὶ ἄλλαι ἀνώνυμοι πολλαί· Ἴστρις νῆσος σταδίων τι′, πλάτος δὲ ρκ′· Ἠλεκτρίδες, Μεντορίδες. αὗται δὲ αἱ νῆσοί εἰσι μεγάλαι. Καταιβάτης ποταμός.

παράπλους τῆς Λιβυρνίδος χώρας ἡμερῶν δύο.

22. 1. {Ἰλλυριοί.} μετὰ δὲ Λιβυρνοὺς εἰσιν Ἰλλυριοὶ ἔθνος, καὶ παροικοῦσιν οἱ Ἰλλυριοὶ παρὰ θάλατταν μέχρι Χαονίας τῆς κατὰ Κέρκυραν τὴν Ἀλκινόου νῆσον. καὶ πόλις ἐστὶν Ἑλληνὶς ἐνταῦθα ᾗ ὄνομα Ἡράκλεια, καὶ λιμήν.

2. εἰσὶ δὲ καὶ οἱ Λωτοφάγοι καλούμενοι βάρβαροι οἵδε· Ἰαδα-σινοί, Βουλινοί, Ὕλλοι· Βουλινῶν ὁμοτέρμονες Ὕλλοι. οὗτοι δέ φασιν Ὕλλον τὸν Ἡρακλέους αὐτοὺς [τοῦ] κατοικίσαι· εἰσὶ δὲ βάρβαροι. κατοικοῦσι δὲ χερρόνησον ὀλίγῳ ἐλάσσω τῆς Πελοποννήσου.

3. ἀπὸ δὲ χερρονήσου ⟨... νῆσός ἐστι⟩ παρὰ στόμιον ὀρθόν· ταύτην παροικοῦσι Βουλινοί. Βουλινοὶ δ' εἰσὶν ἔθνος Ἰλλυ-ρικόν.

παράπλους δ' ἐστὶ τῆς Βουλινῶν χώρας ἡμέρας μακρᾶς ἐπὶ Νέστον ποταμόν.

23. 1. {Νέστοι.} ἀπὸ δὲ Νέστου πλοῦς ἐστι κολπώδης. καλεῖται δὲ Μανιὸς ἅπας οὗτος ὁ κόλπος.

παράπλους δέ ἐστιν ἡμέρας μιᾶς.

2. εἰσὶ δὲ ἐν τούτῳ τῷ κόλπῳ νῆσοι Τραγυράς, Βραττία, Ὀλύντα. αὗται δὲ ἀπ' ἀλλήλων ἀπέχουσι στάδια β′ ἢ ὀλίγῳ πλέον, κατὰ Φάρον καὶ Ἴσσαν. ἐνταῦθα γάρ ἐστι νῆσος Φάρος

⟨καὶ⟩ πόλις Ἑλληνὶς, καὶ Ἴσσα νῆσος· καὶ πόλεις Ἑλληνίδες αὗται.

3. πρὶν ἐπὶ τὸν Νάρωνα ποταμὸν παραπλεῦσαι, πολλὴ χώρα ἀνήκει σφόδρα εἰς θάλασσαν. καὶ νῆσος τῆς παραλίας χώρας ἐγγὺς ᾗ ὄνομα Μελίτη· καὶ ἑτέρα νῆσος ἐγγὺς ταύτης ᾗ ὄνομα Κέρκυρα ἡ Μέλαινα· καὶ ἐξέχει τῷ ἑνὶ τῶν ἀκρωτηρίων νῆσος αὕτη τῆς παραλίας χώρας σφόδρα, τῷ δὲ ἑτέρῳ ἀκρωτηρίῳ καθήκει ἐπὶ τὸν Νάρωνα ποταμόν. ἀπὸ δὲ τῆς Μελίτης ἀπέχει στάδια κʹ, τῆς δὲ παραλίας χώρας ἀπέχει στάδια ηʹ.

24. 1. {Μανιοί.} ἀπὸ δὲ Νέστων ἐστὶν ὁ Νάρων ποταμός· ὁ δὲ εἴσπλους ὁ εἰς τὸν Νάρωνά ἐστιν οὐ στενός· εἰσπλεῖ δὲ εἰς αὐτὸν καὶ τριήρης καὶ πλοῖα εἰς τὸ ἄνω ἐμπόριον, ἀπέχον ἀπὸ θαλάσσης στάδια πʹ. οὗτοι δέ εἰσιν Ἰλλυρίων ἔθνος Μανιοί. λίμνη δ᾽ ἐστὶ τὸ εἴσω τοῦ ἐμπορίου μεγάλη, καὶ ἀνήκει ἡ λίμνη εἰς Αὐταριάτας, ἔθνος Ἰλλυρικόν. καὶ νῆσος ἐν τῇ λίμνῃ ἔνεστι σταδίων ρκʹ· ἡ δὲ νῆσος αὕτη ἐστὶν εὐγέωργος σφόδρα. ἀπὸ δὲ ταύτης τῆς λίμνης ὁ Νάρων ποταμὸς ἀπορρεῖ.

2. καὶ ἀπὸ τοῦ Νάρωνος ἐπὶ τὸν Ἀρίωνα ποταμὸν ἡμέρας ἐστὶ πλοῦς· ἀπὸ δὲ τοῦ Ἀρίωνος ⟨ἐπὶ τὸν Ῥιζοῦντα⟩ ποταμὸν πλοῦς ἡμέρας ἥμισυ.

καὶ Κάδμου καὶ Ἁρμονίας οἱ λίθοι εἰσὶν ἐνταῦθα, καὶ ἱερὸν ἄπωθεν τοῦ Ῥιζοῦντος ποταμοῦ. ἀπὸ δὲ τοῦ Ῥιζοῦντος ποταμοῦ εἰς Βουθόην ὁ πλοῦς καὶ τὸ ἐμπόριον.

25. {Ἐγχελεῖς.} Ἰλλυριῶν ἔθνος εἰσὶν οἱ Ἐγχελεῖς, ἐχόμενοι τοῦ Ῥιζοῦντος.

ἐκ Βουθόης δὲ εἰς Ἐπίδαμνον, πόλιν Ἑλληνίδα, πλοῦς ἡμέρας καὶ νυκτός, ὁδὸς δὲ τριῶν ἡμερῶν.

26. 1. {Ἰλλύριοι.} Ταυλαντίων δέ ἐστι τὸ Ἰλλυρικὸν ἔθνος ἐν ᾧ ἡ Ἐπίδαμνός ἐστι, καὶ ποταμὸς παρὰ τὴν πόλιν παρρεῖ, ᾧ ὄνομα Πάλαμνος.

ἐκ δὲ Ἐπιδάμνου εἰς Ἀπολλωνίαν πόλιν Ἑλληνίδα ὁδὸς ἡμερῶν δύο. ἡ δὲ Ἀπολλωνία ἀπὸ τῆς θαλάττης ἀπέχει στάδια νʹ, καὶ ποταμὸς Αἴας παρρεῖ τὴν πόλιν. ἀπὸ δὲ Ἀπολλωνίας εἰς Ἀμαντίαν ἐστὶ στάδια τκʹ. καὶ ὁ Αἴας ποταμὸς ἀπὸ τοῦ Πίνδου ὄρους παρὰ τὴν Ἀπολλωνίαν παρρεῖ.

2. [—] πρὸς Ὠρικὸν εἴσω μᾶλλον εἰς τὸν κόλπον. τῆς Ὠρικίας καθήκει εἰς θάλατταν στάδια πʹ, τῆς δὲ Ἀμαντίας στάδια ξʹ.

3. Ἄμασιν ὅμοροι ἐν μεσογείᾳ Ἀτιντᾶνες ὑπὲρ τῆς Ὠρικίας καὶ Καρίας μέχρι Ἰδωνίας. ἐν τῇ Κάστιδι χώρᾳ εἶναι λέγεται

πεδίον ⟨ᾧ⟩ ὄνομα Ἐρύθεια. ἐνταῦθα ὁ Γηρυόνης λέγεται οἰ-
κεῖν καὶ τοὺς βοῦς βουκολεῖν. κατὰ ταῦτά ἐστι τὰ Κεραύνια
ὄρη ἐν τῇ ἠπείρῳ, καὶ νῆσος παρὰ ταῦτά ἐστι μικρὰ ᾗ ὄνομα
Σάσων.

ἐντεῦθεν εἰς Ὠρικὸν πόλιν ἐστὶ παράπλους ἡμέρας τρίτον
μέρος.

27. 1. {Ὠρικοί.} οἱ δὲ Ὠρικοὶ κατοικοῦσι τῆς Ἀμαντίας χώρας.
οἵδε [Ἀμαντιεῖς] εἰσὶ μέχρι ἐνταῦθα Ἰλλυριοὶ ἀπὸ Βουλινῶν.

2. τὸ δὲ στόμα τοῦ Ἰονίου κόλπου ἐστὶν ἀπὸ Κεραυνίων
ὀρῶν μέχρι ἄκρας Ἰαπυγίας. ἐπὶ δὲ Ὑδρόεντα πόλιν ἐν τῇ
Ἰαπυγίᾳ ἀπὸ τῶν Κεραυνίων στάδια τοῦ διάπλου ὡς φ΄, ⟨ὅ⟩
ἐστι τὸ στόμα τοῦ κόλπου· τὰ δὲ ἐντὸς ὁ Ἰόνιος. λιμένες εἰσὶ
πολλοὶ ἐν τῷ Ἀδρίᾳ· τὸ δὲ αὐτὸ Ἀδρίας ἐστὶ καὶ Ἰόνιος.

28. {Χάονες.} μετὰ δὲ Ἰλλυριοὺς Χάονες. ἡ δὲ Χαονία ἐστὶν
εὐλίμενος· οἰκοῦσι δὲ κατὰ κώμας οἱ Χάονες.

παράπλους δ᾽ ἐστὶ Χαονίας ἥμισυ ἡμέρας.

29. {Κόρκυρα.} κατὰ δὲ Χαονίαν νῆσός ἐστι Κόρκυρα καὶ πόλις
Ἑλληνὶς ἐν αὐτῇ, λιμένας ἔχουσα τρεῖς κατὰ τὴν πόλιν· τούτων ὁ εἷς κλειστός. ἐπιβάλλει δὲ Κόρκυρα καὶ ἐπὶ τὴν Θεσπρωτίαν πλεῖον ἢ ἐπὶ τὴν Χαονίαν.

ἐπάνειμι δὲ πάλιν ἐπὶ τὴν ἤπειρον, ὅθεν ἐξετραπόμην.

30. {Θεσπρωτοί.} μετὰ δὲ Χαονίαν Θεσπρωτοί εἰσιν ἔθνος.
οἰκοῦσι δὲ καὶ οὗτοι κατὰ κώμας· ἔστι δὲ καὶ αὕτη εὐλίμενος.
ἐνταῦθά ἐστι λιμὴν ᾧ ὄνομα Ἐλαία· εἰς τοῦτον τὸν λιμένα
ποταμὸς ἐξίησιν Ἀχέρων. καὶ λίμνη Ἀχερουσία, ἐξ ἧς ὁ Ἀχέρων ῥεῖ ποταμός.

παράπλους δὲ τῆς Θεσπρωτίας ἥμισυ ἡμέρας.

31. {Κασσωποί.} μετὰ δὲ Θεσπρωτίαν Κασσωπία ἐστὶν ἔθνος.
οἰκοῦσι δὲ καὶ οὗτοι κατὰ κώμας. παροικοῦσι δὲ οὗτοι ἕως εἰς
τὸν Ἀνακτορικὸν κόλπον.

παράπλους δ᾽ ἐστὶ τῆς Κασσωπῶν χώρας ἥμισυ ἡμέρας.
μικρῷ δὲ ἐλάττων ὁ Ἀνακτορικὸς κόλπος ἐστὶν ἀπὸ τοῦ στόματος ἕως εἰς τὸν μυχὸν σταδίων ρκ΄. τὸ δὲ στόμα εὖρος σταδίων δ΄.

32. {Μολοττία.} μετὰ δὲ Κασσωπίαν Μολοττοί εἰσιν ἔθνος.
οἰκοῦσι δὲ οὗτοι κατὰ κώμας· καθήκουσι δὲ κατὰ μικρὸν ἐνταῦθα ἐπὶ τὴν θάλατταν, εἰς μεσογείαν δὲ πολλῇ.

παράπλους δ᾽ ἐστὶ τῆς Μολοττίας χώρας σταδίων μ΄.

33. 1. {Ἀμβρακία.} μετὰ δὲ Μολοττίαν Ἀμβρακία πόλις Ἑλληνίς· ἀπέχει δὲ αὕτη ἀπὸ θαλάττης στάδια π'. ἔστι δὲ καὶ ἐπὶ θαλάττης τεῖχος καὶ λιμὴν κλειστός.

2. ἐντεῦθεν ἄρχεται ἡ Ἑλλὰς συνεχὴς εἶναι μέχρι Πηνειοῦ ποταμοῦ καὶ Ὁμολίου Μαγνητικῆς πόλεως, ἥ ἐστι παρὰ τὸν ποταμόν.

παράπλους δὲ τῆς Ἀμβρακίας στάδια ρκ'.

34. 1. {Ἀκαρνανία.} μετὰ δὲ Ἀμβρακίαν Ἀκαρνανία ἔθνος ἐστί, καὶ πρώτη πόλις αὐτόθι Ἄργος τὸ Ἀμφιλοχικὸν καὶ Εὔριπος καὶ *Θύρρειον ἐν τῷ κοινῷ.* καὶ ἔξω τοῦ Ἀμβρακικοῦ κόλπου ⟨πόλεις⟩ αἵδε· Ἀνακτόριον καὶ λιμήν, Ἀκτὴ καὶ πόλις Λευκὰς καὶ λιμήν· αὕτη ἀνέχει ἐπὶ τὸν Λευκάταν, ὅ ἐστιν ἀκρωτήριον πόρρωθεν ⟨ἐν⟩ τῇ θαλάττῃ ⟨ὁρατόν⟩. αὕτη ἡ πόλις τὸ πρὶν καὶ Ἐπιλευκάδιοι ὠνομάζετο. *Ἀκαρνᾶνες δὲ στασιάσαντες ἔλαβον ἐκ Κορίνθου ἐποίκους χιλίους· οἱ δὲ ἔποικοι ἀποκτείναντες τούτους τὴν χώραν αὐτοὶ ἔχουσιν. αὕτη δ' ἐστὶ νῦν νῆσος τὸν ἰσθμὸν ἀποτεταφρευμένη.* μετὰ δὲ ταῦτα πόλις Φαρά. καὶ κατὰ ταῦτα νῆσός ἐστιν Ἰθάκη καὶ πόλις καὶ λιμήν. μετὰ ταῦτα νῆσος Κεφαληνία.

2. ἐπάνειμι δὲ πάλιν ἐπὶ τὴν ἤπειρον, ὅθεν ἀπέλιπον. μετὰ ταῦτα πόλις Ἀλυζία, καὶ κατὰ ταύτην νῆσος Κάρνος, καὶ πόλις Ἀστακὸς καὶ λιμήν, καὶ ποταμὸς Ἀχελῷος καὶ Οἰνιάδαι πόλις· καὶ εἰς ταύτας [τὰς πόλεις] ἀνάπλους ἐστὶ κατὰ τὸν Ἀχελῷον. εἰσὶ δὲ καὶ ἄλλαι πόλεις Ἀκαρνάνων ἐν μεσογείᾳ.

παράπλους δὲ Ἀκαρνανίας ἐστὶν ἡμερῶν δύο.

3. ἡ δὲ Ἀκαρνανία ἐστὶ πᾶσα εὐλίμενος· καὶ κατὰ ταῦτα νῆσοι παράκεινται πολλαί, ἃς ὁ Ἀχελῷος προσχωννύων ἤπειρον ποιεῖ. καλοῦνται δὲ Ἐχινάδες αἱ νῆσοι· εἰσὶ δὲ ἔρημοι.

35. {Αἰτωλία.} μετὰ δὲ Ἀκαρνανίαν Αἰτωλία ἐστὶν ἔθνος, καὶ πόλεις ἐν αὐτῇ εἰσὶν αἵδε· Καλυδών, Ἁλίκαρνα, Μολύκρεια· καὶ ὁ Δελφικὸς κόλπος· στόμα δὲ τοῦ κόλπου τούτου ἐστὶ στάδια ι', καὶ ἐπ' αὐτοῦ ἱερόν· καὶ Ναύπακτος πόλις· καὶ ἐπ' αὐτῇ πόλεις εἰσὶν ἄλλαι πολλαὶ Αἰτωλοῖς ἐν μεσογείᾳ.

παράπλους δ' ἐστὶ τῆς Αἰτωλίας ἡμέρας μιᾶς.

ἡ δὲ Αἰτωλία παρήκει τὴν Λοκρίδα πᾶσαν ἀπὸ μεσογαίας μέχρι Αἰνιάνων.

36. {Λοκροί.} μετὰ δὲ Αἰτωλοὺς Λοκροί εἰσιν ἔθνος, ἐν οἷς εἰσὶν

⟨οἱ⟩ Ὀζόλαι καλούμενοι, καὶ πόλεις αἵδε· Εὐάνθις, Ἄμφισσα. εἰσὶ δὲ καὶ τούτοις πόλεις ἐν μεσογείᾳ.

παράπλους δ' ἐστὶ τῆς Λοκρῶν χώρας τὸ ἥμισυ ἡμέρας.

37. {Φωκεῖς.} μετὰ δὲ Λοκροὺς εἰσιν ἔθνος Φωκεῖς κατὰ τὸ Κιρραῖον πεδίον, καὶ τὸ ἱερὸν τοῦ Ἀπόλλωνος καὶ Δελφοὶ πόλις καὶ Ἀντίκυρα πόλις, οὗ βέλτιστα ἑλλεβορίζονται.

παράπλους δὲ τῆς Φωκέων χώρας ἥμισυ ἡμέρας.

38. {Βοιωτοί.} μετὰ δὲ Φωκεῖς Βοιωτοί εἰσιν ἔθνος, καὶ πόλεις αἵδε· Κορσιαί, Σίφαι καὶ λιμήν, Εὔτρησις καὶ τεῖχος Βοιωτῶν.

παράπλους δὲ τῆς Βοιωτίας ἥμισυ ἡμέρας ⟨ἢ⟩ ἔλαττον.

39. {Μεγαρεῖς.} μετὰ δὲ Βοιωτοὺς Μεγαρεῖς εἰσιν ἔθνος, καὶ πόλεις αἵδε· Αἰγόσθενα, Πηγαὶ τεῖχος, Γεράνεια, Αἴγειρος.

παράπλους δὲ τῆς Μεγαρέων χώρας στάδια ρ΄.

40. {Κόρινθος.} μετὰ δὲ Μεγαρεῖς ἡ Κόρινθος πόλις καὶ ἱερόν, Λέχαιον, Ἰσθμός.

ἐντεῦθεν ἤδη ἄρχεται ἡ Πελοπόννησος.

ἔστι δ' ἀπὸ θαλάσσης ἡ ὁδὸς πρὸς τὴν ἐπὶ ἡμῶν θάλασσαν διὰ τοῦ Ἰσθμοῦ στάδια μ΄. ταῦτα κολπώδη πάντα.

παράπλους δὲ τῆς Κορινθίων χώρας ἥμισυ ἡμέρας.

41. {Σικυών.} μετὰ δὲ Κόρινθον Σικυὼν πόλις.

ταύτης παράπλους στάδια ρκ΄.

42. {Ἀχαιοί.} μετὰ δὲ Σικυῶνα Ἀχαιοὶ ἔθνος, καὶ πόλεις εἰσὶν ἐν αὐτοῖς αἵδε· Πελλήνη, Αἴγειρα, Αἰγαί, Αἴγιον, Ῥύπες, ἔξω δὲ Ῥίου Πάτραι, Δύμη.

παράπλους δὲ τῆς Ἀχαΐας χώρας στάδια ψ΄.

43. {Ἠλίς.} μετὰ δὲ Ἀχαιοὺς Ἠλίς ἐστιν ἔθνος, καὶ πόλεις ἐν αὐτῇ αἵδε· Κυλλήνη καὶ λιμήν, καὶ ποταμὸς Ἀλφειός· ἔστι δὲ καὶ ἄλλη συνοικία πόλεων Ἠλις ἐν μεσογείᾳ. κατὰ ταύτην τὴν χώραν ἐστὶ νῆσος Ζάκυνθος, ἐν ᾗ καὶ πόλις καὶ λιμήν.

παράπλους δὲ τῆς Ἠλείων χώρας ἄχρι ἐπὶ τοὺς Λεπρεατῶν ⟨ὅρους⟩ στάδια ψ΄.

44. {Ἀρκαδία.} μετὰ δὲ Ἦλιν Ἀρκαδία ἔθνος ἐστί. καθήκει δὲ ἡ Ἀρκαδία ἐπὶ θάλατταν κατὰ Λέπρεον ἐκ μεσογείας. εἰσὶ δὲ αὐτῶν πόλεις ἐν μεσογείᾳ [αἱ μεγάλαι] αἵδε· ⟨ἡ Μεγάλη Πόλις⟩, Τεγέα, Μαντίνεια, Ἡραία, Ὀρχομενός, Στύμφαλος. εἰσὶ δὲ καὶ ἄλλαι πόλεις.

παράπλους δὲ τῆς Λεπρεατῶν χώρας στάδια ρ΄.

45. {Μεσσήνη.} μετὰ δ' Ἀρκαδίαν ἐστὶν ἔθνος Μεσσήνη, καὶ πόλεις ἐν αὐτῇ αἵδε· [πρώτη Μεσσήνη καὶ λιμὴν] Κυπάρισσος ἀπέχουσα ἀπὸ θαλάττης στάδια ζ΄, ⟨Πρωτὴ νῆσος καὶ λιμήν⟩, Ἰθώμη ἐν μεσογείᾳ ἀπέχουσα ἀπὸ θαλάττης στάδια π΄.

παράπλους δὲ τῆς Μεσσηνίας χώρας στάδια τ΄.

46. 1. {Λακεδαίμων.} ⟨μετὰ δὲ Μεσσήνην⟩ Λακεδαίμων ἔθνος, καὶ πόλεις ἐν αὐτῇ εἰσὶν αἵδε· Ἀσίνη, Μοθώνη, Ἀχίλλειος λιμὴν καὶ ἀντίπυγος τούτου Ψαμαθοῦς λιμήν. τούτων ἀμφοτέρων ἐν μέσῳ προέχον εἰς θάλασσαν ἱερὸν Ποσειδῶνος, Ταίναρος. καὶ Λᾶς πόλις καὶ λιμήν, Γύθειον ἐν ᾧ νεώριον καὶ τεῖχος, καὶ ποταμὸς Εὐρώτας, καὶ Βοία πόλις, καὶ Μαλέα ἄκρα. {Κύθηρα.} κατὰ ταύτην κεῖται Κύθηρα νῆσος καὶ πόλις καὶ λιμήν. κατὰ δὲ ταύτην ἐστὶ Κρήτη νῆσος.

2. μετὰ δὲ ταύτην τὴν προειρημένην ἄκραν Μαλέαν Σίδη πόλις καὶ λιμήν, Ἐπίδαυρος πόλις καὶ λιμήν, Πρασία πόλις καὶ λιμήν, Ἀνθάνα πόλις καὶ λιμήν. εἰσὶ δὲ καὶ ἄλλαι πολλαὶ πόλεις Λακεδαιμονίων. ἐν μεσογείᾳ δ' ἐστὶ Σπάρτη καὶ ἄλλαι πολλαί.

παράπλους δὲ τῆς Λακεδαιμονίων χώρας ἡμερῶν τριῶν.

47. 1. {Κρήτη.} κατὰ Λακεδαίμονα νῆσος κεῖται Κρήτη· ἐγγυτάτω γὰρ Λακεδαίμων κεῖται τῆς Εὐρώπης. διάπλους δὲ ἀπὸ Λακεδαίμονος ἕως ἐπὶ τὸ ἀκρωτήριον τῆς Κρήτης ἐφ' ᾧ ἐστι πόλις Φαλάσαρνα, ἡμέρας δρόμος.

ἀπὸ δὲ Φαλασάρνων Κριοῦ Μέτωπόν ἐστιν ἀκρωτήριον. πρὸς νότον δὲ ἄνεμον πλοῦς εἰς Λιβύην, ἐπὶ Χερρονήσου δὲ τὰς Ἀζιρίδας τὰς Κυρηναίων πλοῦς ἡμέρας καὶ νυκτός.

2. ἔστι δὲ ἡ Κρήτη μακρὰ στάδια βφ΄, στενὴ δέ, καὶ τέταται ἀπὸ ἡλίου δυσμῶν πρὸς ἡλίου ἀνατολάς. οἰκοῦσι δὲ ἐν Κρήτῃ Ἕλληνες, οἱ μὲν ἄποικοι Λακεδαιμονίων, οἱ δὲ Ἀργείων, οἱ δὲ Ἀθηναίων, οἱ δὲ ἀπὸ τῆς Ἑλλάδος τῆς ἄλλης ὁπόθεν ἔτυχεν. εἰσὶ δέ τινες αὐτῶν καὶ αὐτόχθονες. πόλεις πολλαὶ ἐν Κρήτῃ.

3. {Κρήτης θέσις.} ⟨ἐπὶ Κωρύκ⟩ῳ ἀκρωτηρίῳ ἐστὶ πρώτη πόλις πρὸς ἥλιον δυόμενον ἡ προειρημένη Φαλάσαρνα καὶ λιμὴν κλειστός. Πολυρρηνία, καὶ διήκει ἀπὸ βορέου πρὸς νότον. Δικτυνναῖον Ἀρτέμιδος ἱερὸν πρὸς βορέαν ἄνεμον, τῆς χώρας Περγαμίας. πρὸς νότον δὲ Ὑρτακίνα. Κυδωνία καὶ λιμὴν κλειστὸς πρὸς βορέαν· ἐν μεσογείᾳ δὲ Ἔλυρος πόλις. πρὸς νότον δὲ Λίσσα πόλις καὶ λιμὴν παρὰ Κριοῦ μέτωπον. [πρὸς βορέαν δὲ ἄνεμον ὄρος κάλλιστον καὶ λιμὴν ἐν αὐτῷ ὅλους καὶ πᾶν] πρὸς βορέαν δὲ ἄν⟨εμον⟩ ἡ Ἀπτεραία χώρα. εἶτα ἡ Λαμπαία, καὶ διήκει αὕτη ἀμφοτέρωθεν, καὶ ποταμὸς Μεσάπος ἐν αὐτῇ ἐστι. 4. μετὰ δὲ ταύτην ὄρος Ἴδα καὶ Ἐλεύθερναι πρὸς βορέαν. πρὸς νότον δὲ Σύβριτα καὶ λιμὴν πρὸς νότον Φαιστός. πρὸς βορέαν Ὀαξὸς καὶ Κνωσσός. πρὸς δὲ νότον Γόρτυνα. Ῥαῦκος ⟨ἐν μεσογείᾳ⟩. ἐν μεσογείᾳ δὲ Λύκτος, καὶ διήκει αὕτη ἀμφοτέρωθεν. ⟨πρὸς βορέαν δὲ ἄνεμον ὄρος Κάδιστος καὶ λιμὴν ἐν αὐτῷ Ὀλοῦς καὶ †πᾶν ...⟩. Πρασός· διήκει ἀμφοτέρωθεν. Ἴτανος ἀκρωτήριον Κρήτης πρὸς ἥλιον ἀνίσχοντα.

εἰσὶ δὲ καὶ ἄλλαι πόλεις ἐν Κρήτῃ· λέγεται δὲ εἶναι ἑκατόμπολις.

48. {Κυκλάδες νῆσοι.} Κυκλάδες δὲ αἵδε εἰσὶ κατὰ τὴν Λακεδαιμονίαν χώραν οἰκούμεναι· Μῆλος καὶ λιμήν, κατὰ δὲ ταύτην Κίμωλος, κατὰ δὲ ταύτην Φολέγανδρος, κατὰ δὲ ταύτην Σίκινος νῆσος καὶ πόλις. κατὰ δὲ ταύτην Θήρα, κατὰ δὲ ταύτην Ἀνάφη, κατὰ δὲ ταύτην Ἀστυπάλαια.

ἐπάνειμι δὲ πάλιν ἐπὶ τὴν ἤπειρον, ὅθεν ἐξετραπόμην.

49. {Ἄργος.} μετὰ δὲ Λακεδαίμονα πόλις ἐστὶν Ἄργος, καὶ ἐν αὐτῇ Ναυπλία πόλις καὶ λιμήν· ἐν μεσογείᾳ δὲ Κλεωναὶ καὶ Μυκῆναι καὶ Τίρυνς.

παράπλους τῆς Ἀργείας χώρας κύκλῳ, ἔστι γὰρ κόλπος ὁ Ἀργολικὸς καλούμενος, στάδια ρν΄.

50. 1. {Ἐπίδαυρος.} μετὰ δ’ Ἄργος ἡ Ἐπιδαυρία χώρα· καθήκει γὰρ εἰς τὸν κόλπον τοῦτον στάδα λ΄.

2. μετὰ δὲ τὴν Ἐπιδαυρίαν χώραν Ἁλία καὶ λιμήν. αὕτη ἐστὶ ἐπὶ τῷ στόματι τοῦ Ἀργολικοῦ κόλπου.

περίπλους ταύτης ἐστὶ σταδίων ρ΄.

51. 1. {Ἑρμίων.} μετὰ δὲ ταύτην Ἑρμιὼν πόλις ἐστὶ καὶ λιμήν.
ταύτης δὲ περίπλους σταδίων π΄.

2. μετὰ δὲ Ἑρμιόνα Σκύλλαιόν ἐστιν ἀκρωτήριον τοῦ κόλπου τοῦ πρὸς Ἰσθμόν· ἔστι δὲ τὸ Σκύλλαιον τῆς Τροιζηνίας. καταντικρὺ δὲ αὐτοῦ ἐστι Σούνιον ἀκρωτήριον τῆς Ἀθηναίων χώρας. κατὰ δὲ τοῦτό ἐστι νῆσος Βέλβινα καὶ πόλις.

3. τούτου τοῦ κόλπου ἀπὸ τούτου τοῦ στόματος εἴσω εἰς τὸν Ἰσθμὸν στάδιά ἐστι ψμ΄. ἔστι δὲ ὁ κόλπος οὗτος αὐτὸς κατὰ στόμα εὐθύτατος.

52. 1. {Τροιζηνία.} μετὰ δὲ Ἑρμιόνα Τροιζὴν πόλις καὶ λιμήν. παράπλους δ' ἐστὶν αὐτῆς στάδια λ΄.

2. μετὰ δὲ ταῦτα νῆσός ἐστι Καλαυρία καὶ πόλις καὶ λιμήν. παράπλους δ' ἐστὶν αὐτῆς στάδια τ΄.

53. {Αἴγινα.} κατὰ δὲ ταύτην νῆσός ἐστι καὶ πόλις Αἴγινα καὶ λιμένες δύο.
ἐπάνειμι δὲ πάλιν ἐπὶ τὴν ἤπειρον, ὅθεν ἐξετραπόμην.

54. {Ἐπίδαυρος.} μετὰ δὲ Τροιζηνίαν πόλις Ἐπίδαυρος καὶ λιμήν. παράπλους δὲ τῆς Ἐπιδαυρίας χώρας στάδια ⟨ρ⟩λ΄.

55. {[Κεγχρεία]. ⟨Κορινθία⟩.} μετὰ δὲ Ἐπίδαυρον ἡ Κορινθίων χώρα ἐστὶν ⟨ἡ⟩ πρὸς ἠῶ, καὶ τεῖχος Κεγχρειαὶ καὶ Ἰσθμός, οὗ ἱερὸν Ποσειδῶνος.

ἐνταῦθα ἡ Πελοπόννησος λήγει.

ἔστι δὲ καὶ ἔξω τοῦ Ἰσθμοῦ χώρα Κορινθίοις, καὶ τεῖχος Σιδοῦς καὶ ἕτερον τεῖχος Κρεμμυῶν.

παράπλους δὲ τῆς Κορινθίων χώρας μέχρι τῶν ὁρίων τῶν Μεγαρέων στάδια τ΄.

56. {Μέγαρα.} ἀπὸ δὲ τῆς Κορινθίων χώρας Μέγαρα πόλις ἐστὶ καὶ λιμὴν καὶ Νίσαια τεῖχος.

παράπλους δὲ τῆς Μεγαρέων χώρας μέχρι Ἰαπίδος, ἔστι γὰρ οὗτος ὅρος τῆς Ἀθηναίων χώρας, στάδια ρμ΄.

57. 1. {Ἀττική.} μετὰ δὲ Μεγαρεῖς εἰσὶν Ἀθηναίων πόλεις. καὶ πρῶτον τῆς Ἀττικῆς Ἐλευσίς, οὗ ἱερὸν Δήμητρός ἐστι καὶ τεῖχος {[καὶ] νῆσος Σαλαμίς}. κατὰ τοῦτό ἐστι Σαλαμὶς νῆσος καὶ πόλις καὶ λιμήν. ἔπειτα ὁ Πειραιεὺς καὶ τὰ σκέλη καὶ Ἀθῆναι. ὁ δὲ Πειραιεὺς λιμένας ἔχει γ΄. **2.** Ἀνάφλυστος τεῖχος καὶ λιμήν. Σούνιον ἀκρωτήριον καὶ τεῖχος, ἱερὸν Ποσειδῶνος. Θορικὸς τεῖχος καὶ λιμένες δύο. Ῥαμνοῦς τεῖχος. εἰσὶ δὲ καὶ ἄλλοι λιμένες ἐν τῇ Ἀττικῇ πολλοί.

περίπλους τῆς Ἀθηναίων χώρας στάδια ͵αρμ΄. ἀπὸ Ἰαπίδος χώρας ἐπὶ Σούνιον στάδια υϟ΄. ἀπὸ Σουνίου μέχρι τῶν ὅρων τῶν Βοιωτῶν στάδια χν΄.

58. 1. κατὰ δὲ τὴν Ἀττικήν εἰσι νῆσοι αἱ Κυκλάδες καλούμεναι, καὶ πόλεις αἵδε ἐν ταῖς νήσοις· {Νῆσοι Κυκλάδες} Κέως· αὕτη τετράπολις, ⟨Ποιήεσσα πόλις⟩ καὶ λιμήν, Κορησσία, Ἰουλίς, Καρθαία. Ἑλένη. Κύθνος νῆσος καὶ πόλις. Σέριφος νῆσος καὶ πόλις καὶ λιμήν. Σίφνος. Πάρος λιμένας ἔχουσα β΄, ὧν τὸν ἕνα

κλειστόν. Νάξος. Δῆλος. Ῥήνη. Σῦρος. Μύκονος· αὕτη δίπολις.
Τῆνος καὶ λιμήν. Ἄνδρος καὶ λιμήν. αὗται μὲν αἱ Κυκλάδες
νῆσοι.

2. ὑπὸ δὲ ταύταις ἕτεραι νῆσοι αἵδε πρὸς νότον· Ἴος καὶ
λιμήν· ἐν ταύτῃ Ὅμηρος τέθαπται. Ἀμοργὸς, αὕτη τρίπολις,
καὶ λιμήν. Ἴκαρος, δίπολις.

3. μετὰ δὲ Ἄνδρον Εὔβοια νῆσος· αὕτη τετράπολις. εἰσὶ δὲ ἐν
αὐτῇ Κάρυστος, Ἐρέτρια καὶ λιμήν, Χαλκὶς καὶ λιμήν, Ἑστίαια
καὶ λιμήν. ἡ δὲ Εὔβοια ἀπὸ Κηναίου Διὸς ἱεροῦ ἐπὶ Γεραιστόν,
Ποσειδῶνος ἱερόν, ἔχει στάδια ͵ατν´· τὸ δὲ πλάτος στενή ἐστιν
ἡ Εὔβοια.

4. ἐν δὲ τῷ Αἰγαίῳ πελάγει εἰσὶ νῆσοι αἵδε· κατ᾽ Ἐρέτριαν
Σκῦρος καὶ πόλις· Ἴκος, αὕτη δίπολις· Πεπάρηθος, αὕτη τρίπολις, καὶ λιμήν· Σκίαθος, αὕτη δίπολις, καὶ λιμήν.

μετὰ ταῦτα ἐπάνειμι πάλιν ἐπὶ τὴν ἤπειρον, ὅθεν ἐξετραπόμην.

59. {Βοιωτοί.} μετὰ δὲ Ἀθήνας εἰσὶ Βοιωτοὶ ἔθνος· καθήκουσι
γὰρ οὗτοι καὶ ἐπὶ ταύτην τὴν θάλασσαν. καὶ ἔστιν ἐν αὐτῇ
πρῶτον ἱερὸν Δήλιον, Αὐλὶς ἱερόν, Εὔριπος, τεῖχος, Ἀνθηδὼν
τεῖχος, Θῆβαι, Θεσπιαί, Ὀρχομενὸς ἐν μεσογείᾳ. εἰσὶ δὲ καὶ ἄλλαι πόλεις.

παράπλους δὲ τῆς Βοιωτίας χώρας ἀπὸ Δηλίου μέχρι τῶν
Λοκρῶν ὁρίων στάδια σν´.

60. {Λοκροί.} μετὰ δὲ Βοιωτοὺς εἰσι Λοκροὶ ἔθνος. καί εἰσι κατ᾽
Εὔβοιαν αὐτοῖς πόλεις αἵδε· Λάρυμνα, Κῦνος, Ὀποῦς, Ἀλόπη·
εἰσὶ δὲ καὶ ἄλλαι πολλαὶ Λοκροῖς.

παράπλους δὲ τῆς χώρας αὐτῶν στάδια σ´.

61. {Φωκεῖς.} μετὰ δὲ Λοκροὺς εἰσι Φωκεῖς· διήκουσι γὰρ καὶ
οὗτοι εἰς τὴν θάλασσαν ταύτην. καὶ πόλεις αὐτοῖς εἰσιν αἵδε·
Θρόνιον, Κνημίς, Ἐλάτεια, Πανοπεύς. εἰσὶ δὲ καὶ ἄλλαι πόλεις
αὐτοῖς ἐν μεσογείᾳ.

παράπλους δ᾽ ἐστὶ τῆς Φωκέων χώρας στάδια σ´.

62. 1. {Μηλιεῖς.} μετὰ δὲ Φωκεῖς εἰσι *Μηλιεῖς* καὶ ὁ κόλπος ὁ
Μηλιεύς. ἐν τούτῳ τῷ κόλπῳ εἰσὶν οἱ Λιμοδωριεῖς καλούμενοι
οἴδε· Ἐρινεός, Βοῖον, Κυτίνιον. ἐνταῦθα Θερμοπύλαι, Τραχίς,
Οἴτη, Ἡράκλεια, Σπερχειὸς ποταμός.

2. {Μαλιεῖς.} μετὰ δὲ Μηλιεῖς ⟨Μαλιεῖς⟩ ἔθνος. ἔστι δὲ
Μαλιεῦσιν ἡ πρώτη πόλις Λαμία, ἐσχάτη δὲ Ἐχῖνος· εἰσὶ δὲ καὶ

ἄλλαι πόλεις Μαλιεῦσι, μέχρι οὗ ὁ κόλπος ἐπιθίγῃ. καὶ τῇ
Μαλιέων χώρᾳ ἐποικοῦσιν ἄνωθεν ἀπὸ μεσογείας Αἰνιᾶνες,
καὶ δι᾽ αὐτῶν ῥεῖ ὁ Σπερχειὸς ποταμός.

63. ἔξω δὲ τοῦ Μαλιαίου κόλπου {Ἀχαιοὶ} εἰσὶ⟨ν⟩ [δὲ] Ἀχαιοὶ
Φθιῶται ἔθνος· εἰσὶ δὲ καὶ ἐν τῷ Παγασητικῷ κόλπῳ ἐπ᾽ ἀριστερᾷ εἰσπλέοντι, ὡς ἐπὶ τὸ ἥμισυ τοῦ κόλπου. Ἀχαιῶν πόλεις
αἵδε· Ἀντρῶνες, Λάρισσα, Μελιταία, Δημήτριον, Θῆβαι· εἰσὶ δὲ
καὶ ἄλλαι πόλεις Ἀχαιοῖς ἐν μεσογείᾳ.

64. 1. {Θετταλία.} μετὰ δὲ Ἀχαιοὺς Θετταλία καθήκει ἐπὶ
θάλατταν ἐκ μεσογείας κατὰ στενὸν εἰς τὸν Παγασητικὸν κόλπον στάδιοι λ΄.

καί εἰσι Θετταλίας πόλεις αἵδε ἐπὶ θαλάττῃ· Ἀμφῆναι,
Παγασαί· ἐν δὲ μεσογείᾳ Φεραί, Λάρισσα, Φάρσαλος, Κιέριον,
Πελινναῖον, Σκοτοῦσα, Κραννών. εἰσὶ δὲ καὶ ἄλλαι πόλεις Θετ-
ταλῶν ἐν μεσογείᾳ. ἡ δὲ Θετταλία παρήκει ἐν μεσογείᾳ ὑπὲρ
Αἰνιάνων καὶ Δολόπων καὶ Μαλιέων καὶ Ἀχαιῶν καὶ Μαγνή-
των μέχρι Τεμπῶν. 2. τοῦ δὲ Παγασητικοῦ κόλπου μῆκός
ἐστιν ἀπὸ στόματος εἰς τὸν μυχὸν Παγασῶν πλοῦς προαριστίδιος. τὸ δὲ στόμα αὐτοῦ ἐστι στάδια ε΄.

ἐν δὲ τῷ Παγασητικῷ κόλπῳ ἐστὶ νῆσος Κικύνηθος καὶ
πόλις.

65. 1. {Μάγνητες.} ⟨μετὰ δὲ Θετταλίαν⟩ ἔθνος ἐστὶ Μάγνητες
παρὰ θάλατταν, καὶ πόλεις αἵδε· Ἰωλκός, Μεθώνη, Κορακαί,
Σπάλαυθρα, Ὀλιζῶν, Τίσαι λιμήν. ἔξω δὲ τοῦ κόλπου Παγασι-
τικοῦ Μελίβοια, Ῥιζοῦς, Εὐρυμεναί, Ἄμυρος. ἐν μεσογείᾳ δὲ
ἐποικοῦσιν ἔθνος Περραιβοί, Ἕλληνες.

2. μέχρι ἐνταῦθά ἐστιν ἀπὸ Ἀμβρακίας συνεχὴς ἡ Ἑλλάς·
ἐπιεικῶς δὲ καὶ ⟨τὰ⟩ ἐπιθαλάσσια ⟨ἐν⟩ Ἑλλάδι ὁμοίως
ἐστίν.

66. 1. {Μακεδονία.} ἀπὸ δὲ Πηνειοῦ ποταμοῦ Μακεδόνες εἰσὶν
ἔθνος, καὶ κόλπος Θερμαῖος.

2. πρώτη πόλις Μακεδονίας Ἡράκλειον· Δῖον, Πύδνα πόλις
Ἑλληνίς, Μεθώνη πόλις Ἑλληνὶς καὶ Ἁλιάκμων ποταμός,
Ἄλωρος πόλις καὶ ποταμὸς Λουδίας, Πέλλα πόλις καὶ βασίλειον ἐν αὐτῇ καὶ ἀνάπλους εἰς αὐτὴν ἀνὰ τὸν Λουδίαν· Ἀξιὸς
ποταμός, Ἐχέδωρος ποταμός, Θέρμη πόλις, Αἴνεια Ἑλληνίς.

3. Παλλήνη ἄκρα μακρὰ εἰς τὸ πέλαγος ἀνατείνουσα, καὶ
πόλεις αἵδε ἐν τῇ Παλλήνῃ Ἑλληνίδες· Ποτίδαια ἐν τῷ μέσῳ

τὸν ἰσθμὸν ἐμφράττουσα, Μένδη, Ἄφυτις, Θραμβηῒς, Σκιώνη, Κανάστραιον τῆς Παλλήνης ἱερὸν ἀκρωτήριον.

4. ἔξω δὲ τοῦ ἰσθμοῦ πόλεις αἵδε· Ὄλυνθος Ἑλληνίς, Μηκύβερνα Ἑλληνίς.

Σερμυλία Ἑλληνὶς καὶ κόλπος Σερμυλικός, Τορώνη πόλις Ἑλληνὶς καὶ λιμήν.

Δῖον Ἑλληνίς, Θυσσὸς Ἑλληνίς, Κλεωναὶ Ἑλληνίς, Ἄθως ὄρος, Ἀκρόθωοι Ἑλληνίς, Χαραδροῦς Ἑλληνίς, Ὀλόφυξος Ἑλληνίς, Ἄκανθος Ἑλληνίς, Ἄλαπτα Ἑλληνίς.

Ἀρέθουσα Ἑλληνίς, Βολβὴ λίμνη, Ἀπολλωνία Ἑλληνίς.

5. εἰσὶ δὲ καὶ ἄλλαι Μακεδονίας ἐν μεσογείᾳ πολλαί. ἔστι δὲ κολπώδης.

παράπλους δὲ περὶ τοὺς κόλπους δύο ἡμερῶν.

μετὰ δὲ Μακεδονίαν Στρυμὼν ποταμός· οὗτος ὁρίζει Μακεδονίαν καὶ Θρᾴκην.

67. 1. {Θρᾴκη.} διήκει δὲ ἡ Θρᾴκη ἀπὸ Στρυμόνος ποταμοῦ μέχρι Ἴστρου ποταμοῦ τοῦ ἐν τῷ Εὐξείνῳ Πόντῳ. εἰσὶ δὲ ἐν Θρᾴκη πόλεις Ἑλληνίδες αἵδε· Ἀμφίπολις, Φάγρης, Γαληψός, Οἰσύμη καὶ ἄλλα ἐμπόρια Θασίων. κατὰ ταῦτά ἐστι Θάσος νῆσος καὶ πόλις καὶ λιμένες δύο· τούτων ὁ εἷς κλειστός.

2. ἐπάνειμι δὲ πάλιν ὅθεν ἐξετραπόμην. Νεάπολις κατὰ ταύτην. Δάτον πόλις Ἑλληνίς, ἣν ᾤκισε Καλλίστρατος Ἀθηναῖος, καὶ ποταμὸς Νέστος, Ἄβδηρα πόλις, Κούδητος ποταμὸς καὶ πόλεις Δίκαια καὶ Μαρώνεια.

3. κατὰ ταῦτα Σαμοθράκη ⟨νῆσος⟩ καὶ λιμήν. κατὰ ταύτην ἐν τῇ ἠπείρῳ ἐμπόρια Δρῦς, Ζώνη, Δουρίσκος. ποταμὸς Ἕβρος καὶ ἐπ᾽ αὐτῷ τεῖχος Αἶνος, πόλις καὶ λιμήν. τείχη Αἰνίων ἐν τῇ Θρᾴκη, Μέλας κόλπος, Μέλας ποταμός, Δερὶς ἐμπόριον, Κῶβρυς ἐμπόριον Καρδιανῶν καὶ ἄλλο Κύπασις.

4. {Ἴμβρος καὶ Λῆμνος.} κατὰ τὸν Μέλανα κόλπον Ἴμβρος ἐστὶ νῆσος καὶ πόλις, καὶ Λῆμνος νῆσος καὶ λιμήν.

5. ἐπάνειμι πάλιν ἐπὶ τὴν ἤπειρον, ὅθεν ἐξετραπόμην. {Χερρόνησος.} μετὰ δὲ τὸν Μέλανα κόλπον ἐστὶν ἡ Θρᾳκία Χερρόνησος. καὶ πόλεις ἐν αὐτῇ αἵδε· Καρδία, Ἴδη, Παιών, Ἀλωπεκόννησος, Ἄραπλος, Ἐλαιοῦς, Μάδυτος, Σηστὸς ἐπὶ τοῦ στόματος τῆς Προποντίδος, ⟨ὅ⟩ ἐστι στάδια Ϝ´. ἐντὸς δὲ Αἰγὸς Ποταμοῦ Κρῆσσα, Κριθώτη, Πακτύη. 6. μέχρις ἐνταῦθα ἡ Θρᾳκία Χερρόνησος. ἐκ Πακτύης δὲ εἰς Καρδίαν διὰ τοῦ αὐχένος πεζῇ

στάδια μ΄, ἐκ θαλάττης εἰς θάλατταν· καὶ πόλις ἐν τῷ μέσῳ ᾗ ὄνομα Ἀγορά. Χερρονήσου μῆκος ἐκ Καρδίας εἰς Ἐλαιοῦντα, ταύτῃ γάρ ἐστι μακροτάτη, στάδια υ΄.

7. μετὰ δὲ τὴν Χερρόνησόν ἐστι Θρᾴκια τείχη τάδε· πρῶτον Λευκὴ ἀκτή, Τειρίστασις, Ἡράκλεια, Γάνος, Γανίαι, Νέον Τεῖχος, Πέρινθος πόλις καὶ λιμήν, Δαμινὸν τεῖχος, Σηλυμβρία πόλις καὶ λιμήν. ἀπὸ τούτου ἐπὶ τοῦ στόματος τοῦ Πόντου εἰσὶ στάδιοι φ΄.

8. {Ἀνάπλους.} καλεῖται δὲ Ἀνάπλους ὁ τόπος ἀνὰ Βόσπορον μέχρι ἂν ἔλθῃς ἐφ᾽ Ἱερόν. ἀφ᾽ Ἱεροῦ δὲ τὸ στόμα ἐστὶ τοῦ Πόντου, εὖρος στάδια ζ΄.

9. εἰσὶ δὲ ἐν τῷ Πόντῳ πόλεις Ἑλληνίδες αἵδε ἐν Θρᾴκῃ· Ἀπολλωνία, Μεσημβρία, Ὀδησὸς πόλις, Κάλλατις, ⟨Ἴστρος⟩ καὶ ποταμὸς Ἴστρος.

10. παράπλους δὲ τῆς Θρᾴκης ἀπὸ Στρυμόνος ποταμοῦ μέχρι Σηστοῦ δύο ἡμερῶν καὶ νυκτῶν δύο· ἀπὸ δὲ Σηστοῦ μέχρι στόματος τοῦ Πόντου δύο ἡμερῶν καὶ νυκτῶν δύο· ἀπὸ δὲ τοῦ στόματος μέχρι τοῦ Ἴστρου ποταμοῦ ἡμερῶν τριῶν καὶ νυκτῶν τριῶν. ὁ σύμπας περίπλους ἀπὸ Θρᾴκης καὶ ποταμοῦ Στρυμόνος μέχρι Ἴστρου ποταμοῦ ὀκτὼ ἡμερῶν καὶ ὀκτὼ νυκτῶν.

68. 1. {Σκυθία, Ταῦροι.} μετὰ δὲ Θρᾴκην εἰσὶ Σκύθαι ἔθνος καὶ πόλεις ἐν αὐτοῖς Ἑλληνίδες αἵδε· Τύρας ποταμός, Νικώνιον πόλις, Ὀφιοῦσα πόλις.

2. ἐπὶ δὲ τῇ Σκυθικῇ ἐποικοῦσι Ταῦροι ἔθνος ἀκρωτήριον τῆς ἠπείρου· εἰς θάλατταν δὲ τὸ ἀκρωτήριόν ἐστιν. ἐν δὲ τῇ Ταυρικῇ οἰκοῦσιν Ἕλληνες, ⟨καὶ πόλεις ἐν αὐτοῖς⟩ αἵδε· Χερρόνησος ἐμπόριον. Κριοῦ Μέτωπον, ἀκρωτήριον τῆς Ταυρικῆς.

3. μετὰ δὲ ταῦτά εἰσι Σκύθαι πάλιν, πόλεις δὲ Ἑλληνίδες αἵδε ἐν αὐτῇ· Θευδοσία, Κύταια καὶ Νύμφαιον, Παντικάπαιον, Μυρμήκιον.

παράπλους εὐθὺς ἀπὸ Ἴστρου ἐπὶ Κριοῦ Μέτωπον τριῶν ἡμερῶν καὶ τριῶν νυκτῶν, ὁ δὲ παρὰ γῆν διπλάσιος· ἔστι γὰρ κόλπος.

4. ἐν δὲ τῷ κόλπῳ τούτῳ νῆσός ἐστι, νῆσος δὲ ἐρήμη ᾗ ὄνομα Λευκή, ἱερὰ τοῦ Ἀχιλλέως.

ἀπὸ δὲ Κριοῦ Μετώπου πλοῦς εἰς Παντικάπαιον ἡμέρας καὶ νυκτός· ἀπὸ δὲ Παντικαπαίου ἐπὶ τὸ στόμα τῆς Μαιώτιδος λίμνης ἐστὶ στάδια κ΄.

5. ἡ δὲ Μαιῶτις λίμνη λέγεται εἰς ἥμισυ εἶναι τοῦ Πόντου.

ἐν δὲ τῇ Μαιώτιδι λίμνῃ εὐθὺς εἰσπλέοντί εἰσιν ἐπ' ἀριστερᾶς
Σκύθαι· καθήκουσι γὰρ ἐκ τῆς ἔξω θαλάσσης ὑπὲρ τῆς Ταυρι-
κῆς εἰς τὴν Μαιῶτιν λίμνην Συρμάται ἔθνος. καὶ ποταμὸς
Τάναϊς ὁρίζει Ἀσίαν καὶ Εὐρώπην.

69. {παράπλους ἁπάσης τῆς Εὐρώπης.} ἀπὸ Ἡρακλείων στηλῶν
τῶν ἐν τῇ Εὐρώπῃ περιπλέοντι τοὺς κόλπους παρὰ γῆν,
λογιζομένῳ ὅσαι γεγραμμέναι εἰσὶ νύκτες ἀντὶ τούτων ἡμέρας, καὶ ὅπου στάδιά εἰσι γεγραμμένα ἀντὶ τῶν φ' σταδίων
ἡμέραν τοῦ πλέοντος, γίνεται τῆς Εὐρώπης ὁ παράπλους [τοῦ
Πόντου ὄντος ἴσου καὶ τοῦ ἡμίσεος μέρους τῆς Μαιώτιδος λίμνης]
ἡμερῶν ρν' τριῶν.

   μέγιστοι δὲ ποταμοί εἰσιν ἐν τῇ Εὐρώπῃ ὁ Τάναϊς, ὁ Ἴστρος, ὁ Ῥοδανός.

70. {Ἀσία.} ἀπὸ Ταναΐδος δὲ ποταμοῦ ἄρχεται ἡ Ἀσία.

   {Σαυρομάται.} καὶ πρῶτον ἔθνος αὐτῆς ἐστιν ἐν τῷ Πόντῳ
Σαυρομάται. Σαυροματῶν δέ ἐστιν ἔθνος Γυναικοκρατούμενοι.
71. {Μαιῶται.} τῶν Γυναικοκρατουμένων ἔχονται Μαιῶται.
72. {Σινδοί.} μετὰ δὲ Μαιώτας Σινδοὶ ἔθνος. διήκουσι γὰρ οὗτοι
καὶ εἰς τὸ ἔξω τῆς λίμνης· καί εἰσι πόλεις ἐν αὐτοῖς Ἑλληνίδες
αἵδε· Φαναγόρου πόλις, Κῆποι, Σινδικὸς λιμήν, Πάτους.
73. {Κερκέται.} μετὰ δὲ Σινδικὸν λιμένα Κερκέται ⟨ἤτοι Τορέται⟩
ἔθνος, **74.** καὶ πόλις Ἑλληνὶς Τορικὸς καὶ λιμήν.   **75.** {Ἀχαιοί.}
μετὰ δὲ Τορέτας Ἀχαιοὶ ἔθνος.   **76.** {Ἡνίοχοι.} μετὰ δὲ Ἀχαιοὺς Ἡνίοχοι ἔθνος.   **77.** {Κοραξοί.} ⟨μετὰ δὲ Ἡνιόχους, Κορα-
ξοὶ ἔθνος.   **78.** {Κορική.}⟩ μετὰ δὲ Κοραξοὺς Κορικὴ ἔθνος.
79. {Μελάγχλαινοι.} μετὰ δὲ Κορικὴν Μελάγχλαινοι ἔθνος, καὶ
ποταμὸς ἐν αὐτοῖς Μητάσωρις καὶ Αἰγίπιος ποταμός.
80. {Γέλωνες.} μετὰ δὲ Μελαγχλαίνους Γέλων.

81. {Κόλχοι.} μετὰ δὲ τούτους Κόλχοι ἔθνος καὶ Διοσκουρίας
πόλις καὶ Γυηνὸς πόλις Ἑλληνὶς καὶ Γυηνὸς ποταμὸς καὶ Χιρό-
βος ποταμός, Χόρσος ποταμός, Ἄριος ποταμός, Φᾶσις ποταμὸς
καὶ Φᾶσις Ἑλληνὶς πόλις· καὶ ἀνάπλους ἀνὰ τὸν ποταμὸν σταδίων ρπ' εἰς πόλιν Αἶαν μεγάλην βάρβαρον ὅθεν ἡ Μήδεια ἦν.
ἐνταῦθά ἐστι Ῥὶς ποταμός, Ἴσις ποταμός, Ληστῶν Ποταμός,
Ἄψαρος ποταμός.

82. {Βούσηρες.} μετὰ δὲ τοὺς Κόλχους Βούσηρες ἔθνος καὶ
Δαραανῶν ποταμὸς καὶ Ἀρίων ποταμός.   **83.** {Ἐκεχειριεῖς.}
μετὰ δὲ Βούσηρας Ἐκεχειριεῖς ἔθνος καὶ ποταμὸς Πορδανὶς καὶ

Ἀραβὶς ποταμός, Λίμνη πόλις, Ὠδεινιὸς πόλις Ἑλληνίς. 84. {Βεχειρική.} μετὰ δ' Ἐκεχειριεῖς Βέχειρες ἔθνος, Βεχειρικὸς λιμήν, Βεχειρὰς πόλις Ἑλληνίς.   85. {Μακροκέφαλοι.} μετὰ δὲ Βέχειρας Μακροκέφαλοι ἔθνος, καὶ Ψωρῶν Λιμήν, Τραπεζοῦς πόλις Ἑλληνίς.   86. {Μοσσύνοικοι.} μετὰ δὲ Μακροκεφάλους Μοσσύνοικοι ἔθνος καὶ Ζεφύριος λιμήν, Χοιράδες πόλις Ἑλληνίς, Ἄρεως νῆσος. οὗτοι ὄρη κατοικοῦσιν.   87. {Τιβαρηνοί.} μετὰ δὲ Μοσσυνοίκους ἔθνος ἐστὶ Τιβαρηνοί.   88. {Χαλύβες.} μετὰ δὲ Τιβαρηνοὺς Χάλυβές εἰσιν ἔθνος καὶ Γενέσιντις λιμὴν κλειστός, Ἀμένεια πόλις Ἑλληνίς, καὶ Ἰασονία ἄκρα καὶ πόλις Ἑλληνίς.

89. {Ἀσσυρία.} μετὰ δὲ Χάλυβας Ἀσσυρία ἐστὶν ἔθνος καὶ ποταμὸς Θερμώδων καὶ πόλις Ἑλληνὶς Θεμίσκυρα, Λύκαστος ποταμὸς καὶ πόλις Ἑλληνίς, Ἅλυς ποταμὸς καὶ Κάρουσσα πόλις Ἑλληνίς, Σινώπη πόλις Ἑλληνίς, Κερασοῦς πόλις Ἑλληνὶς καὶ Ὀχέραινος ποταμός, Ἀρμένη πόλις Ἑλληνὶς καὶ λιμήν, Τετράκις πόλις Ἑλληνίς.

90. {Παφλαγονία.} μετὰ δ' Ἀσσυρίαν ἐστὶ Παφλαγονία ἔθνος· ἔστι δ' ἐν αὐτῇ Στεφάνη λιμὴν ⟨καὶ πόλις Ἑλλην⟩ίς, Κολοῦσσα πόλις Ἑλληνίς, Κίνωλις πόλις Ἑλληνίς, Κάραμβις πόλις Ἑλληνίς, Κύτωρις πόλις Ἑλληνίς, Σησαμὸς πόλις Ἑλληνὶς καὶ Παρθένιος ποταμός, Τίειον πόλις Ἑλληνὶς καὶ λιμὴν Ψύλλα καὶ ποταμὸς Καλλίχωρος.

91. {Μαριάνδυνοι.} μετὰ δὲ Παφλαγονίαν Μαριάνδυνοί εἰσιν ἔθνος. ἐνταῦθα πόλις ἐστὶν Ἡράκλεια Ἑλληνίς, καὶ ποταμὸς Λύκος καὶ ἄλλος ποταμὸς Ὕπιος.

92. {Βιθυνοί.} μετὰ δὲ Μαριανδυνούς εἰσὶ Θρᾷκες Βιθυνοὶ ἔθνος, καὶ ποταμὸς Σαγάριος, καὶ ἄλλος ποταμὸς Ἀρτώνης, καὶ νῆσος Θυνίας· οἰκοῦσι δ' αὐτὴν Ἡρακλεῶται· καὶ ποταμὸς Ῥήβας. εἶτ' εὐθὺς Πόρος καὶ τὸ προειρημένον Ἱερὸν ἐν τῷ στόματι τοῦ Πόντου, καὶ μετὰ τοῦτο πόλις Καλχηδὼν ἔξω ⟨τῆς⟩ Θράκης, μεθ' ἢν ὁ κόλπος ὁ Ὀλβιανός.

παράπλους ἀπὸ Μαριανδυνῶν μέχρι τοῦ μυχοῦ τοῦ κόλπου τοῦ Ὀλβιανοῦ, τοσαύτη γάρ ἐστιν ἡ Βιθυνῶν Θρᾴκη, ἡμερῶν τριῶν.

2. ἀπὸ δὲ τοῦ στόματος τοῦ Πόντου ἕως τὸ στόμα τῆς Μαιώτιδος λίμνης παραπλήσιός ἐστιν ὁ πλοῦς, ὅ τε παρὰ τὴν Εὐρώπην καὶ τὴν Ἀσίαν.

93. {Μυσία.} μετὰ δὲ Θρᾴκην Μυσία ἔθνος. ἔστι δὲ τὸ ἐπ᾽ ἀριστερᾷ τοῦ Ὀλβιανοῦ κόλπου ἐκπλέοντι εἰς τὸν Κιανὸν κόλπον μέχρι Κίου. ἡ δὲ Μυσία ἀκτή ἐστι. πόλεις δ᾽ ἐν αὐτῇ Ἑλληνίδες εἰσὶν αἵδε· Ὀλβία καὶ λιμήν, Καλλίπολις καὶ λιμήν, ἀκρωτήριον τοῦ Κιανοῦ κόλπου, καὶ ἐν ἀριστερᾷ Κίος πόλις καὶ Κίος ποταμός.

παράπλους δὲ τῆς Μυσίας εἰς Κίον ἡμέρας μιᾶς.

94. {Φρυγία.} μετὰ δὲ Μυσίαν Φρυγία ἐστὶν ἔθνος, καὶ πόλεις Ἑλληνίδες αἵδε· Μύρλεια καὶ Ῥύνδακος ποταμὸς καὶ ἐπ᾽ αὐτῷ Βέσβικος νῆσος, καὶ πόλις Πλακία καὶ Κύζικος ἐν τῷ ἰσθμῷ ἐμφράττουσα τὸν ἰσθμόν, καὶ ἐντὸς τοῦ ἰσθμοῦ Ἀρτάκη. κατὰ ταύτην νῆσός ἐστι καὶ πόλις Προκόννησος καὶ ἑτέρα νῆσος εὐλίμενος Ἐλαφόννησος· γεωργοῦσι δ᾽ αὐτὴν Προκοννήσιοι. ἐν δὲ τῇ ἠπείρῳ πόλις ἐστὶ Πρίαπος, Πάριον, Λάμψακος, Περκώτη, Ἄβυδος, καὶ τὸ στόμα κατὰ Σηστὸν τῆς Προποντίδος τοῦτό ἐστι.

95. {Τρωάς.} ἐντεῦθεν δὲ Τρωὰς ἄρχεται, καὶ πόλεις Ἑλληνίδες εἰσὶν ἐν αὐτῇ αἵδε· Δάρδανος, Ῥοίτειον, Ἴλιον· ἀπέχει δὲ ἀπὸ τῆς θαλάττης στάδια κε΄· καὶ ἐν αὐτῷ ποταμὸς Σκάμανδρος. καὶ νῆσος κατὰ ταῦτα κεῖται Τένεδος καὶ λιμήν, ὅθεν Κλεόστρατος ὁ ἀστρόλογός ἐστιν. καὶ ἐν τῇ ἠπείρῳ Σίγη καὶ Ἀχίλλειον καὶ Κρατῆρες Ἀχαιῶν, Κολωναί, Λάρισσα, Ἁμαξιτὸς καὶ ἱερὸν Ἀπόλλωνος, ἵνα Χρύσης ἱερᾶτο.

96. {Αἰολίς.} ἐντεῦθεν δὲ Αἰολὶς χώρα καλεῖται. Αἰολίδες δὲ πόλεις ἐν αὐτῇ εἰσὶν ἐπὶ θαλάττη αἵδε· ⟨Ἄσσος, Γάργαρα, Ἄντανδρος. ἐν μεσογείᾳ δὲ αἵδε·⟩ Κεβρήν, Σκῆψις, Νεάνδρεια, Πιτύεια.

παράπλους Φρυγίας ἀπὸ Μυσίας μέχρι Ἀντάνδρου [—].

97. {Λέσβος.} κατὰ ταῦτά ἐστι νῆσος Αἰολὶς Λέσβος, ε΄ πόλεις ἔχουσα ἐν αὐτῇ τάσδε· Μήθυμναν, Ἄντισσαν, Ἐρεσόν, Πύρραν καὶ λιμένα, Μυτιλήνην λιμένας ἔχουσαν δύο. κατὰ δὲ ταύτην νῆσός ἐστι καὶ πόλις· ὄνομα δὲ ταύτῃ Πορδοσελήνη.

ἐπάνειμι δὲ πάλιν ἐπὶ τὴν ἤπειρον, ὅθεν ἐξετραπόμην ἐπὶ τὰς νήσους.

98. 1. {Λυδία.} ἀπὸ Ἀντάνδρου καὶ τῆς Αἰολίδος τὸ κάτω ἦν πρότερον μὲν καὶ αὕτη ἡ χώρα Μυσία μέχρι Τευθρανίας, νῦν δὲ Λυδία. Μυσοὶ δ᾽ ἐξανέστησαν εἰς τὴν ἤπειρον ἄνω. 2. εἰσὶ δὲ πόλεις ἐν αὐτῇ Ἑλληνίδες καὶ ἐν τῇ Λυδίᾳ αἵδε· Ἄστυρα, οὗ τὸ

ἱερὸν ⟨Ἀρτέμιδος, καὶ⟩ Ἀδραμύττιον. ⟨μετὰ⟩ δὲ ⟨Ἀδραμύττι-
ον⟩ ἡ χώρα Λεσβία· καὶ ὑπὲρ ταύτης ἡ Χίων χώρα καὶ πόλις
Ἀταρνεύς· ὑπὸ δὲ ταῦτα ἐπὶ θάλατταν ⟨πόλις καὶ⟩ λιμὴν Πιτά-
νη καὶ ποταμὸς Κάϊκος. μετὰ Πιτάνην Ἐλαία, Γρύνειον, Ἀχαιῶν Λιμήν· ἐν τούτῳ λέγονται Ἀχαιοὶ βουλεύσασθαι ἐπὶ τὸν
Τήλεφον πότερον στρατεύοιεν ἢ ἀπίοιεν· πόλις Μύρινα καὶ
λιμήν, Κύμη καὶ λιμήν· ὑπὲρ δὲ Κύμης ἐν μεσογείᾳ πόλις
Ἑλληνίς ἐστιν Αἰγαί· καὶ Λεῦκαι καὶ λιμένες καὶ Σμύρνα, ἐν ᾗ
Ὅμηρος ἦν, Φώκαια καὶ λιμὴν καὶ Ἕρμος ποταμός, Κλαζομε-
ναὶ καὶ λιμήν, Ἐρυθραὶ καὶ λιμήν. κατὰ δὲ ταύτας νῆσός ἐστι
Χίος καὶ λιμήν.

3. ἐπάνειμι πάλιν ἐπὶ τὴν ἤπειρον. Αἰραὶ πόλις καὶ λιμήν,
Τέως πόλις καὶ λιμήν, Λέβεδος, Κολοφὼν ἐν μεσογαίᾳ, Νότιον
καὶ λιμήν, Ἀπόλλωνος Κλαρίου ἱερόν, Κάϋστρος ποταμός,
Ἔφεσος καὶ λιμήν, Μαραθήσιον καὶ ἐν τῇ ἠπείρῳ Μαγνησία
πόλις Ἑλληνίς, Ἄναια, Πανιώνιον, Ἐρασιστράτιος, Χαραδροῦς,
Φώκαια, Ἀκαδαμίς, Μυκάλη· ἐν τῇ Σαμίων χώρᾳ ταῦτά ἐστιν.
πρὸ δὲ τῆς Μυκάλης Σάμος ἐστὶ νῆσος πόλιν ἔχουσα καὶ λιμένα κλειστόν. αὕτη ἡ νῆσος οὐκ ἐλάσσων ἐστὶ Χίου.

4. ἐπάνειμι δὲ πάλιν ἐπὶ τὴν ἤπειρον, ὅθεν ἐξετραπόμην. ἐπὶ
τῆς Μυκάλης ἐστὶ πόλις Πριήνη λιμένας ἔχουσα δύο, ὧν τὸν
ἕνα κλειστόν· εἶτα ποταμὸς Μαίανδρος.

παράπλους δὲ Μυσίας καὶ Λυδίας, ἀπὸ Ἀστύρων μέχρι Μαιάνδρου ποταμοῦ, δύο ἡμερῶν καὶ νυκτὸς μιᾶς.

99. 1. {Καρία.} μετὰ δὲ Λυδίαν Καρία ἐστὶν ἔθνος, καὶ πόλεις ἐν
αὐτῇ Ἑλληνίδες αἵδε· Ἡράκλεια, εἶτα Μίλητος, εἶτα Μύνδος
καὶ λιμήν, Ἁλικαρνασσὸς καὶ λιμὴν κλειστὸς καὶ ἄλλος λιμὴν
περὶ τὴν νῆσον καὶ ποταμός, Κάλυμνα νῆσος, Καρύανδα νῆσος
καὶ πόλις καὶ λιμήν· οὗτοι Κᾶρες. νῆσος Κῶς καὶ πόλις καὶ
λιμὴν κλειστός. κατὰ ταῦτα Κεραμιακὸς κόλπος τῆς Καρίας,
καὶ νῆσος Νίσυρος καὶ λιμήν.

2. ἐπάνειμι πάλιν ἐπὶ τὴν ἤπειρον. ἀκρωτήριον τῆς Κνίδου
ἱερόν, Τριόπιον. Κνίδος πόλις Ἑλληνὶς καὶ χώρα ἡ Ῥοδίων ἡ ἐν
τῇ ἠπείρῳ, Καῦνος Καρικὴ πόλις καὶ λιμὴν κλειστός, Κράγος
ἀκρωτήριον.

3. {Ῥόδος.} κατὰ τοῦτο ⟨Ῥόδος⟩ νῆσος ⟨καὶ πόλις· καὶ⟩
τρίπολις ἀρχαία ἐν αὐτῇ, πόλεις αἵδε· Ἰάλυσος, Λίνδος, Κάμει-
ρος. κατὰ δὲ τὴν Ῥόδον αἵδε νῆσοί εἰσιν οἰκούμεναι· Χάλκεια,
Τῆλος, Κάσος, Κάρπαθος· αὕτη τρίπολις.

καὶ ὁ παράπλους Καρίας, ἀπὸ Μαιάνδρου ποταμοῦ ἐπὶ τὸν Κράγον, ὅ ἐστι Καρίας ἀκρωτήριον, δύο ἡμερῶν.
ἐπάνειμι πάλιν ἐπὶ τὴν ἤπειρον, ὅθεν ἐξετραπόμην.

100. 1. {Λυκία.} ἀπὸ δὲ Καρίας Λυκία ἐστὶν ἔθνος· καὶ πόλεις Λυκίοις αἵδε· Τελμισσὸς καὶ λιμήν, καὶ ποταμὸς Ξάνθος, δι᾽ οὗ ἀνάπλους εἰς ⟨Ξάνθον πόλιν⟩. Πάταρα πόλις· καὶ λιμένα ἔχει. Φελλὸς πόλις καὶ λιμήν. κατὰ ταῦτα νῆσός ἐστι Ῥοδίων, Μεγίστη. Λίμυρα πόλις, εἰς ἣν ὁ ἀνάπλους κατὰ τὸν ποταμόν. εἶτα Γαγαία πόλις. εἶτα Χελιδονίαι ἀκρωτήριον καὶ νῆσοι δύο, καὶ Διονυσιὰς νῆσος, ἀκρωτήριον καὶ λιμὴν Σιδηροῦς· ὑπὲρ τούτου ἐστὶν ἱερὸν Ἡφαίστου ἐν τῷ ὄρει καὶ πῦρ πολὺ αὐτόματον ἐκ τῆς γῆς καίεται καὶ οὐδέποτε σβέννυται.
2. καὶ ἐὰν προέλθῃς ἀπὸ θαλάττης ἀνώτερον, ἔστι [—] Φάσηλις πόλις καὶ λιμήν· ἔστι δὲ τοῦτο κόλπος. καὶ Ἴδυρος πόλις, νῆσος Λυρνάτεια, Ὀλβία, Μάγυδος καὶ ποταμὸς Καταρράκτης, Πέργη πόλις καὶ ἱερὸν Ἀρτέμιδος.
ἐπ᾽ εὐθείας δὲ παράπλους ἐστὶν Λυκίας ἀπὸ [—] ἡμέρας καὶ νυκτός· ἔστι γὰρ κολπώδης. ὁ δὲ παρὰ γῆν διπλάσιος τούτου.

101. 1. {Παμφυλία.} μετὰ δὲ Λυκίαν ἐστὶ Παμφυλία ἔθνος, καὶ πόλεις ἐν αὐτῇ αἵδε· Ἄσπενδος πόλις· εἰς ταύτην ὁ ἀνάπλους γίνεται κατὰ ποταμόν, ὁ δὲ ποταμός ἐστιν Εὐρυμέδων. εἶτα πόλις Σύλλειον, ἄλλη πόλις Σίδη, Κυμαίων ἀποικία, καὶ λιμήν.
παράπλους Παμφυλίας ἀπὸ Πέργης ἥμισυ ἡμέρας.
2. εἰσὶ δὲ καὶ ἄλλαι πόλεις Παμφυλίας. Κίβυρα, εἶτα Κορακήσιον.

102. 1. {Κιλικία.} μετὰ δὲ Παμφυλίαν Κιλικία ἐστὶν ἔθνος, καὶ πόλεις ἐν αὐτῇ αἵδε· Σελινοῦς, Χαραδροῦς πόλις καὶ λιμήν, Ἀνεμούριον ἄκρα καὶ πόλις, Νάγιδος πόλις· καὶ νῆσον ἔχει. πρὸς δὲ τὴν Σητὸν λιμένες Ποσείδειον, Σάλον, Μυοῦς, Κελένδερις πόλις, καὶ λιμὴν Ἀφροδίσιος καὶ λιμὴν ἕτερος, Ὄλμοι πόλις Ἑλληνὶς ⟨λιμένα⟩ ἔχουσα, Σαρπηδὼν πόλις ἔρημος καὶ ποταμός, Σόλοι πόλις Ἑλληνίς, Ζεφύριον πόλις, ποταμὸς Πύραμος καὶ πόλις Μαλλός, εἰς ἣν ὁ ἀνάπλους κατὰ τὸν ποταμόν, ἐμπόριον Ἀμάνη καὶ λιμήν, Μυρίανδος Φοινίκων, Θάψακος ποταμός.
παράπλους Κιλικίας ἀπὸ τῶν Παμφυλίας ὁρίων μέχρι Θαψάκου ποταμοῦ τριῶν ἡμερῶν καὶ νυκτῶν δύο.
2. ἐκ δὲ Σινώπης τῆς ἐν τῷ Πόντῳ διὰ τῆς ἠπείρου καὶ τῆς

Κιλικίας εἰς Σόλους ὁδός ἐστιν ἀπὸ θαλάσσης εἰς θάλασσαν
ἡμερῶν ε΄.

103. {Κύπρος.} κατὰ δὲ Κιλικίαν ἐστὶ νῆσος Κύπρος, καὶ πόλεις
ἐν αὐτῇ αἵδε· Σαλαμὶς Ἑλληνίς, λιμένα ἔχουσα κλειστὸν χειμε-
ρινόν· Καρπάσεια· Κερύνεια· Λήπηθις Φοινίκων· Σόλοι, καὶ
αὕτη λιμένα ἔχει χειμερινόν· Μάριον Ἑλληνίς· Ἀμαθοῦς, αὐτό-
χθονές εἰσιν. αὗται πᾶσαι λιμένας ἔχουσιν ἐρήμους. εἰσὶ δὲ καὶ
ἄλλαι πόλεις ἐν μεσογείᾳ βάρβαροι.
    ἐπάνειμι δὲ πάλιν ἐπὶ τὴν ἤπειρον, ὅθεν ἐξετραπόμην.

104. 1. {Συρία καὶ Φοινίκη.} ἔστι μετὰ Κιλικίαν ἔθνος Σύροι. ἐν δὲ
τῇ Συρίᾳ οἰκοῦσι τὰ παρὰ θάλατταν Φοίνικες ἔθνος, ἐπὶ στενὸν
ἔλαττον ἢ ἐπὶ τετταράκοντα σταδίους ἀπὸ θαλάττης, ἐνιαχῇ δὲ
οὐδὲ ἐπὶ σταδίους ι΄ τὸ πλάτος.
    2. ἀπὸ δὲ Θαψάκου ποταμοῦ ἐστι Τρίπολις Φοινίκων, Ἄρα-
δος νῆσος καὶ λιμήν, βασίλεια Τύρου καὶ λιμὴν ὅσον η΄ στάδια
ἀπὸ τῆς γῆς. καὶ ἐν τῇ χερρονήσῳ ἑτέρα πόλις Τρίπολις· αὕτη
ἐστὶν Ἀράδου καὶ Τύρου καὶ Σιδῶνος· ἐν τῷ αὐτῷ τρεῖς πόλεις,
καὶ περίβολον ἑκάστη τοῦ τείχους ἴδιον ἔχει. καὶ ὄρος Θεοῦ
Πρόσωπον. Τριήρης ⟨πόλις⟩ καὶ λιμήν. Βηρυτὸς πόλις καὶ
λιμήν. Βοστρηνὸς ⟨ποταμός⟩. Πορφυρεὼν πόλις. ⟨Λεόντων
πόλις.⟩ Σιδὼν πόλις καὶ λιμὴν κλειστός. Ὀρνίθων πόλις. Σιδωνίων ἀπὸ Λεόντων πόλεως μέχρι Ὀρνίθων πόλεως.
    3. Τυρίων πόλις Σάραπτα. [ἄλλη] πόλις Τύρος λιμένα ἔχουσα
ἐντὸς τείχους· αὕτη δὲ ἡ νῆσος βασίλεια Τυρίων, καὶ ἀπέχει
στάδια ἀπὸ †θαλάττης γ΄.

Παλαίτυρος πόλις, καὶ ποταμὸς διὰ μέσης ῥεῖ. καὶ πόλις Τ[υρίων
    Ἔκδιππα]
καὶ ποταμός. καὶ Ἄκη πόλις, Ἐξώπη πόλις Τυ[ρίων. Κάρμηλος]
ὄρος ἱερὸν Διός. Ἄραδος πόλις Σιδωνίων. [Μάγδωλος πόλις]
καὶ ποταμὸς Τυρίων. Δῶρος πόλις Σιδωνίων, κ[αὶ Ἰόππη πόλις·
    ἐκτε-]
θῆναί φασιν ἐνταῦθα τὴν Ἀνδρομ[έδαν τῷ κήτει. Ἀσκά-]
λων πόλις Τυρίων καὶ βασίλεια. ἐνταῦ[θα ὄρος ἐστὶ τῆς Κοίλης]
Συρίας. παράπλους Κοίλης Συρίας [ἀπὸ Θαψάκου ποταμοῦ μέχρι]
Ἀσκάλωνος στάδια ͵βψ΄.

105. 1.   {Ἀ[ραβία.} μετὰ δὲ Συρίαν εἰσὶν Ἄραβες]
ἔθνος, νομάδες ἱππεύοντες [καὶ νομὰς ἔχοντες παντοδαπῶν βοσ-]
κημάτων, οἰῶν καὶ αἰ[γῶν   ]

καὶ καμήλων· ἔστι δὲ αὔ[τη   ]
ἐστὶ τὰ πολλὰ ἄ[νυδρος   ]
τε τὴν Αἴγυπτον [   ]
ἐν αὐτῇ κολ[π-   ]
ἐστὶν ἐκ τῆς Ἐρ[υθρᾶς θαλάττης   ἔξω-]
θεν θαλ[αττ-   θάλα-]
τταν [   ]
καὶ [   ]
κ[   ]
[   ]
[   ]
[   ]
[παράπλους   ]
[   ]

2. [τῆς Ἀ]ραβίας δὲ αὐτῆς ἀπὸ Συρίας ὁρίων μέχρι στόματος τοῦ
[Νείλου τοῦ ἐ]ν Πηλουσίῳ, τοῦτο γάρ ἐστιν Ἀραβίας ὄρος, στάδια
  ͵ατ'.
[φασὶ δὲ εἶναι καὶ Ἀ]ραβίαν Αἰγύπτου μέχρι τοῦ Νείλου ἐξῆς
  Ἀρα-
[βικοῦ κόλπου.   ] Αἰγύπτιοι· φόρον δὲ φέρουσιν Αἰγύ-
[πτ-   ] ἀεὶ τοῖς Ἄραψιν.

106. 1.   {Αἴγυπτος.}
[μετὰ δὲ Ἀραβίαν Αἴγυπτός] ἐστιν ἔθνος· καὶ πόλεις ἐν αὐτῇ
[αἵδε· Πηλούσιον πόλις καὶ λιμὴν] καὶ βασίλειον, οὗ τὸ στόμα
[τοῦ Νείλου ποταμοῦ Πηλουσιακόν ἐστι] πρῶτον, τῆς Ἀραβίας
[ὄρος. δεύτερον Τανιτικὸν καὶ πόλις βασιλι]κή. τρίτον
[Μενδήσιον καὶ Μένδης πόλις. δ' Φατνιτικ]όν. πέμπτον Σεβεννυ-
[τικὸν καὶ Σεβέννυτος πόλις· Βοῦτος λίμνη, ἔν]θα πόλις καὶ βα-
[σίλειον. ἕκτον Βολβιτινὸν καὶ πόλις βασιλι]κή. ἕβδομον
[Κανωπικὸν καὶ Θῶνις πόλις. μετὰ ταῦτα λίμνη] ᾗ ὄνομά
[ἐστι Μάρεια. αὕτη δὲ ἡ λίμνη ἤδη ἐστὶν ἐν τ]ῇ Λιβύῃ
[   ]ει δὲ ἐ-
[   ]βουλήν
[   ]ε
[   ]
[   ]
[   ]

[   ]
[   ]
[   ]
[Κανωπικόν . . . Σεβεννυτικόν . . .   ]

2. . . . τὸ δὲ Πηλουσιακόν. καὶ πάλιν σχίζεται δίχα· τὸ δὲ
Σεβεννυτικόν, τὸ μὲν εἰς τὸ Μενδήσιον, τὸ δὲ εἰς θάλασσαν·
ἀπὸ δὲ τοῦ Μενδησίου εἰς τὸ Φατνιτικὸν στόμα· ἀπὸ δὲ τοῦ
Πηλουσίου εἰς τὸ Τανιτικὸν στόμα· τὸ δὲ ἀπὸ Κανώπου μέχρι
Σεβεννυτικῆς λίμνης, καὶ στόμα τὸ Βολβιτινὸν ῥεῖ ἐκ τῆς
λίμνης. ἔστι δὲ τὰ πολλὰ τὰ παρὰ θάλατταν Αἰγύπτου λίμναι
καὶ ἕλη.

3. ἔστι δ’ ἡ Αἴγυπτος τοιάδε τὴν ἰδέαν, ὁμοία πελέκει. ἔστι
γὰρ κατὰ θάλατταν πλατεῖα, κατὰ δὲ μεσογείαν στενωτέρα,
κατὰ δὲ Μέμφιν στενωτάτη αὐτῆς· ἔπειτα δὲ εἰς μεσογείαν ἀπὸ
Μέμφεως ἰόντι πλατυτέρα, κατὰ δὲ τὸ ἀνώτερον αὐτῆς πλατυ-
τάτη. τὸ μέρος τὸ ἄνωθεν Αἰγύπτου Μέμφιδός ἐστι τὸ πλεῖστον
ἢ τὸ παρὰ θάλασσαν. τὸ δὲ Κανωπικὸν στόμα ὁρίζει Ἀσίαν καὶ
Λιβύην.

παράπλους δ’ ἐστὶν Αἰγύπτου ἀπὸ Πηλουσίου στόματος
στάδια ‚ατʹ.

4. τῆς δὲ Ἀσίας ὁ περίπλους, ἔστι γὰρ περιφερής, λογιζομένῳ
κατὰ τὸν αὐτὸν τρόπον ὃν περὶ Εὐρώπης γέγραπται, ἡμερῶν
ἐστι πζʹ.

5. ἐπὶ δὲ τῷ στόματι τῷ Κανωπικῷ ἔστι νῆσος ἐρήμη ᾗ ὄνομα
Κάνωπος· καὶ σημεῖά ἐστιν ἐν αὐτῇ τοῦ Μενέλεω τοῦ κυβερνήτου τοῦ ἀπὸ Τροίας, ᾧ ὄνομα Κάνωπος, τὸ μνῆμα. λέγουσι
δὲ Αἰγύπτιοί τε καὶ οἱ πρόσχωροι οἱ τοῖς τόποις Πηλούσιον
ἥκειν ἐπὶ τὸ Κάσιον, καὶ Κάνωπον ἥκειν ἐπὶ τὴν νῆσον οὗ τὸ
μνῆμα τοῦ κυβερνήτου.

107. 1. {Λιβύη.} ἄρχεται ἡ Λιβύη ἀπὸ τοῦ Κανωπικοῦ στόματος
τοῦ Νείλου.

{Ἀδυρμαχίδαι.} ἔθνος Λιβύων Ἀδυρμαχίδαι. ἐκ Θώνιδος δὲ
πλοῦς εἰς Φάρον νῆσον ἔρημον, εὐλίμενος δὲ καὶ ἄνυδρος,
στάδια ρνʹ.

ἐν δὲ Φάρῳ λιμένες πολλοί. ὕδωρ δὲ ἐκ τῆς Μαρείας λίμνης
ὑδρεύονται· ἔστι γὰρ πότιμος. ὁ δὲ ἀνάπλους εἰς τὴν λίμνην
βραχὺς ἐκ Φάρου. ἔστι δὲ καὶ Χερρόνησος καὶ λιμήν. ἔστι δὲ
τοῦ παράπλου στάδια σʹ.

2. ἀπὸ Χερρονήσου δὲ Πλίνθινός ἐστι κόλπος. τὸ δὲ στόμα ἐστὶ τοῦ Πλινθίνου κόλπου εἰς Λευκὴν ἀκτὴν πλοῦς ἡμέρας καὶ νυκτός· τὸ δὲ εἰς τὸν μυχὸν τοῦ Πλινθίνου κόλπου δὶς τοσοῦτον· περιοικεῖται δὲ κύκλῳ. ἀπὸ δὲ Λευκῆς ἀκτῆς εἰς Λαοδαμάντειον λιμένα πλοῦς ἥμισυ ἡμέρας· ἀπὸ δὲ Λαοδαμαντείου λιμένος εἰς Παραιτόνιον λιμένα πλοῦς ἥμισυ ἡμέρας.

3. ἔχεται Ἆπις πόλις. μέχρις οὖν ἐνταῦθα Αἰγύπτιοι ἄρχουσιν.

108. 1. {Μαρμαρίδαι.} ἀπὸ δὲ Ἄπιδος ἔθνος Λιβύων ἐστὶν οἱ Μαρμαρίδαι μέχρι εἰς Ἑσπερίδας.

ἀπὸ δὲ Ἄπιδος ἐπὶ Τυνδαρείους σκοπέλους πλοῦς ἡμέρας. καὶ ἀπὸ Τυνδαρείων σκοπέλων εἰς Πλύνους λιμένα πλοῦς ἡμέρας. ἐκ Πλύνων εἰς Πέτραντα τὸν μέγαν πλοῦς ἥμισυ ἡμέρας. ἐκ Πέτραντος εἰς Μενέλαον πλοῦς ἡμέρας. ἐκ Μενελάου εἰς Κυρθάνειον πλοῦς ἡμέρας. ἀπὸ Κυρθανείου Ἀντίπυγος λιμήν· πλοῦς ἥμισυ ἡμέρας. ἀπὸ δὲ Ἀντιπύγου Πέτρας ὁ μικρὸς λιμήν· πλοῦς ἥμισυ ἡμέρας. ἀπὸ Πέτραντος ⟨τοῦ⟩ μικροῦ Χερρόνησος, Ἀζιρίδες λιμήν· ταῦτα τῆς Κυρηναίων χώρας ἐστί· πλοῦς ἡμέρας.

2. ἐν δὲ τῷ μέσῳ Πέτραντος καὶ Χερρονήσου εἰσὶ νῆσοι Ἀηδωνία καὶ Πλατεῖαι. ὕφορμοι δὲ ὑπ' αὐταῖς εἰσίν. ἐντεῦθεν ἄρχεται τὸ σίλφιον φύεσθαι ἐν γύαις· παρήκει δὲ ἀπὸ Χερρονήσου διὰ τῆς μεσογείας μέχρι Ἑσπερίδων, παρὰ γῆν ἐγγὺς στάδια ͵αφʹ μάλιστα. Ἀφροδισιὰς νῆσος ὕφορμος. Ναύσταθμος λιμήν.

πλοῦς ἀπὸ Χερρονήσου ἡμέρας μιᾶς· ἀπὸ δὲ Ναυστάθμου εἰς λιμένα τὸν Κυρήνης στάδια ρʹ· ἐκ δὲ τοῦ λιμένος εἰς Κυρήνην στάδια πʹ.

3. ἔστι δὲ Κυρήνη ἐν μεσογείᾳ. εἰσὶ δὲ οὗτοι οἱ λιμένες πάνορμοι. καὶ ἄλλαι δὲ καταφυγαὶ ὑπὸ νησιδίοις καὶ ὕφορμοι καὶ ἀκταὶ πολλαὶ ἐν τῇ μεταξὺ χώρᾳ. ἐκ δὲ λιμένος τῆς Κυρήνης μέχρι λιμένος τοῦ κατὰ Βάρκην στάδια φʹ. ἡ δὲ πόλις ἡ Βαρκαίων ἀπὸ θαλάσσης ἀπέχει στάδια ρʹ.

ἐκ δὲ λιμένος τοῦ κατὰ Βάρκην ἐφ' Ἑσπερίδας στάδια χκʹ.

4. ἐκ δὲ Κυρήνης εἰσὶ λιμένες, καὶ χωρία ἐστὶν ἐσχισμένα μέχρι Ἑσπερίδων τάδε· Φυκοῦς κόλπος· ἄνω δὲ ἐνταῦθά ἐστιν ὁ κῆπος τῶν Ἑσπερίδων. ἔστι δὲ τόπος βαθὺς ὀργυιῶν ιηʹ, ἀπότομος κύκλῳ, οὐδαμοῦ ἔχων κατάβασιν· ἔστι δὲ δύο σταδίων πανταχῇ, οὐκ ἔλαττον, εὖρος καὶ μῆκος. οὗτός ἐστι σύ-

σκιος δένδρεσιν ἐμπεπλεγμένοις ἐν ἀλλήλοις, ὡς ὅτι μάλιστα πυκνοτάτοις. τὰ δένδρα ἐστὶ λωτός, μηλέαι παντοδαπαί· ῥοαί, ἄπιοι, μεμαίκυλα, συκάμινα, ἄμπελοι, μυρσίναι, δάφναι, κισσός, ἐλαῖαι, κότινοι, ἀμυγδαλαί, καρύαι.

5. τῶν δὲ χωρίων ἃ οὐκ εἴρηταί ἐστι [δὲ] κατὰ τὸν κῆπον Ἄμπελος, Ἄπιος, ἀλλάσσει στάδια λ΄, Χερρόνησος, κῆποι πλεῖστοι, Ζηνερτίς, Ταύχειρα, Βακαλοῦ κώμη, Ἑσπερίδες πόλις καὶ λιμὴν καὶ ποταμὸς ἐπὶ τῇ πόλει Ἐγχέλειος. κατὰ ταῦτα τὰ χωρία ἀπὸ Χερρονήσου τῶν Ἀζιριδῶν τὰ μὲν Κυρηναίων, τὰ δὲ Βαρκαίων ἐστὶ μέχρι Ἑσπερίδων.

109. 1. {Νασαμῶνες καὶ Μάκαι.} ἀπὸ δὲ Ἑσπερίδων κόλπος ἐστὶ μέγας ᾧ ὄνομα Σύρτις, ὡς δὲ εἰπεῖν ὅτι μάλιστα εἰκάζοντι σταδίων ͵ε. ἔστιν αὐτῇ τὸ πλάτος ἀπὸ Ἑσπερίδων εἰς Νέαν πόλιν τὴν πέραν πλοῦς ἡμερῶν τριῶν καὶ νυκτῶν τριῶν.

2. περιοικοῦσι δὲ αὐτὴν Λιβύων ἔθνος Νασαμῶνες μέχρι τοῦ μυχοῦ τοῦ ἐπ᾽ ἀριστερᾷ.

τούτων δὲ ἔχονται Λιβύων ἔθνος παρὰ τὴν Σύρτιν μέχρι τοῦ στόματος τῆς Σύρτιδος, Μάκαι.

3. εἰς δὲ τὴν Σύρτιν ἀπὸ Ἑσπερίδων εἰσπλέοντι πρῶτοι Ἡράκλειοι Θῖνες· ἔχονται δὲ τούτων Δρέπανον, νῆσοι Ποντίαι τρεῖς, εἶτα τούτων αἱ Λευκαὶ καλούμεναι. ἐν δὲ τῷ κοιλοτάτῳ τῆς Σύρτιδος, ἐν τῷ μυχῷ, Φιλαίνου Βωμοί, ἐπίνειον, Ἄμμωνος ἄλσος [—] τῆς Σύρτιδος. ἀπὸ τούτου τὴν Σύρτιν παροικοῦντες οἱ Μάκαι χειμάζουσιν ἐπὶ θαλάττῃ τὰ βοσκήματα κλείοντες, τοῦ δὲ θέρους ὑπεκλειπόντων τῶν ὑδάτων ἀπελαύνουσι τὰ βοσκήματα εἰς μεσογαίαν ἄνω μεθ᾽ ἑαυτῶν.

4. μετὰ δὲ τὴν Σύρτιν [ἔξω τῆς Σύρτιδος] ἐστὶ χωρίον καλὸν καὶ πόλις ᾗ ὄνομα Κίνυψ, ἔστι δὲ ἔρημος· ἀπὸ δὲ Νέας πόλεως ἀπέχει εἰς τὴν Σύρτιν στάδια π΄ †πάντη. ὑπ᾽ αὐτῷ δ᾽ ἐστὶ ποταμὸς Κίνυψ, καὶ νῆσος ὕπεστι πρὸς τὸν ποταμόν.

5. τὸ δὲ βάθος τῆς Σύρτιδος ἔσω τῶν Ἑσπερίδων πρὸς τοὺς Φιλαίνου Βωμοὺς εἰς τὸν μυχὸν τοῦ κόλπου πλοῦς ἡμερῶν γ΄ καὶ νυκτῶν ⟨β΄⟩. πλάτος δὲ ἀπὸ Κίνυφος ποταμοῦ πρὸς τὰς Λευκὰς νήσους πλοῦς ἡμερῶν τεσσάρων καὶ νυκτῶν τεσσάρων.

110. 1. {Λωτοφάγοι.} τὰ δὲ ἔξω τῆς Σύρτιδος παροικοῦσι Λίβυες Λωτοφάγοι ἔθνος μέχρι τοῦ στόματος τῆς ἑτέρας Σύρτιδος. οὗτοι λωτῷ χρῶνται σίτῳ καὶ ποτῷ. ἀπὸ δὲ Νέας πόλεως τῆς

Καρχηδονίων χώρας *Γάφαρα* πόλις. ταύτης παράπλους ἡμέρας μιᾶς ἀπὸ Νέας πόλεως.

2. ἀπὸ δὲ *Γαφάρων* Ἀβρότονον πόλις καὶ λιμήν. ταύτης ὁ παράπλους ἡμέρας μιᾶς.

3. ἀπὸ δὲ Ἀβροτόνου Ταριχεῖαι, πόλις καὶ λιμήν. παράπλους ἀπὸ Ἀβροτόνου ἡμέρας μιᾶς.

4. κατὰ δὲ ταῦτά ἐστι νῆσος ᾗ ὄνομα Βραχείων, μετὰ Λωτο-φάγους κατὰ Ταριχείας. ἔστι δὲ ἡ νῆσος αὕτη σταδίων τ΄, πλά-τος δὲ μικρῷ ἐλάττων. ἀπέχει δὲ ἀπὸ τῆς ἠπείρου ὡσεὶ στάδια γ΄. ἐν δὲ τῇ νήσῳ γίνεται λωτὸς ὃν ἐσθίουσιν, καὶ ἕτερος ἐξ οὗ οἶνον ποιοῦσιν. ὁ δὲ τοῦ λωτοῦ καρπός ἐστι τῷ μεγέθει ὅσον μεμαίκυλον. ποιοῦσι δὲ καὶ ἔλαιον πολὺ ἐκ κοτίνων. φέρει δὲ καρπὸν ἡ νῆσος πολύν, πυροὺς καὶ κριθάς. ἔστι δὲ ἡ νῆσος εὔγειος. πλοῦς ἀπὸ Ταριχειῶν εἰς τὴν νῆσον ἡμέρας μιᾶς.

5. μετὰ δὲ τὴν νῆσόν ἐστι *Γιχθὶς* πόλις. ἀπὸ δὲ τῆς νήσου εἰς *Γιχθὶν* πλοῦς ἡμέρας ἡμισείας.

6. ⟨. . . Ἐσχίδες . . .⟩ ἀπὸ δὲ Ἐσχίδων ⟨εἰς Νέαν πολιν⟩ πλοῦς ἡμέρας.

7. καὶ νῆσος ἔπεστιν ἐπ᾽ αὐτῇ ἐρήμη. μετὰ δὲ ταύτην Κερκινῖτις νῆσος καὶ πόλις, καὶ κατὰ ταύτην Θάψος. παρά-πλους ἀπὸ ταύτης εἰς Θάψον ἡμέρας καὶ ἡμίσεως.

ἀπὸ δὲ Θάψου ⟨εἰς Λέπτιν τὴν μικρὰν πλοῦς . . .· ἀπὸ Λέπτε-ως εἰς Ἀδρύμητα . . .

8. ἀπὸ δὲ Λέπτεως⟩ τῆς μικρᾶς καὶ Ἀδρύμητός ἐστι κόλπος μέγας εἴσω, ἐν ᾧ ἡ Σύρτις ἐστὶν ἡ μικρά, Κερκινῖτις καλου-μένη, πολὺ τῆς ἄλλης Σύρτιδος χαλεπωτέρα καὶ δυσπλωτο-τέρα, ἧς τὸ περίμετρον στάδια ͵β.

ἐν ταύτῃ τῇ Σύρτιδι ἐνέστηκεν ἡ νῆσος Τρίτωνος καλουμέ-νη ⟨καὶ λίμνη⟩ καὶ ποταμὸς Τρίτων, καὶ αὐτόθεν ἐστὶν Ἀθηνᾶς Τριτωνίδος ἱερόν. στόμα δὲ ἔχει ἡ λίμνη μικρόν, καὶ ἐν τῷ στό-ματι νῆσος ἔπεστιν· καὶ ὅταν ἄναπωτις ᾖ, ἐνίοτε ἡ λίμνη οὐκ ἔχει εἴσπλουν ⟨ναυ⟩σὶν, ὡ⟨ς⟩ φαίνεται. ἡ δὲ λίμνη αὕτη ἐστὶ μεγάλη, τὸ περίμετρον ἔχουσα ὡς σταδίων χιλίων. 9. περι-οικοῦσι δὲ αὐτὴν Λίβυες *Γύζαντες* ἔθνος καὶ πόλις τὸ ἐπέκεινα πρὸς ἡλίου δυσμάς· οὗτοι γὰρ *Γύζαντες* Λίβυες λέγονται ξανθοὶ ἅπαντες καὶ κάλλιστοι. καὶ ἡ χώρα αὕτη ἀρίστη καὶ παμφορω-τάτη, καὶ βοσκήματα παρ᾽ αὐτοῖς ἐστι καὶ μέγιστα καὶ πλεῖστα· καὶ αὐτοὶ πλουσιώτατοι καὶ κάλλιστοι.

10. μετὰ δὲ τὴν Σύρτιν ταύτην Νεάπολίς ἐστι. παράπλους δὲ

ἀπὸ Ἀδρύμητος ἐπὶ Νέαν πόλιν ἡμέρας ἐστίν.

μετὰ δὲ Νέαν πόλιν Ἑρμαία ἄκρα καὶ πόλις. παράπλους ἀπὸ Νέας πόλεως εἰς Ἑρμαίαν ἡμέρας καὶ ἡμίσεως.

ἀπὸ δὲ Νέας ⟨πόλεώς⟩ ἐστιν εἰς ἰσθμὸν στάδια ρπ΄ πεζῇ πρὸς τὴν ἑτέραν θάλασσαν τὴν πρὸς Καρχηδόνα. ἔστι δὲ ἀκτή, δι᾿ ἧς ἰσθμός ἐστιν. ⟨... ποταμὸς ...⟩ παράπλους ἀπὸ τοῦ ποταμοῦ ἐντεῦθεν εἰς Καρχηδόνα ἥμισυ ἡμέρας.

ἡ δὲ Καρχηδονίων χώρα ἐστὶν ἐν κόλπῳ.

111. 1. {Καρχηδών.} μετὰ δὲ τὸν ἰσθμὸν Καρχηδών ἐστι πόλις Φοινίκων καὶ λιμήν. παράπλους ἀπὸ Ἑρμαίας ἥμισυ ἡμέρας εἰς Καρχηδόνα.

2. ἔπεισι δὲ νησία ἐπὶ τῇ Ἑρμαίᾳ ἄκρᾳ, Ποντία νῆσος καὶ Κόσυρος. πλοῦς δὲ ἀπὸ Ἑρμαίας ἐπὶ Κόσυρον ἡμέρας.

3. ἀπὸ Ἑρμαίας ἄκρας πρὸς ἥλιον ἀνίσχοντα, μακρὰν ἀπὸ Ἑρμαίας, εἰσὶ νῆσοι τρεῖς μικραὶ κατὰ τοῦτο, ὑπὸ Καρχηδονίων οἰκούμεναι· Μελίτη πόλις καὶ λιμήν, Γαῦλος πόλις, Λαμπάς· αὕτη πύργους ἔχει δύο ἢ τρεῖς. ἀπὸ δὲ Κοσύρου ἐπὶ Λιλύβαιον ἀκρωτήριον Σικελίας πλοῦς ἡμέρας μιᾶς.

4. μετὰ Καρχηδόνα Ἰτύκη πόλις καὶ λιμήν. παράπλους δὲ ἀπὸ Καρχηδόνος εἰς Ἰτύκην μιᾶς ἡμέρας.

5. ἀπὸ Ἰτύκης εἰς Ἵππου ἄκραν ⟨παράπλους ἡμέρας μιᾶς⟩.

Ἵππου ⟨Ἄκρα⟩ πόλις, καὶ λίμνη ἐπ᾿ αὐτῇ ἐστι, καὶ νῆσοι ἐν τῇ λίμνῃ, καὶ περὶ τὴν λίμνην πόλεις ἐν ταῖς νήσοις αἵδε· Ψέγας πόλις, καὶ ἀπαντίον αὐτῆς νῆσοι Ναξικαὶ πολλαί. Πιθηκοῦσαι καὶ λιμήν. κατ᾿ ἐναντίον αὐτῶν Καλάθη νῆσος καὶ πόλις ἐν τῇ νήσῳ Εὔβοια. Θάψα καὶ πόλις καὶ λιμήν. Ἰγίλγιλις πόλις καὶ λιμήν. Σίδα πόλις. Ἰόμνιον ἄκρα· πόλις καὶ λιμήν. Ἕβδομος πόλις καὶ λιμήν. Ἀκίον νῆσος· πόλις καὶ λιμὴν ἔπεστι. Ψαμαθὸς νῆσος· πόλις καὶ λιμήν. καὶ κόλπος· ἐν δὲ τῷ κόλπῳ Βαρτὰς νῆσος καὶ λιμήν. Χάλκα πόλις ἐν τῷ ποταμῷ. Ἀρύλων πόλις. Μὴς πόλις καὶ λιμήν. Σίγη πόλις ἐν τῷ ποταμῷ. καὶ πρὸ τοῦ ποταμοῦ νῆσος Ἄκρα. πόλις μεγάλη ⟨καὶ⟩ λιμήν. Ἄκρος ἡ πόλις καὶ ὁ κόλπος ἐν αὐτῇ. ἔρημος νῆσος Δρίναυπα ὄνομα.

6. Ἡράκλειος στήλη ⟨ἡ⟩ ἐν Λιβύῃ. ἄκρα Ἀβιλυκὴ ⟨καὶ⟩ πόλις ἐν ποταμῷ καὶ ἀντίον αὐτῆς τὰ Γάδειρα νῆσοι.

ἀπὸ Καρχηδόνος ταύτη ἐστὶν ἐφ᾿ Ἡρακλείους στήλας τοῦ καλλίστου πλοῦ παράπλους ἡμερῶν ἑπτὰ καὶ νυκτῶν ἑπτά.

7. {Γάδειρα.} εἰσὶ νῆσοι αὗται πρὸς τῇ Εὐρώπῃ· τούτων ἡ

ἑτέρα πόλιν ἔχει· καὶ Ἡράκλειοι στῆλαι κατὰ ταύτας, ἡ μὲν ἐν τῇ Λιβύῃ ταπεινή, ἡ δ' ἐν τῇ Εὐρώπῃ ὑψηλή. αὗται δέ εἰσιν ἄκραι καταντικρὺ ἀλλήλων· διέχουσι δὲ αὗται ἀπ' ἀλλήλων πλοῦν ἡμέρας.

8. παράπλους Λιβύης ἀπ' Αἰγύπτου τοῦ Κανωπικοῦ στόματος μέχρι Ἡρακλείων στηλῶν, τιθεμένου τοῦ λογισμοῦ κατὰ ταὐτὰ ἅπερ ἐν Ἀσίᾳ καὶ Εὐρώπῃ γέγραπται, κατὰ τοὺς κόλ-πους κύκλῳ περιπλέοντι ἡμερῶν ν΄ καὶ δ΄.

9. ὅσα γέγραπται πολίσματα ἢ ἐμπόρια ἐν τῇ Λιβύῃ, ἀπὸ τῆς Σύρτιδος τῆς παρ' Ἑσπερίδας μέχρι Ἡρακλείων στηλῶν ⟨τῶν⟩ ἐν Λιβύῃ, πάντα ἐστὶ Καρχηδονίων.

112. 1. μετὰ δὲ Ἡρακλείους στήλας εἰς τὸ ἔξω πλέοντι, ἔχοντι τὴν Λιβύην ἐν ἀριστερᾷ, κόλπος ἐστὶ μέγας μέχρι Ἑρμαίας ἄκ-ρας. ἔστι γὰρ καὶ ἐνταῦθα Ἑρμαία ἄκρα. κατὰ δὲ μέσον τὸν κόλπον κεῖται Ποντίων τόπος καὶ πόλις. περὶ δὲ τὴν πόλιν λίμνη κεῖται μεγάλη, ἐν δὲ τῇ λίμνῃ ταύτῃ κεῖνται νῆσοι πολλαί. περὶ δὲ τὴν λίμνην πέφυκε κάλαμος καὶ κύπειρος καὶ φλέως καὶ θρυόν. αἱ δὲ ὄρνιθες αἱ Μελεαγρίδες ἐνταῦθά εἰσιν, ἄλλου δὲ οὐδαμοῦ, ἂν μὴ ἐντεῦθεν ἐξαχθῶσιν. τῇ δὲ λίμνῃ ταύτῃ ὄνομα Κηφησιάς, τῷ δὲ κόλπῳ Κώτης, ἔστι δὲ Ἡρακλεί-ων στηλῶν καὶ Ἑρμαίας ἄκρας ἐν τῷ μεταξύ.

2. ἀπὸ δὲ τῆς Ἑρμαίας ἄκρας ἕρματα τέταται μεγάλα, ἀπὸ δὲ τῆς Λιβύης ἐπὶ τὴν Εὐρώπην, οὐχ ὑπερέχοντα τῆς θαλάττης· ἐπικλύζει δὲ ἐπ' αὐτὰ ἐνιαχῇ. τέταται δὲ τὸ ἕρμα ἐπὶ ἑτέραν ἄκραν τῆς Εὐρώπης τὸ καταντικρύ· τῇ δὲ ἄκρᾳ ταύτῃ ὄνομα Ἱερὸν Ἀκρωτήριον.

3. ἀπὸ δὲ τῆς Ἑρμαίας ἄκρας ποταμός ἐστιν Ἀνίδης· ἐξίησι δὲ οὗτος εἰς λίμνην μεγάλην. μετὰ δὲ Ἀνίδην [εἶτα] ἐστὶν ἄλλος ποταμὸς μέγας, Λίξος, καὶ πόλις Φοινίκων Λίξος. καὶ ἑτέρα πόλις Λιβύων ἐστὶ πέραν τοῦ ποταμοῦ, καὶ λιμήν.

4. μετὰ δὲ Λίξον Κράβις ποταμὸς καὶ λιμήν, καὶ πόλις Φοινί-κων Θυμιατηρία ὄνομα. ἀπὸ Θυμιατηρίας ⟨πλοῦς⟩ εἰς Σολό-εσαν ἄκραν, ἣ ἀνέχει μάλιστα εἰς τὸν πόντον. τῆς δὲ Λιβύης πάσης αὕτη ἡ χώρα ὀνομαστοτάτη καὶ ἱερωτάτη. ἐπὶ δὲ τῷ ἀκρωτηρίῳ τῆς ἄκρας ἔπεστι βωμὸς μεγαλοπρεπὴς Ποσειδῶ-νος. ἐν δὲ τῷ βωμῷ εἰσὶ γεγραμμένοι ἀνδριάντες, λέοντες, δελφῖνες· Δαίδαλον δέ φασι ποιῆσαι.

5. ἀπὸ δὲ Σολόεντος ἄκρας ποταμός ἐστιν ᾧ ὄνομα Ξιῶν.

περὶ τοῦτον τὸν ποταμὸν περιοικοῦσιν Αἰθίοπες ἱεροί. κατὰ δὲ
ταῦτα νῆσός ἐστιν ᾗ ὄνομα Κέρνη.

παράπλους δὲ ἀπὸ Ἡρακλείων στηλῶν ἐπὶ Ἑρμαίαν ἄκραν
ἡμερῶν δύο. ἀπὸ δὲ Ἑρμαίας ἄκρας εἰς Σολόεντα ἄκραν παράπλους ἡμερῶν τριῶν. ἀπὸ δὲ Σολόεντος εἰς Κέρνην παράπλους
ἡμερῶν ἑπτά.

σύμπας δὲ ὁ παράπλους οὗτός ἐστιν ἀπὸ Ἡρακλείων στηλῶν
εἰς Κέρνην νῆσον ἡμερῶν δώδεκα.

6. τῆς Κέρνης δὲ νήσου τὰ ἐπέκεινα οὐκέτι ἐστὶ πλωτὰ διὰ
βραχύτητα θαλάττης καὶ πηλὸν καὶ φῦκος. ἔστι δὲ τὸ φῦκος
τῆς δοχμῆς τὸ πλάτος καὶ ἄνωθεν ὀξὺ ὥστε κεντεῖν.

7. οἱ δὲ ἔμποροί εἰσι μὲν Φοίνικες· ἐπὰν δὲ ἀφίκωνται εἰς
τὴν νῆσον τὴν Κέρνην, τοὺς μὲν γαύλους καθορμίζουσι, ἐν τῇ
Κέρνῃ σκηνὰς ποιησάμενοι αὐτοῖς· τὸν δὲ φόρτον ἐξελόμενοι
αὐτοὶ διακομίζουσιν ἐν μικροῖς πλοίοις εἰς τὴν ἤπειρον.
8. εἰσὶ δὲ [οὗτοι] Αἰθίοπες πρὸς τὴν ἤπειρον· εἰσὶ δὲ οὗτοι οἱ
Αἰθίοπες πρὸς οὓς διατίθενται. πωλοῦσι δὲ πρὸς δέρματα ἐλά-
φων καὶ λεόντων καὶ παρδάλεων καὶ δέρματα ἐλεφάντων καὶ
ὀδόντας, καὶ τῶν ἡμέρων βοσκημάτων.   9. οἱ Αἰθίοπες χρῶνται κόσμῳ [—] στίκτοις, καὶ ἐκπώμασι τοῦ ἐλέφαντος φιάλαις·
καὶ αἱ γυναῖκες αὐτῶν χρῶνται κόσμῳ ψελίοις τοῦ ἐλέφαντος·
χρῶνται δὲ καὶ πρὸς τοὺς ἵππους ἐλεφαντίνῳ κόσμῳ. εἰσὶ δὲ
οὗτοι οἱ Αἰθίοπες μέγιστοι ἀνθρώπων πάντων ὧν ἡμεῖς ἴσμεν,
μείζους ἢ τετραπήχεις· εἰσὶ δέ τινες αὐτῶν καὶ πενταπήχεις.
καὶ πωγονοφόροι εἰσὶ καὶ κομῆται, καὶ κάλλιστοι πάντων
ἀνθρώπων οὗτοί εἰσι. καὶ βασιλεύει αὐτῶν οὗτος ὃς ἂν ᾖ
μέγιστος. εἰσὶ καὶ ἱππηλάται καὶ ἀκοντισταὶ καὶ τοξόται, καὶ
χρῶνται τοῖς βέλεσι πεπυρακτωμένοις.   10. οἱ δὲ Φοίνικες ἔμποροι εἰσάγουσιν αὐτοῖς μύρον, λίθον Αἰγυπτίαν, ἄλλους ἐξ-
ορύκτους, κέραμον Ἀττικὸν καὶ χοῦς· τὰ γὰρ πλάσματά ἐστιν
ὤνια ἐν τοῖς Χουσὶ τῇ ἑορτῇ.   11. εἰσὶ δὲ οἱ Αἰθίοπες οὗτοι
κρεοφάγοι γαλακτοπόται, οἶνον δὲ ποιοῦσι πολὺν ἀπὸ ἀμπέ-
λων· τὸν δὲ καὶ αὐτοὶ οἱ Φοίνικες ἄγουσιν. ἔστι δὲ αὐτοῖς καὶ
πόλις μεγάλη, πρὸς ἣν οἱ Φοίνικες εἰσπλέουσιν οἱ ἔμποροι.

12. λέγουσι δέ τινες τούτους τοὺς Αἰθίοπας παρήκειν συνε-
χῶς οἰκοῦντας ἐντεῦθεν εἰς Αἴγυπτον, καὶ εἶναι ταύτην ⟨τὴν⟩
θάλατταν συνεχῆ, ἀκτὴν δὲ εἶναι τὴν Λιβύην.

113. 1. διάφραγμα διὰ τῆς θαλάττης ⟨ἀπὸ⟩ τῆς Εὐρώπης εἰς
τὴν Ἀσίαν ἐπιεικῶς εὐθὺ κατ’ ὀρθόν. ἄρχεται δὲ τὸ διάφραγμα

ἀπὸ Εὐρίπου τοῦ κατὰ Χαλκίδα, καὶ ἔστιν ἐπὶ Γεραιστὸν στάδια ψ΄ καὶ ν΄.

ἀπὸ Γεραιστοῦ ἐπὶ Παιώνιον τῆς Ἄνδρου στάδια π΄.

αὐτῆς τῆς Ἄνδρου ἐπὶ τὸν Αὐλῶνα στάδια σπ΄.

τοῦ Αὐλῶνος διάπλους εἰς Τῆνον στάδια ιβ΄.

αὐτῆς δὲ τῆς Τήνου ἐπὶ τὸ ἀκρωτήριον τὸ κατὰ Ῥηναίαν
στάδια ρν΄.

τοῦ δὲ διάπλου εἰς Ῥηναίαν στάδια μ΄.

αὐτῆς δὲ Ῥηναίας καὶ τοῦ διάπλου εἰς Μύκονον στάδια μ΄.

ἀπὸ δὲ Μυκόνου διάπλους ἐπὶ τοὺς Μελαντίους σκοπέλους
προαριστιδίου μικρῷ ἐλάττων, σταδίων μ΄.

ἀπὸ δὲ Μελαντίων σκοπέλων πλοῦς εἰς Ἴκαρον προαριστίδιος.

αὐτῆς δὲ τῆς Ἰκάρου στάδια τ΄ ἐπὶ μῆκος.

ἀπὸ δὲ Ἰκάρου πλοῦς εἰς Σάμον προαριστίδιος.

αὐτῆς δὲ Σάμου στάδια σ΄.

ἐκ Σάμου εἰς Μυκάλην τοῦ διάπλου στάδια ζ΄.

τὸ πᾶν, ἐὰν ἐκ Σάμου πλέωσι πλῷ ἀρίστῳ, στάδια ͵βτο΄, μὴ
προσλογιζομένου τοῦ πλοῦ ⟨τοῦ ἐκ Μυκάλης εἰς Σάμον⟩.

2. ἕτερον διάφραγμα ὀρθὸν κατ᾽ εὐθύ.

⟨ἀπὸ Μαλέας⟩ ἕως Κυθήρων στάδια ⟨ρ⟩λ΄.

αὐτῶν δὲ Κυθήρων μῆκος στάδια ρ΄.

εἰς Αἰγιλίαν πλοῦς προαριστίδιος.

⟨αὐτῆς Αἰγιλίας μῆκος στάδια ν΄.

ἀπ᾽ Αἰγιλίας εἰς Κρήτην, πλοῦς προαριστίδιος.⟩

Κρήτης αὐτῆς μῆκος στάδια ͵βφ΄.

ἀπὸ Κρήτης εἰς Κάρπαθον στάδια †ρ΄.

αὐτῆς Καρπάθου μῆκος στάδια ρ΄.

εἰς Ῥόδον ἀπὸ Καρπάθου πλοῦς στάδια ρ΄.

αὐτῆς Ῥόδου μῆκος στάδια χ΄.

ἀπὸ Ῥόδου εἰς τὴν Ἀσίαν στάδια ρ΄.

ἔστι τοῦ διάπλου τὸ διάφραγμα στάδια ͵δσο΄.

114. Μεγέθη νήσων. μεγίστη Σαρδώ, δευτέρα Σικελία, τρίτη
Κρήτη, τετάρτη Κύπρος, πέμπτη Εὔβοια, ἕκτη Κύρνος, ἑβδόμη
Λέσβος, ὀγδόη Ῥόδος, ἐνάτη Χίος, δεκάτη Σάμος, ἑνδεκάτη
Κόρκυρα, δωδεκάτη †Κάσος, τρισκαιδεκάτη Κεφαλληνία, τεσ-
σαρεσκαιδεκάτη Νάξος, πεντεκαιδεκάτη Κῶς, ἑξκαιδεκάτη Ζάκυνθος, ἑπτακαιδεκάτη Λῆμνος, ὀκτωκαιδεκάτη Αἴγινα, ἐννεα-
καιδεκάτη Ἴμβρος, εἰκοστὴ Θάσος.

TRANSLATION

Italics in parentheses indicate (*a*) a modern, or alternative ancient, name; (*b*) a transliteration. *Italics* outside parentheses indicate (*a*) words highly uncertain (not merely restored or conjectural) in the Greek; (*b*) uncertain sense. Omitted altogether are the names of peoples or regions with which sections of the manuscript begin; these can be consulted in the Greek text if desired. Headings are added by the editor.

( )	words added to the translation to guide the reader
[ ]	words deleted or moved elsewhere
⟨ ⟩	material added in the Greek text
—	parenthetical remark in original
…	lacuna in MS

Introduction

1. And I shall begin from the Pillars of Herakles in Europe (and go) as far as the Pillars of Herakles in Libyē, and as far as the Great Aithiopes (*Ethiopians*). And the Pillars of Herakles are directly facing one another, and they are distant from one another a voyage of a day.

1–69. Europe

1–4. PILLARS OF HERAKLES TO ANTION

Past the Pillars of Herakles in Europe are many trading-towns of the Karchedonioi (*Carthaginians*), and mud and flood-tides and shoals.

2. In Europe the first (people) are the Iberes, a community of Iberia, with the river Iber. And two islands come next here, which have the name Gadeira (*Cádiz*). One of these two has a city that is a day's voyage distant from the Pillars of Herakles. Then a trading-town (*emporion*) ⟨and⟩ city, which has the name Emporion, a Hellenic city; and these people are colonists from the Massaliotai (*men of Marseille*).

Coastal voyage of Iberia: seven days and seven nights.

3. And past the Iberes there follow the Ligyes (*Ligurians*) and Iberes mixed, as far as the river Rhodanos (*Rhône*).

Coastal voyage of the Ligyes from Emporion as far as the Rhodanos river: two days and one night.

4. Past the Rhodanos river there follow the Ligyes as far as Antion (*Antibes*). In this territory there is a Hellenic city, Massalia (*Marseille*), with a harbour, ⟨and Olbia and Antion with a harbour⟩. These cities are colonists from Massalia.

And the coastal voyage of this (territory), from the Rhodanos river as far as Antion, is of days, *two*, and nights, *two*.

And from the Pillars of Herakles as far as Antion, all this territory has good harbours.

5–14. ANTION TO IAPYGIA

5. And past Antion are the Tyrrhenoi (*Etruscans*), a community, as far as Rome, a city. Coastal voyage: days, four, and nights, four.

6. And by Tyrrhenia lies the island of Kyrnos (*Corsica*). And from Tyrrhenia the voyage to Kyrnos is of a day and a half. And there is an island in the middle of this voyage, which is inhabited and which has the name Aithalia (*Elba*); and many other deserted islands.

7. And from Kyrnos island to Sardo island (*Sardinia*): a voyage of the third part of a day, and there is a deserted island in between.

And from Sardo to Libyē: a voyage of a day and a night. And to Sikelia (*Sicily*) from Sardo: a voyage of days, two, and a night.

And I return again onto the mainland, from where I turned away to Kyrnos.

8. After Tyrrhenia there follow the Latinoi (*Latins*) as far as the Kirkaion. Also the monument of Elpenor belongs to the Latinoi.

Of the Latinoi, coastal voyage: a day and a night.

9. And after the Latinoi there follow the Olsoi (*Volsci*).

And of the Olsoi, coastal voyage: days, one.

10. And after the Olsoi there follow the Kampanoi (*Campanians*). And there are these Hellenic cities in Kampania: Kyme (*Cumae*), Neapolis (*Naples*). By these is Pithekoussa (*Ischia*) island with a Hellenic city.

And the coastal voyage of Kampania is of days, one.

11. And after the Kampanoi there follow the Saunitai (*Samnites*).

And the coastal voyage is, of the Saunitai, a day's half.

12. And after the Saunitai there follow the Leukanoi (*Lucanians*) as far as Thouria.

And the voyage beside Leukania (*Lucania*) is of days, 6, and nights, 6.

And Leukania is a headland. In this there are Hellenic cities as follows: Poseidonia (*Paestum*) with Elea, ⟨Laos⟩, a colony of the Thourioi, Pandosia, Klampeteia, Terina, Hipponion, Mesma, and Rhegion, a promontory with a city.

13. 1. And by Rhegion is Sikelia island (*Sicily*), distant from Europe 12 stades *to* Pelorias from Rhegion.

2. And in Sikelia are the following barbarian communities: Elymoi, Sikanoi, Sikeloi, Phoinikes (*Phoenicians*), and Troës (*Trojans*). Now these people are barbarians, but Hellenes also live here. And the promontory of Sikelia is Pelorias.

3. And past Pelorias there are Hellenic cities as follows: Messene with a harbour, Tauromenion, Naxos, Katane, Leontinoi—and to Leontinoi along the Terias river is a voyage upstream of 20 stades—the Symaithos river with a city, Megaris, and a harbour, Xiphoneios. And following Megaris is the city of Syrakousai (*Syracuse*), with two harbours in it, one of these inside a fort and the other outside. And after this is the city of Heloron, and Pachynos promontory. And past Pachynos are the following Hellenic cities: Kamarina, Gela, Akragas, Selinous, and Lilybaion promontory. And past Lilybaion there is a Hellenic city, Himera.

4. And Sikelia is triangular: and each limb of it is of approximately *1,500* stades.

And after Himera city is Lipara island; and a Hellenic city, Mylai, with a harbour. And there is from Mylai up to Lipara island a voyage of a day's half.

5. And I return again onto the mainland, from where I turned away. For past Rhegion the cities are as follows: Lokroi, Kaulonia, Kroton; Lakinion, a sanctuary of Hera; and Kalypso's Island, in which Odysseus dwelt beside Kalypso, and the river

Krathis, and Sybaris and Thouria, a city. These are the
Hellenes in Leukania.

14. And after Leukania are the Iapyges, a community, as far as
the Hyrion mountain in the Adrias (*Adriatic*) gulf.

Coastal voyage beside Iapygia: six days and six nights.

And in Iapygia live Hellenes, and the cities are as follows:
Herakleion, Metapontion, Taras with a harbour. Hydrous upon
the mouth of the Adrias or of the Ionios (*Ionian*) gulf.

15–27. THE ADRIATIC

15. And after the Iapyges, past *Hyrion* are the *Daunitai*, a community. And in this community are the following tongues:
Alphaternioi, Opikoi, *Karakones*, Boreontinoi, and Peuketieis, extending from the Tyrrhenian main to the Adrias.

Coastal voyage of the Daunitid territory: days, two, and a
night.

16. And after the Daunitai is the community of the Ombrikoi
(*Umbrians*), and among them is a city, Ankon. And this community worships Diomedes, having received benefaction from
him: and there is a sanctuary of him.

And the coastal voyage of Ombrike is of days, two, and a
night.

17. And after the Ombric (community?) are the Tyrrhenoi
(*Etruscans*). And these people extend from the Tyrrhenic main
to the Adrias *gulf*: and there is a Hellenic city among them,
⟨Spina,⟩ with a river: and the voyage upstream to the city
along the river is of about 20 stades. [And Tyrrhenia is extending
from the outer sea as far as to the Adrias gulf.]

⟨And of the Tyrrhenoi the coastal voyage is of days, one,⟩
from . . ., a city: and it is a road of days, three.

18. And after the Tyrrhenoi are the Keltoi (*Celts*), a community,
left behind from the expedition, upon a narrow front as far as
the Adrias, ⟨extending from the outer sea as far as to the
Adrias gulf⟩. And here is the inner end of the Adrias gulf.

19. And after the Keltoi are the Enetoi (*Veneti*), a community,
and the river Eridanos (*Po*) among them.

And of the *Enetoi* the coastal voyage in a direct line [from the
city of Pise] is of days, one.

20. And after the Enetoi the Istroi are the community, and the river Istros. This river also discharges into the Pontos in *a scattered bed*, as ⟨the Neilos (*Nile*) does⟩ into Aigyptos (*Egypt*).

And the coastal voyage of the territory of the Istroi: a day and a night.

21. 1. And after the Istroi are the Libyrnoi, a community. And in this community there are cities beside the sea, *Arsias*, *Dassatika*, *Senites*, Apsyrta, Loupsoi, *Ortopeletai*, and *Heginoi*. These people are ruled by women; and the women are (wives) of free men, but mingle with their own slaves and with the men of the nearby lands.   **2.** By this territory are the following islands whose names I am able to state—and there are also many others unnamed—Istris island, of 210 stades and width 120; *Elektrides*; Mentorides; and these islands are great. The Kataibates river.

Coastal voyage of the Libyrnid territory: days, two.

22. 1. And after the Libyrnoi are the Illyrioi (*Illyrians*), a community, and the Illyrioi live beside the sea as far as Chaonia by Kerkyra (*Corfu*), the island of Alkinoös. And there is a Hellenic city here, which has the name Herakleia, with a harbour.

2. The barbarians called Lotophagoi (*Lotus-eaters*) are the following: *Iadasinoi*, Boulinoi, and *Hylloi*; with the Boulinoi the Hylloi are coterminous. And these people say Hyllos son of Herakles settled them; and they are barbarians. And they are settled in a peninsula a little lesser than the Peloponnesos.

3. And past the peninsula ⟨is ... island⟩ *beside a straight mouth*; the Boulinoi live beside this. And the Boulinoi are an Illyric community.

And there is a coastal voyage of the territory of the Boulinoi, of a long day up to the Nestos *river*.

23. 1. And past the Nestos there is a gulf-shaped voyage. And all this gulf is called Manios.

And the coastal voyage is days, one.

2. And there are in this gulf the islands of *Tragyras*, *Brattia*, and Olynta. And these are distant from one another 2 stades or a little more, by Pharos and Issa. For here is the island of Pharos ⟨with⟩ a Hellenic city, and Issa island; and these are Hellenic cities.

3. Before voyaging along the coast up to the Naron river, a lot of territory extends markedly into the sea. And there is an island near the coastal territory, which has the name Melite, and a second island near this, which has the name Kerkyra Melaina (*Black Corcyra*): and this island *projects* very far *with one* of its promontories from the coastal territory, and with the other promontory it comes down to the Naron river. And from Melite it is distant 20 stades, and from the coastal territory it is distant 8 stades.

24. 1. And past the Nestoi is the Naron river: and the voyage into the *Naron* is not narrow, and even a trireme sails into it, and boats do so into the upper trading-town, distant from the sea 80 stades. And these people are a community of the Illyrioi, the Manioi. And there is a lake inland from the trading-town, a great one, and the lake extends to the Autariatai, an Illyric community. And there is an island in the lake of 120 stades, and this island is extremely good for farming. And from this lake the Naron river flows away.

2. And from the Naron up to the *Arion* river is a day's voyage. And from the Arion ⟨up to the Rhizous⟩ river: a voyage of a day's half.

And Kadmos's and Harmonia's stones are here, and a sanctuary above the *Rhizous* river. And from the *Rhizous* river the voyage is to Bouthoë and the trading-town.

25. A community belonging to the Illyrioi are the Encheleis, following the Rhizous.

And out of Bouthoë to Epidamnos, a Hellenic city: a voyage of a day and a night, and a road of three days.

26. 1. Belonging to the *Taulantioi* is the Illyric community in which is Epidamnos; and a river flows beside the city, which has the name Palamnos.

And out of Epidamnos to Apollonia, a Hellenic city: a road of days, two. And Apollonia is distant from the sea 50 stades, and the river Aias flows beside the city. And from Apollonia into Amantia is 320 stades. And the Aias river flows from the Pindos mountain beside Apollonia.

2. . . . . towards Orikos, rather more into the *gulf*. Of the Orikia some 90 stades come down to the sea, and of the Amantia 60 stades.

3. Sharing a border with the *Amantes* in the interior are the Atintanes above the Orikia and *Karia* as far as *Idonia*. In the *Kastid* territory is said to be a plain ⟨which has⟩ the name Erytheia. Here Geryones is said to live and to pasture his oxen. By these places are the Keraunia mountains on the mainland, and there is an island beside these places, a small one, which has the name Sason.

From here to Orikos, a city, is a coastal voyage of a day's third part.

27. 1. And the Orikoi are settled within the Amantian territory. And these people [Amantieis] are Illyrioi as far as here, past the Boulinoi.

2. And the mouth of the Ionios gulf is from the Keraunia mountains as far as cape Iapygia. And up to Hydroëis, a city which is in Iapygia, from the Keraunia (mountains) the stades of the voyage across are about 500, ⟨which⟩ is the mouth of the gulf: and the places inside are the Ionios. There are many harbours in the Adrias (*Adriatic*): and (the) Adrias is the same thing as (the) Ionios.

[28–33. 1. Epeiros]

28. And after the Illyrioi are the Chaones. And Chaonia has good harbours: and the Chaones live in separate villages.

And the coastal voyage of Chaonia is a half of a day.

29. And by Chaonia is the island of Korkyra, and a Hellenic city in it, having three harbours by the city; of these the one is enclosed. And Korkyra belongs also to Thesprotia more than it does to Chaonia.

And I return again onto the mainland, from where I turned away.

30. And after Chaonia are the Thesprotoi, a community. And these people, too, live in separate villages: and this territory also has good harbours. Here there is a harbour, which has the name Elaia. Into this harbour the river Acheron discharges: and a lake, Acherousia, out of which the Acheron river flows.

And the coastal voyage of Thesprotia: a half of a day.

31. And after Thesprotia is Kassopia, a community. And these people, too, live in separate villages. And these people live alongside as far as into the Anaktoric gulf.

And the coastal voyage of the territory of the Kassopoi is a half of a day. And the Anaktoric gulf is a little less, from its mouth as far as into the inner end, than 120 stades. And the mouth is in width 4 stades.

32. And after Kassopia are the Molottoi, a community. And these people live in separate villages: and they come down only a little here to the sea, but over a large extent into the interior.

And the coastal voyage of the Molottian territory is of 40 stades.

33. 2–65. Continuous Hellas

33. 1. And after Molottia is Ambrakia, a Hellenic city: and this is distant from the sea 80 stades. And there is also upon the sea a fort with an enclosed harbour.

2. From here Hellas begins to be continuous as far as the Peneios river and Homolion, a city in Magnesia, which is beside the river.

And the coastal voyage of Ambrakia: 120 stades.

34. 1. And after Ambrakia is Akarnania, a community; and the first city on this spot is Argos the Amphilochic, and Euripos, and *Thyrrheion* in the *federal state*. And outside the *Ambrakic* gulf are the following ⟨cities⟩: Anaktorion with a harbour; Akte; and the city of Leukas with a harbour: this city stands forth upon the Leukatas, which is a promontory ⟨visible⟩ from afar ⟨in⟩ the sea. This city was previously also named Epileukadioi. And the Akarnanes, having fought a civil war, took out of Corinth one thousand new settlers; and the new settlers, having killed *these people*, hold their territory themselves. And this territory is now an island, having been cut off at the isthmus with a ditch. And after these places is the city of Phara; and by these places there is the island of Ithake, with a city and a harbour. After these places the island of Kephalenia.

2. And I return again onto the mainland, from where I departed. After these places the city of Alyzia, and by this the island of Karnos, and the city of Astakos with a harbour, and the river Acheloös, and Oiniadai, a city: and to this [these cities]

there is a voyage upstream along the Acheloös. And there are also other cities of Akarnanes in the interior.

And the coastal voyage of Akarnania is of days, two.

3. And all of Akarnania has good harbours: and by these places many islands lie alongside, which the Acheloös by silting them up is making into mainland. The islands are called Echinades: and they are deserted.

35. And after Akarnania is Aitolia, a community, and in it the cities are as follows: Kalydon, Halikarna, and Molykreia: and the Delphic gulf: and the mouth of this gulf is 10 stades, and upon it is a sanctuary; and Naupaktos, a city: and after it (*sc. Naupaktos*) the Aitoloi have many other cities in the interior.

And the coastal voyage of Aitolia is of days, one.

And Aitolia stretches along all of Lokris from the interior as far as the Ainianeis.

36. And after the Aitoloi (*Aitolians*) are the Lokroi (*Lokrians*), a community, in whom are *the* people called Ozolai and the following cities: Euanthis, Amphissa. And these people also have cities in the interior.

And the coastal voyage of the territory of the Lokroi is the half of a day.

37. And after the Lokroi the Phokeis (*Phokians*) are the community by the Kirrhaion plain; and the sanctuary of Apollo, and Delphoi, a city, and Antikyra, a city, where the best hellebore treatments take place.

And the coastal voyage of the territory of the Phokeis: a half of a day.

38. And after the Phokeis are the Boiotoi (*Boiotians*), a community, and the following cities: Korsiai, Siphai with a harbour, and *Eutresis* with a fort of the Boiotoi.

And the coastal voyage of Boiotia: a half of a day ⟨or⟩ less.

39. And after the Boiotoi are the Megareis (*Megarians*), a community, and the following cities: Aigosthena; Pegai, a fort; Geraneia; and A⟨igei⟩ros.

And the coastal voyage of the territory of the Megareis: 100 stades.

40–55. Peloponnese, with Crete and Southern Cyclades

40. And after the Megareis are Korinthos (*Corinth*), a city with a sanctuary, *Lechaion*, and the Isthmus.

And now from here begins the Peloponnesos.

And from the sea the road towards the sea on our side, through the isthmus, is 40 stades. These places are all gulf-shaped.

And the coastal voyage of the territory of the Korinthioi (*Corinthians*): a half of a day.

41. And after Korinthos is Sikyon, a city.

Of this the coastal voyage: 120 stades.

42. And after Sikyon the Achaioi (*Achaians*), a community, and among them the cities are as follows: Pellene, Aigeira, Aigai, Aigion, and Rhypes; and outside Rhion (are) Patrai and Dyme.

And the coastal voyage of the Achaian territory: 700 stades.

43. And after the Achaioi is Elis, a community, and in it the following cities: Kyllene with a harbour; and the river Alpheios: and there is also another union of cities, Elis, in the interior. By this territory is the island of Zakynthos, in which there is both a city and a harbour.

And the coastal voyage of the territory of the Eleioi (*Eleians*) right up to the ⟨boundaries⟩ of the Lepreatai: 700 stades.

44. And after Elis is Arkadia, a community. And Arkadia comes down to the sea at Lepreon out of the interior. And their [large] cities in the interior are the following: ⟨Megale Polis⟩, Tegea, Mantineia, Heraia, Orchomenos, and Stymphalos. And there are also other cities.

And the coastal voyage of the territory of the Lepreatai: 100 stades.

45. And after Arkadia is the community of Messene, and in it the following cities: [first Messene with a harbour] Kyparissos, distant from the sea 7 stades; ⟨Prote island with a harbour⟩; Ithome in the interior, distant from the sea 80 stades.

And the coastal voyage of the Messenian territory: 300 stades.

46. 1. ⟨And after Messene⟩ Lakedaimon, a community, and in it the cities are the following: Asine; Mothone; Achilleios, a harbour, and back to back with this Psamathous, a harbour. In the middle of both these, projecting into the sea, is a sanctuary of Poseidon, Tainaros; and Las, a city with a harbour; Gytheion, in which is a shipyard with a fort; and the river Eurotas; and Boia, a city; and Malea, a cape. By this (cape) lies Kythera island, with a city and a harbour. And by this is Krete (*Crete*) island.

2. And after this aforementioned cape Malea are Side, a city with a harbour; Epidauros, a city with a harbour; Prasia, a city with a harbour; *Anthana*, a city with a harbour. And there are also many other cities of the Lakedaimonioi (*Lakedaimonians*). And in the interior is Sparta, and many others. And the coastal voyage of the territory of the Lakedaimonioi: days, three.

47. By Lakedaimon lies the island of Krete (*Crete*): for Lakedaimon lies closest to it of (all) Europe. And the voyage across from Lakedaimon as far as to the promontory of Krete upon which is the city of Phalasarna: a day's run.

And past Phalasarna is Kriou Metopon promontory. And towards the south wind is the voyage to Libyē, and up to the *Azirides* of Chersonesos, those of the Kyrenaioi (*Cyrenaeans*): the voyage of a day and a night.

2. And Krete is 2,500 stades long, and narrow, and extends from the settings of the sun towards the risings of the sun. And there live in Krete Hellenes, some of them colonists from the Lakedaimonioi, others from the Argeioi (*Argives*), others from the Athenaioi (*Athenians*), others from the rest of Hellas from wherever it chanced. And some of them are aborigines. (There are) many cities in Krete.

3. ⟨After Koryk⟩os promontory the first city towards the setting sun is the aforementioned Phalasarna with an enclosed harbour. (Then) Polyrrhenia, and it extends from the north towards the south. Diktynnaion, a sanctuary of Artemis, towards the north wind, belonging to the territory that is Pergamian. And towards the south Hyrtakina. Kydonia with an enclosed harbour towards the north. And in the interior Elyros, a city. And towards the south Lissa, a city with a harbour beside Kriou Metopon. [And towards the north wind a very beautiful mountain and a harbour in it, Olous, and all] And towards the north wind the Apteraian territory. Then the Lampaia, and

this extends on both sides, and the river Mesapos is in it.
4. And after this *Mount Ida*, with Eleuthernai towards the
north. And towards the south Sybrita with a harbour towards
the south, (namely) Phaistos. Towards the north Oaxos and
Knossos. And towards the south Gortyna. Rhaukos ⟨in the
interior⟩, and in the interior Lyktos, and this extends on both
sides. ⟨And towards the north wind Mount Kadistos with a
harbour in it, (namely) Olous, and . . .⟩ Prasos; it extends on
both sides. *Itanos*, the promontory of Crete towards the upcoming sun.

And there are also other cities in Krete: and it is said to be
hundred-citied.

48. And the following are the Kyklades (*Cyclades*) by the
Lakedaimonian territory that are inhabited: Melos with a
harbour, and by this Kimolos, and by this *Pholegandros*, and by
this Sikinos, *an island* and a city. And by this Thera, and by this
Anaphe, and by this Astypalaia.

And I return again onto the mainland, from where I turned
away.

49. And after Lakedaimon is the city of Argos, and in it
Nauplia, a city with a harbour: and in the interior Kleonai and
Mykenai and Tiryns.

Coastal voyage of the Argeian territory in a circle, for it is a
gulf, called the Argolic: 150 stades.

50. 1. And after Argos is the Epidaurian territory: for it comes
down to this gulf for 30 stades.

2. And after the Epidaurian territory is the Halia (*territory of
Halieis*) with a harbour. This is upon the mouth of the Argolic
gulf.

The voyage round this is of 100 stades.

51. 1. And after this is Hermion, a city, with a harbour.
And the voyage round this is of 80 stades.

2. And after Hermion is Skyllaion, the promontory of the
gulf towards the Isthmus: and Skyllaion belongs to Troizenia.
And directly facing it is Sounion, the promontory of the territory of the Athenaioi (*Athenians*). And by this is the island of
Belbina with a city.

3. Of this gulf, from this mouth inwards to the Isthmus,

there are 740 stades. And this gulf itself is very straight at the mouth.

52. 1. And after Hermion is Troizen, a city with a harbour.
And the coastal voyage of it is 30 stades.

2. And after these places is the island of Kalauria, with a city and a harbour.
And the coastal voyage of it is *300* stades.

53. And by this is the island and city of Aigina with two harbours.
And I return again onto the mainland, from where I turned away.

54. And after Troizenia is the city of Epidauros with a harbour.
And the coastal voyage of the Epidaurian territory: ⟨1⟩30 stades.

55. And after Epidauros is the territory of the Korinthioi (*Corinthians*), ⟨the part⟩ towards the dawn, and the fort of Kenchreiai, and the Isthmus, where there is a sanctuary of Poseidon.

Here the Peloponnesos ends.

And the Korinthioi also have territory outside the Isthmus, and the fort of Sidous, and the other fort, Kremmyon. And the coastal voyage of the territory of the Korinthioi as far as the bounds of the Megareis (*Megarians*): 300 stades.

56. And past the territory of the Korinthioi is Megara, a city with a harbour, and Nisaia, a fort.
And the coastal voyage of the territory of the Megareis as far as Iapis, for this is a boundary of the territory of the Athenaioi: 140 stades.

57. 1. And after the Megareis are cities of the Athenaioi (*Athenians*). And the first (place) in Attike (*Attica*) is Eleusis, where there is a sanctuary of Demeter and a fort. By this is Salamis, an island with a city and a harbour. Next the Peiraieus and the Legs (*Long Walls*) and Athenai (*Athens*). And the Peiraieus has 3 harbours. 2. (Then) Anaphlystos, a fort with a harbour; Sounion, a promontory with a fort; a sanctuary of Poseidon; Thorikos, a fort with two harbours; Rhamnous, a fort. And there are also many other harbours in Attike.

Voyage round the territory of the Athenaioi: 1,140 stades. From the Iapid territory up to Sounion: 490 stades. From Sounion as far as the boundaries of the Boiotoi (*Boiotians*): 650 stades.

58. 1. And by Attike are the islands called Kyklades (*Cyclades*), and the following cities in the islands: Keos—this one is four-citied: ⟨Poieëssa, a city⟩ with a harbour; Koressia, Ioulis, and Karthaia—Helene; Kythnos island, with a city; Seriphos island, with a city and a harbour; Siphnos; Paros having two harbours, of which the one is enclosed; Naxos; Delos; Rhene; Syros; Mykonos—this one is two-citied; Tenos with a harbour; Andros with a harbour. Now these are the Kyklades islands.

2. But under these are the following other islands towards the south: Ios with a harbour: in this (island) Homer is buried; Amorgos—this one is three-citied—with a harbour; Ikaros—two-citied.

3. And after Andros is Euboia island—this one is four-citied. And there are in it Karystos, Eretria with a harbour, Chalkis with a harbour, Hestiaia with a harbour. And Euboia from (the sanctuary of) Zeus Kenaios up to Geraistos, Poseidon's sanctuary, has 1,350 stades; and in width Euboia is narrow.

4. And in the Aigaion (*Aegean*) main are the following islands: by Eretria Skyros, with a city; Ikos—this one is two-citied; Peparethos—this one is three-citied—with a harbour; Skiathos—this one is two-citied—with a harbour.

After these places I return again onto the mainland, from where I turned away.

59. And after Athenai are the Boiotoi (*Boiotians*), a community: for these people come down to this sea *as well* (as the other). And in it the first (place) is a sanctuary, Delion; Aulis, a sanctuary; Euripos, a fort; Anthedon, a fort; Thebai (*Thebes*); Thespiai; Orchomenos in the interior. And there are also other cities.

And the coastal voyage of the Boiotian territory from Delion as far as the bounds of the Lokroi (*Lokrians*): 250 stades.

60. And after the Boiotoi are the Lokroi, a community. And by Euboia they have the following cities: Larymna, Kynos, Opous, and Alope; and the Lokroi also have many others.

And the coastal voyage of their territory: 200 stades.

61. And after the Lokroi are the Phokeis (*Phokians*): for these people, too, extend to this sea. And they have the following cities: *Thronion*, Knemis, Elateia, and Panopeus. And they have also other cities in the interior.

And the coastal voyage of the territory of the Phokeis is 200 stades.

62. 1. And after the Phokeis are the *Melieis* and the Melieus gulf. In this gulf are the people called Limodorieis, the following: Erineos, Boion, and Kytinion. Here are Thermopylai, Trachis, Oite, Herakleia, and the Spercheios river.

2. And after the Melieis ⟨are the Malieis⟩, a community. And the Malieis have as their first city Lamia, and as the last Echinos: and the Malieis also have other cities, as far as where the gulf reaches. And against the territory of the Malieis live the Ainianes, above from the interior. And through them flows the Spercheios river.

63. And outside the Maliaios gulf are the Achaioi Phthiotai (*Phthiotic Achaians*), a community: and they are also in the Pagasetic gulf, on the left as one sails in, to about halfway up the gulf. The cities belonging to the Achaioi are the following: Antrones, Larissa, Melitaia, Demetrion, and Thebai: and the Achaioi also have other cities in the interior.

64. 1. And after the Achaioi Thettalia (*Thessaly*) comes down to the sea out of the interior on a narrow front to the Pagasetic gulf, 30 *stadioi*.

And belonging to Thettalia there are the following cities upon the sea: Amphenai, Pagasai, and in the interior Pherai, Larissa, Pharsalos, Kierion, Pelinnaion, Skotousa, and Krannon. And there are also other cities of the Thettaloi in the interior. And Thettalia stretches along in the interior above the Ainianes and Dolopes and Malieis and Achaioi and Magnetes, as far as Tempe.   2. And the Pagasetic gulf's length is, from the mouth to the inner end of Pagasai: a voyage before the midday meal. And the mouth of it is 5 stades.

And in the Pagasetic gulf is the island of Kikynethos, with a city.

65. 1. ⟨And after Thettalia⟩ there is the community of the Magnetes (*Magnesians*) beside the sea, and the following cities:

Iolkos, Methone, Korakai, Spalauthra, Olizon, and Tisai, a harbour. And outside the gulf of Pagasai are Meliboia, Rhizous, Eurymenai, and Amyros. And against them in the interior live the community of the Perrhaiboi, Hellenes.

2. As far as here from Ambrakia Hellas is continuous: and probably also ⟨the⟩ seaward parts (of Magnesia) are similarly ⟨in⟩ Hellas.

66–9. MACEDONIA TO THE TANAÏS

66. 1. And past the Peneios river are the Makedones (*Macedonians*), a community, and the gulf of Therma.

2. The first city of Makedonia is Herakleion; (then) Dion; Pydna, a Hellenic city; Methone, a Hellenic city, with the Haliakmon river; Aloros, a city with the river Loudias; Pella, a city with a royal seat (*basileion*) in it, and there is a voyage upstream to it up the Loudias; (then) the Axios river; the Echedoros river; Therme, a city; Aineia, Hellenic.

3. Pallene, a long cape stretching up into the main; and the following Hellenic cities in Pallene: Potidaia, forming a barrier across the isthmus in the middle, Mende, Aphytis, Thrambeïs, Skione, and Kanastraion the sacred promontory of Pallene.

4. And outside the isthmus the following cities: Olynthos, Hellenic; Mekyberna, Hellenic.

Sermylia, Hellenic, with the Sermylic gulf; Torone, a Hellenic city with a harbour.

Dion, Hellenic; Thyssos, Hellenic; Kleonai, Hellenic; Athos Mountain; Akrothoöi, Hellenic; Charadrous, Hellenic; Olophyxos, Hellenic; Akanthos, Hellenic; Alapta, Hellenic.

Arethousa, Hellenic; Bolbe Lake; and Apollonia, Hellenic.

5. And there are also many others belonging to Makedonia in the interior. And it is gulf-shaped.

And the coastal voyage around the gulfs: two days.

And after Makedonia is the Strymon river; this bounds Makedonia and Thrake.

67. 1. And Thrake (*Thrace*) extends from the Strymon river as far as the Istros river in the Euxeinos Pontos (*Black Sea*). And there are in Thrake the following Hellenic cities: Amphipolis, Phagres, Galepsos, Oisyme, and other trading-towns of the

Thasioi (*Thasians*). By these places is Thasos island with a city and two harbours; of these, one is enclosed.

2. And I return again to the point from where I turned away. Neapolis, by this. Daton, a Hellenic city, which Kallistratos of Athenai (*Athens*) founded; and the river Nestos; Abdera, a city; Koudetos river with the cities of Dikaia and Maroneia.

3. By these places is Samothrake ⟨island⟩, with a harbour. By this on the mainland are the trading-towns of Drys, Zone, and Douriskos. The river Hebros with a fort upon it, (namely) Ainos, a city with a harbour. Forts of the Ainioi in Thrake; the Melas gulf; the Melas river; Deris, a trading-town; Kobrys, a trading-town of the Kardianoi, and another, Kypasis.

4. By the Melas gulf is Imbros island, with a city; and Lemnos island, with a harbour.

5. I return again onto the mainland, from where I turned away. And after the Melas gulf is the Thrakian Chersonesos, and in it are the following cities: Kardia, Ide, Paion, Alopekonnesos, Araplos, Elaious, Madytos, and Sestos upon the mouth of the Propontis; ⟨which⟩ is 6 stades (wide). And within Aigos Potamos are Kressa, Krithote, and Paktyë. 6. As far as here it is the Thrakian Chersonesos. And out of Paktyë to Kardia through the neck on foot is 40 stades, out of the sea into the sea; and there is a city in the middle, which has the name Agora. The Chersonesos's length out of Kardia to Elaious—for here it is longest: stades, 400.

7. And after the Chersonesos are Thrakian forts as follows: first Leuke Akte, (then) Teiristasis, Herakleia, Ganos, Ganiai, and Neon Teichos. Perinthos, a city with a harbour; Daminon Teichos; Selymbria, a city with a harbour. From this up to the mouth of the Pontos there are 500 stades.

8. The place is called Anaplous (*Voyage Upstream*) along the Bosporos until you come to Hieron (*The Sanctuary*). And from Hieron it is the mouth of the Pontos, 7 stades in width.

67. 9-92. The Black Sea

9. And there are in the Pontos the following Hellenic cities in Thrake: Apollonia, Mesembria, Odesos Polis, Kallatis, ⟨Istros,⟩ and the river Istros.

10. And the coastal voyage of Thrake from the Strymon river as far as Sestos: two days, and nights, two. And from Sestos as far as the mouth of the Pontos: two days, and nights, two. And from the mouth as far as the Istros river: days, three, and nights, three. The total voyage round, from Thrake and the river Strymon as far as the Istros river: eight days and eight nights.

68. 1. And after Thrake are the Skythai (*Scythians*), a community, and among them the following Hellenic cities: the Tyras river; Nikonion, a city; Ophiousa, a city.

2. And against the Skythike the Tauroi, a community, occupy a promontory of the mainland: and the promontory is (projecting) into the sea. And in the Taurike live Hellenes ⟨and their *poleis* are the following⟩: Chersonesos, a trading-town. Kriou Metopon, a promontory of the Taurike.

3. And after these places are the Skythai again, and the following Hellenic cities in it (*sc. Skythia*): Theudosia, Kytaia with Nymphaion, Pantikapaion, and Myrmekion.

Coastal voyage direct from (the) Istros up to Kriou Metopon: three days and three nights; and that beside land is double, for it is a gulf.

4. And in this gulf there is an island—and the island is deserted—which has the name Leuke, sacred to Achilles.

And from Kriou Metopon is a voyage to Pantikapaion of a day and a night: and from Pantikapaion up to the mouth of the Maiotis lake (*Sea of Azov*) is 20 stades.

5. And the Maiotis lake is said to amount to half of the Pontos. And in the Maiotis lake, as one sails directly in, on the left are Skythai: for there come down out of the outside sea, above the Taurike, to the Maiotis lake the Syrmatai, a community. And the river Tanaïs (*Don*) bounds Asia and Europe.

69. Length of Europe

69. From the Pillars of Herakles in Europe, as one sails around the gulfs beside land—if, for so many nights as have been written (above), one reckons days in place of these; and, where stades are written, in place of the 500 stades *a day of a man sailing*—the coastal voyage of Europe becomes [the Pontos being *equal to* the half portion of the Maiotis lake] days, 150 (and) three.

And the greatest rivers in Europe are the Tanaïs, the Istros, and the Rhodanos.

70–106. Asia

70–92. TANAÏS TO PROPONTIS

70. And past the Tanaïs river Asia begins.

And the first community of it is, in the Pontos, the Sauromatai. To the Sauromatai belongs the community of the Gynaikokratoumenoi.   71. After the Gynaikokratoumenoi there follow the Maiotai.   72. And after the Maiotai are the Sindoi, a community: for these people extend also to the outside of the lake, and there are Hellenic cities among them, the following: Phanagorou Polis; Kepoi; Sindikos, a harbour; and Patous.   73. And after Sindikos harbour are the Kerketai ⟨or rather Toretai⟩, a community, 74. and a Hellenic city, Torikos, with a harbour.   75. And after the Toretai are the Achaioi (*Achaians*), a community.   76. And after the Achaioi are the Heniochoi, a community.   77. ⟨And after the Heniochoi are the Koraxoi, a community.⟩   78. And after the Koraxoi is Korike, a community.   79. And after Korike are the Melanchlainoi, a community, and among them the river Metasoris, and the Aigipios river.   80. And after the Melanchlainoi is Gelon.

81. And after these are the Kolchoi, a community, with Dioskourias, a city; and Gyenos, a Hellenic city, with the Gyenos river and the Chirobos river; the Chorsos river, the Arios river, the Phasis river with Phasis, a Hellenic city; and there is a voyage upstream up the river of 180 stades to the city of Aia, a great barbarian one, where Medeia was from. Here is the Rhis river, the Isis river, Lēstōn Potamos, and the Apsaros river.

82. And after the Kolchoi are the Bouseres, a community, and the river of the Daraanoi, and the Arion river.   83. And after the Bouseres are the Ekecheirieis, a community, and the river Pordanis, and the Arabis river; Limne, a city; Hodeinios, a Hellenic city.   84. After the Ekecheirieis are the Becheires, a

community; Becheirikos, a harbour; Becheiras, a Hellenic city.
85. And after the Becheires are the Makrokephaloi, a community, and Psōrōn Limen; Trapezous, a Hellenic city.   86. And
after the Makrokephaloi are the Mossynoikoi, a community,
with Zephyrios Limen; Choirades, a Hellenic city; Ares's Island.
These people occupy mountains.   87. And after the Mossyn-
⟨oik⟩oi is the community of the Tibarenoi.   88. And after
the Tibarenoi are the Chalybes, a community; and Genesintis,
an enclosed harbour; Ameneia, a Hellenic city; and Iasonia, a
cape and Hellenic city.

89. And after the Chalybes is Assyria, a community, and the
river Thermodon, and a Hellenic city, Themiskyra; the Lykastos river with a Hellenic city; the Halys river and Karoussa, a
Hellenic city; Sinope, a Hellenic city; Kerasous, a Hellenic city
with the Ocherainos river; Harmene, a Hellenic city with a
harbour; and Tetrakis, a Hellenic city.

90. And after Assyria is Paphlagonia, a community. And in it is
Stephane, a harbour ⟨and a Hellenic ci⟩ty; Koloussa, a Hellenic
city; Kinolis, a Hellenic city; Karambis, a Hellenic city; Kytoris,
a Hellenic city; Sesamos, a Hellenic city with the Parthenios
river; and Tieion, a Hellenic city with the harbour of Psylla and
the river Kallichoros.

91. And after Paphlagonia are the Mariandynoi, a community.
Here is the city of Herakleia, Hellenic, with the river Lykos and
another river, the Hypios.

92. 1. And after the Mariandynoi are the Thrakes Bithynoi
(*Bithynian Thracians*), a community, and the river Sagarios, and
another river, Artones, and the island of Thynias—and men of
Herakleia live on it—and the river Rhebas. Then directly
(after) are the Strait and the aforesaid Hieron in the mouth of
the Pontos, and after this the city of Kalchedon outside
Thrake, after which is the Olbian gulf.
    Coastal voyage from the Mariandynoi as far as the inner
end of the Olbian gulf—for so great is the Thrake of the Bithynoi: days, three.   ⌒

    2. And from the mouth of the Pontos as far as the mouth of
    the Maiotis lake, the voyage is of similar size, both that
    along Europe and that along Asia.

93–102. MYSIA TO KILIKIA

93. And after Thrake is Mysia, a community. And it is the left side of the Olbian gulf as one sails out into the Kian gulf as far as Kios. And Mysia is a headland. And the Hellenic cities in it are as follows: Olbia with a harbour; Kallipolis with a harbour; the promontory of the Kian gulf; and on the left Kios, a city, and the Kios river.

And the coastal voyage of Mysia to Kios: days, one.

94. And after Mysia is Phrygia, a community, and the following Hellenic cities: Myrleia with the Rhyndakos river, and upon it Besbikos island, and the city of Plakia, and Kyzikos in the isthmus, forming a barrier across the isthmus, and within the isthmus Artake. By this is an island and city of Prokonnesos, and a second island, with good harbours, Elaphonnesos: and Prokonnesioi farm it. And on the mainland is the city of Priapos; (then) Parion, Lampsakos, Perkote, and Abydos; and this is the mouth of the Propontis by Sestos.

95. And from here Troas (*the Troad*) begins, and the Hellenic cities in it are as follows: Dardanos, Rhoiteion, and Ilion—and it is distant from the sea 25 stades—with the river Skamandros in it. And an island lies by these places, Tenedos, with a harbour, where Kleostratos the astronomer is from. And on the mainland Sige and Achilleion and Krateres Achaiōn, Kolonai, Larissa, and Hamaxitos with a sanctuary of Apollo, where Chryses served as priest.

96. And from here it is called Aiolid territory. And the Aiolid cities in it, upon the sea, are as follows: ⟨Assos (and/or) Gargara (and) Antandros; and in the interior as follows:⟩ Kebren, Skepsis, Neandreia, and Pityeia.

Coastal voyage of Phrygia from Mysia as far as Antandros:
. . .

97. By these places is an Aiolid island, Lesbos, having in itself 5 cities, the following: Methymna, Antissa, Eresos, Pyrrha with a harbour, and Mytilene having two harbours. And by this there is an island with a city: and the name that this has is Pordoselene.

And I return again onto the mainland, from where I turned away onto the islands.

98. 1. Past Antandros and downwards from *Aiolis, this* territory *too* was previously Mysia as far as Teuthrania, but is now Lydia; and the Mysoi migrated up into the mainland. 2. And there are the following Hellenic cities in it and in Lydia: Astyra, where there is the sanctuary ⟨of Artemis, and⟩ Adramyttion. And ⟨after Adramyttion⟩ the territory is Lesbian; and above this is the territory of the Chioi (*Chians*) and the city of Atarneus: and below these places upon the sea the ⟨city and⟩ harbour of Pitane with the river Kaïkos. After Pitane are Elaia, Gryneion, and Achaiōn Limen: in this the Achaioi are said to have taken counsel against Telephos, whether to march or to depart; the city of Myrina with a harbour; Kyme with a harbour—and above Kyme in the interior is a Hellenic city, Aigai—and Leukai with harbours, and Smyrna, in which Homer was; Phokaia with a harbour and the Hermos river; Klazomenai with a harbour; and Erythrai with a harbour. And by these is the island of Chios with a harbour.

3. I return again onto the mainland. *Airai*, a city with a harbour; Teos, a city with a harbour; Lebedos; Kolophon in the interior; Notion with a harbour; the sanctuary of Apollo Klarios; the Kaÿstros river; Ephesos with a harbour; Marathesion with, on the mainland, Magnesia, a Hellenic city; Anaia, Panionion, Erasistratios, Charadrous, Phokaia, Akadamis, and Mykale—these places are in the territory of the Samioi (*Samians*). And in front of Mykale is Samos island, having a city and an enclosed harbour. This island is not lesser than Chios.

4. And I return again onto the mainland, from where I turned away. Upon Mykale is the city of Priene, having two harbours, of which the one is enclosed: then the river Maiandros (*Maeander*).

And the coastal voyage of Mysia and Lydia, from Astyra as far as the Maiandros river: two days and nights, one.

99. 1. And after Lydia is Karia, a community, and in it the following Hellenic cities: Herakleia; then Miletos; then Myndos with a harbour; Halikarnassos with an enclosed harbour and another harbour around the island, and a river; Kalymna island; Karyanda island, with a city and harbour—these people are Kares (*Karians*). The island of Kos, with a city and an enclosed harbour. By these places is the Keramiac gulf of Karia, and the island of Nisyros, with a harbour.

2. I return again onto the mainland. A sacred promontory ⟨of Knidos⟩, Triopion; Knidos, a Hellenic city, with the territory of the Rhodioi (*Rhodians*) on the mainland; Kaunos, a Karic city with an enclosed harbour; Kragos, a promontory.

3. By this is ⟨Rhodos⟩ (*Rhodes*) island, ⟨with a city: and⟩ an ancient triple city in it, namely the following cities: Ialysos, Lindos, and Kameiros. And by Rhodos the following islands are inhabited: Chalkeia, Telos, Kasos, and Karpathos—this one is three-citied.

And the coastal voyage of Karia, from the Maiandros river up to *Kragos*, which is (the) promontory of Karia: two days.

I return again onto the mainland, from where I turned away.

100. 1. And past Karia is Lykia, a community: and the Lykioi have the following cities: Telmissos with a harbour and the river Xanthos, through which is a voyage upstream to ⟨Xanthos, a city⟩; Patara, a city, and it has a harbour; Phellos, a city with a harbour—by these places is an island of the Rhodioi, Megiste; Limyra, a city, to which the voyage upstream is along the river. Then Gagaia, a city; then Chelidoniai, a promontory with two islands; and Dionysias island; the promontory and harbour of Siderous. Above this is a sanctuary of Hephaistos in the mountain, and much spontaneous fire burns out of the land and is never extinguished.

2. And if you go forward higher from the sea there is . . ., (then) Phaselis, a city with a harbour—and this is a gulf; and Idyros, a city; the island of Lyrnateia; Olbia; Magydos with the river Katarraktes; and Perge, a city with a sanctuary of Artemis.

And in a direct line the coastal voyage of Lykia from . . . is of a day and a night, for it is gulf-shaped: and that beside land is double this.

101. 1. And after Lykia is Pamphylia, a community, and in it the following cities: Aspendos, a city—to this the voyage upstream takes place along the river, and the river is the Eurymedon; then the city of Sylleion; another city, Side, a colony of the Kymaioi, with a harbour.

Coastal voyage of Pamphylia from Perge: a half of a day.

2. And there are also other cities of Pamphylia: Kibyra, then Korakesion.

102. 1. And after Pamphylia is Kilikia (*Cilicia*), a community, and in it the following cities: Selinous; Charadrous, a city with a harbour; Anemourion, a cape with a city; Nagidos, a city: and it has an island. And towards *Setos* are *the harbours* Poseideion; Salon; Myous; Kelenderis, a city with the harbour of Aphrodisios and another harbour; Holmoi, a Hellenic city having ⟨a harbour⟩; Sarpedon, a deserted city with a river; Soloi, a Hellenic city; Zephyrion, a city; the river Pyramos and the city of Mallos, to which the voyage upstream is along the river; the trading-town of *Amane* with a harbour; Myriandos Phoinikōn (*of the Phoenicians*); and Thapsakos, a river.

Coastal voyage of Kilikia from the bounds of Pamphylia as far as the Thapsakos river: three days and nights, two.

2. And out of Sinope in the Pontos, through the mainland and Kilikia to Soloi, the road from sea to sea is of days, 5.

103. CYPRUS

103. And by Kilikia is the island of Kypros (*Cyprus*), and in it the following cities. Salamis, Hellenic, having an enclosed winter harbour. Karpaseia; Keryneia; Lepethis Phoinikōn (*of the Phoenicians*); Soloi—this too has a winter harbour; Marion, Hellenic; and Amathous—they are aborigines; all these have deserted harbours. And there are also other cities in the interior (that are) barbarian.

And I return again onto the mainland, from where I turned away.

104–6. SYRIA–PHOENICIA TO EGYPT

104. 1. There is after Kilikia the community of the Syroi (*Syrians*). And in Syria there live, in the seaward part, the Phoinikes (*Phoenicians*), a community, upon a narrow front less than up to 40 stades from the sea, and in some places not even up to 10 stades in width.

2. And past the Thapsakos river is Tripolis Phoinikōn (*of the Phoenicians*). Arados island with a harbour, a royal seat (*basileia*) of Tyros (*Tyre*) with a harbour roughly 8 stades from

the land. And in the peninsula is a second city of Tripolis: this belongs to Arados and Tyros and Sidon; in the same place are three cities, and each has its own circuit of the enclosure wall. And a mountain, Theou Prosopon. Trieres, ⟨a city⟩ with a harbour. Berytos (*Beirut*), a city with a harbour. ⟨The river⟩ *Bostrenos*. Porphyreōn, a city. ⟨Leontōn Polis.⟩ Sidon, a city with an enclosed harbour. Ornithōn Polis. Belonging to the Sidonioi is (the area) from Leontōn Polis as far as Ornithōn Polis.

3. Belonging to the Tyrioi is the city of Sarapta. The city of Tyros, having a harbour within a fort; and this island is a royal seat of the Tyrioi, and is distant 3 stades from the *sea*. Palaityros, a city; and a river flows through the middle. And a city of the Tyrioi, ⟨Ekdippa⟩, with a river. And Ake (*Akko*), a city. Exope, a city of the Ty⟨rioi. Karmelos (*Carmel*)⟩, a mountain sacred to Zeus. Arados, a city of the Sidonioi. ⟨Magdolos, a city⟩ and river of the Tyrioi. Doros (*Dor*), a city of the Sidonioi. ⟨Ioppe (*Jaffa*), a city;⟩ they say it was here that Androm⟨eda⟩ was ⟨ex⟩posed ⟨to the monster. Aska⟩lon, a city of the Tyrioi and a royal seat. Her⟨e is the boundary of Koile⟩ (*Hollow*) Syria.

Coastal voyage of Koile Syria ⟨from the Thapsakos river as far as⟩ Askalon: 2,700 stades.

105. 1. ⟨And after Syria are the Arabes,⟩ a community, horse-riding herders ⟨and having pastures of all kinds of ani⟩mals: sheep and goats . . . . and camels; and thi⟨s⟩ is . . . . is for the most part w⟨aterless⟩ . . . . Aigyptos . . . . in it a gul⟨f⟩ . . . . is out of the E⟨rythraian sea⟩ . . . . . . ⟨ou⟩ter se⟨a⟩ . . . . ⟨s⟩ea . . . . and . . . . k . . . . (*gap of c.35 words*) . . .
⟨The coastal voyage of . . .⟩

2. . . . and of ⟨A⟩rabia itself, from the bounds of Syria as far as the mouth of the ⟨Neilos (*Nile*) i⟩n Pelousion—for this is the boundary of Arabia—1,300 stades.

⟨And they say A⟩rabia belongs to Aigyptos as far as the Neilos next to the Ara⟨bian gulf⟩ . . . . the Aigyptioi; and they bring tribute (to) Aigy⟨pt-⟩ . . . . always to the Arabes.

106. 1. ⟨And after Arabia is⟩ the community of ⟨Aigyptos⟩ (*Egypt*); and the cities in it are ⟨the following: Pelousion, a city

with a harbour⟩ and a royal seat, where the mouth ⟨of the river Neilos, the Pelousiac, lies⟩ first, Arabia's ⟨boundary. Second the Tanitic, and a roy⟩al ⟨city⟩. Third the ⟨Mendesian with Mendes, a city. 4th Phatniti⟩c. Fifth Sebenny⟨tic, with Sebennytos, a city; Boutos, a lake, wh⟩ere there is a city and a ro⟨yal seat. Sixth the Bolbitic, with a roy⟩al ⟨city⟩. Seventh ⟨the Kanopic, with Thonis, a city.

After these places a lake⟩ which has the name ⟨Mareia. And this lake is already i⟩n Libyē . . . . and it . . . . council . . . . e . . . (gap of about 60 words) . . . . ⟨the Canobic . . . the Sebennytic . . .⟩

2. . . . the other the Pelousiac. And again it is split apart: and the Sebennytic (goes) on the one hand into the Mendesian, on the other hand into the sea. And from the Mendesian (the river goes) into the Phatnitic mouth; and from the Pelousian into the Tanitic mouth. And the one from Kanopos (goes) as far as the Sebennytic lake, and the Bolbitine mouth flows out of the lake. And mostly the seaward parts of Aigyptos are lakes and marshes.

3. And Aigyptos is as follows in shape: similar to an axe. For it is by the sea broad, and by the interior narrower, and by Memphis the narrowest of itself; and next, as one goes into the interior from Memphis, wider; and by the uppermost part of itself widest. The part of Aigyptos above Memphis is the most substantial compared to the part beside the sea. And the Kanopic mouth bounds Asia and Libyē.

And the coastal voyage of Aigyptos from the Pelousian mouth is 1,300 stades.

106. 4. Length of Asia

4. And of Asia the voyage round—for it is convex in shape— as one reckons in the same manner in which it has been written about Europe, is of days, 87.

5. And upon the Kanopic mouth there is a deserted island, which has the name Kanopos; and on it there are monuments, the tomb of the ship-captain of Menelaos from Troy, who had the name Kanopos. And both the Aigyptioi and the neighbours to the places say that Pelousios came to Kasion, and Kanopos came to the island where the memorial of the ship-captain is.

107–11. Libyē

107–9. NON-CARTHAGINIAN LIBYĒ

107. 1. Libyē begins from the Kanopic mouth of the Neilos.

A community of the Libyes (*Libyans*), the Adyrmachidai. And out of Thonis the voyage to Pharos, a deserted island—and it has good harbours and no water—is of 150 stades.

And in Pharos are many harbours. And they draw water out of the Mareia lake, for it is drinkable. And the voyage upstream to the lake is short out of Pharos. And there is also Chersonesos with a harbour. And the coastal voyage has 200 stades.

2. And past Chersonesos is the Plinthinos gulf. And the mouth of the Plinthinos gulf to Leuke Akte: a voyage of a day and a night; and that to the inner end of the Plinthinos gulf: twice as much; and it is surrounded by inhabitants in a circle. And from Leuke Akte to Laodamanteios, a harbour: a voyage of half of a day. And from Laodamanteios harbour to Paraitonios, a harbour: a voyage of half of a day.

3. There follows Apis, a city. So as far as here the Aigyptioi rule.

108. 1. And past Apis is a community of the Libyes, the Marmaridai, as far as to Hesperides. And from Apis up to Tyndareioi Skopeloi: a voyage of a day.

And from Tyndareioi Skopeloi to Plynoi, a harbour: a voyage of a day. Out of Plynoi to Petras the Great: a voyage a half of a day. Out of Petras to Menelaos: a voyage of a day. Out of Menelaos to Kyrthaneion: a voyage of a day. Past Kyrthaneion is Antipygos, a harbour: a voyage of half of a day. And past Antipygos is Petras the Small, a harbour: a voyage a half of a day. Past Petras ⟨the⟩ Small is Chersonesos and *Azirides*, a harbour—these places are in the territory of the Kyrenaioi (*Cyrenaeans*)—a voyage of a day.

2. And in the middle of Petras and Chersonesos are the islands of Aëdonia and Plateiai. And there are anchorages under them. From here the silphium begins to grow in fields: and it stretches along from Chersonesos through the interior as far as Hesperides, nearly 1,500 stades beside the land. (Then) Aphrodisias island, an anchorage; Naustathmos, a harbour.

Voyage from Chersonesos: days, one. And from Naustathmos to the harbour of Kyrene: 100 stades. And out of the
harbour to Kyrene: 80 stades.

3. And Kyrene is in the interior. And these are all-weather
harbours. And there are other refuges under islets, and there
are anchorages and many headlands in the territory between.
And out of the harbour of Kyrene as far as the harbour by
Barke, 500 stades. And the city of the Barkaioi is distant from
the sea 100 stades.

And out of the harbour by Barke up to Hesperides, 620
stades.

4. And out of Kyrene there are harbours, and there are the
following *divided localities* as far as Hesperides: Phykous, a gulf;
and inland here is the garden of the Hesperides. And it is a
place 18 fathoms deep, sheer in a circle, nowhere having a
descent; and it is of 2 stades every way, not less, width and
length. This is shaded with trees woven in one another as
densely as possible. The trees are lotus (and) fruit-trees of all
kinds: pomegranate-trees, pear-trees, arbutus fruits, mul-
berries, vines, myrtles, bay-trees, ivy, olive-trees, wild olive-
trees, almond-trees, and nut-trees.

5. Among the localities that have not been mentioned is, by
the garden, Ampelos; Apios—it is distant 30 stades; Chersonesos; very many gardens; Zenertis; Taucheira; *Bakalou* Kome;
Hesperides, a city with a harbour, and a river upon the city,
the *Encheleios*. By these localities past the Chersonesoi of the
Azirides, some are of the Kyrenaioi, others of the Barkaioi as far
as Hesperides.

109. 1. And past Hesperides there is a great gulf, which has the
name Syrtis, and, so to say, as one guesses approximately, of
some 5,000 stades. In width it is, from Hesperides to Neapolis
(*Lepcis Magna*) on the other side, a voyage of days, three, and
nights, three.

2. And there live around it a community of the Libyes, the
Nasamones, as far as the inner end on the left.

And after these there follow a community of the Libyes
beside the Syrtis, as far as the mouth of the Syrtis, (namely)
the Makai.

3. And as one sails into the Syrtis from Hesperides the first (place) is Herakleioi Thines; there follow after these Drepanon, the three islands of Pontiai, then after these the so-called Leukai. And in the most hollow part of the Syrtis, in the inner end, is Philainou Bomoi, a dependent harbour; *the grove of Ammon* ... *of the Syrtis*. From this, living beside the Syrtis, the Makai winter at the sea, shutting away their animals; and in the summer, with the waters receding, they drive away their animals up into the interior with themselves.

4. And after the Syrtis there is a fine locality and a city, which has the name Kinyps; and it is deserted. And from Neapolis into the Syrtis it is distant *80* stades: and under it is the river Kinyps, and an island is below it towards the river.

5. And the depth of the Syrtis inside Hesperides towards Philainou Bomoi, to the inner end of the gulf: voyage of days, 3, and nights, ⟨2⟩. And width from Kinyps river towards the Leukai islands: voyage of days, four, and nights, four.

110–11. CARTHAGINIAN TERRITORY

110. 1. And beside the places outside the Syrtis live the Lotophagoi (*Lotus-eating*) Libyes, a community, as far as the mouth of the other Syrtis. These people use lotus as food and drink. And past Neapolis (*Lepcis Magna*) in the territory of the Karchedonioi (*Carthaginians*) is *Gaphara*, a city. Of this (territory), coastal voyage: days, one, from Neapolis.

2. And past *Gaphara* is Abrotonon, a city with a harbour. Of this, the coastal voyage: days, one.

3. And past Abrotonon is Taricheiai, a city with a harbour. The coastal voyage from Abrotonon: days, one.

4. And by these places there is an island, which has the name Bracheion, after the Lotophagoi (and) by Taricheiai. And this island is of 300 stades, and in width a little less. And it is distant from the mainland about 3 stades. And in the island grows a lotus which they eat, and another out of which they make wine. And the fruit of the lotus is in size as big as an arbutus fruit. And they make much oil out of wild olive-trees. And the island bears much produce, namely wheat and barley. And the island has good earth. Voyage from Taricheiai to the island: days, one.

5. And after the island is *Gichthis*, a city. And from the island to *Gichthis*: voyage of half a day.

6. ⟨. . . Eschides . . .⟩ And from *Eschides* ⟨to Neapolis⟩: voyage of a day.

7. And an island is at hand by it, deserted. And after this is Kerkinitis (*Gharbi*), an island with a city; and by this is Thapsos. Coastal voyage from this to Thapsos: a day and a half.

And from Thapsos ⟨to Leptis the Small is a voyage of . . .; and from Leptis to Adrymes (*Hadrumetum*) . . .

8. And past Leptis⟩ the Small and Adrymes there is a great gulf inside, in which is the Small Syrtis, called Kerkinitis, much more dangerous and hard to sail than the other Syrtis, whose circumference is 2,000 stades.

In this Syrtis stands the so-called island of the Triton ⟨with a lake⟩ and the river Triton, and just here there is a sanctuary of Athena Tritonis. And the lake has a small mouth, and in the mouth an island is at hand; and whenever there is an ebb tide, sometimes the lake does not have a voyage in *for* ⟨ships, as it⟩ *appears*. And this lake is great, having its circumference of about 1,000 stades. 9. And Libyes live around it, the Gyzantes, a community, and a city beyond (the lake) towards the sun's setting; for these *Gyzantes* Libyes are said to be all fair-haired and very beautiful. And this territory is excellent and very productive, and among them there are animals both very large and very numerous; and they themselves are very rich and very beautiful.

10. And after this Syrtis is Neapolis (*Nabeul*). And the coastal voyage from Adrymes up to Neapolis is of a day.

And after Neapolis is Hermaia (*Cap Bon*), a cape with a city. The coastal voyage from Neapolis to Hermaia is of a day and a half.

And from Nea⟨polis⟩ to the isthmus is 180 stades on foot towards the other sea, towards Karchedon (*Carthage*). And it is a headland, through which is (the) isthmus. . . . ⟨river⟩ . . . Coastal voyage from the river, from here to Karchedon: a half of a day.

And the territory of the Karchedonioi is in a gulf.

111. 1. And after the isthmus is Karchedon, a city of the

Phoinikes (*Phoenicians*) with a harbour. Coastal voyage from Hermaia: a half of a day to Karchedon.

2. And islets are at hand upon Hermaia Cape, Pontia island and Kosyros. And the voyage from Hermaia up to Kosyros: a day.

3. Past Hermaia Cape towards the upcoming sun, *a long way* from Hermaia, are three small islands by this place, inhabited by Karchedonioi: Melite (*Malta*), a city with a harbour; Gaulos (*Gozo*), a city; Lampas (*Lampedusa*)—this one has two or three towers. And past Kosyros up to Lilybaion, the promontory of Sikelia (*Sicily*): a voyage of days, one.

4. After Karchedon is Ityke, a city with a harbour. And the coastal voyage from Karchedon to Ityke: 1 day.

5. From Ityke to Hippou Akra: ⟨a voyage of days, one⟩.

Hippou ⟨Akra⟩, a city, and after it there is a lake, and islands in the lake, and around the lake the following cities in the islands: Psegas, a city, and right by it many Naxian islands: Pithekousai with a harbour; opposite it Kalathe island, and a city in the island, Euboia. Thapsa with a city and a harbour. *Igilgilis*, a city with a harbour. Sida, a city. *Iomnion*, a cape; a city and a harbour. Hebdomos, a city with a harbour. Akion island; and a city with a harbour is upon it. Psamathos island; a city with a harbour, and a gulf; and in the gulf is Bartas, an island with a harbour. Chalka, a city in the river. Arylon, a city. Mes, a city with a harbour. Sige, a city in the river; and before the river is the island of Akra. A great city ⟨with⟩ a harbour. Akros, the city and the gulf in it. A deserted island, Drinaupa by name.

6. The Pillar of Herakles in Libyē. Cape Abilyke, ⟨and⟩ a city in a river, and opposite it the Gadeira islands.

From Karchedon in this direction, up to the Pillars of Herakles, with the best sailing the coastal voyage is of days, seven, and nights, seven.

7. These islands are beside Europe; one of these two has a city: and the Pillars of Herakles are by these, the one in Libyē low and the one in Europe high. And these are capes directly facing one another; and these are apart from one another a voyage of a day.

111. 8. Length of Libyē

8. The coastal voyage of Libyē from Aigyptos, (from) the Kanopic mouth as far as the Pillars of Herakles, the reckoning being put in the same terms as has been written in Asia and Europe, as one sails around in a circle along the gulfs: days, *50* and 4.

9. As many townships or trading-towns as have been written in Libyē, from the Syrtis beside Hesperides as far as the Pillars of Herakles in Libyē, are all of the Karchedonioi.

112. Beyond the Pillars of Herakles

112. 1. And after the Pillars of Herakles, as one sails to the outside holding Libyē on the left, there is a great gulf as far as Hermaia Cape. For here, too, is a Hermaia Cape. And by the middle of the gulf lies Pontiōn, a place with a city. And around the city lies a great lake, and in this lake lie many islands. And around the lake grows reed, and galingale and wool-tufted reed and rush. And the Meleagrid birds are here, and nowhere else unless they are exported from here. And this lake has the name Kephisias, and the gulf (has the name) Kotes, and it is in between the Pillars of Herakles and Hermaia Cape.

2. And past Cape Hermaia there extend great reefs, and from Libyē up to Europe, not projecting above the water: and it washes over them in places. And the reef extends up to the other cape of Europe directly facing it: and this cape has the name Hieron Promontory.

3. And past Cape Hermaia is the river Anides: and this discharges into a great lake. And after Anides there is another great river, the Lixos, and a city of the Phoinikes, Lixos; and there is a second city of the Libyes beyond the river, with a harbour.

4. And after Lixos is the Krabis river with a harbour and a city of the Phoinikes, Thymiateria by name. From Thymiateria ⟨is a voyage⟩ to Soloësa Cape, which projects somewhat into the inner-sea. And out of all Libyē this territory is the most renowned and sacred. And upon the promontory of the cape there is a magnificent altar of Poseidon. And on the altar are carved human statues, lions, and dolphins; and they say Daidalos made them.

5. And past Soloëis Cape there is a river, which has the name Xion. Around this river live the Sacred Aithiopes (*Ethiopians*). And by these places there is an island, which has the name Kerne.

And the coastal voyage from the Pillars of Herakles up to Hermaia Cape: days, two. And from Cape Hermaia to Cape Soloëis, coastal voyage: days, three. And from Soloëis to Kerne, coastal voyage: days, seven.

And the total of this coastal voyage is, from the Pillars of Herakles to Kerne island, days, twelve.

6. And the places beyond Kerne island are sailable no further because of the shallowness of the sea and (because of) mud and seaweed. And the seaweed is the breadth of a hand and is sharp above, so that it stabs.

7. And the traders are Phoinikes; but whenever they arrive at the island of Kerne, they anchor the round-boats, having made tents on Kerne for themselves; but taking out the cargo they themselves transport it in small boats to the mainland. 8. And there are Aithiopes towards the mainland; and it is these Aithiopes towards whom they set out (their wares). And they sell (them) for skins of deer and lions and leopards, and skins and teeth of elephants and (skins) of domestic animals. 9. The Aithiopes use for adornment ... pricked with decoration, and for drinking-vessels bowls of ivory; and their women use for adornment bracelets of ivory; and they also use ivory decoration on their horses. And these Aithiopes are the largest of all the humans of whom we know, larger than four cubits, and some of them are even five cubits, and they are beard-wearing and long-haired; and these people are the most beautiful of all humans, and there rules over them whoever is tallest. They are also horsemen and javelin-men and archers, and use their weapons fire-hardened. 10. And the Phoinikes (that are) traders import to them perfumed oil, Aigyptian stone, *other mined* (ones), Attic tile and pitchers: for the artefacts are on sale at the festival of the Choës. 11. And these Aithiopes are meat-eating milk-drinkers, and make much wine from vines: and this the Phoinikes themselves also bring. And they also have a great city, towards which the Phoinikes sail in, the traders.

12. And some say that these Aithiopes stretch along inhabiting continuously from here to Aigyptos (*Egypt*), and that this sea is continuous, and that Libyē is a headland.

113–14. Endmatter

113. 1. Partition through the sea ⟨from⟩ Europe to Asia, fairly direct in a straight fashion. And the partition begins from Euripos by Chalkis, and up to Geraistos it is 850 stades.

From Geraistos up to the Paionion in Andros, 80 stades.

Of Andros itself up to the Aulon, 280 stades.

Voyage across the Aulon to Tenos, 12 stades.

And of Tenos itself up to the promontory by Rhenaia, 150 stades.

And of the voyage across to Rhenaia, 40 stades.

And of Rhenaia itself and the voyage across to Mykonos, 40 stades.

And from Mykonos the voyage across up to the Melantioi Skopeloi, a little less than a voyage before the midday meal, of 40 stades.

And from the Melantioi Rocks, a voyage to Ikaros before the midday meal.

And of Ikaros itself, 300 stades lengthwise.

And from Ikaros, a voyage to Samos before the midday meal.

And of Samos itself, 200 stades.

Out of Samos to Mykale, 7 stades of the voyage across.

The whole, if they sail out of Samos with the finest sailing, 2,370 stades, without reckoning in addition the voyage ⟨out of Mykale to Samos⟩.

2. Another partition, straight in a direct fashion.

⟨From Malea⟩ as far as Kythera, ⟨1⟩30 stades.

And the length of Kythera itself, 100 stades.

To Aigilia, a voyage before the midday meal.

⟨Length of Aigilia itself, 50 stades.

From Aigilia to Krete, a voyage before the midday meal.⟩

Length of Krete itself, 2,500 stades.

From Krete to Karpathos, †100 stades.

Length of Karpathos itself, 100 stades.

To Rhodos from Karpathos, a voyage of 100 stades.

Length of Rhodos itself, 600 stades.

From Rhodos to Asia, 100 stades.

The partition of the voyage across is 4,270 stades.

114. SIZES OF ISLANDS. Greatest Sardo, second Sikelia, third Krete, fourth Kypros, fifth Euboia, sixth Kyrnos, seventh Lesbos, eighth Rhodos, ninth Chios, tenth Samos, eleventh Korkyra, twelfth †Kasos, thirteenth Kephallenia, fourteenth Naxos, fifteenth Kos, sixteenth Zakynthos, seventeenth Lemnos, eighteenth Aigina, nineteenth Imbros, twentieth Thasos.

COMMENTARY

1–69. Europe

PS divides his text between the three continents—Europe (1–69), Asia (70–106), and Libyē (107–11)—marking the end of each with a summative sailing distance (assuming these passages are original; see Introduction, III). Europe he divides into smaller geographical blocs, some defined only implicitly. Those explicitly defined are (*a*) from the Pillars of Herakles to Antion (*Antibes*), at 4; (*b*) the Adriatic (15–27); (*c*) 'continuous Hellas' (33–65), with the beginning and end of the Peloponnese defined inside it (40–55) and, within that, a detour to Crete (47) and the southern Cyclades (48). (In Crete we briefly abandon coastwise narration.) Intersecting with Thrake (67) is the beginning, defined only in passing (67. 8–9), of the Black Sea ('Euxeinos Pontos' at 67. 1, elsewhere 'Pontos'), which runs to 92. 2; by this point we are well into Asia. PS thus allows topography to modify his division of the world into *ethnos* territories. This reflects a geographer's concerns rather than a strictly ethnic, historical, or coastal arrangement, but he is not wholly systematic: Epeiros is unnamed and its constituent peoples in limbo between the Adriatic and 'continuous Hellas'.

The density of coverage increases from the Pillars to Greece.

Barr. 26–8

1–4. Pillars of Herakles to Antion

In Spain and France, treated in a few lines, there were not many Greek settlements. Greek traders may, perhaps, have been excluded from the western Mediterranean by the Carthaginians, perhaps after the evacuation of Alalia (see n. on 6 Kyrnos), just as the Romans were by treaty in 509 and/or 348 (Polyb. 3. 22 and 24; Livy 7. 27. 2; Walbank 1957, 338–47; Roller 2006, 14, cf. 60–9 *passim*); but it seems unlikely, given that there were Greek cities further W than Italy and that there is no evidence for a ban.

Even the hypothetical exclusion of Greeks can hardly explain the slightness of the information in this passage as compared with others. The people of Massalia could surely have told PS more than he tells us. Writing before Pytheas's voyage (Introduction, VII), he may have used a Massaliote source that withheld, or a non-Massaliote source that lacked, information about the West. Beaumont 1939, 80, even suspects a Punic source; this could, of course, be a Phoenician or Carthaginian informant at Athens.

1. Pillars of Herakles in Europe: PS uses at least two sources for the area of the straits. (*a*) At 1, 69, and 111. 9 he refers to 'pillars' in both Europe and Libyē, but at 111. 6–7 there is only one in each continent. (Elsewhere when he uses 'pillars', those in each continent could be singular or plural.) (*b*) At 1 and 111. 7 the pillars are a day apart; but at 4, 69, 111. 6 and 8–9, and 112. 5 (twice) he reckons distances to or from the pillars, which should therefore be at a single location. Furthermore, 111. 7 clearly compares the peaks framing the narrows (see n. on 111. 6 Abilyke). (*c*) 111. 7 unnecessarily repeats information about the Gadeira Is. from 2.

This confusion may relate to the report in Strabo (3. 5. 5) that Dikaiarchos (connected somehow to our author: see Introduction, VII), Eratosthenes, Polybios, and 'most of the Hellenes' put the Pillars around the narrows whereas the Carthaginians and Libyans locate them at Gades. It is possible that the Pillars, originally envisaged as the western supports of the world, perhaps around Gadeira, were later rationalized as the peaks N and S of the narrows (see Antonelli 1995, more precise than Cataudella 1989–90). The stated distance of a day between the Pillars may really be that from Gadeira to the narrows (see n. on 'a day', below)

Two other points are less of a problem. (*d*) At §2 Gadeira is a day from the Pillars; yet at 111. 6 it is 'opposite' (*antion*) C. Abilyke and at 111. 7 'by' or 'opposite' (*kata*) the Pillars; this is not necessarily contradictory, since *antion* and *kata* do not entail proximity. Furthermore, it is in the last passage that we find the comparison between the peaks at the straits, not around *Cádiz*. (*e*) Two spellings are used, *Herakleiai stelai* (1) and *Herakleioi stelai* (111. 6–7, 112. 1; other instances are genitive plural, compatible with either form); this could be due either to MS error, as the three-termination form is certain only at §1, or to compilation from different sources.

Great Aithiopes: this is PS's first mention of the Aithiopes, here located in NW Africa. See n. on 112. 5 'sacred Aithiopes'.   **a day:** using the formula at 69, this should be *c*.500 stades (*stadia*) or *c*.90 km. From *Gibraltar* to *Ceuta* is only 23 km, while the shortest crossing, further W, is only 14 km. The duration may refer to the crossing from Gadeira to a city on the African side (Allain 133–4); more likely it was originally the distance from the narrows to Gadeira (as at 2). See also n. on 'Pillars', above.   **trading-towns of the Karchedonioi:** none of which PS names. There are early Phoenician sites both W and E of the Straits; those in Portugal include *Cerro* *da Rocha Branca* (in the *Algarve*), Abul (on the R. *Sado*), *Quinta do Almaraz* (on R. *Tagus*), and *Santa Olaia* (on R. *Mondego*; B. Lowe, pers. comm.). PS, however, probably believes he is referring to places E of Gadeira, since he said he would begin from the Pillars (cf. n. on 'Pillars', above). Apart from the legendary voyage to Tartessos by Kolaios of Samos in C7m (Hdt. 4. 152), there is Attic pottery as far N as *Galicia* from C5l (B. Lowe, pers. comm.), which may relate to how PS got information. The omission of Tartessos, the lower *Guadalquivir* valley NW of *Cádiz*, is remarkable given its reputation in Greek sources; it is perhaps due to PS's focus on moving E from Gadeira. **mud and flood-tides and shoals:** Peretti 1979, 164, takes 'flood-tides' to refer to the higher Atlantic tides, which could be observed at Gades. Such vagueness, however, may reflect travellers' excuses for not having gone further, or traders' attempts at mystification intended to boost their authority and discourage others (cf. 112. 1 and 6).

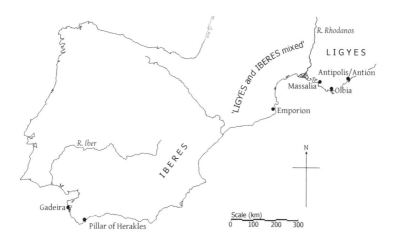

Map 1. Iberian peninsula and France.

2. Of the few known Greek settlements in Spain and France, PS mentions only Emporion and notably omits Rhode (*Inv.* **4**).   **Iberes:** PS puts the Iberes first in Europe, but Hekat. FF 38–52 distinguishes from them the Mastianoi or Mastienoi 'by the Pillars of Herakles', while Polyb. 3. 37 places 'Iberia' within the Pillars. PS may be combining sources none of which covered the Atlantic; or his choice of Pillars as starting-point may have a literary motive.   **Iber:** probably the *Tinto* of SW Spain (one anc. name of which was Iberus), not the *Ebro* of NE Spain; so there is no reason to move the next two sentences to §1 (as Müller 15–16 does).   **Gadeira:** *Cádiz* (Lat. Gades), the renowned Phoenician trading city of Gadir. For PS, it is a *polis* but not a Greek one.   **one of these two:** Erytheia, the smaller and more southerly island (*Barr.* 26 D5 Aphrodisias/Erythea, Lat. Iunonis Insula).   **a day's voyage:** see n. on 1 'a day'. Gadeira is *c*.100 km from *Gibraltar*.

Barr. 25

Emporion: or Emporiae (*Inv.* 2), founded trad. *c*.600 from Massalia or Phokaia. This is its first mention in ancient sources. On Emporion as an *emporion* (place for trade), see M. H. Hansen 2006a, 10–11 (= M. H. Hansen 1997a, 88 n. 37). The next 'Hellenic city' is Massalia (4). **these people:** the awkward switch from singular to plural (Klausen 277) is characteristic of PS (cf. 24. 1, 31. 1) and may reflect the compilation process.   **seven days and seven nights:** implying *c*.7,000 st. (1,300 km). Polyb. 3. 39 gives figures totalling 7,200 st. (*c*.1,330 km). The coasting distance is *c*.1,240 km, so the stated duration is reasonable.

3. there follow: PS uses this verb six times at 3–12 and only twice elsewhere; it may indicate a distinct source on western Europe. **the Ligyes and Iberes mixed:** the Cl Greeks seem to have located the Ligurians on both sides of the *Rhône*. Only later were they viewed as extending into Italy (Strabo 5. 1. 1, 3, and 4). However, there may be no exact match between the Ligyes and the Latin Ligures, and both may be more construct than reality (Arnaud 2001). Views of the Iberes, too, changed. Strabo 3. 4. 19 says earlier writers extended Iberia eastwards to the *Rhône* whereas his contemporaries limited it to the area beyond (i.e. S of) the Pyrenees.   **Rhodanos:** E limit of the Iberes, but the Ligyes extend W of it; not a frontier as such. **Coastal voyage:** for the *paraplous* cf. Polyb. 3. 39. 7 (1,600 st.; but the text is problematic, see Walbank 1957–79, i. 371–2).

Barr. 15

4. Ligyes: see 3 n.   **Antion:** the third settlement that PS names. It appears three or four times in this section, and in §5 as the point after which Tyrrhenia begins. It is probably a by-form of Antipolis (*Antibes; Barr.* 16 D2), or a false form reflecting the habit of abbreviating '*polis*' in the MS. (It is probably not Antion in NW Italy, *Anzo di Framura, Barr.* 39 F5, where there seems to be no evidence for Greek settlement. At Pliny 3. 4/35 it is Athenopolis.) If so, this is the earliest attestation of *Antibes*, a colony of Massalia. The Greeks' hazy notions of the extent of the Ligyes may explain why the way is open for widely separated locations to be proposed for Antion.   **Hellenic**

city: the second occurrence of this term (next in 10).   **Massalia:** *Marseille* (*Inv.* 3).   **with a harbour:** the first occurrence of this or a similar phrase.   **⟨and Olbia and Antion with a harbour⟩:** Olbia was a C4s foundation from Massalia. I do not add Tauroëis (as some do), as it may not have been founded until C3l (see *Inv.* 3).   **days, two, and nights, two:** 'days, 4, and nights, four', MS, implying 4,000 st. (740 km). If Antion is *Antibes* (above) this is too large by a factor of 3; the error may be due to corruption of δύο (two) into δ′ (4) (Müller). **from the Pillars:** PS sums up a long section of coast, treating Antion as the end of one geographical unit and the start of another. His next summing-up is at the end of Illyria, also the end of the Adriatic (27. 2).   **harbours:** in fact the Spanish coast has few good harbours, while the shallow sea off the *Rhône* delta was tricky to navigate (Cary 250).

5–14. ANTION TO IAPYGIA

PS gives no name to the Italian peninsula (on the disputed extent of 'Italia', see Fischer-Hansen *et al.* 2004a, 249–50). For the mainland as far as the 'heel' of Italy he offers few details but mentions most of the known Greek *poleis* (19 out of 23 in *Inv.*); in Sicily the reverse. At several points he is out of date (see nn. below). His sources may include writers from the numerous Greek colonies, though the philosophical circles with which he is associated (Introduction, VII) seem to have found information on Italy hard to come by (Fraser 1994, 182–7).

Barr. 41

5. Tyrrhenoi: Etruria is defined by Strabo 5. 2. 1 as extending to the R. Tiber, upon which Rome lies. PS names none of their settlements (Pisē occurs at 19, but in a probable later note or 'gloss'), perhaps because their large towns were inland or for the same reason that he omits Carthaginian towns in Sicily (13).   **as far as Rome:** in Greek *Rhōmē*. Mentioned in advance as the endpoint of Tyrrhenia, but not under Latium at 8, where we would expect it. PS does not attach it to either region, perhaps regarding it as liminal (cf. Cary 130). Despite being invisible from the sea, and thus not a navigational landmark, it is a significant reference point for PS because of its growing power. According to later belief the Etruscans ruled Rome until 509, after which the independent city encroached on them in turn, capturing e.g. Veii (*c*.16 km from Rome) in 396. PS is capable of treating major places lightly (Fabricius 1846, 7), and Greek contact was limited until C4l; but Rome's territory was still relatively small in C4m (Klausen 253–4) even though in 351 it conquered Tarquinii (*c*.90 km away). The minimal space given to it is thus not a sign that our text is archaic, though PS could be using slightly out-of-date material as elsewhere in Italy. **days, four, and nights, four:** implying *c.*4,000 st. (740 km). Similarly, Pliny 3. 5. 5/49 and 51 gives distances totalling 495 Roman miles (3,960 st.) from the R. Macra, just E of *Antibes,* to the Tiber.

Map 2. Italy.

Barr. 48

6. Kyrnos: despite its limited renown, the island was valuable to outsiders, perhaps because of timber (Cary 148–9), and had harbours (Diod. 5. 13. 3). Yet Greek literary knowledge was limited and PS gives no detail, even though he may be using Carthaginian or Phoenician sources (Introduction, V). This may be because, once the Phokaian colony of Alalia was abandoned after a costly naval victory over the Carthaginians (Hdt. 1. 166), there were probably no Greek *poleis.* **a day and a half:** implying *c.*750 st. (140 km); but Diod. 5. 13. 1 and 3 puts 'Aithaleia' *c.*100 st. (19 km) from the coast and Kyrnos only 300 st. (56 km) from it. Clearly PS is not referring to the shortest crossing. **Aithalia:** *Elba* (Lat. Ilva). Much closer to Italy than to Corsica; but 'in the middle' need not mean 'halfway'. It has copper ores (Cary 125). **deserted islands:** probably some or all of *Gorgona, Capraia, Pianosa,* and *Montecristo. Barr.* 41 D5 Igilium (*Giglio*) was probably inhabited, at least from Hl times.

7. Sardo: outside interest may have been prompted by mineral resources, but it lay off the main routes (Cary 149–50). PS gives no details, presumably the reasons are the same as for Kyrnos. **third part of a day:** implying *c.*167 st. (31 km). Strabo's 60 st. (5. 2. 6) and Pliny's 8 miles (i.e. 64 st.; 3. 6/83) are accurate if they refer to the shortest voyage; PS may mean a journey between two settlements near the strait (we cannot know which ones). **deserted island:** probably the Cuniculariae Is. on the Sardinian side of the strait, or smaller islets on the Corsican side. **a day and a night:** implying *c.*750 st.; actually *c.*180 km (880 st.). Strabo 5. 2. 8 (300 miles) and Pliny 3. 7/84 (200 miles) greatly over-estimate it. One is never out of sight of land (Cary 29), so this will have been a regular crossing; cf. map at Horden and Purcell 2000, 127 (adapted, Arnaud 2005, 30–1), showing how rarely in the western Mediterranean one is out of sight of land. **days, two, and a night:** implies *c.*1,500 st. (*c.*280 km); accurate. **to Libyē . . . to Sikelia:** as at a few other points, PS adds information about 'branch routes' off his main itinerary (Introduction, VIII). This was not a purely hypothetical route, at least in the Roman period: ships' anchors found off Tunisia are evidence for direct voyages (Weitemeyer and Döhler 2009). **I return . . . turned away:** PS's first use of this expression. See Introduction, VIII.

Barr. 42–3

8. Latinoi: Roman control of Latin and Volscian territory was not complete until *c.*300 (*OCD³* on Latium); hence for PS the two are distinct regions. PS again has little to say about a region without prominent Greek cities. It lacked tempting minerals, though Theophrastos notes timber (*HP* 5. 8. 3; Cary 128–9). PS does not use *ethnos* to define peoples between the Latinoi and the Leukanoi (12), either through inadvertent variation or because of a change of source. **Kirkaion:** the 'shrine of Kirke', Odysseus's Circe, at one of the most prominent capes on this coast (*Barr.* 44 D3; *Monte Circeo*). The Kirkaion and Elpenor (next n.) are mentioned by Theophrastos (*HP* 5. 8. 3). **Elpenor:** at Hom. *Od.* 11. 51–83, Odysseus tells the ghost of Elpenor (his companion who got drunk, fell off the roof of Kirke's house, and was killed) that he will build him a shrine on the seashore, a promise he keeps (12. 8–15). See previous n. **a day and a**

night: implying *c.*1,000 st. (200 km), beginning where *Lazio* begins today, N of Rome. This point is much further N than is implied at 5; if Tyrrhenia does extend to Rome, PS's figure here is double what it should be. Strabo (5. 3. 5) gives 260 st. for Antion to Ostia; Pliny (3. 5/56) 50 miles for Latium. The error may derive from using sources of different dates.

9. Olsoi: 'Ouolskoi', Strabo 5. 3. 2, etc. Their territory was part of 'added Latium' (Latium Adiectum), between Old Latium (Latium Vetus) and Campania. Around 500 it expanded from the Apennines to the sea (Cary 130; *OCD*[3] on Volsci); PS's short coast may reflect a stage in Roman expansion between C5l and the 'Latin war' of 341–338. His information is out of date, but not by much.

10. Kampanoi: the earliest use of the name (Fischer-Hansen *et al.* 2004a, 251). They were a formal *ethnos* from 438 (Diod. 12. 31. 1; Marcotte 1986, 172; Cornell 1995, 305). This small region was fertile, with good harbours and potting clay (Cary 133–4), though Pithekoussa (below) was probably sited for access to Etruscan metals (Cary 135).   **Hellenic cities:** PS's third use of this term (last used of Massalia, 4). He ignores probable Samnite influence in Campania (see 11, 15 nn.).   **Kyme:** Cumae; *Inv.* **57.** The Campanians captured it in 423 (Livy 4. 44) or *c.*421 (Diod. 12. 76. 5), so PS's information is later. **Neapolis:** *Inv.* **63;** *Napoli, Naples*). Founded *c.*470 from Kyme (Ps.-Skymnos 242–3; cf. Strabo 5. 4. 7).   **Pithekoussa:** a *polis* (*Inv.* **65**) on *Ischia* I. in the bay of Naples, said to have been founded from Eretria and Chalkis (Strabo 5. 4. 9), perhaps in C8. Archaeology suggests a decline after *c.*700 (Flensted-Jensen and Hansen 2007, 215). It may have become a dependent *polis* of Syracuse, or PS may be using old information.

11. Saunitai: historians used to view the Samnites as a league of upland tribes, some of whom formed a federal state that expanded its territory in C4 until it extended from coast to coast. Recent work (Dench 1995, 175–217; Richardson 2009) points to a less formal association, less systematic conquest (though there were incursions in both directions), and a more fluid identity. Even the name may be one that others gave them; its first attestation in the region is in a local form in C2 (Vetter 1953, 149). PS places them between Campania and Lucania, where one would expect to find the Alfaterni; and appears to ignore their presence in Campania, which the Romans captured in the first Samnite war (343–341). See also introduction to 15. (I thank Amy Richardson for discussion of these and other points.)   **and the … voyage:** 'and' is *kai*, not the normal *de*. The only other *kai* introducing a *paraplous* is at 99. 3. There seems no particular reason for it, other than variation for variation's sake.

12. Leukanoi: more fertile than Samnium (Cary 139), Lucania attracted Greeks at different periods. The territory of the Bruttii (anc. Bruttium, the 'toe' of Italy; mod. *Calabria*, a name that has migrated from the 'heel', see 14) is passed over in silence, even though in 356 they rebelled against Lucanian rule and formed themselves into a (probably federal) community (Diod. 16. 15. 2; Marcotte 1986, 172–3; *OCD*³ on Bruttii). PS's information is out of date (Müller 19). **as far as Thouria:** an advance mention; see 13. 5 n. **days, 6, and nights, 6:** implying *c.*6,000 stades (*c.*1,110 km), which is much too long and equals the length of Iapygia (14), itself too great (Müller 19, emending to 3 and 3); probably a copyist's error. **Poseidonia:** *Inv.* 66. Lucanian from a date between 438 and 424 (Strabo 6. 1. 3; Müller 19). **Elea ... ⟨Laos⟩:** *Inv.* **54, 58. Pandosia:** *Inv.* **64.** Unlocated (Edlund-Berry and Small 2000, 702). An Achaian foundation (Ps.-Skymnos 326–9) of uncertain date. **Klampeteia:** *Barr.* 46 D3 Clampetia; 'Plateëis', MS. Fischer-Hansen *et al.* 2004a, 257, make Plateëis a non-*polis*; but Clampet(e)ia or Lampeteia (Polyb. 13. 10. 2) will be the correct name. **Terina ... Hipponion:** *Inv.* **73, 53. Mesma:** *Inv.* **60,** also Medma; C4 coins give the name as Mesma (Fischer-Hansen *et al.* 2004a, 278). **Rhegion:** *Inv.* **68** (*Reggio di Calabria*).

13. 1. Sikelia: PS keeps the coast on his r. hand for the first and only time, apart from the brief tours of two multi-*polis* islands (58. 1 Keos; 99. 3 Rhodos). This clockwise *periplous* requires him to cross his own route at 13. 5. It would have been more natural to begin with the N coast, fronting the waters he has just described, whereas the E coast looks into the almost separate sea that is the eastern Mediterranean (on this division see Cary 146; Braudel 1972, i. 116, 114 fig. 10). The change of orientation may not be mere literary *variatio*: it hints at the use of a specialized source on Sicily, an impression reinforced by the use of measurements in stades. (Peretti 1979, 170–9, discusses §13.) Political coverage is incomplete: PS lists only 15 out of 47 Greek *poleis* in *Inv.*, omitting both inland and coastal places. The inclusion of the ex-*poleis* of Himera and Naxos suggests the use of pre-C4 material, as does the division into barbarian peoples: in C4 it would have made more sense to divide the island between Greek tyrants and the Carthaginians (Marcotte 1986, 173). **Europe:** PS does not name the mainland of Italy, or even Leukania, but emphasizes Europe as the entity to which all these *ethnē* belong. Cf. 47. 1. **12 stades:** on the *stadion* measure, see Introduction, IV. PS's figure (*c.*2.2 km) is reasonably accurate for the narrowest crossing (3.0 km), which is also 12 st. at Polyb. 1. 42. 5 and Pliny 3. 5/73. See n. on 'from Rhegion', below. PS's first distance in stades is thus a local one; there is another at 13. 3, a long sea-distance at 13. 4, then no more in stades until 17 and 21. The omission of the difficult currents of the strait of Messina (mythologized as the whirlpool of Charybdis) confirms that the periplous is not meant as an aid to navigation. **Pelorias:** Lat. Pelorus/Regium.   **from Rhegion:** unless we radically alter the text or change '12', we must accept that PS mistakenly believes the shortest crossing is from Rhegion, further S, where the strait is 10 km wide.

13. 2. barbarian: PS uses this term only here (twice) and at 22. 2 (twice), 81, and 103. His list of five non-Greek peoples mirrors that of Thucydides (though see next n.). It was already out of date in C5 (OCD³ on Sicels; Sicily).   **Elymoi:** a non-Greek people of Eryx and Egesta, rarely recorded and sometimes regarded as descendants of the Trojans (Thuc. 6. 2); PS, however, mentions them as separate groups.   **Sikanoi, Sikeloi:** Thuc. 6. 2 regards the Sicanians as Iberians living in western Sicily, and the Sicels as migrants from mainland Italy.   **Phoinikes:** Thuc. 6. 2 sees the Phoenicians as once widespread but now confined to the W. PS does not name their cities (Motya, Panormos, Soloëis). See also n. on 104. 1 Phoinikes. This antiquated term may have nationalistic overtones, reflecting Timoleon of Corinth's success in deposing Sicilian tyrants (c.344–c.337) and restricting the Carthaginians to the W (Marcotte 1986, 176); but, at least when listing ethnic groups, PS may simply be drawing on out-of-date information.   **Troës:** see n. on Elymoi, above.

13. 3. Messene: Inv. 51 (Messina). Zankle was renamed Messana in 486, and was under Syracusan control by C4m (OCD³ on Messana).   **Tauromenion:** Inv. 48 (Taormina), founded c.390 (Diod. 14. 59. 2; Flensted-Jensen and Hansen 1996) though there may have been earlier Greek settlement (Fischer-Hansen et al. 2004b, 231). See next n.   **Naxos:** Inv. 41; only c.2 km S of Tauromenion. Reputedly the oldest Greek colony in Sicily, founded from Euboian Chalkis in trad. 735/4 (Thuc. 6. 3. 1). It was reportedly destroyed in 403 by Dionysios I of Syracuse, but there is C4–C3 occupation (Fischer-Hansen et al. 2004b, 219). The mention of Naxos and Tauromenion as if both are extant—whereas the latter effectively replaced the former—has been seen (by Peretti and others) as evidence of an early 'core' text (like the inclusion of Himera, below). But if the text was updated to keep it useful, why were obsolete names not removed? Since it is, rather, a C4m compilation (Introduction, III), it may be that the author used old sources and did not realize Naxos was no longer a polis. Alternatively, it was still a dependent polis of Tauromenion; or we have here a historical note about a once important place (M. H. Hansen, pers. comm.). **Katane:** *Inv.* 30 (*Catania*). **Leontinoi:** *Inv.* 33 (*Lentini*), 'the only primary colony of the Greek West situated inland'. **Terias:** *Barr.* 47 G4. **Symaithos:** but between Katane and Leontinoi, Thuc. 6. 65 (and *Barr.*). **Megaris:** *Inv.* 36 Megara Hyblaia. Megaris may have been its name when it was repopulated in the late 340s, in the time of Timoleon (Marcotte 1986, 174). **Xiphoneios:** cf. *Barr.* 47 G4 C. Xiphonias (*Porto Megarese*). **Syrakousai ... two harbours:** *Inv.* **47,** with two excellent natural harbours (*OCD*³ on Syracuse). **Heloron:** *Inv.* 18; fortified under Timoleon (Talbert 1974, 152; Marcotte 1986, 174). **Pachynos:** the SE cape of Sicily. **Kamarina:** *Inv.* **28;** see n. on Selinous, below. **Gela:** *Inv.* **17.** See n. on Selinous, below. **Akragas:** *Inv.* 9 (Lat. Agrigentum). See next n. **Selinous:** *Inv.* **44.** The preceding four *poleis* were destroyed by the Carthaginians in C5l; the first three revived after 339/8 (Marcotte 1986, 175), while Selinous kept going but veered between Syracusan and Carthaginian control (Fischer-Hansen *et al.* 2004b, 221–2), being Carthaginian in the 330s. PS is more likely to be using an old source than information updated as recently as 339/8. **Lilybaion:** the W cape of Sicily. Also a Carthaginian town; but PS omits Carthaginian towns in western Sicily, displaying a bias seen elsewhere in his western European *periplous* (cf. n. on 5 Tyrrhenoi). **Himera:** *Inv.* **24.** One of the few Greek *poleis* on the N coast, partly an area of Carthaginian settlement. PS mentions Mylai (below) but omits nearby Tyndaris (founded 396). The mention of Himera raises a similar issue to Naxos (above), though not so critically. It was reportedly destroyed by the Carthaginians in 409/8 (Diod. 13. 62. 4, 13. 114. 1), Thermai Himeraiai (11 km to the W) being founded in 408/7 to replace it. In 313 Himera became Carthaginian 'just as (it) had formerly been' (Diod. 19. 71. 7); when it had ceased to be so is unclear—not necessarily by Timoleon's treaty of 339/8 (Talbert 1974, 83–5). Even if it was again a *polis* by 339/8, we may more easily suppose PS to be using old information than to be perfectly up to date.

13. 4. triangular: the use of geometrical figures to characterize land masses does not entail that the author was using maps (Introduction, V). The same comparison of Sicily is made indirectly by Timaios F 164 (Diod. 5. 21. 3); Timosthenes (C3 geographer, cited by Agathemeros 20); Polyb. 1. 42. 3; Poseidonios (cited by Strabo 6. 2. 1; cf. 2. 1. 30; 6. 1. 5); and later authors. Cf. Dueck 2005, 24–38. **each limb ... 1,500 stades:** the numeral is corrupt in the MS, but plausibly restored. A total circuit of 4,500 st. is close to the 'nearly 8 days' of Thuc. 6. 1. But Sicily is not equilateral (Peretti 1979, 174–5); the E coast is *c.*1,000 rather than *c.*1,500 st. **Lipara island:** *Lipari*; also a *polis*, *Inv.* **34.**

Depending on how we punctuate this passage, it could mean 'Lipara, an island and Hellenic *polis*; (then) Mylai'; or 'Lipara island; and a Hellenic *polis*, Mylai'. The latter seems more in PS's style (cf. 13. 3 on Himera).   **Mylai:** *Inv.* **38.** It seems to have varied between *polis* and non-*polis* status (Flensted-Jensen and Hansen 2007, 215–16). At Thuc. 3. 90 it is a possession or dependency of Messana.

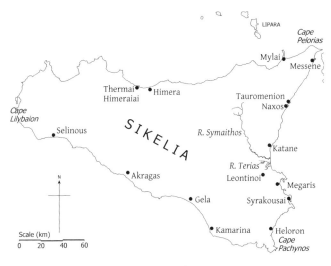

Map 3. Sicily.

13. 5. After his right-handed (clockwise) circuit of Sicily, PS resumes his left-handed (anti-clockwise) *periplous* of the Italian peninsula. **Lokroi:** *Inv.* **59** Lokroi Epizephyrioi. After 356 it belonged, with Rhegion and Kroton, to Bruttium (see 12 n.).   **Kaulonia ... Kroton:** *Inv.* **55, 56;** see previous n.   **Lakinion:** an important pan-Italian sanctuary of Hera Lakinia by C5l (see under *Inv.* **56**). For Polyb. 34. 10. 10 it is a major landmark.   **Kalypso's Island:** not 'Kalypso Island'. It is unlocated (Edlund-Berry and Small 2000, 704). PS and Pliny give independent, possibly early, traditions about heroic voyages reflecting a pre-colonial network of Greek cult sites; the mention of Odysseus is the only Homeric reference in PS's account of Magna Graecia (Greek southern Italy) (Vandermersch 1994, 244–5, 246–7, *contra* Peretti).   **river Krathis:** *Barr.* 46 D2 (*Crati*). Cf. n. on 112. 4 Krabis. Ps.-Arist. *Mir. ausc.* 169. 846b33–4 mentions the rivers Sybaris and Krathis near 'Thourion' (Thouria, below). Paus. 8. 15. 9 says it was named after the Arkadian Krathis.   **Sybaris:** *Inv.* **70;** a byword for prosperity followed by calamity. It used to be claimed that (as the

sources tell us) it was destroyed by Kroton *c.*510 and had no successor until Thourioi was founded in the 440s ('Thouria' below), so
that PS is either in error or using old information. But Sybaris survives until C5m as a dependent *polis* of Kroton (Fischer-Hansen *et al.*
2004a, 297–8). Those evacuated when Thourioi was set up founded a
new Sybaris (not yet located; known to archaeology as 'Sybaris V'; cf.
*OCD*³). This was destroyed by the Bruttii after 356 (Diod. 12. 22. 1; cf.
n. on 12 Leukanoi, above). PS may thus be *c.*20 years out of date (he
also omits the Bruttii at 12) but his probable associate Theophrastos
makes the same mistake of mentioning Sybaris in the present tense
at *HP* 1. 9. 5 (cf. Fraser 1994, 182).   **Thouria:** *Inv.* **74** Thourioi,
founded by an Athenian-led multi-state expedition in 444/3 (Diod.
12. 10. 4, etc.).   **Hellenes:** in PS only twice here and at 14, 47, 65,
and 68. See Introduction, V.

14. Iapyges: Iapygia (Hdt. 3. 138, 4. 99, 7. 170), Lat. Calabria, the
Sallentine peninsula or 'heel' of Italy; now southern *Puglia.* (Anc.
Calabria has migrated to the 'toe', while anc. Apulia is now northern
Puglia.) PS's Iapygia includes the gulf of Taras. On its varying extent
in the sources, see Wilkes and Fischer-Hansen 2004, 322.   **Hyrion:**
an advance mention (cf. at 15). Cf. *Barr.* 45 C1 Urias Sinus (*Lago di
Varano*), a bay on the N side of the *Gargano* peninsula.   **Adrias gulf:**
see introduction to (*c*) below.   **Herakleion:** *Barr.* 45 E4 Heraclea
(*Policoro*); *Inv.* **52.** Founded from Taras in 433/2 (Diod. 12. 36. 4, etc.),
either 5 km N of *Inv.* **69** Siris (*Barr.*) or at Siris itself. See also n. on
Taras, below.   **Metapontion:** *Inv.* **61.**   **Taras:** *Inv.* **71** (*Taranto*; Lat.
Tarentum).   **Hydrous:** *Otranto* (Lat. Hydruntum), a scarcely hellen-
ized non-*polis* founded by Cretans (Wilkes and Fischer-Hansen 2004,
326; Steph. Byz. 169. 3–4). Called Hydroëis at 27. 2. After this PS omits
Brentesion (Hdt. 4. 99; Lat. Brundisium), probably because it was
Messapian rather than Greek (Cary 142; Radke 1964a; *OCD*³ on Brundisium). The next settlement named is Ankon (16), *c.*560 km to the
NW. In this case the gap may reflect not so much anti-barbarian bias
as a genuinely 'harbourless' coast (Beaumont 1936, 161).   **Adrias
. . . Ionios:** see *apparatus criticus* for the possibility that 'Ionios' was
not in the original text; the same might be true at 27. 2, though it is
less likely (see n. there). However, although 'Adrias' may be an
earlier name (e.g. Hekat. F 90) for a specific part of the gulf, 'Ionios'
was also in general use from C5 (Beaumont 1936, 204). ('Iŏnios', with
a short first 'o', is unrelated to 'Iōnian'.)

15–27. THE ADRIATIC

This is the first 'authentic' account of the Adriatic (Wilkes 1992, 94–

101, at 94) and the main source for the names of the lesser islands (Wilkes and Fischer-Hansen 2004, 325). (See previous n.)

For the W coast PS does little more than enumerate regions and peoples, with occasional cities.

For the E he has more to say and probably uses another source, which may run out at 28 where the tone becomes drier. At 26. 1 he begins to give *paraploi* in stades (having previously done so only for Sicily, 13), which are regular up to eastern Phokis (61). The many islands, promontories, lakes, and harbours receive more detailed topographical, ethnographic, and economic observations than in 1–14, as well as Homeric references and local distances. This side held more attraction for Greeks than the almost harbourless west (overview at Wilkes and Fischer-Hansen 2004, 321–5); on the commodities that stimulated their interest, see D'Andria 1990, 283. The richer information may partly reflect their more intensive activity, particularly after the new foundations of Dionysios I of Syracuse in the 380s (Caven 1990, 149–52). However, detail is still limited and sometimes inaccurate, suggesting either that Greek contacts were not yet highly developed (Wilkes 1992, 101) or that PS did not have access to Syracusan sources about the new colonies. Either view may explain the misconception about the *Danube* (20).

Other authors extend the Adriatic further S (*OCD*[3] on Adriatic sea; Ionian sea), so PS is taking a stance in a geographical debate.

For the coast as far as Albania, see *Geographical Handbooks* 1944–5b, 121–216. For the Albanian coast (from S to N), see *Geographical Handbooks* 1945, 65–83. On PS's treatment of the Adriatic, see also Colonna 2003; Counillon 2007b.

Barr. 42, 44

15. 'Daunitai', MS, is probably correct (see next n.), but PS's list of five peoples includes at least two from the W coast (Alfaterni, Opici) and is probably a list of Samnites (cf. 11 above) whom he misplaces here—though he appears to say that some or all of them extend 'from the Tyrsenian main to the Adrias'. This phrase may be genuine rather than interpolated, since twice in the following paragraphs a people extends from sea to sea (Tyrrhenoi, 17; Keltoi, 18, if correctly restored). (See also Peretti 1979, 180–97.) The use of 'mouths' (*stomata*) to mean 'languages' is a late feature (Müller 24); the preceding *ētoi* ('or indeed') confirms that this is a two-word, or slightly longer, gloss—not that the whole list is late, as Müller believes).   **Daunitai:** Daunia is the N part of anc. Apulia (Radke 1964b), a region with limited agricultural potential, better known for horse-rearing (Cary 140). The Daunians are viewed as a Iapygian people well known to the Greeks of Taras from C5l and also to peoples across the Adriatic (*OCD*³ on Daunians). Marcotte 2000, cxxvi–cxxvii, favours this name rather than 'Saunitai' (Samnites), proposed by earlier editors, since it appears to be borrowed from PS by Ps.-Lykophron (*Alexandra*, 1063; cf. on 108. 2 'fields') and is confirmed by Steph. Byz. on Daunion; cf. also Dion. Hal. *Ant. Rom.* 7. 3. 1 (C1 BC). On the other hand, even if this name was in PS's original text, it is based on a misunderstanding since the Daunioi do not appear to have controlled such a large area as he implies (Peretti 1979, 180 n. 181). See previous n.   *Alphaternioi*: 'Laternioi', MS; Alfaterni (*Barr.*), ESE of Naples.   **Opikoi**: otherwise unknown by this name, but Thuc. 6. 4. 5 locates Campanian Kyme in 'Opikia' (cf. n. on 10 Kyme) while Aristotle fr. 609 Rose locates a Latin place in 'Opike'. They are clearly a west coast tribe (Antonelli 2002, 204).   *Karakones*: 'Kramones', MS; probably the Carecini (*Barr.*) or Carricini of the Apennine uplands. **Boreontinoi**: probably the Frentani (Peretti 1979, 190, 191), an upland Samnite tribe with a stretch of the E coast (Strabo 5. 2. 2). The prefix 'Boreo-' ('north') looks like an attempt to hellenize the name. **Peuketieis**: there is confusion between the Peuketiantes of SE Italy (neighbours of the Oinotrians, Hekat. F 89) and the Picentes of Picenum in NE Italy, who attacked Rome (schol. Kallimachos fr. 106 Pfeiffer, where they are 'Peuketioi'); see Antonelli 2002. Some of the latter were deported to Campania by the Romans in 268; so, as there were neither Picentes nor Peuketians on the W coast in C4, the Peuketieis will be an E coast people, the same as the Peuketiantes. Assuming that it was possible to call them Samnites (in a loose sense; see n. on 11 Saunitai), PS's report that they (or all five peoples) extend from sea to sea may originally have been a statement about the Samnites as a whole.   **days, two, and a night:** implying *c.*1,500 st. (*c.*280 km), which would take us from Hyrion to Ankon (16).

16. Ombrikoi: Umbria was probably the upland region between the Sabines and Samnites of the central Apennines (which here approach the coast) and the region known as Cisalpine Gaul, though it is an elastic term (*OCD*³ on Umbrians). Ancona (below) is sometimes located in Picenum.   **Ankon:** *Inv.* 76 (*Ancona*), founded *c.*387 by Dionysios I (Strabo 5. 4. 2).   **Diomedes:** the great warrior of the *Iliad* (esp. bks 5–6). In post-Homeric legend he migrates to Apulia and receives land from king Daunos (*OCD*³ on Diomedes 2). Coppola 1993 discusses PS's evidence for a temple of Diomedes here. On the prevalence of his cult in the Adriatic, see Strabo 5. 1. 8–9; d'Ercole 2000; Wilkes and Fischer-Hansen 2004, 322; Castiglioni 2008. Fraser 1994, 183–4, notes that the cult is attested oftener in C4. Since PS's probable associate Theophrastos (*HP* 4. 5. 6) reports that plane-trees occur in the Adriatic only around the sanctuary of Diomedes, and that Dionysios planted planes at Rhegion, one wonders whether the cult was not promoted by the Syracusan ruler. At any rate, PS appears to have contemporary information.   **days, two, and a night:** implying *c.*1,500 st. (*c.*280 km); this is excessive, as from Ankon (the implicit end of the previous *paraplous*, at 15) it would take us *c.*100 km beyond the principal mouth of the *Po*. Most likely the measurement is wrongly repeated from 15 and should be emended, perhaps to a day and a night.

Barr. 40

Sections 17–20 contain a number of serious corruptions. Counillon 2007b would leave most of them unchanged rather than tempt readers to regard the printed text as final. I prefer to show possible reconstructions (those of Peretti seem well founded) while indicating where text has been removed and relocated.

17. Tyrrhenoi: for their W coast see 5. See generally Peretti 1979, 198–218.   **these:** as at 2, PS slips from singular into plural (Allain 143).   ⟨**Spina**⟩: *Inv.* **85**, at the mouth of the *Po*. Most scholars (e.g. Wilkes and Fischer-Hansen 2004, 334) consider that Spina is meant, whether or not the name stood here; *contra*, Counillon 2007b, 20. See also n. on 19 Eridanos. There were probably no Greek *poleis* from here to 22. 1 Herakleia.

18. Keltoi: since 'Celts' is usually equivalent to 'Gauls', this relates to the ancient name of the *Po* region, Cisalpine Gaul (Gallia Cisalpina), conquered by Rome in 222. According to Livy 5. 34–5, the region was assaulted by peoples from beyond the Alps, who replaced the Etruscans between C6 and C4e. The 'expedition' is usually thought to be that of *c.*390 in which Rome was captured; another historical occasion might be intended, but this reported invasion was used by Greek historians to synchronize Roman and Greek history (Counillon 2007b, 20 n. 8). It is also recorded by the philosopher Herakleides Pontikos (F 23. 3 = fr. 102 Wehrli), whose work PS probably knew (Introduction, VII).   **outer sea:** while one should generally be cautious (not all editors are) about modifying the order of material in the text, it is sometimes justified. I follow Peretti in transferring these words from 17.

Barr. 19

19. Enetoi: the Veneti lived NE of the *Po* at the head of the Adriatic (*OCD*³ on Veneti 2), in an area of wetlands known for horse-breeding (Cary 119–20; cf. Alkman's 'Enetic steed', fr. 1. 50–1 Page).   **Eridanos:** the *Po* (Lat. Padus/Eridanus), with several distributaries, the main one in the area of Spina (17); yet if PS mentions Spina he puts it in Tyrrhenia. Perhaps he understands that it is on the southernmost mouth while the Enetoi live by the more northerly ones.

Barr. 20

20. Istroi: inhabitants of the Histria or Istria peninsula (mod. *Istria*, in Croatia). As no major river debouches here, PS's Istros (below) should be further W, in modern Italy; so his Istroi begin W of the peninsula.   **river Istros:** PS believes that the *Danube* (see also 67. 1, 9–10; and 69) has a second mouth in the Adriatic (as at Ps.-Arist. *Mir. ausc.* 105. 839b9–11). Timagetos, *On Harbours* (C3), F 1a Müller, puts it in the 'Celtic sea', a rare phrase probably denoting the *Golfe du Lion* S of France (cf. App. *Mith.* 434). The headwaters, and some tributaries, of the *Sava* and *Danube* arise in the Julian Alps in NW Slovenia, as do several rivers of NE Italy, notably the *Tagliamento.*   **in a *scattered bed … Egypt:*** this tentative conjecture refers to the 'outspread bed' of the supposed Adriatic mouth of the *Danube*, presumably the wetlands of the *Veneto* province or the rivers of *Friuli-Venezia Giulia*. However, it entails an extension of the sense of *eunē*, 'bed' (also made by Müller 26 in a different reconstruction), which normally denotes the item of furniture. That the Nile was named here is convincingly argued by R. Hansen 1879. Other reconstructions make the Adriatic Istros face Egypt, so that PS may be evoking Hdt.'s reference (2. 33–4) to the Nile as opposite the *Danube* (Counillon 2007b, 22 n. 21; González Ponce 1994, 164).   **Istroi:** 'Istrianoi', MS, the *ethnikon* of Istros in the Black Sea (*Inv.* **685**), which has perhaps influenced the text here. Same suggestion, for different reasons: Suić 1955b, 169.

21. 1. Libyrnoi: for their extent see next n.   **Arsias:** 'Lias', MS. The suggested restoration is based on the R. Arsia in SE *Istria* (Pliny 3. 19/129; cf. Suić 1955a, 295) and the possible town of the same name (Pliny 3. 19/132). In R times the Liburni extended from the Arsias to the Titius (below; see n. on 21. 2 Kataibates) (*OCD*[3] on Liburni); if we restore Arsias, that becomes true for C4 also. This is the only purported list of *poleis* in PS that contains only non-*poleis* (Counillon 2007b, 22 n. 18).   **Dassatika:** 'Idassa', MS; anc. Tarsatica (*Trsat*). **Senites:** 'Attienites', MS; anc. Senia (*Senj*).   **Apsyrta:** 'Dyyrta', MS, may be Apsyrta (Suić 1955b, 151–2, 168, prefers 'Apsyrtai'), or Crepsa (*Cres*), or the Apsyrtides group, of which it is the largest.   **Loupsoi … Ortopeletai … Heginoi:** Lopsica (*Sveti Juraj*, near *Senj*), Ortopla (*Stinica*), and Vegium (*Karlobag*).   **ruled by women:** cf. 70 on the Gynaikokratoumenoi of the E Black Sea. On the independence of Libyrnian women cf. Theopompos F 39.

21. 2. of which I have the names to tell: a rare venture into the 1st person (Counillon 2007b, 22).   **Istris:** Curicta (*Krk*); alternatively, the *Istria* peninsula (Counillon 2007b, 21).   *Elektrides*: if correctly restored (the MS is meaningless), we have the earliest mention of these 'Amber Islands' (Ps.-Skymnos 374; not in *Barr*.). It could read 'Kassiterides' ('tin islands').   **Mentorides:** Cissa (*Pag*) and islets to SW.   **Kataibates:** 'Katarbates', MS, emended by Rendić-Miočević 1950 (cf. Suić 1955b, 162 nn. 67–8) and Nenci 1977. Probably the *Krka*, meeting the sea N of *Zadar*.

22. 1. Illyrioi: the Illyrians (22–7) occupy an area smaller than Roman Illyricum (Wilkes 1969, 5 n. 1). In Hdt. 4. 49 it runs from the Enetoi to Epeiros (Wilkes and Fischer-Hansen 2004, 321). PS defines Illyria geographically, in terms of its neighbours (Counillon 2007b, 23). (Peretti 1979, 219–37, discusses the Boulinoi and §22 generally.)   **as far as Chaonia:** advance mention; see 28. (Now in Albania.)   **Kerkyra . . . Alkinoös:** advance mention (see 29, where MS has 'Korkyra'). Alkinoös is its king in the *Odyssey*; oddly, he is not named at 29. One harbour was named after him, according to a late source (schol. Dion. Peri. 492). For his shrine see Thuc. 3. 70. 4; Gehrke and Wirbelauer 2004, 363.   **Herakleia:** *Inv.* **80;** location unknown; possibly Herakleia on Pharos (*Hvar*; Zaninović 1991–2). The first *polis* in *Inv.* that PS names since 16 Ankon (or 17 Spina, if correctly restored).

22. 2. Lotophagoi: no other source locates the Lotus-eaters here (Allain 145); they are usually in Libyē (see 110. 1).   *Iadasinoi*: or Iadastinoi, both conjectures offered by Peretti 1979, 224–8, 237; 'Hierastamnai', MS. Cf. perhaps Iader (*Zadar*), though at 44° 6′ N it should precede the *Krka* (see n. on 21. 2 Kataibates); or the Himani, Pliny 3. 21/139? Because of problems with the sequence of places (see Suić 1955b, 130–1), Counillon 2007b, 23, believes that among PS's sources was a *periplous* running in the reverse direction. Cf. n. on 23. 3 Kerkyra Melaina.   **Boulinoi:** located by scholars at *Ploča* by C. Diomedes (*Primorje*), *c*.43° 30′ N. The name varies: Boulinoi (Ps.-Skymnos 404), Boulimeis (Dion. Peri. 386), Ballini (Livy 44. 30), Bylliones (Strabo 7. 7. 8), Bulini (Pliny 3. 21/139).   *Hylloi*: 'Hyllinoi', MS, perhaps rightly. *Barr*. 20 D6 Hylloi, a few km inland on the same peninsula as the Boulinoi (with the town of *Primošten*). Counillon 2007b, 22, punctuates 'Boulinoi; Hyllinoi bordering on the Boulinoi; Hylloi'. **Hyllos . . . barbarians:** Ps.-Skymnos 409–14 cites Timaios (F 77; writing at Athens after *c*.315) and Eratosthenes (C3) for the Hylloi, founded by Hyllos, being 'barbarized' by their neighbours—a different account from here (Counillon 2007b, 23 n. 32).   **a little lesser than the Peloponnese:** wildly inaccurate (Pliny 3. 22/141 gives the Hyllis peninsula a circumference of only 100 miles), but from the sea the archipelago can seem like a peninsula (Counillon 2007b, 23 n. 31).

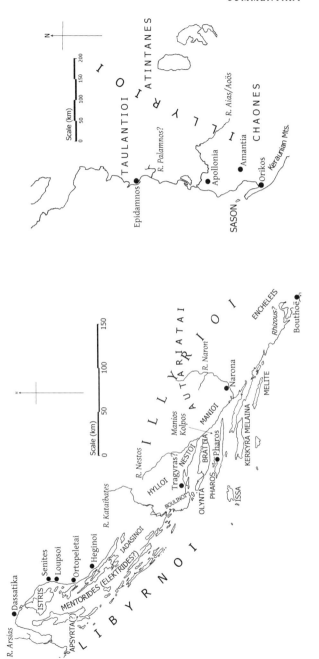

Map 5. Illyria.

Map 4. The Dalmatian coast.

22. 3. ⟨is ... island⟩: perhaps Bova (*Čiovo*), the largest islet off C. Hyllis (above), rather than Issa (*Vis*), which is at 23. 2.   **Nestos river:** emended from 'Nestos gulf'. See next n.

23. 1. Nestos: *Cetina*; the coastal gorge faces the island of *Brač*. Peretti 1979, 238–45, discusses the Nestoi and §23 generally.   **gulf ... Manios:** *Hvraski Canal*. For the Manioi see 24. 1. If we retain 'gulf' at the end of 22. 3, the giving of two names to this gulf (or coast made up of gulfs) would suggest that PS is trying to reconcile different sources (Counillon 2007b, 24–5 with n. 35). Cf. n. on 100. 2 'gulf-shaped'.

23. 2. Tragyras: 'Proteras', MS; the change (by Müller) is speculative, but cf. the mainland town of Tragurium (*Trogir*).   **Brattia:** *Brač* I., opposite *Split*. 'Krateiai', MS, probably a misreading (Suić 1955b, 129, 172; Kirigin 1990, 292 fig. 1; Wilkes 1969, 5); some forms of beta and kappa are repeatedly confused in the MS.   **Olynta:** Olunta (*Šolta* I.). **Pharos ... Issa ... cities:** Pharos is *Inv.* **84** (*Stari Grad* on *Hvar*); founded from Paros in 385/4 (Ephoros F 89, etc.), perhaps with help from Dionysios I of Syracuse (Diod. 15. 13. 4, 14. 1–2; cf. Kirigin 1990, 296). Issa is *Inv.* **81** (on *Vis*), SW of Pharos; a Syracusan foundation (Ps.-Skymnos 413–14, etc.), perhaps under Dionysios I, though there is a Greek presence earlier. For 'the island of Pharos ⟨with⟩ a Hellenic city the MS gives 'new Pharos middle Hellenic'; Müller 29 restores 'new Pharos, a Hellenic island', but PS nowhere else uses 'new' (*neos*) or describes a *polis* as new or an island as 'Greek'. In any case, Pharos was partly Illyrian (see under *Inv.* **81**); and if it is called Hellenic, why is not Issa? The reconstructed words 'and these are Hellenic cities' are pleonastic, but that is not a fault to which PS is immune.

23. 3. a lot of territory: an odd phrase, but plausible for the long *Pelješać* peninsula (Counillon 2007b, 24).   **Naron ... Melite:** the R. *Neretva* and *Mljet* I.   **Kerkyra Melaina:** *Inv.* **83** Melaina Korkyra (*Korčula*; Lat. Corcyra Nigra), S of Pharos. Called 'black' or 'dark' because of its lush greenery (Wilkes 1969, 8). Again there are hints that PS is using a reverse *periplous* (Counillon 2007b, 24). Cf. n. on 22. 2 Iadasinoi.

Barr. 49

24. 1. Nestoi: on the mainland opposite Brattia I. Despite the phrasing, they have not been mentioned yet (other than in the heading added later at 23. 1), though we have met the R. Nestos. **these people:** Allain 147 takes this to refer to the population of the area, though they could be the people of the town.   **upper trading-town:** presumably anc. Narona; see n. on 'a lake inland', below.

Manioi: cf. the Manios gulf, 23. 1. Peretti 1979, 246–61, discusses the Manioi and §24 generally.   **a lake inland:** probably L. *Svitava* (*c.*43° 2′ N, 17° 45′ E; Bosnia-Herzegovina), at sea level but *c.*25 km inland, which discharges into the Naron (*Neretva*) on the opposite bank to anc. Narona *c.*8 km to the WNW (*Vid*). If the rivers are identified differently, the lake could be further SE: either the gulf of *Kotor* (Montenegro; see n. on 24. 2 'up to the Rhizous river'; Martinovic 1966) or L. *Scodra* (*Skhöder, Skadar*) on the Montenegrin–Albanian frontier (Suić 1955b, 127, 174–5, and Suić 1953, as cited by Wilkes 1969, 5–6; Wilkes 1992, 99).   **Autariatai:** *Barr.* 20 E6, in the upper Naro valley (Bosnia-Herzegovina).   **island:** probably one of the now landlocked hills around L. *Svitava* (Bosnia-Herzegovina; see n. on 'a lake inland', above).

24. 2. *Arion* river: in the vicinity of *Dubrovnik* (Croatia; Counillon 2007b, 25). Editors disagree about whether to emend the name to Drilon, Rhizous, or Rhizon.   ⟨**up to the Rhizous river**⟩: cf. the town of Rhizon at *Barr.* 20 F7 (*Risan*, Montenegro) on the lengthy gulf of *Kotor.* Some addition is necessary to complete the second 'voyage', but there is danger in tidying up the text too much. The author may have inserted notes into an existing list (Counillon 2007b, 25–6). **Kadmos's and Harmonia's stones ... *Rhizous*:** Kadmos and his followers were exiled from Thebes and lived among the Encheleis (Hdt. 5. 61, etc.). Strabo 7. 7. 8 refers to the descendants of Kadmos and Harmonia as ruling the 'Encheleioi'. See n. on 25 Encheleis. See next n.   **Bouthoë:** *Budva, c.*12 km S of Rhizon. Founded by Kadmos (Steph. Byz. on Kadmos); see previous n. A Greek non-*polis* (Wilkes and Fischer-Hansen 2004, 326).

25. Encheleis: 'Eel-men', inland from the gulf of Rhizon. Also Encheleai (Hekat. F 103), Encheleioi (Ps.-Skymnos 437–9), Enchelanes (Steph. Byz.); their city is Brygoi (Ps.-Skymnos), is Enchelanai (Polyb. 5. 108). See n. on 24.2 Kadmos.   **Epidamnos:** *Inv.* 79 (*Durrës*, Albania); one of the few good natural harbours in the eastern Adriatic (Cary 293); another is at Apollonia (26. 1 below). A C7l colony of Kerkyra (Thuc. 1. 24. 1, etc.). Also called Dyrrhachion from C5 (Wilkes and Fischer-Hansen 2004, 330).

26. 1. *Taulantioi*: inland from Epidamnos (*Barr.*). The name is restored (see app. crit. with Counillon 2007b, 26 n. 51), but the text may still be corrupt, as the sense is rather contorted. (Peretti 1979, 262–75, discusses the Taulantioi and §26 generally.)   **Palamnos:** identified as R. *Lizana*, Garzón Díaz 2008, 298 n. 168; or possibly the *Leshniqe* at 41° 16′ N.   **Apollonia:** *Inv.* 77 (*Pojan*).   **Aias:** R. Aoös (*Vijosë* or *Vjosë*), the largest in the area, meeting the sea a few km S of

Apollonia.   **Amantia:** *Inv.* **86,** in Epeiros (near *Plocë*). A *c*.C5m foundation replacing Thronion, a non-*polis* SSE of Apollonia (Wilkes and Fischer-Hansen 2004, 342).   **Pindos mountain:** the mountain range bounding modern Greece and Albania.

26. 2. Orikos: *Inv.* **103;** *Orikumi,* at the head of the gulf of the same name. Flensted-Jensen and Hansen 2007, 224, note that Orikos is a *limēn* in Hekat. F 106 and Hdt. 9. 93. 1, and may have become a *polis* by C4m. Though the text is corrupt, Hammond 1967, 512 n. 2, believes it means 'that Oricum lies further up the gulf of Valona than Amantia does'. Alternatively PS is using a reverse *periplous* for a source (Counillon 2007b, 26, 27; cf. nn. on 22. 2 Iadasinoi; 23. 3. Kerkyra Melaina); but Hammond's plausible substitution of 'gulf' for 'Ionios' counters this. From this point, PS names no *polis* in *Inv.* until 29. 1 Korkyra.   **the Amantia:** clearly the *polis* territory rather than the urban centre (Funke *et al.* 2004, 342).

26. 3. the interior: PS's first use of this term (next at 32; see n. on 34. 2 'cities in the interior').   **Atintanes:** at Atintanis (Çermenike, Albania), *c*.80 km inland and NE from the places named at 26. 1–2. *Karia:* Hammond 1967, 522, supports this reading, citing inscriptions from Epeiros with related *ethnika,* and the place-name Kareia. *Idonia:* Hammond 1967, 513, 522–3, retains this reading rather than 'Dodonia', as Dodona is too far away.   *Kastid* **territory:** or 'Kestrid', though Hammond 1967, 523, prefers the MS form. Kestris is *Barr.* 54 B2 'Kestria?' (*Aëtos*). PS temporarily leaps forwards to find the Keraunia mountains, then follows them back N.   **Erytheia:** not in *Barr.* Erytheia was the name of Geryon's daughter (see next n.) as well as of his island (Hes. *Th.* 290, 983), located near Gadeira (see n. on §2 'one of these two').   **Geryones:** usually 'Geryon', whose cattle Herakles captured (e.g. Stesichoros, Davies 1991, S17, S19; Arr. *Anab.* 2. 16. 5).   **Keraunia mountains:** *Cikes;* we are still in the area of the gulf of Orikos.   **on the mainland:** the use of *ēpeiros,* 'mainland', as a place-name seems almost certain already in Xenophon, writing in the 350s (*Hell.* 6. 1. 7; Funke *et al.* 2004, 338); so PS could have used it as the name of a region. But since he does not use it at 28–31, he probably intends the common noun here, as in the same phrase at 67. 3, 94, 95, 98. 3, and 99. 2 (cf. similar uses at 68. 2, 98. 1, 102. 2, 110. 4, 111. 7 and 8; and his repeated 'I return onto the mainland'). See introduction to (*d*) below.   **Sason:** *Sazani.* PS essentially jumps back: he has gone inland, identified the Keraunia Mts further S, then followed them NW towards the sea by Orikos with Sason I. offshore. Is this further evidence of his using a source arranged from S to N? (Cf. n. on 26. 2 Orikos, with cross-references there.)   **From here to Orikos:** i.e. from Amantia (though the distance from Sason I. is about the same). PS ends his awkward digression with a *paraplous* that joins up with that at 26. 1 (Apollonia to Amantia).

27. 1. these people are Illyrioi . . .: see 22. 2. PS marks the end of Illyria as he leaves it. If we retain 'the Amantieis' from the MS, Amantia must extend from the R. Nestos to Orikos; this is not impossible, given the uncertainty over the extent of Illyria at this period (Counillon 2007b, 26 n. 51).

27. 2. Ionios gulf . . . cape Iapygia: see 14 and n. on 'Adrias or Ionios'. **Hydroëis:** see n. on 14 Hydrous.   **stades . . . 500:** Here PS, as elsewhere, punctuates his narrative with a transit forward or back across open water. The distance implies a day's sailing; it is actually *c*.73 km (*c*.395 st.), thus accurate.   **same thing as (the) Ionios:** see n. on 14 'Adrias or Ionios' for a possible MS problem. The preceding use of Ionios, however, is likely to be genuine, otherwise this comment (original or not) would be unnecessary.

[28–33. 1. Epeiros]

We enter Epeiros ('Mainland'), the region S of Illyria (now in southern Albania and NW Greece), though PS does not name it. Of 14 Epeirote tribes listed by Theopompos (F 382 = Strabo 7. 7. 5) the most important were those PS mentions: the Chaones (28), Thresprotoi (30), and Molottoi (32), the last dominant from between 365–356 and *c*.330, particularly when Philip handed Kassopian towns to Alexander the Molossian after 342. The Kassopians remained allies of the Molossians, not subjects, but Thesprotia was taken over *c*.335 and Chaonia in or after 317 (Marcotte 1986, 176, 178; cf. M. H. Hansen and Nielsen 2004, 106). PS conveys none of these developments and does not use the name Epeiros (it is thus unlikely that he intended it earlier: see n. on 26. 3 'on the mainland') or the *ethnikon* Epeirotai (Marcotte 2000, 207–8; Marcotte 1986, 176–7). On the other hand, he may be aware of Molossian expansion to the coast (32). He appears to be ignoring the present rather than using old sources. His repeated assertion that the peoples live in *komai*, 'villages', may be a topographical comment and is not necessarily an implicit assertion that they did not live in *poleis* (see M. H. Hansen 1995; M. H. Hansen and Nielsen 2004, 74–9); but he does omit their towns and may thus share the prejudice of those who saw Epeirotai as dubiously Hellenic (cf. Polyb. 18. 5). Yet they spoke a form of Greek and the Molossians were admitted to Panhellenic festivals (Wilkes 1992, 102, 104).

28. Chaones: the first of the three Epeirote peoples, already named at 22. 1.   **in separate villages:** PS uses these words only in 28–32. See introductory n. to 28–33. 1.   **a half of a day:** actually 600 or 660 stades (Fabricius 1878, 13 n. 7), implying a longer sailing time; but PS gives no clear start and finish (Allain 150).

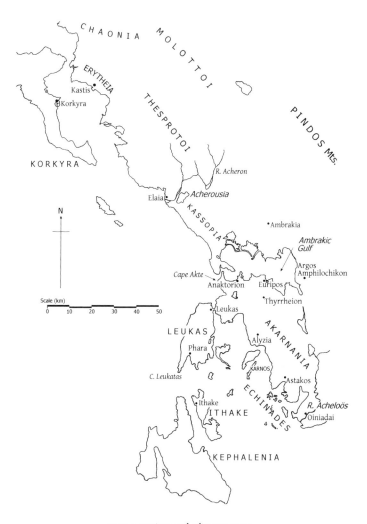

Map 6. Epeiros and adjacent areas.

Barr. 54

29. Korkyra: or (as at **22. 1**) Kerkyra (*Corfù*, Greece); *Inv.* **123.** For PS, the last Greek place not in 'continuous Hellas'; also the first *polis* he names that is in *Inv.* since 26. 2 Orikos. PS, like other ancient authors, does not consider the Ionian Is. to be a group, like the Cyclades, but locates Leukas, Ithake, and Kephalenia with respect to Akarnania (34), and Zakynthos with respect to Elis (43). He omits the Paxoi Is. (no *poleis*) S of Korkyra.   **three harbours:** Thuc. 3. 72 mentions two harbours (his words do not exclude a third), Hyllaïkos and another, usually thought to be that of Alkinoös. (The latter is in a late source, schol. Dion. Peri. 492.) The identity of the third is uncertain (Gehrke and Wirbelauer 2004, 362–3). There are other anchorages (Müller). **enclosed:** i.e. a naval base; see n. on 103 Cyprus. It may be the Hyllaïkos (Allain 150).   **Thesprotia:** advance mention (see next n.).

30. Thesprotoi: Thesprotia sometimes included Dodona (not mentioned by PS; wrongly restored by some editors at 26. 3) and always included the oracle of the dead, or Nekyomanteion, between L. Acherousia and the sea (*OCD*³ on Thesprotia).   **in separate villages:** see n. on this phrase at 28. Thuc. 2. 80 says that, like the Chaonians, they had no king.   **harbour … Elaia:** *Cheimerion.* A non-*polis* in Funke *et al.* 2004, 340, where it is the harbour of *Inv.* 95 Elea; the latter is some way inland (39° 25′ N, 20° 35′ E).   **Acheron:** mod. *Acheron.*   **a lake, Acherousia:** a few km inland (*Barr.* 54 C3).   **a half of a day:** about half the real distance (Müller 34).

31. Kassopia … villages: cf. the *polis* of Kassope a little inland (*Kamarina; Inv.* 100), synoikized in C4m (M. H. Hansen 2004c, 117–18) yet omitted by PS together with its dependent *poleis* (which are in a list of *theorodokoi* from Epidauros, in a section probably dating from 356: *IG* iv² 1. 95. 24–6).   **Anaktoric gulf:** the small bay on which the city of Anaktorion (34) stands. It is really part of the Ambrakic gulf, the broad inlet halfway from Corfu to the gulf of Corinth, a mention of which is restored at 34. If we do not alter the text here (hard to justify), it may be that PS names this rather than the Ambrakic gulf because, as one enters the gulf, it is this bay that opens up first and whose entrance is the landmark for sailors. 'A little less than' may imply that a more precise measurement along the shore has been 'rounded up' (cf. similar qualifications at 38, 110. 4, 113. 1; also 104. 1, slightly different in kind).   **a little less … than 120 stades:** *c.*22 km, suiting only the Ambrakic gulf as a whole (over 30 km, Marcotte 1985, 254).

32. Molottoi: see nn. on 28 'in separate villages'; and, for Molossian access to the sea, introduction to (*d*) above. PS again leaps back to the N and inland.   **the interior:** the second use of the term; cf. nn. on 26. 3 'the interior' and 34. 2 'in the interior'.

33. 2–65. CONTINUOUS HELLAS

Like PS, Herakleides Kretikos in C3 defines Hellas so as to end at Homolion in Magnesia (fr. 3. 8 Pfister). PS, however, distinguishes the Greek homeland from parts of the *oikoumenē* where Hellenic settlement is discontinuous, temporarily dropping 'Hellenic city' in favour of 'city'. (On his definition of Hellas, see Peretti 1961, 23–4; M. H. Hansen 2004c, 150–1; M. H. Hansen 2006b, 33–4; and nn. on 33. 2 Hellas; 40 'from here begins the Peloponnese'.) This spatial, geographical criterion appears in almost identical words at Dion. Kall. 31–4, using PS or a common source (possibly Phileas of Athens, *c*.C5), see Marcotte 1986, 168–9 (and cf. first n. on 47. 1). By excluding Epeiros and Macedonia from Hellas, PS may be making a nationalistic point in the aftermath of Chaironeia (ibid. 176), though at the cost of making outsiders of the East Greeks (see §§95–8). Illogically, however, he inserts Crete (§47) and nearly all the Aegean islands (§§48, 58) without observing that they are not part of continuous Hellas. In view of the geographical intentions of PS, it is perhaps more likely that he, rather than Phileas, adopted 'continuity' as a principle of organization.

The passage gives an impression of fuller coverage but is no more detailed than what precedes it; there are simply more *poleis*. After Attica (57), PS limits himself to an almost bare list of regions (or islands) and their *poleis*. There are fewer enlivening details, apart from Homer's burial-place (58. 2) and the occasional sanctuary and river. In another change in presentation, having hitherto introduced most sections with the name of a people, PS now sometimes uses the name of a region.

The irregularity with which harbours occur suggests multiple sources or inconsistent method. Lakedaimon has eight, Attica five, other parts of continuous Hellas one or none. Lack of knowledge, or of interest, is possible, as even Corinth's harbours, though named (40, 55), are not called harbours. He also gives up counting harbours after the Cyclades (58).

The prevalence of *paraploi* in stades, a style first introduced partway through Illyria (26), does not bear on the question of navigation versus geography. Some data do point to the use of documents about routes, such as the exceptional use of day–night distances for Lakedaimon (46. 2) and for the crossings to Crete and Libyē (47. 1). As these are followed immediately by the southern Cycladic route to the Dodecanese (48), PS may be using a specific itinerary. But he inserts Crete into his account of the Peloponnese because he perceives a geographical relationship, not because of the travel link between them.

For Crete itself, he abandons coastwise progression for the first time, zigzagging along the island from W to E in what Counillon 2001a has aptly called a geographer's presentation. The inclusion of inland *poleis* elsewhere, notably in Arkadia, confirms that his main interest is not in navigation but in geography, in the creation of a verbal or mental map.

Barr. 55

33. 1. Ambrakia: *Inv.* 113 (*Arta*), a city (not an *ethnos* region) on the river-plain N of the Ambrakian gulf. It is the last city called 'Hellenic' until we leave 'continuous Hellas' (66).   **80 stades:** Dion. Kall. 27–8 agrees; in Strabo (7. 7. 6) it is only 'a little way' (*mikron*) from the mouth of the gulf.   **fort ... enclosed harbour:** Hammond 1967, 137–8 (cf. 514–15), locates Ambrakos (Polyb. 4. 61. 7) here and identifies the site as *Phidokastro*. Dion. Kall. 28–30 agrees about the 'enclosed harbour', on which see 103 n.

33. 2. Hellas begins to be continuous: see introductory n. to 33. 2–65, above.   **Peneios river:** the border between Thessaly and Macedonia (cf. n. on 65. 2 Hellas).   **Homolion:** *Inv.* 448 (*Palaiokastro Karitsas*; not *Barr.* 55 D1 *Lapsochorio*, where it is normally put), in Magnesia on the Aegean coast. First attested in an inscription of 362/1 (Bousquet 1989, no. 1). Mentioned in advance, but not at 65. 2, where one would expect it (see n. there on 'Hellas is continuous').   **a city in Magnesia:** probably a topographical remark (taking *Magnētikēs* as partitive genitive, sc. *gēs* or *chōras*) rather than political ('a Magnesian city', i.e. a possessive adjective with *poleōs*). See also 64. 1 n.

34. 1. Akarnania: PS begins it not on its sea-coast but inside the Ambrakian gulf.   **Argos the Amphilochic:** *Inv.* 115 (*Agios Ioannis* near *Neochori*), at the inner end of the Ambrakic gulf. Strabo 10. 2. 2 and Pliny 4. 1/5 also put Argos in Akarnania, unlike Ps.-Skymnos 455–61 and Dion. Kall. 46–7 (Allain 151). Cf. Marcotte 1986, 178. **Euripos:** *Inv.* 119 (*Rouga*), on the S side of the Ambrakic gulf. Named in a list of *theorodokoi* from Nemea in 323/2 (S. G. Miller 1988, 148 with pl. 46 *a*).   **Thyrrheion ... federal state:** *Inv.* 139 (*Thyrio*, f. *Agios Vasileios*), on a hill above the S side of the gulf. Thyrrheion led minority Akarnanian resistance to Athenian control, which ended *c.*340 or in 338, just before the *Periplous* was written. PS means to convey that not all Akarnanians are in the *koinon* (Marcotte 1985, 257–8).   **outside the Ambrakic gulf:** 'Anaktoric', MS, puts Anaktorion outside its own gulf. Müller 36 alters radically; the simple emendation by Marcotte 1985, 254–5, is preferable. See n. on 31 Anaktoric gulf.   **Anaktorion:** *Inv.* 114 (*Agios Petros* near *Nea Kamarina*), in a bay at the W end of the S shore of the Ambrakic gulf.

It had an extra-urban sanctuary of Apollo Aktios, 40 st. from the city, on a cape (*akra*, Strabo 10. 2. 7); see Gehrke and Wirbelauer 2004, 356–7, and next n.   **Akte:** not in *Barr.* Rather than simply 'a headland' (*aktē*), this is the name of the headland after which Apollo was named (previous n.). Steph. Byz. (on Akte) notes Akte as a place-name in Akarnania; he does not say what kind of place.   **Leukas:** its *polis* is *Inv.* **126.**   **Leukatas:** *Barr.* 54 C4 Leukata(s).   **fought a civil war ... hold their territory themselves:** i.e. that of the Epileukadioi. This is the longest historical aside in the *periplous*, perhaps intended as an explanation for the dredging of the channel. The rare term ἔποικοι, 'new settlers', occurs in an account of similar strife at Arist. *Pol.* 5. 3. 1303a27–b3.   **now an island:** cf. Strabo 10. 2. 8 for Leukas as a former promontory of Akarnania. Pliny 4. 1/5 recounts the excavation and subsequent silting up of the channel.   **Phara:** *Inv.* **133;** otherwise unrecorded; perhaps in SW Leukas (at *Pyrgi*; *Barr.* 54 C4), or on one of the islets between Leukas and Ithake, or in the mainland territory (*peraia*) of Leukas (Gehrke and Wirbelauer 2004, 370, citing Wirbelauer 1998, 221–2, for the suggestion that we restore 'Palairos', a known *polis*; *Inv.* **131**).   **Ithake:** Odysseus's home; dominated by nearby Kephal(l)enia. Its *polis* is *Inv.* **122.**   **Kephalenia:** its four *poleis* (*Inv.* **125** Kranioi, **132** Paleis, **135** Pronnoi, **136** Same) are not named.

34. 2. Alyzia: *Inv.* **112** (*Kandila*).   **Karnos island:** *Barr.* 54 C4 (*Kalamos*).   **Astakos:** *Inv.* **116.**   **Acheloös:** *Barr.* 55 C3.   **Oiniadai:** *Inv.* **130** (*Trikardo*).   **cities ... in the interior:** including *Inv.* **117** Derion, **124** Koronta, **129** Medion, **134** Phoitiai, **140** Torybeia, and **138** Stratos, the last probably the most important. Until 26. 3 and 32 PS does not use 'the interior'; at 43–66. 5 he does so regularly; occasionally at 96–109. 3. In continuous Hellas, however, he names inland *poleis* only from Elis (43) to Boiotia (59).

34. 3. Echinades: *Barr.* 54 D5.

35. Aitolia: definition and extent, Freitag *et al.* 2004, 379–80. PS does not demean the Aitolians, as he does the Epeirotes, by claiming that they do not live in *poleis*.   **Kalydon:** *Inv.* **148** (N of *Evinochori*). **Halikarna:** *Inv.* **146** Halikyrna (*Chilia Spitia/Agios Symeon*), more naturally named before Kalydon.   **Molykreia:** *Inv.* **150** Molykreion (*Velvina/Elliniko*).   **Delphic gulf:** gulf of Corinth, so called nowhere else (Müller 37).   **10 stades:** 7 st. in Thuc. 2. 86, Agathemeros 5. 24; under a mile, Pliny 4. 2/6; actually 2.0 km (*c.*11 st.).   **sanctuary:** probably that of Poseidon, cf. Thuc. 2. 84. 4; Freitag *et al.* 2004, 385, under *Inv.* **150**).   **Naupaktos:** *Inv.* **165.** Its inclusion in Aitolia dates this information not earlier than 338 (Marcotte 1986, 170). Philip promised it to the Aitolians (Strabo 9. 4. 7) but may not have been able to deliver until after Chaironeia (338).   **many other cities . . . in the interior:** e.g. *Inv.* 142 Agrinion, 143 Aigition, 147 Kallion, and 156 Trichoneion. Cf. n. on 34. 2 'cities in the interior'. 'Many cities', by withholding information, embodies a rhetorical claim to authority; similarly at 46. 2, 47. 2, 60, and 66. 5 (plus other places where PS refers to 'many (other) islands').   **along all of Lokris:** that is, West Lokris (36); for Doris, Malis, and Phokis stand between Aitolia and East Lokris (60).   **Ainianeis:** see 62. 2. An advance mention. Again PS is not limited to coasts.

36. Lokroi . . . Ozolai: West or Ozolian Lokris, W of the gulf of Krisa below Delphi. (Name and geography: Rousset 2004b, 391–2.) East or Opountian Lokroi: see 60. 'In whom are the . . . Ozolai' presumably means PS envisages the East and West Lokroi as a single *ethnos* containing two or more parts. Again he organizes his narrative on a geographical, not linear or political, basis.   **Euanthis:** *Inv.* 166 Oiantheia (*Tolofon*, f. *Vitrinitsa*).   **Amphissa:** *Inv.* 158 (*Salona*).   **cities in the interior:** e.g. *Inv.* 157 Alpa/Alope, 161 Hypnia, 164 Myania, and 168 Tritea—none of them far inland. Cf. n. on 34. 2 'cities in the interior'.   **the half of a day:** less than a day, Dion. Kall. 69; actually c.320 st. (Müller 38). The same distance is given to Phokis (37); at 60–1 the two regions again have equal *paraploi*, but in stades.

37. Phokeis: like Lokris, Phokis has two coasts (cf. 61); unlike it, it is not divided into two parts. (Region: Oulhen 2004, 399–402. History: McInerney 1999.)   **Kirrhaion plain:** cf. *Inv.* 183 Kirrha.   **Delphoi, a city:** *Inv.* 177, with discussion of the *polis*–sanctuary relationship. PS, however, does not refer to Delphi as a cult place; of the four Panhellenic sanctuaries, only that of Poseidon at the Isthmos is noted (55).   **Antikyra, a city:** *Inv.* 173 (*Kastro tou Stenou*).   **hellebore:** either 'where they are helleborized best' (passive) or 'where they helleborize themselves best' (middle). Hellebore is a medicinal plant, also linked with Antikyra by Theophrastos (*HP* 9. 9. 2, 9. 14. 4), Strabo (9. 3. 3), and Pausanias (10. 36. 7). The verb also occurs in other C4 authors (Demosthenes, *De corona*, 121, from 330 BC; cf. Diphilos's comedy *Helleborizomenoi*), but is rare before the R period.   **a half of a day:** see 36 n.

38. Boiotoi: this passage, though corrupt, is the earliest (Roesch 1980, 126) and best (Marcotte 2000, 212) ancient description of the W coast. Western Boiotia is virtually fenced off from the eastern part by mountains (Cary 72–3). (Boiotia's name and definition: M. H. Hansen 2004b, 431–3. PS's text: Roesch 1980, too radical.) The absence of Chaironeia, here and at 59 (Allain 153), may be due to its inland location or to PS's reluctance to mention the site of a recent

calamity, the Greek defeat of 338.   **Korsiai:** *Inv.* **202** Chorsiai
(*Nichori*).   **Siphai:** *Inv.* **218** (*Aliki*).   *Eutresis: Inv.* **205** (*Arkopodi*), a
dependent *polis* of Thespiai, named at 59 (and see end of next n.).
Müller 38 punctuates so as to distinguish Eutresis, inland, from the
harbour of Siphai. 'Eutritos', MS, is closer to 'Eutresis' but might be
'Kreusis', an important harbour town (non-*polis*, M. H. Hansen 2004b,
434–5).   **a fort of the Boiotoi:** we could be dealing with a place-
name, 'Teichos Boioton', taking *Boiōtōn* as the federal *ethnikon* of the
third ('hellenistic') Boiotian league, set up in either 338 (M. H.
Hansen 2004b, 431–2, 435) or 335 (Marcotte 1986, 178–9). Given,
however, that PS is writing soon after 338 and the league's date is
uncertain, *teichos* is best treated as a common noun. Furthermore, PS
never demonstrably uses *kai teichos* to mean simply 'and (next) a
fort', without a place-name preceding or following; so the fort
should be in the territory of Eutresis. (Roesch proposed 'a fort of the
Thespians'.) PS uses *teichos* only in Greece and western Thrace,
between 33 and 67.

Barr. 58

39. Megareis: the Megaris (Megarid) is a single-*polis* territory with
two coasts, the second described at 56. PS postpones Megara the *polis*
(*Inv.* **225**) until then.   **Aigosthena . . . Pegai:** *Inv.* **224, 226.** This is the
only direct evidence of their C4 *polis* status; but the heading of the
list, 'the following cities', is not reliable (Flensted-Jensen and Hansen
2007, 207–11, esp. 210). See n. on Aigeiros, below.   **Geraneia:** the
principal mountain range of the Megarid.   **A⟨igei⟩ros:** 'Aris', MS.
Theopompos F 241 uses this form of Aigeiroussa (so says Steph. Byz.
on the latter) and calls it a *polis*; it may be *Megalo Vathychori* (Hammond 1954, 118–20), though Wiseman 1978, 21–2, and Muller 1982,
387 n. 32, doubt it.

40–55. Peloponnese, with Crete and Southern Cyclades

Unlike Demosthenes (19. 103), PS does not separate the Peloponnese
from Hellas, but includes it in 'continuous Hellas'. See also introduction to (*e*) above. (I thank T. H. Nielsen for advice, especially on
43–4.) PS refers five times to 'the interior' but names only a selection
of major inland towns.

40. Korinthos: *Inv.* **227,** a one-*polis* territory. Having two coasts, it is
covered twice (see 55), like Boiotia and Megaris.   **sanctuary:**
probably neither the temple of Apollo in Corinth—PS generally
mentions landmarks only outside towns—nor the temple of Poseidon
at Isthmia (on the other coast; see 55). Müller 39 suggests Hera's
sanctuary on the *Perachora* peninsula, across the gulf, though he does

not wish to restore her epithet 'Akraia'.   *Lechaion:* the N harbour of
Corinth.   **Isthmus:** *isthmos* without qualification often denotes the
isthmus of Corinth (LSJ entry, II.2), though PS also uses it elsewhere
as a common noun (e.g. 34. 1).   **from here begins the Peloponnesos:** it ends at 55. (Dion. Kall. 108 uses almost identical words, but
they are a prose interpolation, perhaps from Herakleides Kritikos
(Marcotte 1990, 34–8, 169) rather than PS.) See also introduction to
(*e*) above.   **the sea on our side:** some take this as evidence that PS
was an Athenian; but a writer from any Aegean *polis* might use these
words.   **all gulf-shaped:** referring to Korinthia rather than the gulf
of Corinth as a whole, since PS has not yet given the length of the
former; but it is an odd comment on such a short stretch of coast.

41. Sikyon: *Inv.* **228**, W of Corinth, with a small one-*polis* territory
(Sikyonia).

42. Achaioi: Achaia, the N coast, includes part of the mountain massif
inland. (Name, geography, history: Morgan and Hall 2004, 472–7.) A
multi-*polis* territory; its *poleis* had strong associations from early
times. PS lists seven cities, though there were traditionally twelve
(listed, Hdt. 1. 145). Boura (*Inv.* **233**) and Helike (*Inv.* **235**) may be
absent because they were destroyed by an earthquake in 373, though
Helike soon revived. Pharai (*Inv.* **241**) and Tritaia (*Inv.* **244**) may be
omitted because they lie inland, while PS may include inland Pellene
(below) because it is notable and near the coast. The absentee that is
hard to explain is coastal Olenos (*Inv.* **238**) between Patrai and Dyme;
but it disappeared *c.*300 or later, so perhaps was already in decline.
Pellene, Aigeira, Aigai, Aigion, and Rhypes: *Inv.* **240, 230, 229, 231,**
and **243**.   **outside Rhion:** i.e. outside the gulf of Corinth. PS probably means (*a*) Peloponnesian Rhion (mod. *Rio*), a cape rather than a
settlement (not in *Inv.*), not (*b*) Rhion in Aitolia ('Molykric Rhion',
Thuc. 2. 86. 2–3; 'Antirrhion', Strabo 8. 2. 3; mod. *Andirio*), a non-*polis*
settlement, the dependent harbour of Molykreia (§35; Freitag *et al.*
2004, 381).   **Patrai and Dyme:** *Inv.* **239, 234.**

43. Elis: the chief city of the NW Peloponnese (*Inv.* **251**); also one
name for the region, also called 'Eleia'. Unlike e.g. Arkadia and
Achaia, Elis was never united in a federation; instead, like Lakedaimon, it had a central *polis* that reduced others to the status of
perioikoi, dependent neighbours. (Political organisation: Roy 1997.)
PS omits the Panhellenic sanctuary of Zeus at Olympia, which lay in
southern Elis on the N bank of the Alpheios, as well as the area of
Pisatis around it (Roy 2002a) containing the sometime *polis* of Pisa
(*Inv.* **262**).   **Kyllene:** *Inv.* **254**, probably the only significant harbour
on this coast (Baladié 1980, 267–8), serving mainly the *polis* of Elis. PS

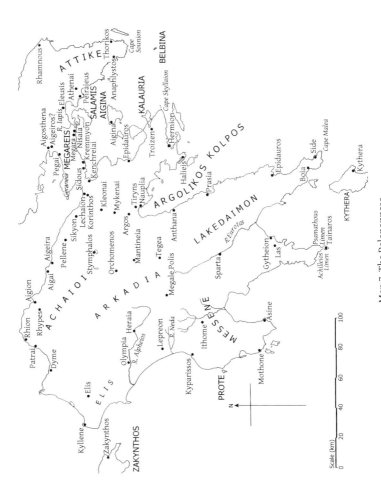

Map 7. The Peloponnese.

is the only evidence that Kyllene was a *polis*; he may be right, though uncertainty arises in several cases where he applies the term to the harbour of an inland *polis* (Flensted-Jensen and Hansen 2007, 218), e.g. Harmene (89) and Notion (98. 3).   **Alpheios:** one of the two great rivers of the Peloponnese. Like the Eurotas (46), it is included either because it was a landmark in one of PS's sources and/or because of its historical significance.   **amalgamation of cities:** *synoikia*, cf. *synoikismos*, the process of combining the populations of several settlements into a new one, with or without their actual relocation. Elis was synoikized in 471 (Roy 2002b).   **in the interior:** see n. on 34. 2 'cities in the interior'.   **Zakynthos:** *Inv.* **141;** a colony of the Achaioi (§42; Thuc. 2. 66). Unlike Strabo (10. 2. 18), PS does not give the crossing from here to Libyē.   **the ⟨boundaries⟩ of the Lepreatai:** see n. on 44 Lepreon.

44. Arkadia: at first sight paradoxical, in a purported *periplous*, for it occupies the central Peloponnese and usually had no coastal *poleis*. Only at Phigaleia, in most periods, was there a connection with the Ionian sea via the R. Neda (Cooper 1972, 359–62). However, if PS's source dated from the 360s or later, the region could have been said to have a short W coast (see next n.). But he would surely have included Arkadia even if landlocked, for he combines coastal measurement with a geographical tessellation of the world accessible to the Greeks. He is silent on internal ethnic subdivisions of the Arkadians, which were important in C4 (Nielsen 2002, 271–307). The region was organized as a federal state in the 360s and possibly for later parts of C4 (Nielsen 2002, 474–99). (*Poleis*: Nielsen 2002. Name and extent: Nielsen 2004a, 505–6, with 540–1 on Triphylia.)   **Lepreon:** *Inv.* **306,** usually Triphylian but here Arkadian, which fits a C4m date. It was Eleian in C5, but was now probably the main town of the new Triphylian state, which it represented in the Arkadian league (*IG* v. 2. 1. 20, 360s BC; Nielsen 1997, 153–4; Nielsen 2005). In C4l Dikaiarchos (Introduction, VII) similarly referred to Arkadia as having a coastline (fr. 79 Mirhady = Cic. *Att.* 6. 2. 4), contradicting Homer, who says (*Il.* 2. 610–14) that the Arkadians know nothing of the sea (cf. Paus. 8. 51. 7; Shipley under review; Marcotte 1986, 182).   **in the interior:** though Cl Arkadia (not including Triphylia) had *c*.39 inland *poleis* (Nielsen 2004a), PS names only six: the four main ones in the E and (probably) two in the W, Heraia and Megalopolis. See n. on 34. 2 'cities in the interior'.   **Tegea, Mantineia:** *Inv.* **297, 281.**   **Heraia:** *Inv.* **274.** It existed from Ar times and probably became more important after the defeat of Sparta at Boiotian Leuktra in 371, when it was synoikized (Strabo 8. 3. 2) and joined the Arkadian league (*IG* v. 2. 1 = *Syll.*³ 183), though the date of the synoikism is a modern inference (Nielsen 2002, 172–4).   **Orchomenos:** *Inv.* **286.   Stymphalos:** *Inv.* **296.** Its circuit wall is C4m or C4l, and the town was orthogonally planned *c.*375–350. Paus. 8. 22. 1–2 claims that 'old Stymphalos' was on a different site; but if PS did refer to Megalopolis (next n.), he probably refers to the 'new' Stymphalos.   **⟨Megale Polis⟩:** *Inv.* **282,** later Megalopolis (presumably a back-formation from the *ethnikon*, *Megalopolitēs*); the most prominent C4m Arkadian city, founded in 369 as the new 'capital'. (Territory: Petronotis 1973; Pikoulas 1988.) The MS omits it. If PS did so, it was not because it was inland: he names other Arkadian *poleis*, all inland apart from Lepreon. Omission might be evidence that at least part of the text was written before the 360s, or that he is using an earlier source. As the MS stands ('and their large cities in the interior are these: Tegea', etc.), the question arises what 'great' means; it is unclear, since PS omits some *poleis* that are 'great', in size (e.g. Phigaleia, *Inv.* **292;** Psophis, *Inv.* **294**) or power (e.g. Kleitor, *Inv.* **276**). (On the criteria by which sources describe *poleis* as 'great' or 'small', see M. H. Hansen 1997b, 25–31; Nixon and Price 1990.) However, a relatively simple emendation (see *apparatus criticus*) restores the name. (PS omits the famous Apollo temple at Bassai in Phigaleia's *chora*.)   **other cities:** see generally Nielsen 2002.

45. community of Messene: 'Messene', not Messenia, is the regular Cl name of the region (Shipley 2004b, 562). It was possible to call Messene a region before 369, but PS's information clearly postdates its independence from Sparta (see n. on 'Ithome', below). (Outline of geography and history: Shipley 2004b, 547–50.)   **Kyparissos:** *Inv.* **317.   Prote:** a non-*polis* (Shipley 2004b, 558). (Archaeology: Dimakis 1984, over-interpreting Steph. Byz. on Prote.) The name, accented differently, would mean 'first'; evidently a copyist, not realizing it was a name, put it before Kyparissos and added the chief *polis* of the region, Messene, not knowing this was the same as Ithome (next n.). This is one of three possible transpositions in 45–6 (see nn. on 46. 1 Asine and Achilleios), but it is easily accounted for by mis-transmission.   **Ithome:** the *polis* of the Messenians liberated in 369 (not all were: see n. on 46 Asine); later Messene (Shipley 2004b, 561–2). **300 stades:** implying that Messenia extends N to Pylos (Müller 40).

46. 1. Lakedaimon, a community: 'Lakedaimon' denotes either (1) the city of Sparta or (2) its territory—either the core territory of the *polis* in the upper Eurotas valley, or the SE Peloponnese as a whole (with the dependent *poleis* of Sparta's *perioikoi* or 'circumhabitants': Shipley 2004a; 2006, citing earlier works). Sense (2) is meant here (scholars often call this area Laconia or Lakonia, but these are not ancient terms). It is not called an *ethnos* in other Cl texts; one would

expect that term to be applied to the people (Lakedaimonioi, Lako-
nes). But PS calls Elis (43) and Messene (45) *ethnē*, so this may be
stylistic variation. He may use a new source here: see introduction to
(*e*) above. The selection of towns reflects a coastal bias—no major
coastal town is absent—but there are surprising inclusions (e.g. Las
and Side, very minor places) and omissions (Kotyrta, Kyparissia,
Teuthrone, and Zarax, all important harbours).   **Asine:** *Inv.* 313
(medieval Coron; *Koroni*), The Messenian *polis*, not the less well-
attested Laconian Asine on the E side of C. Tainaron (a non-*polis*,
Shipley 2004a, 574). Both are E of Mothone (Strabo 8. 4. 4), yet the MS
puts Asine first. There is no obvious reason for scribal confusion
here (contrast n. on 45 Prote), so the error may be original—perhaps
the result of using a reverse *periplous* (see also n. on 'Achilleios'
below); for other possible reverse *periploi* see 23. 3, 100. 2, 109. 5. It
seems best not to emend the text. See also next n.   **Mothone:** *Inv.*
319 (medieval Modon; *Methoni*). The inclusion of Asine and Mothone
within Lakedaimon is evidence that Sparta retained southern Messenia after 369, almost certainly until 338 (Shipley 2000) or shortly
after. Although he names the other two S capes of the Peloponnese
(Tainaron, Malea), PS omits C. Akritas between Mothone and Asine
(Strabo 8. 4. 4), where the Messenian gulf begins.   **Achilleios ...**
Psamathous: 'Achilles' Harbour ... Sandy Harbour'. PS explicitly
locates them on opposite sides of C. Tainaron. The only suitable
'back-to-back' harbours (both, as it happens, sandy) are *Porto Kagio*
on the E (a good anchorage, *Mediterranean Pilot* 1987, 70–1 no. 3.119;
cf. *Geographical Handbooks* 1944–5a, i. 55–6) and *Marmari* on the W,
only 0.6 km away. Though small, they were doubtless recorded by
PS's source because they offered alternative shelters in different
winds (cf. Cary 28–9). The word order in the MS implies that Achilleios is on the W side, Psamathous on the E, as in Artemidoros (=
Steph. Byz. on Psamathous) and Strabo (8. 5. 2). Steph. Byz. (on
Achilleios Dromos) locates a *kome* and harbour of Achilleion 'in
Messene', which is probably Achilleios. Earlier scholars were misled
by Pausanias's having mentioned first Achilleios, then Psamathous,
on the way from Gytheion to Tainaron (3. 25. 4). Fabricius wished to
transpose the names (see Müller 41), but Paus. surely visited the W
harbour first, then crossed the ridge to the other. The question is
important because there are two other probable transpositions in
45–6 (see nn. on Prote and Asine, above). Only that of Asine and
Mothone, however, potentially implies that PS drew upon a reverse
periplous. (Pausanias 3. 24. 10 reports that the locals believed Achilles
had links to the area, and that he killed the eponymous hero of Las,
below.)   **Tainaros:** not a Cl *polis* (Shipley 2004a, 576). The sanctuary

of Poseidon was one of the most important pan-Lakedaimonian shrines.   **Las:** *Inv.* **337.** See also n. on Achilleios, above. **Gytheion:** *Inv.* **333.** Site of the Spartan shipyards attacked by Athens in 445 (Diod. 11. 84. 6). It was probably a *polis* then, but was not a large settlement before C4 (Falkner 1994). Xen. *Hell.* 6. 5. 32 seems to imply that it was fortified in 370–369. Müller 41 punctuates so as to separate the fort from Gytheion; but see n. on 38 'with a fort of the Boiotoi'.   **Eurotas:** included as a landmark, or for its historical importance (like the Alpheios, 43); it is too shallow to be navigable. **Boïa:** *Inv.* 327.   **Malea:** the SE cape of the Peloponnese, notoriously dangerous to sailors—but it is not in PS's geographical agenda to say so.   **Kythera:** the *polis* is *Inv.* **336.**   **by this is Krete:** repeated, in effect, at 47. 1. As with Kyrnos and Sardo (6–7), PS waits till he has finished his mainland region before recounting the island off it (his agenda is geographical, not navigational); but on this occasion he signals the island in advance.

46. 2. **Side:** *Inv.* **344** (probably *Velanidia*).   **Epidauros:** *Inv.* **329;** or Epidauros Limera, 'Harboured Epidauros', though Limera was not part of its 'official' name.   **Prasia:** *Inv.* **342** Prasiai.   *Anthana*: *Inv.* **324** (probably *Nisi Agiou Andrea*), in the district of Thyreatis or Thyrea (probably the territory of Thyrea, *Inv.* **346**) in the Kynouria region. Thyreatis was Spartan until Philip II removed it in 338 (Shipley 2000, 378); Anthana may have been one of two known coastal forts in the area. We could keep the MS reading 'Methana' and move the passage to 52. 1, where Methana is absent; but 'Anthana' is an easy emendation (see Phaklaris 1990, 47–55, *contra* Pritchett 1989, 91–101).   **Sparta:** *Inv.* **345.** Its inclusion, like that of other inland cities in the Peloponnese, shows that PS's agenda is geographical, not navigational. He does, however, omit several inland *poleis*, notably Geronthrai (*Inv.* **333**) and Sellasia (*Inv.* **343**).   **many other cities:** true until 195, when Sparta lost most of its still substantial 'perioikic' territories (Shipley 2000, 387). See n. on 35 'many other cities'.   **days, three:** other *paraploi* from Sikyon (41) to Lokris (62) are in stades. Perhaps PS could not get detailed, up-to-date information about the coast given the secrecy of the Spartans (contrast the precise data on the sections of Attica, 57); or perhaps, since PS transposes Asine and Methone (46), one of his sources was a W–E *periplous*.

Barr. 60

47. 1. Phileas of Athens (see n. on 33. 2 Hellas), whom Dion. Kall. 110–30 cites for Crete, is a source, or one of PS's sources, for 47 (Marcotte 1990, 172–85). PS differs from both authors, however, in adopting a

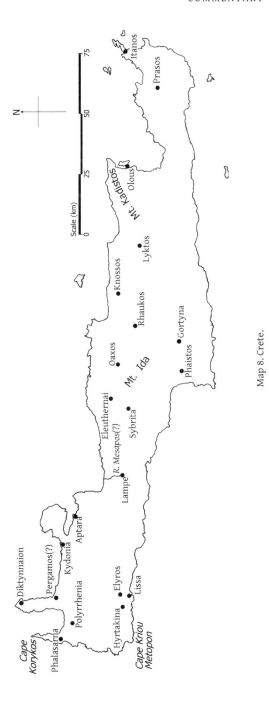

Map 8. Crete.

Itanos
Prasos
Mt. Kadistos
Olous
Lyktos
Knossos
Rhaukos
Gortyna
Oaxos
Mt. Ida
Phaistos
Eleuthernai
R. Mesapos(?)
Sybrita
Lampe
Diktynnaion
Pergamos(?)
Kydonia
Aptara
Polyrrhenia
Hyrtakina
Elyros
Lissa
Cape
Korykos
Phalasarna
Cape Kriou
Metopon

Scale (km)
0   25   50   75

N

geographical rather than a periplographic or political arrangement. But this may rather be an innovation by his source than by himself. Unlike Strabo and Pliny, he is not influenced by graphic representations (e.g. maps) or itineraries (Counillon 2001a, 391–4). With a cartographic perspective thus excluded, several gaps identified by Peretti and others cease to matter. (Peretti 1979, 418–34, discusses §47. Name and scope of Crete and offshore islets: Perlman 2004, 1144–5.) In the E, PS omits e.g. the important *polis* of Hierapytna (*Inv.* 962). In the W, coverage of *poleis* is fuller (Allain 157); but he several times names *polis* territories (Apteraia, Polyrrhenia, Pergamia, Lampaia) rather than *poleis* as such. Thphr. *HP* 3. 3. 4 (plausibly emended) mentions the 'Pra(i)sia', Aristoxenos the Pergamia (see nn. below); were PS and the Peripatetics using similar sources?   **By Lakedaimon:** as already indicated, with respect to Kythera, at 46. 1. **Europe:** cf. 13. 1 n.   **the promontory of Krete:** it is tempting to restore 'Korykos', but PS seems to prepare us for a retrospective reference at 47. 3; see n. there.   **Phalasarna:** see 47. 3 n.   **a day's run:** the same phrase at Hanno 8 (see introductory n. to 112) and Hdt. 2. 5 (of a voyage inland into Egypt). Allain 157 suggests 'some nautical significance', perhaps direct transit or a long day's sail (cf. 'a long day' at 22. 3).   **is Kriou Metopon promontory:** these words form an iambic trimeter in Greek, presumably accidental. Kriou Metopon means 'Goat's Brow'.   **the *Azirides* of Chersonesos:** 'Aliadai', MS, which is disputed (see app. crit.); the same place may represented by 108. 1 Achitidai and 108. 5 Antides. Like Fabricius and Peretti, however, I adopt Bursian's 'Azirides' (cf. Aziris, Hdt. 4. 157). For this Chersonesos see 108. 1, 2, 5; Strabo 17. 3. 22; Ptol. *Geog.* 4. 5. Despite being a cape, it is too low to be seen from far away; sailors crossing from Crete might first see the cliffs to the W and the notch formed by the *wadi* of Azirides, *c.*20 km further W.   **a day and a night:** Müller 42 reckons it as *c.*1,750 st. (over 2 days and 1 night), noting that Pliny 4. 12/60 (citing Agrippa) gives 125 miles (1,000 st.), which is also too short, while Strabo 17. 3. 22 gives 2,000 st. Mt Ida provides a backsight for most of the journey (Cary 29).

47. 2. 2,500 stades: as at 113. 2 and Dion. Kall. 113–14, who read PS; other sources vary. This is *c.*460 km; the actual length is *c.*250 km (*c.*1,350 st.). Müller 42 suggests that the figure reflects the indentations of the coast.   **settings ... risings:** Allain 158 detects an 'archaic flavor', but the reason may be that this is almost the only place where PS uses cardinal directions; cf. 58 'south', 110. 9 'settings of the sun', 111. 3 'the rising sun'. It seems only some of PS's sources used these directions. Cf. n. on 47. 3 'setting sun'.   **colonists:** Dion. Kall., who read PS, is the only other author to claim (114–17) that some Cretans were of Athenian origin. It may be that the Athenian status of each author induced him to make this unlikely claim (Marcotte 1986, 168–9), though PS may be a resident at Athens, rather than Athenian as such (Introduction, II). The listing of ethnic population groups recalls 13. 2 on Sicily.   **aborigines:** also at 103, of Amathous in Cyprus.   **many cities:** the sentiment is repeated at 47. 4, suggesting compilation from more than one source; see *Inv.* for the others (49, of which PS names 20); also n. on 35 'many other cities'.

47. 3. ⟨Koryk⟩os: the NW tip of Crete (also called Kimaros, Strabo 10. 4. 2), information PS seems to have promised at 47. 1, since he has not yet pointed out any cape without also naming it (and will not do so until 68. 2, though see n. on Itanos below).   **setting sun:** cf. 'settings of the sun ... risings of the sun' at 47. 2, but 'setting sun ... upcoming sun' in this paragraph. Deliberate *variatio*, or a change of source?   **Phalasarna:** *Inv.* 981. The words 'with an enclosed harbour' (i.e. a naval base, Counillon 1998b) must refer to Phalasarna rather than inland Polyrrhenia, named next.   **Polyrrhenia:** *Inv.* 983 Polyrhen. 'Polyrrhenia' may denote the *chora*.   **from the north towards the south:** see n. on 47. 2 'settings'.   **Diktynnaion:** a sanctuary of Diktynna on C. Tityros; built by Samians, Hdt. 3. 59. 1–3. Cf. Perlman 2004, 1171, 1181, 1183.   **Pergamian territory:** lit. 'the land Pergamia', unusual word order for PS. The settlement or *polis* is probably Pergamos, Perlman 2004, 1146 (*Grimbiliana-Agia Eirini*); cf. Bennet and Reger 2000, 926. It may be in the *Kisamos* region SW of the Diktynnaion (Counillon 2001a, 387). Aristoxenos, contemporary and possible associate of PS, is the only other Cl author who mentions it, locating the Spartan Lykourgos's tomb in 'the Pergamia' (fr. 44 Wehrli = Plut. *Lyc.* 31. 4).   **Hyrtakina ... Kydonia ... Elyros ... Lissa:** *Inv.* 963, 968, 959, and 973 (Lisos).   **Apteraian territory:** of *Inv.* 947 Aptara.   **the Lampaia:** of *Inv.* 970 Lappa (or Lampe, Lampai). **Mesapos:** the R. Messapolis, Dion. Kall. 128. Not certainly identified (Counillon 2001a, 388 n. 17).

47. 4. *Mount Ida*: 'Osmidas', MS, must be removed from the list at Perlman 2004, 1145 nn. 3 and 6.   **Eleuthernai:** *Inv.* 957.   **Sybrita:** *Inv.* 990; inland, so not a harbour as the MS implies. I tentatively punctuate to make Phaistos its harbour town (with Counillon 2001a, 387), implying a misunderstanding by PS or his source (Phileas?) since Phaistos is *c*.5 km inland (perhaps less in antiquity if the plain to its NW has expanded through alluviation).   **Phaistos ... Oaxos ... Knossos ... Gortyna ... Rhaukos ... Lyktos:** *Inv.* 980 (see previous n.), 950 Axos, 967 Knosos, 960 Gorty(n)s, 986, and 974.   **Mount Kadistos:** Müller's reconstruction presumes that Kadistos and Olous are on the cape E of *Irakleio*.   **Olous:** *Inv.* 978.   **Prasos:** *Inv.* 984.

'Prasis', MS. Two of the rare Cl mentions are by PS's likely associate Theophrastos: *HP* 3. 3. 4 Praisia (better Prasia, given τιρασίαν in MSS); fr. 113 Wimmer = 560 Fortenbaugh = Strabo 10. 4. 12 Prasos. *Itanos*: 'Granos', MS, could be the Cretan *polis* of Dragmos (Xenion, *FGrH* 460 F 2; Counillon 2001a, 387 n. 15, 389). But PS mentions only a cape, and we have no idea where Dragmos lay. 'Itanos' is a less radical change. It is a *polis* (*Inv.* 965) and a cape (Steph. Byz. on Itanos). The long, hilly cape beside it (*Sidero*) is anc. Samonion; Strabo (e.g. 10. 4. 3, 5, and 12) measures distances from it. Accordingly, *Barr*. 60 F2 places C. Itanon (*sic*) at *Plaka c.*8 km to the S. But would PS's source mention *Plaka* and not *Sidero*? We could understand 'Itanos; (then) the promontory . . .', i.e. Samonion; but PS rarely leaves a promontory unnamed (see nn. on ⟨Koryk⟩os, above, and 61 Knemis). Itanos may be an alternative or earlier name of Samonion; or we might read 'Itanos, ⟨city and⟩ promontory . . .' (see app. crit.).

upcoming sun: i.e. to the east. Contrast 'the sun's risings', 47. 2. **hundred-citied:** most famously at Hom. *Il.* 2. 649; cf. Strabo 10. 4. 15 (100 or 90 cities). Perlman 2004 identifies a minimum of 49. PS more or less repeats what he says at 47. 2 about the numerous other *poleis*. See n. on 35 'many other cities'.

Barr. 57

48. Kyklades . . . by the Lakedaimonian territory: if Pholegandros (below) is correctly restored, PS covers exclusively Dorian islands here—after Dorian Laconia (46) and Crete (47)—reserving the Ionian until later (58). (Region: Reger 2004, 732–3.) He does not, however, categorize them as Dorian and Ionian. Furthermore, while the Dorian group lie on a sea route towards Rhodes, the principle of organization is not purely periplographic (see Counillon 2004, 18), for the endpoint is unstated. It is, as elsewhere, to create a 'verbal map' that allows the reader or listener to conceive the thing described; so the Laconia–Melos link allows us to relate the new information to what went before. (See, further, n. on 58.) PS omits islands without a *polis* (though see n. on Pholegandros, below), but does not always note the *polis*.   **Melos . . . Kimolos:** Dorian; the *poleis* (not mentioned) are *Inv.* 505, 496.   **Pholegandros:** 'Nochioros' (meaningless), MS. Some editors restore Oliaros (*Andiparos*), a non-*polis* dependency of Ionian Paros (Reger 2004, 767–8), which would go better in 58. Rather, Dorian Pholegandros (or possibly Polyaigos) stood here (Müller 44; Counillon 2001b, 18).   **Sikinos:** *Inv.* **518,** Dorian.   **Thera . . . Anaphe . . . Astypalaia:** Dorian islands; the *poleis*, not mentioned, are *Inv.* **527, 474,** and **476.**

49. *Argolis.* Here at the end of Lakedaimon, PS omits Thyreatis and

Kynouria, outlying areas of Spartan territory until 338, when they became Argive (Shipley 2000). As in Arkadia, he is not interested in sub-regions. In Argolis itself he omits the prominent, independent, inland *polis* of Phleious (*Inv.* **355**), as well as the Panhellenic sanctuary of Zeus at Nemea, originally controlled by Kleonai but later (by C4l) under Argos (S. G. Miller 1982; 1990; Perlman 2000, 131–52). (Jameson *et al.* 1994b discuss PS's representation of the eastern Argolid or Akte, 'Peninsula'.)   **Argos:** *Inv.* **347;** its *polis* territory is Argeia, used here for the area directly controlled by Argos; this includes the dependent *poleis* of Kleonai, Mykenai, and Tiryns but not the Akte (see previous n.). PS does not use 'Argolis', which usually includes the Akte; this wider region occupies 49–52 and 54 but is not identified as an entity. (Overviews: see Tomlinson 1972; Pariente and Touchais 1998. Name, extent: Piérart 2004, 599–600. Southern Argolis: Jameson *et al.* 1994a.)   **Nauplia:** a non-*polis*, or possibly a dependent *polis* of Argos (Piérart 2004, 601–2; Flensted-Jensen and Hansen 2007, 218.   **Kleonai:** *Inv.* **351;** an inland town, naturally connected with the N coast but a dependent *polis* of Argos by C4. On its *chora*, see Sakellariou and Faraklas 1971. PS operates a geographical scheme, not a navigational agenda. (I thank T. H. Nielsen for his thoughts on this.)   **Mykenai:** Mycenae, *Inv.* **353.** Argos took its territory in C5, having destroyed the *polis* after the Persian wars (Diod. 11. 65. 2–5, etc.). See next n.   **Tiryns:** *Inv.* **356.** Destroyed in C5 (Hdt. 6. 83. 1–2; Paus. 2. 17. 5, 8. 46. 3). Either PS's source was out of date, or it included Mycenae and Tiryns as prominent landmarks—hardly for their intrinsic importance, unless retrospectively.   **a gulf ... Argolic:** this interrupts the flow but is in PS's style.

50. 1. **Epidaurian territory:** it begins here and resumes (with the *polis*) at 54 after being interrupted by the enclaves of Halieis, Hermion, and Troizen, plus Kalaureia I. Epidauros, like Tyrrhenia, Boiotia, and Megaris, stretches from sea to sea; PS normally mentions such regions twice. (Territory: Pharaklas 1972a.)   **comes down to this gulf for 30 stades:** i.e. has a coastline 30 st. (*c.*6 km) long on the Argolic gulf, between Nauplia and Halieis.

50. 2. **Halia:** the territory of Halieis (*Inv.* **349**), founded C5m and abandoned by *c.* the 280s (Jameson *et al.* 1994a, 88). See also Pharaklas 1973.   **voyage round:** PS uses *periplous* only four times of a region's coast rather than his usual *paraplous*, 'coastal voyage'. It is probably correct here, at 51 (Hermion), and at 57. 2 (Attica), since corruption of the common into the rare is unlikely (see, however, 67. 10 n.). At 106. 4 he uses *periplous* of a continent (in contrast to 69 and 111. 8) on the grounds that Asia is convex (*peripherēs*); but here he probably does not mean to say that Halieis has a convex coast: Attica does, but Hermion does not. It may reflect the style of his source or sources for this part of Greece (Shipley 2010, 104–5).

51. 1. Hermion: *Inv.* **350.** Territory: Pharaklas 1973.   **voyage round:** see n. on 50. 2.

51. 2. Skyllaion: the E extremity of Argolis. Since PS says it belongs to Troizen, he could have deferred it to 52; he may mention it early to define the Saronic gulf (a name he does not use). (Saronic gulf as region: Figueira 2004, 620.)   **Troizenia:** an advance mention (see previous n.).   **Sounion:** *c.*50 km ENE of Skyllaion.   **by this:** i.e. opposite Skyllaion, not opposite Sounion.   **Belbina:** *Agios Georgios,* halfway from Skyllaion to Sounion. The *polis* is *Inv.* **359.**

51. 3. 740 stades: this figure is too large for the SW side of the Saronic gulf, unless it includes indentations (Müller 45). See further on '1,140 stades' at 57. 2.   **very straight at the mouth:** the divergent coasts are straight, i.e. the Saronic has a wide mouth.

52. 1. Troizen: *Inv.* **357.** 'Troizenia', MS, probably reflecting late antique style. The *polis* is Troizen in pre-Hl sources. (On the area: Pharaklas 1972b.) PS omits Methana (*Inv.* **352;** Mee and Forbes 1997), though see n. on 46. 2 Anthana.

52. 2. Kalauria: *Inv.* **360.** (Territory: Pharaklas 1972b.)   *300* **stades:** some emend to 30 st., the distance from C. Skyllaion to Kalaureia; but corruption of τ (300) into λ (30) is not easy. Müller 45 prefers 300, noting that PS does not make Skyllaion the start of Troizen; either 80 st. for Hermione (51) is too large, or PS omits Troizenian territory up to Skyllaion.

53. Aigina: the island dominating the view from Athens; its *polis* is *Inv.* **358.** Its links with the Peloponnese were at least as strong as with Attica, which may be why it is treated here as lying off Kalaureia and Epidauros rather than Piraeus. Strabo even locates it 'in Epidauria', describing it between the Argolic Akte and Corinth (8. 6. 16). (History: Figueira 1981; Figueira 1991.)   **two harbours:** the second is presumably that in the E of the island, near the temple of Aphaia.

54. Epidauros: *Inv.* **348.** See 50. 1 n.   **a harbour:** really a bay, with shelter from all but the E wind.   **130 stades:** '30' (MS) is too short; either 130 or 230 is preferable.

55. ⟨the part⟩ towards the dawn: i.e. the E part of Korinthia (see 40). As with the 'sun' phrases at 47. 2, the phrase suggests PS is using a regional *periplous*.   **Kenchreiai:** Corinth's port on the Saronic gulf. A non-*polis*, Legon 2004, 466. (Different from the non-*polis* of that

name in Argolis, Piérart 2004, 601.)   **sanctuary of Poseidon:**
Isthmia, overlooking the Saronic gulf.   **the Peloponnesos ends:** see
40 n.   **Sidous ... Kremmyon:** dependent non-*polis* settlements of
Corinth E of the isthmus (Legon 2004, 466).

56. Megara: see 39 n.   **Nisaia:** the dependent port of Megara on the
Saronic gulf; Legon 2004, 463.   **Iapis:** probably the *Ammosoúra*,
descending to the sea W of Mt Kerata E of Megara (Chandler 1926, 12
and pl. 1). Iapis is otherwise recorded only by the poet Kallimachos
in C3 (Steph. Byz. on Iapis). This apparently obscure information
may point to PS using a local Attic or Megarian source, or drawing
on personal knowledge (Shipley 2010, 106–7). Until 104. 3 this is the
only statement of the form 'X is the border of Y'.

Barr. 59

57. 1. cities: PS is not calling Eleusis and other Attic demes *poleis*. He
is right to use this term, for Salamis was a *polis* (below). He probably
means to convey that Athens is a multi-*polis* region like certain
others (Shipley 2010, 103–4). But he also calls the region Attike three
times, 'the land of the Athenians' once, and in 59 Athenai: conscious
variatio, as elsewhere? (Name and extent of Attica, overview of
settlements: M. H. Hansen 2004a, 624–6.) PS mentions five non-*polis*
towns on the coast, but does not tell us (as in e.g. Arkadia and
Lakedaimon) that there are large towns inland. He may be
consciously selecting coastal fortifications, given the frequency of
'fort' in this section (Shipley 2010, 108).   **Eleusis ... a fort:** *Inv.* 362;
it has a *polis* no. in *Inv.* only because of its brief independence in 403–
401. PS is not saying it was a separate *polis* from Athens, as Salamis
was; he does not say it is the first (*prōtē*, feminine adjective) *polis* you
come to, but the place you encounter *first* (*prōton*, adverb). The
earliest fortifications are C6l (*OCD³*).   **Salamis:** *Inv.* 363. An Athenian cleruchy and, as such, a dependent *polis* of Athens rather than a
deme (Flensted-Jensen and Hansen 2007, 217; M. H. Hansen 1996, 30–
2).   **Peiraieus and the Legs:** the Long Walls were built *c.*460 and
rebuilt in 393 (*OCD³*). Another piece of local knowledge, perhaps.
Athenai: *Inv.* **361.   3 harbours:** Kantharos (the main one),
Mounichia, Zea. Thuc. 1. 93 also refers to three (not named).

57. 2. Anaphlystos: a major fort. Xen. *Poroi*, 4. 43, identifies it and
Thorikos as the two Athenian forts in the silver-mining district.
Sounion . . . Thorikos . . . Rhamnous: with Eleusis, Piraeus, and
Anaphlystos these are the major coastal fortifications. PS correctly
gives Thorikos two harbours, but omits that of Rhamnous.   **many
other harbours:** having named all the major ones, PS hints at special
knowledge, for the rest are decidedly minor. (For a possible list, and

for their naval and economic roles, see Shipley 2010, 109–10.) The emphatic placing of Delion as the first place in Boiotia (59) makes Oropos implicitly Athenian; its omission is odd, since having been Boiotian from 366 it was Athenian from 338 to 322 (Marcotte 1986, 171). PS's measurements of Attica are long enough to include it, and he was happy to include an obscure landmark to indicate the beginning of Attica (56). Perhaps he does not wish to remind Athenians of its recent loss and recovery (Shipley 2010, 107); or perhaps its status was not yet resolved when he wrote (in 338/7?).   **Voyage around:** *periplous* again; see 50. 2 n.   **1,140 . . . 490 . . . 650:** the second figure is 60 in the MS, impossibly short; the conjecture of 490 (Gail 1825) makes the total of the second and third figures correct (if the first is correct!) and conforms to geographical reality. PS gives only two other long but precise distances (divisible by 10 but not by 100), both in Greece (51. 3, 58. 3). They are probably totals of shorter distances—measured by sea, rather than on land by bematists or surveyors, or why are they not still more precise? Did PS have access to administrative documents? See further Shipley 2010, 105–6.   **Iapid territory:** an odd phrase if Iapis is merely a ravine or watercourse (see 56). Perhaps it was more than that; but PS does not normally name sub-regions.

Barr. 60

58. 1. Kyklades: PS fails to remind us that he covered the southern (Dorian) Cyclades earlier (48). Here he covers the Ionian, though he does not call them that. Again he mentions only islands with *poleis*. As at 48, the text at first sight is arranged as a voyage, with most islands arranged in an anti-clockwise tour from Keos to Andros, followed by a short hop to the non-Cycladic islands of Euboia and the (mod.) *Northern Sporades*. But it is not a real route. Ios and Amorgos, which could easily have been fitted into this circuit, are delayed to a point between Andros and Euboia; Ikaros is appended to them. The last three, though all Ionian, make an uneasy trio. Ikaros had much closer connections to Samos (98. 3) than to the Cyclades. The sequence Delos–Rhene–Syros–Mykonos is also impractical; a sailor approaching from Naxos would prefer Mykonos–Delos–Rhene–Syros or the converse. Once again PS arranges his material not navigationally but to give the reader a mental map (see 48 n.). Rather than an Athenocentric perspective (the view of Counillon 2001b, 17–19), he may have chosen a starting-point near Attica in order to make a topographical segue (as with 48 Melos). He makes it easier to visualize the relationship by starting, not with the nearest island to Attica, obscure Helene, but with the nearest well-known island, Keos. This entails a 180 degree 'about turn' to reach Kythnos.

Keos … four-citied: the island had four *poleis* but is also referred to elsewhere as a single political entity. Koressia, Ioulis, and Karthaia, but probably not Poieëssa, formed a short-lived federation in the 360s (Reger 2004, 748). PS makes a clockwise circuit (cf. 13. 1 n.) from the point nearest Attica.   ⟨**Poieëssa, a city**⟩ **with a harbour:** *Inv.* **494;** a scribe has failed to copy the text between two similar words (by *saut du même au meme*, West 1973, 24–5), from -πολις to πόλις. Marcotte 1986, 179–82, argues that it may have ceased to be a *polis* c.375–330, so that 'four-citied' was purely conventional (as in Dion. Kall. 135 much later); but PS is not seriously inaccurate, for it survived as a town, may have been fortified in 354–338, and reverted to *polis* status at least by C4l/C3e (*Inv.*).   **Koressia:** *Inv.* **493.** A dependency of Ioulis for a time in C4s (Reger 2004, 750), but still a *polis*. (Site, territory: Cherry *et al.* 1991, esp. Whitelaw 1991.)   **Ioulis … Karthaia:** *Inv.* **491, 492.   Helene:** *Makronisos.* The *polis* (not mentioned) is *Inv.* **479.   Kythnos … Seriphos … Siphnos:** the *poleis* (not mentioned) are *Inv.* **501, 517,** and **519.   Paros … two harbours:** the *polis* (not mentioned) is *Inv.* **509.** The main harbour is there; *Inv.* makes no suggestion as to the second; it was perhaps at the *Naousa* bay in the N. 'Enclosed' means a secure naval harbour (Counillon 1998b).   **Naxos … Delos:** the *poleis* (not mentioned) are *Inv.* **507, 478.   Rhene:** usually Rhenaia or Rheneia (the *polis*, not mentioned, is *Inv.* **514**).   **Syros:** the *polis* (not mentioned) is *Inv.* **523.** In several islands, PS has omitted mention of a *polis* or *poleis*; contrast the repetitive list at 66. 4. Since he mentions some, the inconsistency may simply be due to poor transmission.   **Mykonos … two-citied:** two *poleis* are confirmed by *Syll.*³ 1024 (C3l; Reger 2001; cf. Flensted-Jensen and Hansen 2007, 217). The main one is *Inv.* **506;** the other is unknown but was probably at *Palaiokastro.*   **Tenos … Andros:** the *poleis* (not mentioned) are *Inv.* **525, 475.**

58. 2. **under these:** ὑπό certainly does not imply the use of a map. It may mean 'beyond', in the sense that things further away appear to be lower (a nautical usage?). PS otherwise uses ὑπό in a spatial sense only at 98. 2 (with accusative rather than dative), where 'beyond' seems meant (and ὑπέρ might be conjectured) and 108. 3 (with dative), meaning 'under' (in the lee of islets). See 58. 1 n.   **other islands:** see 48 n.   **Ios … Homer is buried:** the *polis* (not mentioned) is *Inv.* **484.** Strabo reports the same of Homer, but with 'some say' (10. 5. 1). It is odd that PS puts Ios outside the Kyklades, as it lies within the quadrilateral defined by Paros, Naxos, Sikinos, and Thera.   **Amorgos … three-citied:** they are Aigiale (*Inv.* **471**), Arkesine (**472**), and Minoa (**473**). *Tripolis* is also used of Peparethos, 58. 4; Karpathos, 99. 3; the 'triple city' of Rhodes, 99. 3; and twice in

Syria–Phoenicia, 104. 2.   Here we leave the Cyclades, as usually defined.   **Ikaros ... two-cited:** included here, rather than with Samos at 98. 3, perhaps because it is visible from the eastern Cyclades. The *poleis* are Oine (*Inv.* **480**) and Therma (**481**). Pliny 4. 12/68 describes it as having two cities out of an original three (unnamed); Strabo 14. 1. 19 names Oinoe and Drakanon.

Map 9. The SW Aegean.

58. 3. Euboia: on its name and urban history, see in brief Reber *et al.* 2004, 643–4.   **Karystos ... Eretria ... Chalkis:** *Inv.* **373, 370,** and **365**. **Hestiaia:** or Histiaia; *Inv.* **372**. Also known as Ore(i)os (Theopompos F 387 = Strabo 10. 1. 3); both names were used in C4m. PS may be the last occurrence of the toponym (*Inv.* cites a C4f treaty), though the *ethnikon* Histiaiëus occurs in the Hl period.   **Zeus Kenaios:** at C. Kenaion.   **Geraistos:** a non-*polis* (Reber *et al.* 2004, 645).   **1,350 stades:** see n. on '1,140 stades' at 57. 2.

58. 4. by Eretria Skyros: surprising at first sight, as they are on opposite coasts of Euboia; but Eretria's territory extended to the NE coast. The *polis* of Skyros is *Inv.* **521.** PS lists this and the next three Northern Sporades in geographical order from ESE to WNW, and ignores smaller islets.   **Ikos ... two-citied:** *Alonnisos*; its main *polis* is *Inv.* **482.** As Flensted-Jensen and Hansen 2007, 217, observe, there is no other evidence for a second town, though Reger 2004, 741, cautions that sources and archaeology are minimal.   **Peparethos ... three-citied:** *Skopelos* I.; the main *polis* is *Inv.* **511,** plus *Inv.* **510** Panormos and **512** Seleinous. The cases of Amorgos (58. 2) and Ikos (previous n.) show that it may only be a lack of inscriptions that makes PS the sole evidence for their *polis* status (Flensted-Jensen and Hansen 2007, 217–18).   **Skiathos ... two-citied:** the main *polis* is *Inv.* **520.** As for Peparethos (previous n.), there is no other evidence that there were ever two urban centres at the same time; but we know that an older centre, Palaiskiathos, existed in 408/7 (*IG* i³ 109; Flensted-Jensen and Hansen 2007, 217).   **the mainland, from where I turned away:** at 58. 1.

Barr. 55

59. Boiotoi ... this sea: the words 'these people, too, come down to this sea' would most naturally refer back to the Athenians (57), but it would be a pointless comment. A simple emendation (see app. crit.) gives 'these people come down to this sea as well', a reference back to the other Boiotian coast at 38. (Perhaps a copyist, faced with οὗτοι καὶ, was influenced by διήκουσι δὲ καὶ οὗτοι at 17 and οἰκοῦσι δὲ καὶ οὗτοι at 30–1.) See also n. on 61 Phokeis.   **first:** adverb (as at 57. 1), not adjective: Delion is the first place, not the first sanctuary, in Boiotia.   **Delion ... Aulis:** non-*poleis*, M. H. Hansen 2004b, 433. **Euripos, a fort:** Strabo 9. 2. 8 refers to towers either side of the narrows, possibly built by Kassandros *c.*313 BC (Diod. 19. 77. 4). But PS may record earlier fortifications, though the punctuation, and therefore the sense, is uncertain.   **Anthedon:** *Inv.* **200.   Thebai:** *Inv.* **221.** Its inclusion implies a date before September 335 (date from Bosworth 1994, 797) or after 316 (Marcotte 1986, 170–1).   **Thespiai ... Orchomenos:** *Inv.* **222, 213.   other cities:** the important ones are all inland (e.g. *Inv.* **220** Tanagra, **222** Thespiai, **198** Akraiphia).

60. Lokroi: though PS does not say so, these are the eastern or Opountian Lokrians; see n. on Opous, below. For the West Lokrians, see 36. (Region: Nielsen 2000; Nielsen 2004b, 664–5; Fossey 1990; Katsonopoulou 1990.) Cary 67–8 stresses the limited coastal plains and Lokris's role as a 'land of passage'. (I thank T. H. Nielsen for help on East Lokris.)   **Larymna:** *Inv.* **383.** Its inclusion in Lokris is further evidence that PS is writing in or after 338, since the Boiotians lost Larymna (which Epameinondas had fortified) from 338 to *c.*270

(Marcotte 1986, 171).   **Kynos:** *Inv.* **382.** See also n. on Alope, below.
Opous: *Inv.* **386** (*Atalandi*). Despite its large territory and hegemonic
role in East Lokris (Nielsen 2000), PS does not use the term
'Opountian Lokrians' (e.g. Hdt. 7. 203; Thuc. 2. 32. 1).   **Alope:** *Inv.*
378; near the coast, like Kynos; so both can be described as 'by
Euboia' (if that indicates a coastal location and is not meant to
distinguish the East from the West Lokrians).   **many others:** e.g.
Alponos (*Inv.* **379**), Halai (**380**), Knemis or Knemides (**381**), Naryka
(**384**), Nikaia (**385**), Skarpheia (**387**), and Thronion (**388;** but see 61 n.).
See n. on 35 'many other cities'.   **200 stades:** the same as for eastern Phokis (61); both are too short. The two regions also have equal
paraploi for their W coasts at 36–7, but in the form 'half of a day'.

61. Phokeis … this sea: 'these people, too' would most naturally
refer to the Boiotians (59) and Lokrians (60). Perhaps (as suggested at
59) we should read οὗτοι καὶ, referring back to the Phokians at 37.
Thronion: so MS, apparently referring to the East Lokrian *polis* of this
name N of Mt Knemis (*Inv.* **388**), not named in 60. Alternatively, this
conceals Teithronion (*Inv.* **194**), an inland Phokian *polis* S of Knemis.
The Phokians did capture Thronion from the East Lokrians in 353
(Diod. 16. 33. 3), but presumably lost it, at the latest, when Philip II
defeated them in 346. Since PS could be using an out-of-date source,
both readings are possible and we should not alter the text. (I thank
T. H. Nielsen for discussion.)   **Knemis:** *Inv.* **381** Knemi(de)s on the
coast, though Knemis may be a cape (Serv. *Aen.* 3. 399) and a mountain (previous n.) rather than a *polis*. Perhaps, as may be the case
with 47. 4 Itanos, PS fails to make clear that a *polis* and a promontory
share a name.   **Elateia … Panopeus:** *Inv.* **180, 190** (Phanoteus).
other cities: PS names Delphoi and Antikyra at 37, reserving those N
of Mt Parnassos for the present section. Among inland *poleis* he
might have named *Inv.* **172** Amphikaia (or Amphikleia) and **187** Neon
(or Tithorea).   **200 stades:** see n. on '200 stades' at §60.

62. 1. We enter the group of nine regions that, in Hl times, were seen
as parts of Thessaly but which Cl sources treat separately (Decourt *et
al.* 2004, 676). PS mentions all except Athamania, far inland to the W.
Since he gives only one *paraplous* (64. 2) and repeatedly uses the
Meliac and Pagasetic gulfs as reference points, he seems to regard all
these areas as closely connected. This passage may derive from a
specific source, but there is no over-arching label as for the Illyrians
(22), and no summative *paraplous*.   **Melieis:** the region is Malis or
Melis. See Decourt *et al.* 2004, 685–6 (region), 709–13 (*poleis*).
Melieus gulf: also Maliakos Kolpos (Maliacus Sinus, *Barr.*); 'Maliaios'
at 63. Before naming Malian *poleis*, PS inserts those of Doris (see next
n.).   **Limodorieis:** 'Starving Dorians'; not in *Barr.* The three *poleis*

are not in Malis but in the small, landlocked region of Doris SW of the Malian gulf, the legendary homeland of Dorians everywhere (Dorieis). (Region: Rousset 2004a, 674.) It was not part of 'greater' Thessaly. The MS does not mention the Dorieis, only the possibly fictitious or facetious Limodorieis. According to late sources (e.g. Ps.-Plutarch, *Proverbs the Alexandrians Used*, 1. 34 (Leutsch and Schneidewin 1839, 326), the name refers to a legend, unconnected with this region, about Dorians leaving the Peloponnese for Rhodos and Knidos during a famine (the Rhodian *tripolis* features in the story, as at §99 below). Müller 49 would remove the comment as an interpolation; but if both Dorieis and Limodorieis originally stood in the text, the former could easily have been omitted during copying. Doris comes earlier than one might expect: it would normally be reached from a point W of Trachis or Herakleia (below). **Erineos, Boion, and Kytinion:** *Inv.* **391, 390,** and **392;** in Doris, see previous n. **Thermopylai:** the first place PS names that is genuinely in Malis, as are the next four. **Trachis:** *Inv.* **432,** the predecessor of Herakleia (below); they may never have co-existed, so PS may combine information of different dates (Decourt *et al.* 2004, 713). Cf. 13. 3 Tauromenion and Naxos. (Not the unlocated Trachis in Phokis, *Inv.* **195,** not included by PS.) **Oite:** not a *polis*, but a mountain inland. PS may mean the people of the area, the Oitaioi: see Decourt *et al.* 2004, 684–5 (region), 709 (*poleis*). **Herakleia:** *Inv.* **430,** founded for the Malians by the Spartans *c*.426 (Thuc. 3. 92) near, or on the site of, Trachis (see above). From 370 both Malian and Oitaian (Xen. *Hell.* 6. 4. 27), but by 323 probably Oitaian (Decourt *et al.* 2004, 685). **Spercheios:** a major river, discharging into the W (inner) end of the Malian gulf.

62. 2. ⟨**Malieis**⟩: see 62. 1 n. (Müller 49 rejects the idea that one of the references to 'Malieis' conceals 'Lamieis', the men of Lamia.) **Lamia … Echinos:** *Inv.* **431, 429** (*Achinos*), both N of the Spercheios. **against … live:** one of the few places (with Thuc. 6. 86, 7. 27) where the rare verb ἐποικέω has a sense stronger than merely 'settle in'. **Ainianes:** also at 35. PS jumps back S of the Spercheios to Ainis, a small inland region W of Mt Oita and Doris, and S of Thessalia. See Decourt *et al.* 2004, 683–4 (region), 708–9 (*poleis*; PS names none); and first n. on 62. 1.

63. Achaioi Phthiotai: mainly in the uplands of the Othrys range, inland and N from the Maliac gulf, with a short coast. See Decourt *et al.* 2004, 686–8 (region), 713–18 (*poleis*). **Pagasetic gulf:** later Demetriac gulf, after the C4l city of Demetrias. **halfway up:** the language reveals PS's concern with the extent and relationships of topographic units rather than navigational landmarks. **Antrones:** *Inv.* **433** (*Glypha/Achilleio*). **Larissa:** *Inv.* **437** (*Pelasgia*; distinct from 64. 1

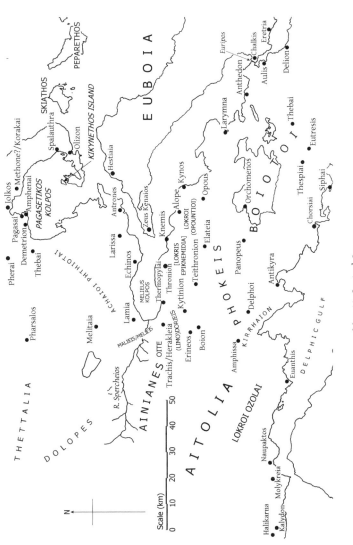

Map 10. Central Greece.

Larissa); also Larissa Kremaste. Though set back from the coast on a mountain spur, it should have preceded Antrones; one would not land at Antrones to visit it, for a high ridge separates them.   **Melitaia:** *Inv.* **438** (*Avaritsa*; 39° 2′ N, 22° 27′ E). A surprising place to mention, far inland to the N of Othrys, overlooking the inland basin of Achaia Phthiotis.   **Demetrion:** another name for Pyrasos (*Inv.* **442**; *Kantiraga*) at the NW corner of the Pagasetic gulf. 'Demetrion' (apparently current in Strabo's day, 9. 5. 14) reflects the well-known sanctuary of Demeter (not e.g. the C4l city of Demetrias, named after Demetrios I).   **Thebai:** *Inv.* **444,** or Thebai Phthiotides, behind the wide coastal plain W of the Pagasetic gulf (*Akitsi/Mikrothives*, 39° 15′ N, 22° 46′ E, rather than at *Nea Anchialos*).   **other cities:** despite including Melitaia (above), PS omits other inland *poleis*: Ekkarra and Kypaira further W, Proerna and Thaumakoi further N, and more surprisingly Peuma closer to the coast (*Inv.* **434, 436, 441, 443,** and **439**).

64. 1. Thettalia: Attic spelling; also Thessaliotis. The heartland of 'greater' Thessaly (see n. on 62. 1), a large, landlocked region with extensive inland arable and a continental climate. PS includes inland cities in the fertile heartland (Cary 62–3). See (Decourt *et al.* 2004, 677–83 (region), 691–707 (*poleis*).   **Amphenai:** *Inv.* **393** (*Sesklou?* or *Soros, Barr.*), only *c.*3 km beyond Demetrion (63) and *c.*1.6 km from Pagasai (but see next n.).   **Pagasai:** *Inv.* **407** (*Soros*); see previous n. A good harbour (*Inv.*).   **Pherai:** *Inv.* **414**; *Barr.* D2 (*Velestino*).   We turn away from the coast, as PS says, and move inland to Pelinnaion in the NW of the Thessalian plain, then halfway back to the coast at Skotoussa and Krannon (SW of Larissa).   **Larissa, Pharsalos, Kierion, Pelinnaion, Skotousa, and Krannon:** *Inv.* **401** (distinct from 63 Larissa), **413, 398, 409, 415,** and **400** (also Ephyra).   **other cities:** *Inv.* lists 25 in Thessaly proper (nos **393–417**), of which PS has named 6. Some are very closely spaced.   **above:** i.e. behind, inland from. PS rightly stresses the vast extent of Thessalia proper.   **Dolopes:** a hill people S of the plain of Thessaliotis.   **Magnetes:** see 65. 1 n. **Tempe:** the gorge of the Peneios (*Barr.* 55 D1). An advance mention. Although 'greater' Thessaly (see above) has a coast W of Magnesia, Thessalia proper had sea access only here.

64. 2. Kikynethos: *Inv.* **451,** attested only here and in Artemidoros (cited at Strabo 9. 5. 15); somewhere on the islet in the SE corner of the gulf of Pagasai (*Barr.* 55 E3 Cicynethus; *Palaia Trikeri*).

65. 1. of the Magnetes: in the MS the name is in the genitive case; but 'a community belonging to the Magnesians' (for this usage cf. 70) is false, for the *poleis* are those of the Magnesians themselves. Changing to the nominative case makes the statement true (literally 'the *ethnos* that is the Magnetes'). For Magnesia see Decourt *et al.* 2004, 688–9 (region), 718–21 (*poleis*). It is formed by a mountain range *c*.65 km long, parallel to the shore, cutting off Thessalia proper from the Aegean except at the N end (vale of Tempe, see 64. 1).   **Iolkos, Methone, Korakai, Spalauthra, Olizon:** *Inv.* **449** (at *Volos*), **454** (*Nevestiki, Barr.*), **452** (*Nevestiki, Inv.*; or unlocated, Fossey and Morin 2000, 834), **458,** and **455.** With Olizon we have turned the corner as we exit the Pagasetic gulf.   **Tisai:** 'Isai', MS; Ap. Rhod. 1. 568 mentions a Cape Tisaia (not noted in *Inv.*).   **Meliboia:** *Inv.* **453** (either *Kastro Velika, Inv., c.*39° 44′ N, or unlocated, Fossey and Morin 2000, 835).   **Rhizous:** *Inv.* **457.**   **Eurymenai:** *Inv.* **447,** 'at the entrance to the Tempe valley at the site traditionally identified with Homolion'; or to the SE below Mt Ossa, *Barr.*   **Amyros:** *Inv.* **445,** inland. 'Myrai', MS; restored on the basis of Decourt *et al.* 2004, 718. It more naturally precedes Rhizous.   **Perrhaiboi:** Perrhaibia is an inland region N of Thessaly proper. Although he has named several cities in Thessaly, PS is silent here. See Decourt *et al.* 2004, 689-90 (region), 721–7 (11 *poleis*).

65. 2. Hellas is continuous: we might expect a mention, here or at 65. 1, of the R. Peneios and the *polis* of Homolion, both named at 33. 2 when PS defined 'continuous Hellas' (see n. there for the link with Phileas). But Homolion is absent, and the Peneios named almost casually at the start of Macedonia (66. 1). We need not suppose (with Fabricius) that both have dropped out. Rather, the coordination between the passages proves the unity of the *periplous*: at 66. 1 PS expects us to recall his earlier remark. The omission of Homolion at 65. 1 remains surprising, as it was explicitly Magnesian at 33. 2; in this case MS corruption may be to blame (there is corruption at 65. 2, though we would look for Homolion at 65. 1).   **probably . . . Hellas:** ἐπιεικῶς in Cl authors has two main senses, 'fairly' (i.e. 'approximately') and 'probably' (LSJ on ἐπιεικής III. 1–2). The latter seems appropriate here, the former at 113. 1. The text cannot be restored with certainty but the sense seems to be that, though there is some dispute, Magnesia's coast is rightly included in continuous Hellas. (The received text of Dion. Kall. 35–6 implies that Phileas did not put Magnesia in Hellas; but Marcotte 1990, following Leue 1884, acutely replaces 'Magnesia' with 'Macedonia', so this is irrelevant to 65. 2.)

66–9. MACEDONIA TO THE TANAÏS

The account of Macedonia, Thrake, and Skythia is spare, with one historical note (67. 2), several major rivers, one mountain (Olympos being omitted at the start), and a striking three-part summative *paraplous* of Thrake. PS calls some *poleis* Hellenic once more, but not systematically: in Thrake he omits to describe as Hellenic all the *poleis* from Abdera to Selymbria. See also next n. PS gives no sense that Chalkidike has a special identity, failing to name it or two of its three peninsulas.

Map 11. Northern Greece and Macedonia.

66. 1. In Macedonia the *poleis* PS calls Hellenic (the majority) are separate from the Macedonian state; the rest (Dion, Herakleion, Aloros, Pella, Therme) are within it (Hatzopoulos 1996, 472–3; Flensted-Jensen and Hansen 2007, 220–1). In reality the former, particularly in Chalkidike (66. 3), were not independent after 348; PS may be making a nationalistic point.   **Peneios:** see n. on 65. 2 Hellas.   **gulf of Therma:** *Barr.* 50 C4 Thermaicus Sinus.

66. 2. **Herakleion:** *Inv.* **537.**   **Dion:** *Inv.* **534** (not Euboian Dion, *Inv.* **368,** or Chalkidic, **569**). Named after Zeus, whose sanctuary was a chief cult place of Macedonia. PS probably means us to understand that Dion was a Macedonian rather than Hellenic *polis*, since he calls the next place a Hellenic *polis* (Flensted-Jensen and Hansen 2007,

220–1). Dion is in the original Macedonian heartland of Pieria. PS does not mention Mt Olympos (2,919 m), overlooking Herakleion and Dion on the W.   **Pydna:** *Inv.* **544.** Sometimes independent; allied with Athens from 364 (or 363) to 357, when Philip II recaptured it (*Inv.*). This is the first use of 'Hellenic city' since 33. 1 Ambrakia. **Methone:** *Inv.* **541.** A Greek colony destroyed by Philip 353, but called a *polis* by Strabo 7, fr. 22.   **Haliakmon:** meeting the sea just N of Methone.   **Aloros:** little-known, *Inv.* **532.** Its *polis* status is certain only for the Hl period (Flensted-Jensen and Hansen 2007, 219) but likely for C4 (*Inv.*).   **Loudias:** 'Lydias', MS, probably a scribal error, though 'Loudias' is attested only later (Strabo 7, frs 20, 22, 23). **Pella … royal seat:** *Inv.* **543.** A Paionian town where Ionians settled in the Ar period; residence of the kings from Amyntas III, *c*.393–370. Philip II built a palace; but PS may mean the earlier palace of Archelaos (Allain 168).   **upstream:** Strabo 7, fr. 22, gives the distance as 120 st.   **Axios … Echedoros:** the *Axios* (*Vardar*) and Echeidoros (*Gallikos*).   **Therme:** *Inv.* **552** (either *Thessaloniki* or *Mikro Karabournaki* to the S), in Mygdonia, N of Chalkidike. Like Pydna, a *polis* with separatist ambitions (*Inv.*). On Mygdonia see Flensted-Jensen 2004b, 810 (region), 816–19 (*poleis*).   **Aineia:** *Inv.* **557,** founded by Aineias (Aeneas). A cape at Ps.-Skymnos 627–8.

66. 3. Chalkidike contains one-sixteenth of all Greek *poleis* (*Inv.* **556–621**). PS does not name it or differentiate it from Macedonia; perhaps because it had been conquered by Philip in 348, though elsewhere he seems to be anti-Macedonian. He names the W arm, Pallene, but not Sithonia and Athos (or Akte), though he mentions Mt Athos. (See Flensted-Jensen 2004b, 810–14, region; 821–48, *poleis*.) Several *poleis* allegedly destroyed by Philip (including Mekyberna, Akanthos, Torone, and Aphytis) remained in existence (*OCD*[3] on Chalcidice). Their inclusion, therefore, does not refute the case for dating the work to the 330s.   **Pallene:** the W arm of Chalkidike.   **Potidaia:** *Inv.* **598.** Reportedly destroyed by Philip *c*.356, when its land was given to Olynthos, it was refounded in 316 as Kassandreia (Strabo 7, fr. 25). Either PS's information is out of date or Poteidaia, like Mekyberna (below), survived as a settlement. See n. on Skione, below.   **Mende:** *Inv.* **584.** See n. on Skione, below.   **Aphytis:** *Inv.* **563.** PS's contemporary Aristotle (*Pol.* 6. 4) notes that its population is large in relation to its territory (cf. Nagle 2006, 48–52). See n. on Skione, below. **Thrambeïs:** *Inv.* **616** Therambos (Hdt. 7. 123. 1). See next n.   **Skione:** *Inv.* **609.** In strict coastal order one expects Poteidaia, Mende, Skione, Thrambeïs, Aphytis. Neither are we zigzagging down the cape, or Skione would precede Thrambeïs.   **Kanastraion:** the tip of Pallene.

66. 4. outside the isthmus: the paragraphing adopted in this edition assumes that these words govern only Olynthos and Mekyberna; but it is possible that PS did not understand the relationship of the towns on Pallene to the others in Chalkidike. **Olynthos:** *Inv.* **588.** Destroyed by Philip II in 348 and never again a *polis*, though it endured as a settlement (Flensted-Jensen 2004b, 835). (Domestic buildings: Cahill 2002.) **Mekyberna:** *Inv.* **583,** probably the harbour of Olynthos. **Sermylia:** *Inv.* **604.** **Sermylic gulf:** *Barr.* 51 B4 Toronaikos Kolpos. PS fails to name the middle peninsula of Chalkidike, Sithonia. **Torone:** *Inv.* **620.** **Dion:** *Inv.* **569.** PS again jumps silently between peninsulas, not naming Athos (cf. below). See next n. **Thyssos:** *Inv.* **618.** Given its location, PS could have named it first if he had been following a strict *periplous.* **Kleonai:** *Inv.* **580.** **Athos:** the peak (1,978 m) at the end of Athos, the E arm of Chalkidike, which PS does not name as such. Hdt 7. 22 notes its size and fame. Again PS does not follow a coastal *periplous*; if anything, he makes an anti-clockwise circuit, starting from and returning to the NE coast near the mainland. **Akrothoöi:** *Inv.* **560.** **Charadrous:** *Inv.* **565;** unlocated, Borza 2000, 781; recorded only by PS; presumably between Akrothoöi and Olophyxos. **Olophyxos:** *Inv.* **587;** perhaps *Vatopedi* or *Iviron* (Flensted-Jensen 2004b, 833), in which case we have almost returned to our starting-point, Dion. **Akanthos:** *Inv.* **559.** Given its location, PS could have said 'outside the isthmus', as in the case of Pallene. **Alapta:** *Inv.* **561;** unlocated, Borza 2000, 780). **Arethousa:** *Inv.* **546;** may have existed in C5. Here we move far beyond the Athos peninsula into Mygdonia, at the NE limit of Chalkidike. Surprisingly, given his philosophical links (Introduction, VII), PS omits Stagiros or Stageira (*Inv.* **613**), the home of Aristotle, on the coast before Arethousa. **Bolbe Lake:** upstream from Arethousa. **Apollonia:** *Inv.* **545,** S of L. Bolbe (rather than the Apollonia on the sea coast E of the Strymon).

66. 5. many others: PS names 27 *poleis* in what he calls Macedonia (including Chalkidike); *Inv.* lists 17 in Macedonia and 82 in 'Thrace west of the Strymon' (including 8 in Mygdonia and 66 in Chalkidike). See n. on 35 'many other cities'. **Strymon:** the naming of this river as the E border of Macedonia has been thought consistent with a date of composition in or before 335 (Marcotte 1986, 171); but it is now clear that even after Alexander's death the Strymon was regarded as the E limit of Macedonia (Hatzopoulos 1996, 185–6). **two days:** but Müller 53–4 reckons 3,300 st. from the Peneios to the Strymon (not allowing for the flexions of the coast as PS purports to do), and suggests 4 days and 4 nights.

67. 1. Thrake: it has an Aegean and a Black Sea coast (note also Bithynian Thrake in Asia Minor, 92). On its component regions, see Flensted-Jensen 2004b, 810–14; Loukopoulou 2004a, 870–1; 2004b, 854–6; 2004c, 900–2; Archibald 2004, 885–92; Loukopoulou and Łaitar 2004, 912–13.   **Istros:** the *Danube*, named at 20 and here in advance of its proper place (see 67. 9–10; also 68. 3, 69).   **Euxeinos Pontos:** PS uses this name only here; elsewhere just Pontos (20. 1, 67. 7–70 *passim*, 92 *bis*, 102. 2). See n. on 67. 9.   **Amphipolis:** *Inv.* 553, in Bisaltia, N of Mygdonia; founded 437/6 from Athens near the existing settlement of Ennea Hodoi (Thuc. 4. 102. 3).   **Phagres:** *Inv.* 636. Founded by people expelled from Pieria by Perdikkas I of Macedonia (Thuc. 2. 99. 3).   **Galepsos:** *Inv.* 631. (Not Galepsos, or Gale, on Sithonia, *Inv.* 571.) **Oisyme:** *Inv.* 635; originally Thasian; later, under Macedonian rule, named Emathia.   **Thasioi:** 'Sagioi', MS, would be the Thracian Saioi (cf. Archilochos fr. 5 West); but the 'trading-towns' named are Greek *poleis*.   **Thasos . . . enclosed:** the *polis* is *Inv.* 526. 'Enclosed' means a secure naval harbour (Counillon 1998b).

67. 2. Neapolis: *Inv.* 634, on the coast opposite Thasos. (Not Neapolis on Pallene, *Inv.* 586.)   **by this:** these words may seem to go with Datos, which follows; but Counillon 1998a, 116, argues that they refer to the last-named place, Neapolis (cf. 111. 7), so that PS puts Neapolis opposite Thasos (Datos and Neapolis being mainland cities). Except at 26. 3 and 108. 5, PS always uses such a phrase of an island and the mainland to which it relates.   **Daton:** *Inv.* 629 Daton or Datos; 'Datos', as a city name, replaced the regional name 'Daton' (Counillon 1998a, 119–21), which denoted the Angites valley (Borza 2000, 774). The colony postdates *c.*361 (see next n.; Desanges 92; Counillon 1998a, 117 and n. 8). Its foundation cannot, however, date PS's work to *c.*360 (Counillon 1998a, 123 n. 39, *contra* Fabre 1965).   **Kallistratos of Athenai:** a leading politician of the Second Athenian Confederacy, exiled in the late 360s. For his city-founding in Thrace, see Isoc. *De pace*, 24. Some see his inclusion as evidence that PS was Athenian (Marcotte 1986; Counillon 1998a, 124); but, like other such evidence, it is consistent with his having merely lived at or near Athens. He is not writing for Athenians alone, or he would have written 'of Aphidna', not 'of Athenai'. Probably he is writing for intellectual readers who included non-Athenians (Introduction, VII). **river Nestos:** opposite Thasos, E of Neapolis.   **Abdera:** *Inv.* 640. **Koudetos river:** not in *Barr.* (unlocated, Borza 2000, 781). Possibly the Kampsatos, Hdt. 7. 109.   **with . . . Dikaia and Maroneia:** *Inv.* 643 and 646. Despite the repeated 'and' or 'with' (*kai*), by which PS often indicates a close connection, Maroneia is not near the Koudetos.

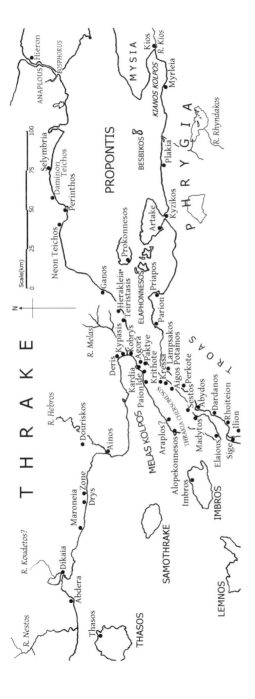

Map 12. Aegean Thrace and Propontis.

67. 3. Samothrake: the *polis* is *Inv.* **515** (not mentioned, but PS includes Aegean islands only if they have *poleis*).   **Drys, Zone:** *Inv.* **644** and **651**.   **Douriskos:** a non-*polis*, Loukopoulou 2004a, 871; a few km inland on the W bank of the Hebros (in mod. Greece).   **Hebros:** the major river of this region.   **Ainos:** *Inv.* **641,** at the mouth of the Hebros (on the E or Turkish bank).   **forts of the Ainioi:** i.e. in the territory of Ainos (above).   **Melas gulf:** 'Black gulf', *c.*60 km E of Ainos, next to the Thracian Chersonese.   **Melas river:** 'Black river'; *Kavak Suyu*?   **Deris:** *Inv.* **662** (*Kocaçesme*?). See n. on Kypasis, below. **Kobrys:** a non-*polis*, Loukopoulou 2004c, 903; 1.6 km S of the *Kavak Suyu*. See n. on Kypasis, below.   **Kardianoi:** see n. on 67. 5 Kardia. **Kypasis:** a non-*polis*, Loukopoulou 2004c, 903; 3 km N of the *Kavak Suyu*). Deris, Kobrys, and Kypasis are at the head of the Melas gulf, but Kypasis is between the other two.

67. 4. Imbros: strategically situated near the Thracian Chersonese; usually an Athenian possession. The *polis* is *Inv.* **483.**   **Lemnos:** its two *poleis* are not named (*Inv.* **502** Myrina, **503** Hephaistia).

67. 5. Thrakian Chersonesos: the Thracian Chersonese (*Gallipoli* peninsula).   **Kardia:** *Inv.* **665;** resettled C6m from Athens.   **Ide ... Paion:** *Inv.* **664, 670;** otherwise unknown.   **Alopekonnesos:** *Inv.* **659.** The preceding four places are in the correct sequence on the Aegean (NW) shore of the Chersonesos.   **Araplos:** *Inv.* **660;** unlocated, Borza 2000, 780; otherwise unknown. Loukopoulou 2004c, 903, lists Drabos (a possible reading here) as a non-*polis* (cf. Strabo, 7 fr. 52; Müller 55); but Drabos should precede Alopekonnesos (Allain 172). **Elaious:** *Inv.* **663.** Settled from Athens in C6m on a C7l site. **Madytos, and Sestos:** *Inv.* **669, 672;** in the straits, before and after the opening of the Hellespont. See next n.   **Propontis:** PS does not name the Hellespont as separate from, or a part of, the Propontis, but simply makes Sestos the start of the latter. He maintains a strict *periplous* organization, interposing his account of the Black Sea between his description of the N and S shores (though he mentions Sestos again at 94 despite it being on the 'wrong' shore). In this instance, then, he does not privilege topography over coastal contiguity; perhaps because all these places are subject to an overriding division between Europe and Asia.   **6 stades:** the Hellespont narrows to 1.4 km (*c.*7½ st.) at a point *c.*5 km S of Sestos. Hdt. 7. 34 says 7 st.; the next earliest source, Xen. *Hell.* 4. 8. 5, gives 8 st.; most ancient authors follow Hdt. (Müller 55). See also n. on '7 stades' (referring to the Bosporos) at 67. 8.   **Aigos Potamos:** 'Goat's River'. There is no definite instance of PS putting *potamos* ('river') after its name, so we may treat Potamos as part of the name here. Though PS does not say so, Aigos Potamos or Potamoi is also a *polis*, *Inv.* **658.** He locates the next three places 'within' it, i.e. further into the Propontis. See n. on Krithote, below.   **Kressa:** *Inv.* **666**, not definitely attested elsewhere. See next n.   **Krithote ... Paktyë:** *Inv.* **667, 671**; both founded by Miltiades in C6l (cf. Strabo 7 fr. 55; Pliny 4. 11/48). The preceding four places are in the correct order.

67. 6. 40 stades: same figure in Strabo 7, fr. 54.   **Agora:** 'Marketplace'. *Inv.* **661** Chersonesos or Agora (settled from Athens in C6l by Miltiades, Hdt. 6. 38. 1); *Barr.* 51 H3 (*Bolayır*).   **stades, 400:** 'slightly more than 400', Strabo 7, fr. 52.

67. 7. Thrakian forts: i.e. Greek forts in Thrake, not forts of the (non-Greek) Thracians.

Barr. 22, 52–3

Leuke Akte: 'White Headland'. Not in *Barr.*   **Teiristasis:** *Inv.* **681** Tyrodiza.   **Herakleia:** a non-*polis*, Loukopoulou and Łaitar 2004, 913 (*Heraklitza/Erikli*; but in *Barr. Erikli* is *Inv.* **677** Neapolis). (Not to be confused with Roman Perinthos, below).   **Ganos, Ganiai:** non-*poleis*, Loukopoulou and Łaitar 2004, 913. *Barr.* equates Ganos with Serreion Teichos. At Aischines 3. 82 Ganos and Ganias (*sic*) occur together; Ganias is presumably PS's Ganiai.   **Neon Teichos:** 'New Fort'; a non-*polis*, Loukopoulou and Łaitar 2004, 914 (*Servili* in *Barr.*).   **Perinthos:** *Inv.* **678** (renamed Herakleia in R times).   **Daminon Teichos:** *Inv.* **675** (Daunion Teichos, *Barr.*). Teichos is part of the name, since the ethnic is Damnioteichites (*IG* i³ 272) or Daunioteichites (*IG* i³ 271). 'Daminon Teichos' is unparalleled and may be a scribal error.   **Selymbria:** *Inv.* **679**.

67. 8. Anaplous ... Bosporos: Anaplous is otherwise attested as a place-name only in Byzantine times, referring to the narrows between Byzantion and Kalchedon (C. 71) and a settlement on the W shore (*Barr.* 53 B2). The Bosporos is named again at 92.   **Hieron:** convincingly relocated, and its cultic and navigational significance explored, in Moreno 2009. PS abandons the formal *periplous* principle by including the main landmark on the E shore (Hdt. 4. 85; Polyb. 4. 43. 1)—though he does not mention the major *polis* of Kalchedon on that shore until 92. Other than Hieron, he skips over the Bosporos entirely. The glaring omission is Byzantion (Constantinople, *İstanbul*) at the start, perhaps the accidental result of combining data from incomplete or regional *periploi* (C. 44). At 92 PS barely mentions Kalchedon opposite Byzantion. Other omissions are less significant: no other settlement on either shore appears to have been a Cl *polis*. **7 stades:** the sources disagree about the width of the Bosporos (C. 71). Hdt. gives 4 st. (4. 85), Polyb. *c.*5 st. (4. 43. 2), Agathemeros 6 st. (3. 10). The actual figure is 0.7 km (4 st.).

The late Latin poet Avienus (*OM* 370–4) attributes to Damastes of Sigeion (C5; *FGrH* 5 F 4) the statement that the strait of *Gibraltar* is 7 st. wide—an absurd under-estimate—and to Skylax of Karyanda the view that it has the same width as the Bosporos—an equally gross error if the Thracian Bosporos is meant, but a fair comparison with the Kimmerian (Panchenko 2005; cf. 68. 4). Damastes presumably found this equation (but no distance) in a source now lost; took it to refer to the Thracian Bosporos; took the width of the latter from another source or personal knowledge (his home was nearby); and deduced that the strait of *Gibraltar* was 7 st. wide. He may have found the equation or the distance (not both) in SK; but more likely he carelessly inferred that SK made the equation. Noticing the figure of 7 st. in our *periplous* (which, for him, was by SK), he made the leap from 'Skylax gives the same width to the Bosporos as Damastes does to the strait of *Gibraltar*' to 'Skylax says they are the same'. We cannot, therefore, deduce from this passage that SK wrote about the Mediterranean or visited the West (*contra* Panchenko 2005, who fails to distinguish our *periplous* from the work of SK).

67. 9–92 (first part). The Black Sea

PS is less interested in demonstrating the unity of the Black Sea than in marking the divisions between Thrace and Skythia, and between Europe and Asia. Despite the large number of 'sections' in the conventional arrangement, these pages (under a thousand words) are even less detailed than what goes before them, and there are no *paraploi* except at the end. He gives us the data with which we could calculate the distance from the mouth of the Pontos as far as Panti-kapaion, though he has no interest in the figure except as part of his summation of Europe; but for the E half of the sea he can only offer the information that it is the same length as the W half (92. 2). Yet Hdt. (1. 104, 4. 85–6, cf. 4. 101) had already indicated the dimensions of the parts of the sea.

PS is a major source of *polis* names in the BS; but while he mentions most of the *c*.30 that are known, he is unreliable as to their status (Avram *et al.* 2004, 925, 928). Some places he claims as Hellenic *poleis* may be geographical features (e.g. Lykastos, Karambis, Iasonia) or non-Greek towns (Choirades, see Hekat. F 204). Some definite Greek *poleis* are not called Hellenic (Dioskouris, Limne). Chersonesos (*Inv.* **695**) appears only as an *emporion*. Others are omitted. Byzan-tion's absence is explained above (see n. on 67. 8 Hieron), and Istros can be plausibly restored (67. 9); but others in the NW (*Inv.* **690** Olbia, **693** Tomis, **684** Dionysopolis) and S (*Inv.* **723** Kromna, **722** Kotyora), plus Hermonassa (*Inv.* **697**) on the Kimmerian Bosporos, are notably missing. The lack of references to the lands behind the coast is also in contrast to some other passages of PS, as is the lack of ethnographic colour despite the plurality of meaningfully named barbarian peoples, and despite the example of Hdt. book 4. The use of multiple itineraries could explain some of the omissions, and also why PS gives no sense of spatial unity to the Bosporos and Pontos (C. 81).

While Athenian interest in the southern Black Sea was less strong than we once thought, it was stronger in C4m than before (H. B. Mattingly 1996). It seems clear, therefore, that PS's information reflects a much earlier period (as argued by Baschmakoff 1948 and upheld by Arnaud 1992, 60). Peretti 1979, 456–69, similarly, regards PS's ethnic geography of northern Anatolia as preserving very early data; this is not inconsistent with a C4m date for the work. (Black Sea as region, geography, resources, urban history: Avram *et al.* 2004, 924–8. PS's treatment: Counillon 2004 (cited here as 'C.' for §§67–92). Overview of Greek activity: Boardman 1999, 238–64, 281–2, ruling out a presence before C7.)

67. 9. Apollonia: *Inv.* **682** (*Sozopol*, Bulgaria). PS has jumped *c.*180 km from Hieron. See n. on Kallatis, below.   **Mesembria:** *Inv.* **687** Mesambria (settled from Kalchedon and Megara *c.*513/2; *Nesebur*), *c.*25 km N of Apollonia. See n. on Kallatis, below.   **Odesos Polis:** *Inv.* **689** (*Varna*). The MS spelling 'Odesos' is supported by coins (C. 71). PS may have regarded 'Polis' as part of the name (as a category noun it would be redundant, given 'cities' just before). See next n.   **Kallatis:** *Inv.* **686** (founded from *Inv.* **715** Herakleia (91), *c.*C6l or *c.*380; *Mangalia*, Romania), *c.*100 km N of Odesos. The preceding four places were the most important in the western Black Sea in C4m, but PS surprisingly—in view of his connections and interests—omits C5 Athenian foundations such as Agathepolis before Apollonia (above) (*Barr.* 22 E6, in Bulgaria) and Orgame further N (*Inv.* **692**; *Barr.* 22 F4, 23 B4, in Romania). See C. 71–2. The former may have been a non-*polis* Avram *et al.* 2004, 929, under 'Aulaiouteichos'), the latter (*Inv.* **692**) a dependent *polis* of Istros and a minor place; but the omission of other Athenian foundations (C. 72 n. 199) points to a more systematic explanation. See next n.   ⟨**Istros**⟩: the omission of this major *polis* (*Inv.* **685** Istria) could be due to compilation from sources laid out in different ways, or the name could have dropped out by *saut du même au même* (West 1973, 24–5).

67. 10. coastal voyage … voyage round: on these terms, see 50. 2 n. The switch from *paraplous* to *periplous* makes one suspect that the latter is corrupt, though Thrace as a whole might be called convex and suspicion does not justify for emendation.   **eight days and eight nights:** yet the figures total 7 days and 7 nights (Müller).

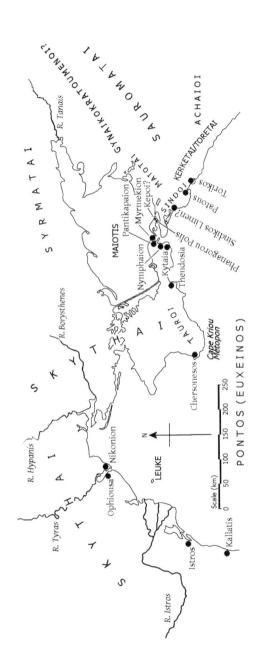

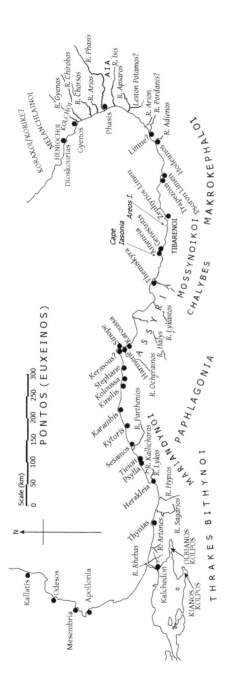

Map 13. The Black Sea.

68. 1. Skythai: on §68, and on European Skythia and Taurike, see C. 73–81. Sources and scholarship locate them in different regions between the *Danube* and *Don*. PS does not say where Skythia ends; perhaps implicitly at the *Don* (68. 5), as at Hdt. 4. 21.   **Tyras river:** the *Dniester*. As it stands, it is a striking example of PS including non-*poleis* in what purports to be a list of *poleis*. But the *polis* of Tyras (*Inv.* **694;** *Belgorod Dnestrovskij*, Ukraine) may have dropped out (e.g. 'Tyras, ⟨a city and⟩ a river' or 'Tyras, ⟨a city, and the Tyras⟩ river'); see n. on Ophiousa, below.   **Nikonion:** *Inv.* **688** (*Roksolanskoye*), on the l. (NE) bank of the R. Tyras opposite the *polis* of Tyras (Strabo 7. 3. 16 puts 'Nikonia' and Ophiousa on opposite banks). The *polis* existed from C4m or earlier. Agbunov 1979 identifies a C4s decline caused by the silting up of the river.   **Ophiousa:** *Barr.* 23 D2 Tyras/Ophiousa; but separate and unlocated, *Inv.* **691;** attested only here and possibly absorbed by Tyras at an unknown date. If rightly located on the SW shore of the lake or lagoon at the mouth of the Tyras, it should precede Nikonion. One of PS's sources may be an anti-clockwise *periplous* (C. 76).   PS omits the major *polis* of Olbia (*Inv.* **690**). The omission of this as well as Byzantion (at 67. 8) does not look coincidental; perhaps his sources included a direct crossing from the R. Tyras to Chersonesos (68. 2; C. 73, 76, 80–1); 68. 3 shows that ships made that crossing. Cf. also n. on 90 Karambis. (Less significantly, PS omits Karkinitis or Kerkinitis, *Inv.* **698,** probably a dependency of Chersonesos by C4m.)

68. 2. Tauroi: described more fully by Hdt. 4. 99.   **Chersonesos:** in the *Crimea* or 'Taurike Chersonesos'; the *polis* is *Inv.* **695** (*Cherson*), founded from Herakleia (91) and Delos in C4 or earlier; this is the earliest testimony. It may be the 'old Chersonesos' that Strabo 7. 4. 2 describes as 'destroyed'.   **Kriou Metopon:** 'Goat's Brow' (cf. another, 47. 1); C. *Sarych*, the southernmost point of the *Crimea* and the terminus of direct crossings from Istros (68. 1) and Karambis (90). **Taurike:** the territory of the Tauroi.

68. 3. Theudosia: *Inv.* **707** (*Feodosiya*).   **Kytaia:** *Inv.* **701** (near *Zavetnoye*), founded by Greeks from western Asia Minor in or before C5e; this is the earliest testimony.   **Nymphaion:** *Inv.* **704** (*Gero-yevka*).   **Pantikapaion:** *Inv.* **705** (*Kerch*).   **Myrmekion:** *Inv.* **703** (*Karantinnaya*; founded probably by Ionians c.580–560, but this is the earliest testimony). The next *polis* in *Inv.* that PS names is Phanago-rou Polis (72).   **coastal voyage:** odd, since PS first gives a direct crossing. The text may be corrupt. Cf. 100. 2.   **straight ... three days and three nights:** too long, implying c.3,000 st. (c.560 km); actually c.300 km. Perhaps 'straight' is an error and the duration refers to coasting. (Agbunov 1981, 143, quotes it as 390 km in 3 days, ignoring the nights, and therefore represents the transit as faster than it is. See n. on 68. 4 'a day and a night'.) The starting-point is probably the R. Istros, not the *polis* of Istros, as the *paraplous* at 67. 10 ends there.   **that beside land:** one of two places where PS distinguishes coastal sailing from a direct crossing, the other being 100. 2. See previous n.

68. 4. the island is deserted … Leuke: 'White Island'; sanctuary of Achilles from at least C6 (Avram *et al.* 2004, 929, under 'Hieron Achilleos').   **a day and a night:** implying *c.*1,000 st. (*c.*185 km), much too short (unlike the previous crossing, 68. 3): the coasting is *c.*290 km, and even with direct crossing of bays it is still *c.*240 km. See n. on 68. 3 'straight'. Perhaps PS or his source knew an Istros–Kriou Metopon–Pantikapaion transit of 4 days and 4 nights that has been wrongly divided; or rapid currents may explain the short duration, at least of the second part (Agbunov 1981, 143). (On direct crossings of the Black Sea, see Arnaud 1992; Avram *et al.* 2004, 924.)   **20 stades:** actually *c.*120 st. (Müller).

68. 5. Maiotis lake … half of the Pontos: Ps.-Arr. *Eux.* 44 uses almost identical words. It is untrue in respect of area, but a reasonable view of their relative lengths. The vagueness may reflect a period when Greek voyages were rarer (Arnaud 1992, 62), though not as rare as when Hdt. 4. 86 says Maiotis is only slightly smaller than the Pontos. The appeal to external authority in 'is said' may reflect a plurality of sources (C. 81).

for … Syrmatai: 'for' makes sense if PS is referring to the Skythai of the Black Sea; 'outside sea' here means the Pontus (outside L. Maiotis), not the 'Outer Ocean' (C. 78). PS distinguishes Syrmatai from Sauromatai (70), but this may be fictive (Gardiner-Garden 1988; Braund 2000a, 1213–14); or they may be Satarchae or 'Scythae Satarci' of Mela and Pliny (C. 78). He does not name the Kimmerian Bosporos (strait of *Kerch*) linking the Black Sea to the Sea of Azov; omits notable settlements; and fails to convey the size of the Tauric Chersonese. Contrast Hdt. 4. 99–100 (C. 78–9).   **Tanaïs:** the *Don* (now in Russia), meeting the sea by the town of the same name. Hdt. 4. 45 puts the start of Asia at the R. Kolchos (in Georgia), but notes that others put it at the Tanaïs and the Kimmerian Bosporos. (On continental divisions in Cl geography see Romm 1992. Ethnography of eastern Black Sea: Counillon 2007a.)

69. Length of Europe

69. *Summation of Europe.* The total does not match the data given earlier (many of which may be corrupt); see n. on 'days', below. Counillon (82) thinks the passage is by a later editor—perhaps Markianos—as otherwise such an editor would have corrected it or commented on it. But an editor may have corrected silently, yet new errors crept in afterwards. Indeed, as C. 82 concedes, the passage coheres with the general image of the world offered by PS. There are verbal echoes of §2, and close similarities to the other two summations (106. 4, 111. 8) as well as other passages, such as in the use of present participles in the dative. Key terms in the three places (e.g. *logizomai, logismos, peripherēs*) are standard in Cl writers (notably Arist. *Mete.* 2. 5. 362b23–4: see Introduction, III and VII), and none of the vocabulary is anachronistic. Once the 'bizarrerie' (Counillon) about L. Maiotis is removed, these passages are entirely consistent with one of the aims of the work, that of measuring the world. **500 stades a day:** the reckoning of 500 stades per day (as opposed to night) is standard in Greek geography (Arnaud 1993, 234).   **the Pontos … Maiotis lake:** garbled and probably repeated from 68. 5. The error was perhaps caused by the similarities between *hēmisu*, *hēmeras*, and *hēmerōn* (involving the introduction of *isou* and *merous*) and between *pleontos* (*vel sim.*) and *Pontou*. Alternatively, the words 'as far as the Maiotis lake' stood here or above and prompted the confusion (the summative *paraplous* at 111. 8 has an endpoint of this kind, though that at 106. 4 does not). (I thank C. Pelling for advice.) **days, 150 plus three:** Müller 58–9 discusses the total of previous measurements, arriving at 147; but his table contains at least one error and depends on conjectures in earlier passages as well as estimates for coasts without a *paraplous*. There are so many uncertainties that one is impressed that the total is even close to 153. This in itself suggests that most of the numbers in the preceding text are correctly transmitted.   **greatest rivers:** Müller xlii regards this statement as non-original; but it is in keeping with similar statements by Herodotos (4. 48–57, cf. 82, Skythia; Istros and Nile, 50; cf. 7. 196, Eridanos of Achaia Phthiotis).

70–106. Asia

70–92. TANAÏS TO PROPONTIS

See introductory n. at 67. 9. The increasing level of detail from Kolchis onwards reflects the point where the Caucasus range runs out and is followed by the Georgian lowlands; it may mark a change of source. On 82-5, and on the character of the S coast as far as

Trapezous, see C. 93–9.

70. Asia: Polyb. 3. 37. 3 similarly divides Europe from Asia at the Tanaïs (*Don*). *AWP* 13 agrees in ending Europe at L. Maiotis, whereas Hdt. (4. 45) favours the R. Phasis (cf. Lordkipanidze 2000, 23–4). **Sauromatai:** Hdt. 4. 57 likewise makes them the first people E of the Tanaïs. PS seems to be expressly revising what Hdt. says (4. 110, 123, etc.) about the Sauromatai living three days inland (Counillon 2007a, 39). They are often identified with the nomadic Sarmatai of later sources. See n. on 68. 5 Syrmatai.   **Gynaikokratoumenoi:** 'Woman-ruled', cf. 21. 1 on the Libyrnians. Ephoros F 160 (cited by Ps.-Arr. *Eux.* 45, which is similar to Ps.-Skymnos fr. 16 Marcotte) also refer to this group of Sauromatai.

71. Maiotai: Maietai, Hdt. 4. 123. Ephoros (previous n.) also makes them a tribe of the Sauromatai.

72. Sindoi: Sindike is the peninsula E of the Kimmerian Bosporos. Hdt. 4. 86 gives 3 days and 2 nights for the direct crossing from here to Themiskyra (89), which he converts to 330,000 fathoms (3,300 st.). **Phanagorou Polis:** 'Phanagoras's City', *Inv.* **706** Phanagoria. The naming of a city's founder, unusual in PS (cf. 67. 2), may reflect Hekataios (C. 85).   **Kepoi:** 'The Gardens'; *Inv.* **699** (location uncertain, despite *Barr.* 87 (inset, L2) and Braund 2000b, 1246, *Artyukhov/Sennaya*).   **Sindikos:** *Barr.* 84 C4. Location disputed (C. 85), though see n. on 73 Sindikos Limen.   **Patous:** a *polis* only here, Avram *et al.* 2004, 926 (*Novorossiysk*); assumed to be Bata, the last place in Sindike at Strabo 11. 2. 14 (C. 85–6), though at 73 PS has Sindikos Limen just before the Kerketai.

73. Sindikos Limen: possibly Gorgipp(e)ia, *Inv.* **696,** founded by Leukon I of the Bosporan kingdom (r. 389–349) but probably a trading town from C6. The omission of the name Gorgippia is not evidence of PS's date, given other omissions in the Black Sea.   **Kerketai, ⟨or rather Toretai⟩:** marked separately from the Toretai at *Barr.* 84 C4–D4. Though sometimes named separately (e.g. Toretai alone, Rhodes–Osborne 65c = Tod ii. 171c, *c.*344/3–*c.*311/0 BC), they are combined using these words at Ps.-Arr. *Eux.* 22B, the source of the supplement here.

74. Torikos: a non-*polis* in the bay of *Gelendzhik*, recorded only here (Avram *et al.* 2004, 926, 930.

Barr. 87

At 75–80, the communities on this inhospitable coast, overlooked by the Caucasus Mts, are hard to pinpoint (C. 86–90).

75. Achaioi: SE of the Kerketai, *Barr.* 84 E4; named by Pherekydes F 143 in C6.

76. Heniochoi: 'Drivers'. Inland from Dioscurias/Sebastopolis (*Inv.* **709** Dioskouris, in Georgia; see 81). Strabo 11. 2. 12 makes them Laconian Argonauts who settled here.

77. ⟨Koraxoi⟩: *Barr.* 87 F1, W of the Heniochoi. Cf. the Kolaxaian horse at Alkman 1. 59. They are named by Hellanikos F 70 alongside the Heniochoi (76), and by PS's contemporary Aristotle (*Mete.* 1. 13. 351a11, discussing rivers).

78. Korike: not in *Barr.*; the Koloi 'by the Caucasus', Hekat. F 209, mentioning the 'Kolika mountains'; so an upland region (C. 88).

79. Melanchlainoi: 'Black-Cloaks'. N of 81 Dioskourias; Braund and Sinclair 2000, 1239). At Hdt. 4. 107, etc., they wear the black cloaks of their name; he puts them near the Tanaïs, so PS's source places them further SE; from the same source he may take Patous (72), Torikos (74), and the two rivers below (C. 88–9).   **Metasoris ... Aigipios:** unknown rivers; N of *Sukhumi*, Braund and Sinclair 2000, 1240; 1239.

80. Gelon: not in *Barr.* The Gelonoi who feed on lice (Hdt. 4. 102, etc.) may have been invented to explain 'Gelon', probably a river; and are perhaps from the same source as the names in 79 (C. 89–90). 'Gelon' may conceal Gelonos, their city among the Boudinoi at Hdt. 4. 108 (inland from the Sauromatai and beyond the Melanchlainoi).

81. Kolchoi: not the small area of Kolchis S of Trabzon (*Barr.* 87 E4), but a substantial region of western Georgia. The absence of the names found in Pliny 6. 4/13–14 reflects the vagueness or mutability of its boundaries and settlements (C. 91).   **Dioskourias:** *Inv.* **709** Dioskouris (*Sukhumi*).   **Gyenos:** *Inv.* **710** (near *Ochamchire*). The listing of six towns (including three Greek *poleis*) between Kolchis and Trapezous is unique before the Roman period, and may reveal otherwise unattested Greek settlement in or before C4 (C. 98).   **Gyenos river:** *Mokvi*.   **Chirobos river:** see n. on 'Phasis river', below. **Chorsos river:** *Enguri*; same as Chobos (Pliny 6. 4/14), Braund and Sinclair 2000, 1231.   **Arios river:** *Barr.* 87 G2, 'Arios'/Charieis (*Khobi*).   **Phasis river:** *Rioni*.   **Phasis ... city:** *Inv.* **711** (unlocated). A minor place, possibly a dependency of Sinope (as Dioskouris and Gyenos may be) (Avram *et al.* 2004, 926). See n. on Gyenos, above. **180 stades:** 300 st. in Steph. Byz. on Aia.   **Aia:** an area between the Phasis and its tributaries. Ps.-Arr. *Eux.* 3–4B repeats PS almost verbatim. See n. on Gyenos, above.   **Medeia:** the Kolchian princess in the Argonauts myth. For her presence in a geographical narrative, cf. Trogus in Justin 42. 3. 9; Clarke 1999, 96.   **Rhis river:** unlocated,

Braund and Sinclair 2000, 1240. Possibly the Surius of Pliny 6. 4/12 (Müller 62).   **Isis river:** *Natanebi*, near the S limit of the Georgia lowlands as the mountains close in upon the coast.   **Lēstōn Potamos:** 'Pirates' River', possibly near the town and river of Apsaros, where the coast is steep-to; may be the *Tchoroki* (Braund and Sinclair 2000, 1233), but see next n.   **Apsaros river:** *Tchorokhi* estuary, Georgia. Arr. *Peripl.* 11. 4 makes the Apsaros, where the coast bends N (he is going anti-clockwise), the 'limit, in terms of length, of the Pontos'.

82. Bouseres: not in *Barr.*; presumably in modern Turkey; 'Dizeres', Hekat. F 207; 'Byzeres' in other sources (e.g. Ap. Rhod. 2. 394, 1242). At Ps.-Arr. *Eux.* 1B the area where they lived is occupied by the Zydritai (*Barr.* 87 G3; Arr. *Peripl.* 11. 3).   **river of the Daraanoi:** not in *Barr.*   **Arion river:** *Abu* (*Barr.*).

83. Ekecheirieis: not in *Barr.*; only here and Ps.-Arr. *Eux.* 42. 1 (Ekcheirieis). Counillon (97–9) discusses the names Bouseres, Ekecheiries, and Becheirike (see also 84 n.). *Eux.* reports that the area where they lived is now occupied by the Machelones and Heniochoi (for the latter see 81; for both, Arr. *Peripl.* 15). *Ekecheiria* in Greek means 'armistice', but if the name is correctly transmitted it need only mean that Greeks turned a foreign name into something they could understand.   **river Pordanis:** not in *Barr.*; may be the Prytanis (Arr. *Peripl.* 8; *Barr.* 87 F4 *Furtuna Dere*).   **Arabis river:** not in *Barr.*; may be Arrian's Zagatis (Müller 63).   **Limne:** meaning 'Lake' but possibly a corruption of 'Athene' (Arr. *Peripl.* 8; Müller 63). See n. on 81 Gyenos.   **Hodeinios:** *Inv.* 727 (Odeinios; *polis* status doubted), first attested here; cf. R. Adienos, Arr. *Peripl.* 7. 3; Ps.-Arr. *Eux.* 39 (Adineos, also Adienos); *Kıbledağı Dere*, *Barr.* The aspirate is clear in the MS; has the name been assimilated to *ho deina* (ὁ δεῖνα), 'such-and-such'? See n. on 81 Gyenos.

84. Becheires ... Becheirikos ... Becheirias: not in *Barr.*; discussed by Peretti 1979, 100; see also n. on Ekcheirieis (83). Becheiras is *Inv.* 713, attested only here (*polis* status doubted). (See n. on 81 Gyenos.) Ps.-Arr. *Eux.* 38 reports that the Kolchoi now live where the Becheires did.

85. Makrokephaloi: 'Long-heads', as in *AWP* 14. 1–5; elsewhere Makrones (Hekat. F 206, Xen. *Anab.* 4. 7. 27, Ps.-Skymnos fr. 21 Marcotte, Ps.-Arr. *Eux.* 38, etc.). The differences from Hekat. indicate an intermediate or distinct source (C. 99).   **Psōrōn Limen:** 'Itching Harbour' (lit. harbour of itches, scabs, or mange). *Araklıçarşısı* (*Barr.* 87 F4) or *Trabzon Limanı* (C. 99).   **Trapezous:** *Inv.* 734; dependency of Sinope.

86. For this mountainous coast PS selects defensible harbours as fixed points on a maritime route, but omits two C4 *poleis*: Kerasous (*Inv.* **719**; Xen. *Anab.* 5. 3–7 *passim*; see 89 for other places with this name) and Kotyora (*Inv.* **722**; Xen. *Anab.* 5. 5 *passim*, 5. 8. 24), both dependencies of Sinope (Avram *et al.* 2004, 925); they were no doubt absent from his source (C. 108–12).   **Mossynoikoi:** 'Hut-dwellers', a tributary people of the Persians in Hdt. 3. 94; 7. 78. Their name (first in Hekat. FF 204–5) was supposed to derive from their wooden house, *mosyn* (C. 100). Xen. *Anab.* 5. 4–5 describes their customs; they were well known to the Greeks.   **Zephyrios Limen:** 'West Wind Harbour'; *Zefre* (*Barr.*) or *Gül Burnu* (C. 108–9).   **Choirades:** *Inv.* **714** (*Gedik Kaya*, C. 110; Bryer and Winfield 1985, 127; unlocated, *Inv.*, *Barr.*); a *polis* of the Mossynoikoi, i.e. non-Hellenic, Hekat. F 204; possibly later Pharnakia (see under *Inv.* **719** Kerasous).   **Ares's Island:** *Giresun Adası.*

87. Tibarenoi: stereotypical traits are attributed to them: e.g. a love of laughter (Ephoros F 43), fighting battles on pre-arranged dates (schol. Ap. Rhod. 2. 1010), throwing old people off cliffs (Porphyry, *De abst.* 4. 21). See C. 103.

88. As in 86, named places are closely spaced, reflecting a concern with safe anchorages and protection from the interior (C. 112), presumably deriving from PS's source(s).   **Chalybes:** see C. 104–8; Peretti 1961, 28–30. Non-Greeks, traditionally masters of iron-working. Named by e.g. Hekat. F 199, etc.; Hdt. 1. 28; Xen. *Anab.* 4. 4–5, 5. 5. 1 (Chalybes in uplands and on coast); Ephoros F 162. Counillon (105–7) argues that PS is here using not only Hekataios but also a later or independent source.   **Genesintis:** the E point of C. Iasonion (*Yasun Burnu*; see n. on Iasonia, below), the chief cape between Trapezous (*Trabzon*) and Amisos (*Samsun*). Like Kerasous (omitted at 86) and Kotyora, which are Sinopean fortified harbours, Genesintis (or Genetes) reflects the organization of the Sinope–Trapezous route and possibly a C5 Athenian source (C. 113). 'Enclosed' means a secure naval harbour (Counillon 1998b).   **Ameneia:** *Inv.* **730** Stameneia (Hellenic *polis* status doubtful), on the N coast of *Yasun Burnu*. A *polis* of the Chalybes, Hekat. F 202.   **Iasonia:** NW point of *Yasun Burnu*; the *polis* (not in *Barr.*) is *Inv.* **716**.

89. Assyria is clearly a larger area and further E than in *Barr.* Counillon (120) notes a pattern of obscure and/or short-lived settlements, reflecting PS's use of a *periplous* specific to this region. It differs from his account of the NW and N Black Sea, where he names fewer minor places. Counillon (114–17) notes the omission of Chadisios (known from Hekat. and Menippos); the designation of Lykastos, uniquely, as 'a river and a Hellenic *polis*'; the omission of the R. Iris, which may reflect the use of a *periplous* alongside an ethnographic catalogue; and the omission of Amisos (*Inv.* 712; *Samsun*), which may be due to textual corruption). The reliability of 'Hellenic *polis*' in 89 may be doubted (Flensted-Jensen and Hansen 2007, 221).   **Assyria:** Hdt. 1.72 says Hellenes call the Cappadocians 'Syrians', though he then calls them 'Cappadocian Syrians'. Strabo 12. 3. 9 discusses their varying names, in his day Leukosyroi ('White Syrians'). At Ap. Rhod. 2. 964 the region is Assyriē; our text may have been altered from 'Syria' to reflect this (C. 113 n. 374).   **river Thermodon:** *Terme Çay*, running through Themiskyra.   **Themiskyra:** *Inv.* 732 (Hellenic status doubted). Otherwise only at Hdt. 4. 86. 3 and in late authors. Implicitly in the Amazons' territory, Ap. Rhod. 2. 994–7.   **Lykastos river:** *Merd Irmağı*, W of Themiskyra and immediately E of Amisos. The *polis* is *Inv.* 726, named in no other pre-Hl source. PS omits Amisos; see introductory n. to 89.   **Halys:** *Kızıl Irmak*, the great river of NW Turkey, with a projecting delta *c.*40 km wide between Amisos and Sinope.   **Karoussa:** *Inv.* 718 (no details known); *Gerze*, S of Sinope. We have jumped *c.*70 km W of the Halys, so *kai* is translated 'and' here rather than 'with'.   **Sinope:** *Inv.* 729; on the most prominent cape on the S coast, midway along its length. Its inclusion in Assyria is odd, as the Halys (above) is normally made the frontier between Assyria and Paphlagonia; this could be connected with the spread of Persian power to Sinope in C4m, or the ancient mistake of supposing that a line from Issos to Sinope marked the neck of Anatolia (supposedly only five days' travel, Hdt. 2. 34; but see 102. 2 n.). See C. 118. **Kerasous:** between Sinope and the Ocherainos (below); not in *Barr.* Counillon (119–20) puts it in the plain between Sinope and Harmene, probably as a short-lived *polis*.   **Ocherainos river:** *Kara Su* (*Barr.*; C. 119).   **Harmene:** *Akliman*, with a well-protected small bay; probably the main *emporion* of Sinope (C. 119). A non-*polis* (Avram *et al.* 2004, 929; cf. Flensted-Jensen and Hansen 2007, 218, comparing Kyllene as the harbour of Elis, §43); but no worse attested as a *polis* than e.g. *Inv.* 713 Becheirias and *Inv.* 720 Kinolis (M. H. Hansen, pers. comm.).   **Tetrakis:** *Inv.* 731 (unlocated; otherwise unknown); Flensted-Jensen and Hansen 2007, 221, incline to doubt PS. Counillon (120) suggests it is one of three sites W of Sinope; one is anc. Potamoi (Markianos, *Epit. Men.* 9; *Şerefiye*, Counillon; or *Gebelit*, Foss 2000, 1221).

Barr. 86

90. Paphlagonia: W of Sinope the shore again trends S of W. On the region see C. 121–30 (esp. 130), who observes that the number of poorly attested place-names reflects C5s–C4e, when the Athenians were developing new routes (cf. frequency of 'Hellenic') and were

interested in a direct route to the *Crimea*. This, he suggests, explains
the separation of Paphlagonia from Assyria, the Mariandynoi, and
Herakleia; and could explain the negative attitude of the Sinopeans
to Xenophon's idea of founding a city here (*Anab.* 5. 5. 7–12).   **Stephane:** *Istifan* (*Barr.*); or *Çaylioğlu* by the promontory of *Usta Burnu*,
the W limit of Sinopean territory (C. 123).   **Koloussa:** *Inv.* 721;
Güllüsu (*Barr.*); or one of the capes between Kinolis and Stephane (C.
127–8). Otherwise unknown.   **Kinolis:** *Inv.* 720; *Ginoğlu* (*Barr.*) or
Konaklı Liman (C. 128 n. 436). An *emporion*, Arr. *Peripl.* 21; an *oppidum*,
Pliny 6. 2/5 (these not cited in *Inv.*). Archaeology points to occupation from C5 (Eser 2004).   **Karambis:** *Inv.* 717; *Fakas*? A town only
here and at Pliny 6. 2/6; a promontory, Ps.-Skymnos fr. 28 Marcotte,
etc., suggesting it ceased to be a *polis*. A jumping-off point for the
direct crossing (*c*.260 km, *c*.1,400 st.) to the *Crimea* (C. 125–6; Strabo
12. 3. 10), especially if one had to avoid Sinope further E; but PS does
not mention the crossing.   **Kytoris:** *Inv.* 724 Kytoros (*Kidros/Süt-
lüce*; *Cide*, Google Earth), with one of the best harbours in northern
Turkey (C. 126). One of four Milesian settlements—the others are
Tieion (below), Kromna (*Inv.* 723), and Sesamos (below)—that were
synoikized as Amastris *c*.300–290. C4 Kytoris was perhaps a dependent *polis* of Sinope. PS's evidence suggests that all four towns in
Amastris were C4m *poleis* (Flensted-Jensen 1995, 219).   **Sesamos:**
Inv. 728; *Amasra*, the 'akropolis' of the new Amastris (C. 126). See
previous n. A good anchorage on the way to Karambis (above; C. 126–
7).   **Parthenios:** *Bartın Su*, reaching the sea W of Sesamos. One of
the most important rivers of this coast (C. 127).   **Tieion:** *Inv.* 733
(*Hisarönü*). A small settlement, like Kromna, Sesamos, and Kytoris
(Avram *et al.* 2004, 925–6); good harbour (C. 127, *contra* L. Robert). See
under Kytoris, above.   **Psylla:** *Çatal Ağzı*, *c*.8 km WSW of Tieion (90
st. W according to Menippos ap. Markianos, *Epitome of Menippos*, 1. 8;
Arr. *Peripl.* 13. 5); or one of several places between *Türkeli* and *Kilimli*
(C. 128).   **river Kallichoros:** *Ilık Su*, though C. 129–30 prefers a river
closer to Psylla, perhaps the *Kilimli* or *Zonguldak*. He suggests retain-
ing Kallichōros ('good place'), MS, rather than Kallichŏros ('place of
good dancing'), which would imply a link with Dionysos and point to
the Hl period.

91. Mariandynoi: a probably Thracian people (Burstein 1976, 6–11).
The sparsity of information in PS, as compared with NW Anatolia in
general, is perhaps due not to the presence of a non-Greek
population (C. 131) but rather to PS's sources. See also next n.
Herakleia: *Inv.* 715 (*Ereğli*). A major *polis* with extensive territory and
a semi-free dependent population of Mariandynoi. PS omits its dependent anchorages; the implied extent of territory suits 425–400

rather than C4m (C. 131–2).   **river Lykos:** *Gülünç Su*, meeting the sea just S of Herakleia.   **river . . . Hypios:** *Büyük Melen Su/Akarsu*, W of the Lykos (C. 132).

92. 1. Asiatic Propontis and sub-regions: Avram 2004, 974–6.   **Thrakes Bithynoi:** this section is even more laconic than 91. Like Xen. *Anab.* 7, PS implies it is hostile territory, but the omission of the Kalpe district, where Xenophon famously wanted to build a *polis*, is still notable (C. 133).   **Sagarios:** meeting the sea at 30° 40′ E (*Sakarya*).

Barr. 52

Artones: we jump *c.*100 km W to the Şile (29° 35′ E), almost certainly the Artanes of Menippos (Marcian, *Epit. Men.* 8); Arr. *Peripl.* 17; Ps.-Arr. *Eux.* 3. In reality the leap is less, for those sources agree it is W of Thynias (below). Even so, the step from Thynias to the Artones is *c.*60 km (*c.*320 st.) coasting. Either PS is using an anti-clockwise *periplous*, or the error reflects the editing of sources into *periplous* format (C. 133, who notes that the rivers represent daily stages on a voyage).   **Thynias . . . men of Herakleia:** a prominent cape (*İğneada*, *Barr.*; 30° 16′ E) with an offshore islet (max. length *c.*0.5 km). (*Nēsos* can mean 'island' or 'peninsula'.) It should have preceded the Artones; see previous n. For Herakleiote control of Thynias see Avram *et al.* 2004, 955, 956. PS's language suggests a non-*polis* (C. 133).   **river Rhebas:** the town (*Rıva*) and river (*Rıva Deresi*) are *c.*5 km E of the N entrance to the Bosporos, a place where ships exiting the Bosporos and turning E would put in (C. 133). (Not the R. Rhebas, *Gökçesu*, at *Barr.* 52 F4 in Mysia.)   **Strait:** *poros*, MS; if not corrupt, this should be a synonym for Bosporos and is possibly used as a name, Poros.   **aforesaid Hieron:** a reference back to 67. 8.   **Kalchedon:** or Chalkedon (*Inv.* **743**); at the S entrance to the Bosporos opposite Byzantion, but founded first (Hdt. 4. 144. 1). As at 67. 8, we pass through the Bosporos in a few scant words. Despite referring back to Hieron, PS seems uninterested in the strait; he may be using a Herakleiote *periplous* (C. 134).   **outside Thrake:** perhaps because Kalchedon was conquered by Byzantion in 357 (C. 134; *Inv.* **743**).   **Olbian gulf:** the inner E corner of the Propontis (*İzmit Körfezi*), known as the gulf of Astakos. Olbia is at 93.   **days, three:** implying *c.*1,500 st.; Müller 68 reckons 1,300.

92. 2. of similar size: whether or not this passage is original (as C. 134 suggests), it is oddly (or significantly) placed, for the measurement of the Black Sea is introduced after we have already left it and is made in the reverse direction. It lacks a figure in days, and stands at the end of neither an *ethnos* (we are now 'oustide Thrace') nor the relevant geographical bloc (the Black Sea). The sentence uses different terms from §69.

93–102. MYSIA TO KILIKIA

Parts of this passage are relatively detailed and are enlivened with mythological or historical allusions. For Ionia (98. 2–4) the listing of *poleis* is almost complete; even some non-*polis* settlements appear (e.g. in the Samian *peraia*). This probably reflects literary or documentary research rather than navigational know-how. After Ionia, however, diverting details are few and the passage ends with an erroneous statement about the land crossing of Asia Minor.

93. Mysia: the region containing *Inv.* **828** Pergamon, a minor *polis* until C4l. (Fluidity of Mysia's frontiers: Avram 2004, 974–6.) PS's Mysia has two coasts (see n. on 98. 1 'this territory too').   **Kian gulf:** in Strabo (12. 4. 3) simply 'another gulf' (after the Astakenos Kolpos) containing Prousias, 'formerly named Kios'.   **as far as Kios:** an advance mention; see n. below.   **Olbia:** *Inv.* **753,** a dependency in the territory of *Inv.* **737** Astakos (this is the first attestation); not in *Barr.* (though see n. on 92 'gulf of Olbia'). Strabo (12. 4. 8) cites Skylax of Karyanda for Phrygians and Mysians around L. Askania. We need not infer, from the absence of the lake here, that Strabo knew a fuller version of our *periplous,* for Skylax repeatedly compared things in India with things in Asia Minor, as Panchenko 2002 deduces from passages in Philostratos (C3 AD), *Life of Apollonios.* Philostratos, indeed, compares the Indian Mt Aornos to mountains in NW Asia Minor (2. 10), a comparison he may have taken from Skylax, who in theory could have mentioned L. Askania.   **Kallipolis:** *Inv.* **744,** unlocated (between Astakos and Kios; not in *Barr.*); it existed at least from C5l.   **Kios:** *Inv.* **745.**   **days, one:** implying *c.*500 st.; Müller 68 reckons over 800, and considers that PS uses a longer day's sailing in respect of Asia Minor than elsewhere (on stades and days' sailing see Arnaud 1993). It could, however, be a simple under-estimate.

94. Phrygia: on its definition, see Avram 2004, 974–6.   **Myrleia:** *Inv.* **752,** founded from Kolophon in or before C5; probably named Brylleion until *c.*C4m (perhaps really the same name); in C4 a dependent *polis* of Kios.   **Rhyndakos:** meeting the sea *c.*30 km W of Myrleia (*Orhaneli/Koca Dere*).   **Besbikos:** off the mouth of the Rhyndakos (*İmrali*).   **Plakia:** *Inv.* **757,** an Athenian foundation with non-Greek elements (*Kurşunlu?*).   **Kyzikos:** *Inv.* **747** (*Kelkiz Kale*). An excellent natural harbour (Cary 158).   **Artake:** *Inv.* **736,** founded from Miletos before 493 (*Erdek*), on the SW shore of Arktonnesos.   **Prokonnesos:** *Inv.* **759** (*Marmara*), off Arktonnesos. Neither here nor at 95 (Tenedos) does PS use his stock phrase 'I return again to the mainland', which we last met at 67. 5 (after Lemnos); it reappears at 97 (after Lesbos), after which it is more common (though not ubiquitous). **Elaphonnesos:** *Ekinlik Adası*, much smaller than Prokonnesos. **Priapos . . . Parion:** *Inv.* **758** (*Karabiğa*) and **756** (*Kemer*).

Barr. 51

Lampsakos: *Inv.* **748** (*Lapseki*, at NE entrance to Hellespont). **Perkote:** *Inv.* **788** (6 km E of *Umurbey*). **Abydos:** *Inv.* **765** (*Maltepe*). Strabo (13. 1. 4) says Skylax of Karyanda and Ephoros (F 163a) begin Troas at Abydos; PS actually makes Abydos the last town in Phrygia. Strabo appears to have used both the original (Indian) *periplous* of Skylax and the *Periplous*. **Propontis:** see 67. 5. **by Sestos:** as elsewhere (e.g. 7), PS interrupts (or enhances) linear progress and links back to an earlier passage (67. 5 and 10).

Barr. 56

95. Troas: on its definition and history see Mitchell 2004, 1000–1.) See n. on 94 Abydos. **Dardanos:** *Inv.* **774** (3 km S of *Kepez*). **Rhoiteion:** *Inv.* **790** (*Baba Kale*), on the coast. **Ilion:** *Inv.* **779**; successor to Bronze Age *Hisarlık*, *c.*5 km inland. **Skamandros:** Homer's R. Scamander (*Menderes Çay*). **Tenedos:** island off Troas (*Bozcaada*). PS does not mention the *polis* (*Inv.* **793**) but implies it exists by naming a famous citizen (next n.). **Kleostratos:** though PS uses the present tense, K. was the C6l author of *Astrologia*, credited with introducing the signs of the zodiac to Greeks (Fotheringham 1919; 1920; 1925; Webb 1921; 1928). The surviving fragments may not be genuine (*OCD*[3] on astronomy; constellations and named stars). **Sige:** probably *Inv.* **791** Sigeion (*Yenişehir*). **Achilleion:** *Inv.* **766** (*Beşika Burnu*). **Krateres Achaiōn:** 'Achaians' Mixing-bowls'; also called simply Achaiïōn (Strabo 13. 1. 32 and 36; *Hantepe*). **Kolonai, Larissa, and Hamaxitos:** *Inv.* **782** (*Beşiktepe*), **784** (*Limantepe*), **778** (*Beşiktepe, Gulpınar*). The last means 'Wagon Road'. They are in the correct sequence. **Apollo:** Apollo Smintheus, Strabo 13. 1. 61. **Chryses:** Apollo's priest whose daughter Chryseis was seized from Achilles by Agamemnon (*Iliad* 1). (The temple of Apollo Smintheus at *Gulpınar* is Hl.)

96. Aiolid territory: on Aiolis see Rubinstein 2004a, 1033–6, noting that Hdt. and Xen. knew two regions of this name, the more southerly lying in the same satrapy as Ionia (see 98. 2); PS presents only the more northerly here. 〈**Assos . . . Gargara (and) Antandros**〉: Müller 69 (followed by Peretti 1963, 40–1; Marcotte 1986, 170 n. 33; Allain 184) adds Assos (*Inv.* **769**; *Beyramkale*), Gargara (**775**; near *Arıklı*), and Antandros (**767**; *Devren/Avcılar*). All are on the S coast of Troas, from W to E. Antandros is already in the MS at the end of 96 (also 98. 1) in a reference back to here, so is certain; but we cannot be sure both Assos and Gargara stood here. The addition of 'as follows' (*haide*) allows the omission of the *poleis* to be explained by *saut du* *même au même* (West 1973, 24–5). See n. on 34. 2 'cities in the interior'.   **Kebren:** *Inv.* **780,** inland (*Fuğla Tepe, Çal Dağ*).   **Skepsis:** *Inv.* **792,** further inland; Aiolian city resettled from Miletos, perhaps post-494 (*Kurşunlu Tepe*).   **Neandreia:** *Inv.* **785,** attested from 454/3 but with Ar monuments (*Çığrı Dağ*). It is further W than Kebren and Skepsis, so out of place; indeed, it is only a short way inland from Kolonai (95).   **Pityeia:** not in *Barr.* A non-*polis*, Mitchell 2004, 1002. Strabo 13. 1. 44 does not specify whether it is a district or a town, but appears to locate it inland from and NE of Skepsis. (Not *Barr.* 56 F3 Pityaia in the headwaters of the Kaikos; see 98. 2.)   **Phrygia:** for PS, Troas and (northern) Aiolis are part of Phrygia (Allain 184). He may view Phrygia as extending round behind the others.

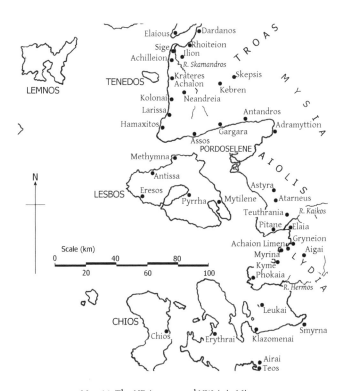

Map 14. The NE Aegean and NW Asia Minor.

97. Lesbos: PS correctly identifies the five Cl *poleis*. As in Rhodes (below), he makes an anti-clockwise circuit, starting at the part closest to the mainland. (*Poleis*: M. H. Hansen *et al.* 2004, 1018–20.) **Methymna:** *Inv.* **797** (*Mithymna*), the second most powerful *polis*. **Antissa, Eresos, Pyrrha:** *Inv.* **794** (*Skalochori/Obriokastro*), **796** (*Skala*),

799 (*Megali Limni*).   **Mytilene:** *Inv.* **798** (*Mytilini*), the largest *polis* on Lesbos. ('Mitylene', MS, a post-Cl spelling.)   **I return again . . .:** first use of this phrase since 67. 5; hereafter it is more common, though not used on every possible occasion (see e.g. n. on 99. 1 Kos).   **Pordoselene:** *Inv.* **831** (*Alibey Adası*), largest of the Hekatonnesoi (Hdt. 1. 151. 1) between Lesbos and Troas. May be identical with *Inv.* **823** Nasos on that island (Mitchell 2004, 1049).

Barr. 61

98. 1. was . . . Mysia . . . now Lydia: the text as restored (after Müller) refers back to the other part of Mysia (93–4). PS follows Persian satrapal divisions but notes that this part of Lydia was once in Mysia (Rubinstein 2004a, 1033). On Mysia, see Rubinstein 2004a, 1033–6. **Teuthrania:** *Inv.* **833** (*Kalerga*), on the Kaikos; mentioned in advance as the S limit of the former Mysia.

98. 2. Astyra: *Inv.* **770**; at 98. 4 it is the point from which the *paraplous* of 'Mysia and Lydia' is measured. Mitchell 2004, 1005, favours *Kilisetepe Kaplıcaları* (*Barr.* 56 D2, N of the R. Euenos), though he and co-authors at Foss *et al.* 2000, 843–4, give two alternatives.   **⟨of Artemis⟩:** Allain 185 prefers not to add the name, but there are spare letters in the MS which may be a remnant.   **Adramyttion:** *Inv.* **800** (*Karataş/Ören*), allegedly Lydian in origin; further S than the likely location of Astyra, but NE of 97 Por(d)oselene, and thus out of place. **the territory is Lesbian . . . territory of the Chioi:** these phrases, like 98. 3 'territory of the Samioi', refer to the mainland possessions (*peraiai*) of large islands (see Constantakopoulou 2007, 228–53). For the Mytilenean—not Lesbian—*peraia*, see in brief M. H. Hansen *et al.* 2004, 1026; for the Chian, Rubinstein 2004b, 1065.   **Atarneus:** *Inv.* **803** (*Kale Tepe* near *Dikili*); between Pordoselene and Teuthrania, so out of sequence. Müller xlvi rebuts those who would use Atarneus as evidence of PS's early date; but PS says 'the Chians' territory *and* Atarneus', which does not necessarily mean A. was in the *peraia* at the time of writing, so this is not dating evidence. Chios probably lost its *peraia* under the King's Peace of 386 (Rubinstein 2004b, 1065). **Pitane:** *Inv.* **830** (*Çandarlı*), just before (i.e. W of) the Kaikos. We enter southern Aiolis (cf. 96 n.), which is not named—perhaps because PS respects satrapal boundaries. Pitane is one of the original twelve Aiolian *poleis* (Hdt. 1. 149. 1). Of Hdt.'s eleven survivors (the Ionians having taken Smyrna) PS names only the first (Kyme) and the last four (Pitane, Aigai, Myrina, Gryneion), omitting **818** Larisa, **824** Neon Teichos, **832** Temnos, **814** Killa, **825** Notion (not the Ionian *polis*; see 98. 3), and **802** Aigiroёssa.   **river Kaïkos:** *Bakır Çay.*   **Elaia:** *Inv.* **807** (*Kazıkbağları*).   **Gryneion:** *Inv.* **809** (*Termaşalık Burnu*), an original

Aiolian *polis*.   **Achaiōn Limen:** 'Achaians' Harbour', further S in the same bay.   **Telephos:** the Arkadian king of Mysia who clashed with the Achaeans on their way to Troy, was wounded by Achilles, and was later healed by him.   **Myrina:** *Inv.* **822,** at the mouth of the R. Titnaios or Pythikos (*Koca Çay*). An original Aiolian *polis*.   **Kyme:** *Inv.* **817** (*Nemrut Limanı*), *c*.16 km coasting from Myrina around C. Hydra. An original Aiolian *polis*.   **Aigai:** *Inv.* **801** (*Nemrut Kale*): more easily reached by river from Myrina than overland from Kyme, so out of place. An original Aiolian *polis*.   **Leukai:** *Inv.* **819** (*Üçtepeler*); here coastal. Taken with Pliny 5. 31/119, who says its promontory was once an island, this indicates that alluviation linked it to the mainland by C4 (cf. Rubinstein 2004a, 1046).   **Smyrna ... Homer:** *Inv.* **867** (*İzmir*). See n. on Pitane, above; Aiolian, later Ionian, but disbanded by the Lydians C6m and inhabited 'village style' (Strabo 14. 1. 37) until refounded by Antigonos *c*.330 (Rubinstein 2004b, 1099, with archaeological evidence). It is probably not chronologically significant that PS does not call it a *polis*; he is unsystematic about site classification in this passage, and probably includes Smyrna (which did exist as a settlement in C4m) for its Homeric link.

PS does not name Ionia—oddly, given the inclusion of the Panionion (below); neither does he indicate a new region or identity, but simply locates the *poleis* implicitly in Lydia (whose end he announces at the start of Karia, 99. 1). As before (see n. on 98. 2 Pitane), the reason may be respect for satrapal boundaries. Similarly, Herodotos (1. 142) locates the three most southerly Ionian *poleis* (Miletos, Myous, Priene) 'in Karia' and the next six (Ephesos, Kolophon, Lebedos, Teos, Klazomenai, Phokaia) 'in Lydia', though he lists separately the two island *poleis* (Samos, Chios) and mainland Erythrai. Of these twelve PS omits Myous (*Inv.* **856**). Unlike Hdt., he implicitly places Priene in Lydia (98. 4), as well as the two islands and Erythrai; and inserts non-*poleis* (e.g. 98. 3 Notion) and non-canonical Ionian *poleis* (e.g. 98. 3 Airai, 99. 1 Herakleia) between the Ionian *poleis*.   **Phokaia:** *Inv.* **859** (*Foça*); should have stood immediately after Kyme.   **Hermos:** the *Gediz Çay*, between Phokaia and Smyrna.   **Klazomenai:** *Inv.* **847** (*Klazumen*), Ionian *polis*.   **Erythrai:** *Inv.* **845** (*Ildır*), Ionian *polis* opposite Chios.   **Chios:** the *polis*, not explicitly classified despite its importance (though its *ethnikon* was used a few lines above), is *Inv.* **840**. In C4m it was dominated by Maussollos of Karia (r. 377–353) and his successors, but this hardly explains its omission, which is probably an oversight if not due to MS error.

Barr. 56–7

98. 3. Airai: 'Agra', MS; *Inv.* **837** (discussing name), a minor Ionian *polis*; *Barr.* 56 D5 Gerraidai (*Sığacık Liman*), *c*.3 km N of Teos.   **Teos:**

Ionian *polis*, *Inv.* **868** (*Sığacık*). Teos, Lebedos (next n.), or both may have declined by C4m, for Alexander's successor Antigonos planned to amalgamate them (Austin 2006, no. 48 = Welles 1934, no. 3–4; *Syll.*³ 344).   **Lebedos; Kolophon:** *Inv.* **850, 848,** Ionian *poleis.* See previous n.   **Notion:** 'South Wind City'; *Inv.* **858**; harbour town of Kolophon. See n. on 43 Kyllene. There is evidence of Notion's *polis* status in 403/2 and C4l (Flensted-Jensen and Hansen 2007, 219). (Not *Inv.* **825** Notion in Aiolis; see above under 98. 2 Pitane.)   **Apollo Klarios:** Klaros, site of the sanctuary, just N of Kolophon.   **Kaÿstros:** the Caÿster (*Küçük Menderes*).   **Ephesos:** *Inv.* **844** (*Selçuk*). One of the chief Ionian *poleis*, S of the Kaÿstros.   **Marathesion:** *Inv.* **853** (*Ambar Tepe*), in the Samian *peraia*.   **Magnesia:** *Inv.* **852** (*Tekke*); not included among Ionian *poleis* by Hdt. 1. 142. PS puts it between Marathesion and Anaia, only *c.*4 km apart on the coast—oddly, for most seafarers will have reached it by road from Ephesos. Perhaps the interposition implies a regular road from Marathesion up the R. Kenchrios between Marathesion and Anaia.   **Anaia:** *Inv.* **838** (*Kadikalesi*). Like Marathesion, Anaia and the next six places (to Mykale) are in the Samian *peraia* (see Shipley 1987, 31–7, 266–8), except Panionion, which belonged to Priene.   **Panionion:** near *Güzelçamlı.* Common sanctuary of the Ionians; see Metcalfe 2005, 46–121.   **Erasistratios:** not in *Inv.* or *Barr.*, but explained by Suda, on Erasistratos, by reference to the anatomist of that name from Ioulis (*c.*315–240), who cured Antiochos I of love-sickness (Plut. *Dem.* 38; App. *Syr.* 59–61) and was buried on Mykale; but this story postdates PS by at least half a century. PS is the earliest record of the place; its name suggests a hero-shrine of an unknown Erasistratos.   **Charadrous:** unattested elsewhere (not in *Barr.*); unlocated, Rubinstein 2004b, 1059. **Phokaia:** unlocated, Rubinstein 2004b, 1061; not in *Barr.* Not the Ionian *polis* (98. 2) but an unidentified settlement on Mykale, otherwise recorded only by Steph. Byz., at the end of his entry on Phokaia. **Akadamis:** not in *Inv.* or *Barr.* Presumably named after the hero Hekademos, so a sanctuary, not a *polis*; it can be restored in Hiller von Gaertringen 1906, no. 37 (C2e; Shipley 1987, 34 n. 50).   **Mykale:** probably the famous promontory (*Samsun Dağı*) rather than the settlement of that name, since PS locates Samos 'in front of' it (below). The settlement (not in *Barr.*) is known from Hiller von Gaertringen 1906, p. 466, and implied by the Mykaleis, a civic subdivision of Samos (Shipley 1987, 287, 292).   **territory of the Samioi:** the *peraia*; see n. on 98. 2 'territory is Lesbian'.   **Samos . . . enclosed:** large island with Ionian *polis*, *Inv.* **864**. PS specifies the *polis* (as he omits to do at 98. 2 Chios), despite writing when the island is an Athenian cleruchy (365–322); he may be following a source or, as he may have done elsewhere (see n. on 13. 3 Naxos), includes a former *polis* for its historical importance. The 'enclosed' (i.e. naval) harbour had a famous mole (Hdt. 3. 60).   **not lesser than Chios:** Chios is much larger in area (842 sq km as against 476 sq km) but similar in length, which is often PS's criterion.

Map 15. The SE Aegean and SW Asia Minor.

98. 4. **Priene:** *Inv.* **861** (*Güllübahçe*). Ionian *polis*, here in Lydia but in Karia at Hdt. 1. 142.   **coastal voyage of Mysia and Lydia:** Counillon 2007c, 37, sees a contradiction between this *paraplous* and that at 96 ('of Phrygia from Mysia'); but there is none, since there are two parts to Mysia in PS's scheme (see n. on 98. 1).   **Maiandros:** the R. Meander.

99. 1. Karia: on the region, see Flensted-Jensen 2004a, 1108–9.
Herakleia: *Inv.* **910** Latmos/Herakleia (*Kapıkırı*), in Cl times on a gulf
of the sea but now inland from Miletos. PS is the earliest source for
the name Herakleia (unless we date this passage C4l; see below).
'Latmos' went out of use *c*.C4l (*Inv.*), though the city's refoundation
(not necessarily its renaming) may have been instigated earlier by
Maussollos of Karia (r. 377–353), as suggested by Hornblower 1982,
319–20. Despite Flensted-Jensen and Hansen 2007, 205, and Counillon
2007c, 38–9, the use of 'Herakleia' does not mean this passage was
compiled or revised in or after 323–313 (the date of the Latmos-
Pidasa synoikism under the Macedonian satrap Asandros: *SEG* 47
1563; translated, van Bremen 2003, 314–15), which uses only
'Latmos'. F.-J. and H. themselves (n. 9) recognize that both names
may have been in use for a time. Indeed, usage may have changed
more than once in tandem with political control (Hornblower 1982,
320).   **Miletos:** *Inv.* **854** (*Balat*). The southernmost Ionian *polis*, a
major one, but put in Karia by PS, as by Hekat. F 240; Hdt. 1. 142.
Myndos: *Inv.* **914** (*Gümüslük*). Its new (Maussollan?) site was at the
end of the promontory further round which lies Halikarnassos.
Halikarnassos: *Inv.* **886** (*Bodrum*); an Ionic city (*OCD*³), but not one of
the original Ionian *poleis*. If PS meant the urban site, he should have
put it after Karyanda, Kalymna, and Kos (Müller 73); but he may
mean the N part of its territory, which—especially after the
synoikisms enacted by Maussollos (Hornblower 1982, 78–105)—will
have reached to the N coast of the peninsula, only *c*.6 km wide here.
the island: Müller 72 takes this for Arkonnesos (*Kara Ada*), which, at
c.349 m high and *c*.4 km offshore, extends across the view from the
harbour of Halikarnassos (cf. Strabo 14. 2. 16). The definite article, if
genuine, may suggest compression of an original source.   **Kalymna:** one of the larger Dodecanese islands. See n. on Halikarnassos,
above. (The name 'Dodecanese', however, is a Byzantine period in-
vention: Craik 1980, 4.)   **Karyanda island:** the *polis* (home of Skylax
of Karyanda) is *Inv.* **896;** it may have lain upon the island (*Salih Adası*)
before it was relocated a few km WSW onto the mainland, probably
in early Hl times (Flensted-Jensen 2004a, 1121). See also n. on Halikarnassos, above.   **these people are Kares:** it is unclear whether
this refers to Karyanda alone or to more than one of the above cities.
But since Karyanda was a Greek *polis*, the words may be misplaced
(Allain 188). Indeed, Kalymna is also Greek.   **Kos:** the *polis* is *Inv.*
497, synoikized in 366/5 from two or more *poleis* including Kos
Meropis (e.g. Hdt. 1. 144. 3). See also n. on Halikarnassos, above. PS
does not use his usual phrase 'I return to the mainland', though he
could have done so, but delays it until after Nisyros.   **Keramiac**

gulf: PS omits the cities in it (notably *Inv.* **878** Bargasa, **900** Keramos) and seems interested only in the outer coast of Karia (Counillon 2007c, 40).   **Nisyros:** the *polis* (not mentioned) is *Inv.* **508**.

99. 2. promontory ⟨of Knidos⟩, Triopion: the tip of the peninsula (*Deveboynu Burun*) on which Knidos lies; a non-*polis* settlement in C4 (Flensted-Jensen 2004a, 1110) and a Dorian cult centre (Hdt. 1. 144). 'Of Knidos' should be added here, rather than at the next use of 'promontory' a few lines below. The rubricator, who added these words in red at the top of the page, linked them with an asterisk to the passage about Kragos; this cannot be right, for Kragos (like Kryassos, the alternative conjecture) is near or at the E frontier of Karia. Triopion, on the other hand, is aptly called a 'promontory of Knidos', i.e. in Knidian territory; the name will have dropped out by *saut du même au même* (West 1973, 24–5). (I thank Stephen Mitchell for advice on this passage.)   **Knidos:** *Inv.* **903** (*Tekir*, 27° 22′ E). Against the notion that the Ar–Cl site was *c.*28 km to the E at *Datça*, 27° 41′ E, see Flensted-Jensen 2004a, 1123 (archaeological evidence). **territory of the Rhodioi:** the *peraia* or mainland territory of Rhodes after its synoikism in 408/7 (Fraser and Bean 1954; Gabrielsen 2000).

Barr. 65

Kaunos: *Inv.* **898** (*Dalyan*). PS jumps *c.*100 km E, omitting the island of Syme and the large Chersonesos promontory.   **Kragos:** in other sources Kragos (leaving aside other places of this name in Asia Minor) is a well-known mountain (*Barr.* 65 B5) and (probably) cape SSE of Telmessos, which PS makes the first town in Lykia (100. 1). Müller therefore prefers to read (here and at 99. 3) Kryassos, a town somewhere in Karia (Steph. Byz.; Plut. *Mor.* 246 e 7, etc.); it may be connected with C. Crya in eastern Karia (Mela 1. 83; cf. *Inv.* **907** Krya in Karia, though Artemidoros ap. Steph. Byz. on Krya puts this *polis* in Lykia). But corruption of ΚΡΥΑϹϹΟϹ into ΚΡΑΓΟϹ is more than a small step; nor is it easy to imagine an ancient editor making that change, in this Karian paragraph, if he knew Kragos was E of Telmessos and thus in Lykia. Accordingly we should, if possible, retain Kragos. This entails that PS misplaces Telmessos, perhaps as a result of compiling from different sources. (See n. on 100. 1 Telmissos for the city's Karian or Lykian identity in C4.) It is not impossible that PS named Kryassos (or Krya) at 99. 2 and Kragos at 99. 3; this would account for the otherwise unnecessary repetition of 'promontory' but would not solve the contradiction with respect to Telmessos.

Be it Kragos or Kryassos or both, PS has arranged 99–100 oddly (Counillon 2007c, 35). He moves rapidly via the Rhodian *peraia* to the limit of Karia, before turning back to the islands; then gives the *paraplous* of Karia; and only then says he is returning to the mainland. He

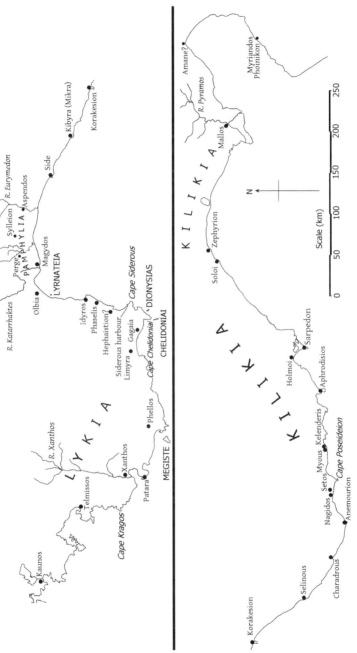

Map 16. Southern Asia Minor.

could have completed the mainland *ethnos* before moving offshore (as at 6–7), or interrupted the *ethnos* with an island excursion (as at 34), which would have allowed him to mention the Rhodian *peraia* either immediately before or immediately after Rhodes. (See also n. on 99. 3 Telos.)

99. 3. Rhodos island, ⟨with a city⟩: the old *poleis* (below) were synoikized in 408/7 (Diod. 13. 75. 1; *Inv.* **1000**), though in many respects they already acted as one community (Nielsen and Gabrielsen 2004, 1196, 1197).   **ancient triple city:** PS is not merely giving a historical note in the present tense but is listing real places: Ialysos, Lindos, and Kameiros (Thuc. 8. 44) survived as dependent *poleis* of Rhodos (Nielsen and Gabrielsen 2004, 1196, 1197). 'Triple city' is *tripolis* in Greek, also used below of Karpathos; see n. on 58 Amorgos. PS's circuit of Rhodes is clockwise, starting with the *polis* nearest the mainland, as on Keos (58).   **Ialysos, Lindos, and Kameiros:** *Inv.* **995**, **997**, and **996**.   **Chalkeia:** Chalke (*Chalki*), perhaps regularly approached from Kameiros; the *polis* (not mentioned) is *Inv.* **477**. **Telos:** within sight of Knidos; its *polis* (not mentioned) is *Inv.* **524**. The order of islands is odd. Moving seawards from Knidos, one might list Telos, Chalke, Rhodes, Karpathos, and Kasos (from N to S), reserving Kaunos for later. The anti-clockwise 'route' that PS takes from Rhodes to Karpathos is geographical in concept rather than political (Counillon 2007c, 41) or navigational.   **Kasos:** the *polis* (not mentioned) is *Inv.* **490**. Listed at 114, wrongly, as one of the largest islands (see n. there).   **Karpathos ... three-citied:** the island may have had four *poleis* earlier (Strabo 10. 5. 17), but PS is probably right to give it three (unnamed). The certain ones are Arkeseia (*Inv.* **486**; *Arkassa*), Brykous (**487**; *Agios Ioan0nis*), and Karpathos (**489**; unlocated). A fourth entity, Eteokarpathioi (**488**), has been described as a 'semi-independent *koinon*' of the others, lacking an urban centre; though sometimes regarded as a *polis* (Flensted-Jensen and Hansen 2007), it probably ceased to exist after C5 (Reger 2004, 746). Alternatively, the fourth may be Potidaion, which struck coins in C6 (Flensted-Jensen and Hansen 2007, 219–20). For 'three-citied' (possibly also used of Rhodos at 99. 3), see n. on 58 Amorgos.   **and the coastal voyage:** Counillon 2007c, 35 n. 7, thinks the use of *kai* to begin a *paraplous* reflects the unusual arrangement of this passage; but the only other example (11) has no obvious explanation. It could be a case of simple *variatio*.   **Kragos ... promontory of Karia:** its second mention here is as the end of a *paraplous*, but 'promontory' repeats information given at 99. 2; the text may be damaged. See n. on 99. 2 Kragos. (For the misplaced marginal note 'of Knidos', see n. on 99. 2 'promontory'.)   **I return again:** see n. on 99. 2 Kragos.

100. 1. Lykia: on the region, see Keen and Hansen 2004, 1138–40. **Telmissos:** elsewhere Telmessos (*Fethiye*), a non-*polis* (Keen and Hansen 2004, 1139–40) *c.*50 km E of Kaunos. One must distinguish, from W to E, (T1) Telemessos/Telmessos/Telmissos (*Inv.* **936**) near Halikarnassos, western Karia; (T2) Telmissos–*Fethiye*, SW Lykia, named here; (T3) Termessos Mikra (Oinoanda), NW Lykia, founded from T4 *c.*200 BC; (T4) Termessos, W Pamphylia (or W Pisidia), just E of Lykia. Of these PS names only T2. Its inclusion in Lykia is not evidence that PS wrote this passage after Alexander's entry into Asia Minor, despite Flensted-Jensen and Hansen 2007, 205 (where T2 is confused with T4), and Counillon 2007c 35–6, who tentatively proposes a date in the 310s. It is, however, evidence that PS is using C4 (and not earlier) information, since T2 became Lykian only C5l/C4e when captured by Perikles of Limyra (Theopompos F 103. 17). It reverted to Karia after *c.*360 (Hornblower 1982, 120–1; Counillon 2007c, 35), and will have been within Pixodaros's satrapy of Karia–Lykia (341/0–336/5; date at Hornblower 1982, 46–50). It was removed from Karia in 333 when Alexander created a satrapy of Lykia–Pamphylia (Arr. *Anab.* 3. 6. 7; Justin 13. 4. 15) for Nearchos, who later recaptured the town from a rebel (Polyain. 5. 35). Telmissos's placement within Lykia therefore suits either C5l–C4e or post-333. Since PS shows no other awareness of events after Alexander's accession, he may simply be using old information.   **Xanthos:** the *Esen Çay*.   **voyage upstream:** or rather, inland along a gulf *c.*8 km deep (now an alluvial plain).   **to ⟨Xanthos, a *polis*⟩:** *Inv.* **943** (*Kınık*), on a hill at the N (inner) corner of the former bay. The supplement is necessary, as Patara is on the coast beyond the river mouth (Strabo 14. 3. 4). Xanthos is a Lykian city in Hdt. 1. 176. 3; hellenization was promoted by the Hekatomnids of Karia in C4m.   **Patara:** a non-*polis* settlement (Keen and Hansen 2004, 1139; *Gelemiş*; later Arsinoë). Strabo 14. 3. 6 gives it a harbour.   **Phellos:** inland non-*polis* (*Çukurbağ*; Keen and Hansen 2004, 1138, 1139, 1211). Its Lykian identity may reflect its capture from Pamphylia (where Hekat. F 258 places it) by Pixodaros (Flensted-Jensen and Hansen 2007, 205). The E border of Lykia varied; PS 100. 2 locates the end of Lykia after Perge (30° 51′ E), in the plain of *Antalya*, whereas Strabo (14. 4. 1) begins Pamphylia further W, at Olbia (30° 36′ E), at the W end of the plain.   **Megiste:** *Kastellorizo*, with a non-*polis* town (Keen and Hansen 2004, 1140).   **Limyra:** NE of *Finike*; a non-*polis* (Keen and Hansen 2004, 1138, 1139). **Gagaia:** *Yenice*. Keen and Hansen 2004, 1140 (cf. 1138), suggest that, though allegedly founded by Rhodians, it was not Hellenic.   **Chelidoniai:** *Beş Adalar* ('Five Islands'). **Dionysias island:** also Krambousa (*Sulu Ada*).   **Siderous:** the promontory is *Adrasan Burnu*; the

harbour is Posidarisous (if correct at *Stad.* 230–1), *Ceneviz Limanı.*
Hephaistos ... spontaneous fire: *Barr.* 65 D5 Hephaistion (*Yanar Taş*,
'Flaming Rock'), where methane emissions burn naturally at an
altitude of *c.*180 m on a mountain spur (see Hosgormez *et al.* 2008 for
the geology). (See also Ps.-Arist. *Mir. ausc.* 127. 842b25–6; Bean 1968,
168–70 = Bean 1979, 138, against the view that this is anc. Chimaira;
he prefers to locate that in western Lykia, with Strabo 14. 3. 15).

100. 2. **higher from the sea:** the text is faulty, placing the harbour
town of Phaselis inland. Müller suggests that a 'Mt Phaselis' has
dropped out; but the peak behind Phaselis is Olympos or Phoinikous
(2,339 m); the similarity of the latter name to Phaselis may have
induced a kind of *saut du même au même* (West 1973, 24–5).   **Phase-**
lis ... and this is a gulf: *Inv.* 942 (*Tekirova*). Allain 190 suggests that
the phrase refers to the gulf with Phaselis on its W shore; but this
'Pamphylian Sea' is so wide that sailors would hardly see it as a gulf
rather than the open sea.   **Idyros:** *Inv.* 1002 (*Kemer?*). Hekat. F 260
locates it in Pamphylia. Cf. next n.   **Lyrnateia:** a non-*polis* in Pamphylia (Keen and Fischer-Hansen 2004, 1212; *Reşat Ada*). Hekat. F 261
(= Steph. Byz. on Lirnyteia) locates it in Pamphylia.   **Olbia:** a non-
polis in Pamphylia (Keen and Fischer-Hansen 2004, 1212; *Koruma* in
the city of *Antalya*). See n. on 100. 1 Phellos.   **Magydos:** *Lara*
Manastır on the E (l.) bank of the Katarraktes; a non-*polis* in Pamphylia (Keen and Fischer-Hansen 2004, 1212).   **Katarraktes:** the
Düden Çay. Strabo 14. 4. 1; *Stad.* 221.   **Perge ... sanctuary of**
Artemis: *Inv.* 1003 (*Aksu*). See n. on 100. 1 Phellos. Its inclusion in
Lykia rather than Pamphylia (implying the most easterly border of
Lykia for any period: Keen 1998, 18), might potentially date this
passage after Alexander (Counillon 2007c, esp. 36 n. 10), but in the
absence of other evidence that PS refers to events after 335 this
would be a radical step. It is theoretically possible that Hekatomnid
rule at some point extended this far E.   **gulf-shaped:** true only
when Lykia extends as far E as Perge.   **that beside land:** for the
second time (cf. 68. 3) PS distinguishes a direct crossing from coastal
sailing. But the implied use of *paraplous* for the direct route is surprising, unless it can denote any sailing where a certain land mass is
kept to left or right.

101. 1. **Pamphylia:** on the region, see Keen and Fischer-Hansen 2004,
1211–12, arguing that Pamphylia and Kilikia saw hellenization before
Alexander, for which PS is part of the evidence. (Extent of Pamphylia: also 100. 1 n.)   **Aspendos:** *Inv.* 1001 (later Primoupolis; *Belkis*),
on the W bank of the Eurymedon.   **Eurymedon:** the *Köprü Çay.*
Sylleion: a non-*polis* (Keen and Fischer-Hansen 2004, 1212; *Asar Köy*),
*c.*15 km WNW of Aspendos but listed after it, so perhaps reached by

road from it. Alternatively, if it was once on the coast, the order is inverted.   **Side:** *Inv.* **1004** (*Selimiye*). PS is the earliest evidence for its foundation from Aiolian Kyme (98. 2), though no Ar Greek finds are known. (If PS wrote before *c.*334, the claim was not concocted in the age of Alexander, as suggested in *Inv.*).   **a half of a day:** too short, if Kibyra and Korakesion (101. 2) are in Pamphylia rather than Kilikia. Pliny 5. 22/93 implies an earlier border further W, which would suit a shorter *paraplous*; Hekat. F 266 and later Artemidoros (ap. Strabo 14. 5. 3) put it further E than PS, as does Pliny for his day.

101. 2. also other cities: elsewhere PS always mentions 'other cities' before a region's *paraplous*. He may be combining different sources (Müller 76).   **Kibyra:** certainly Kibyra Mikra (*Karaburun*; 36° 38′ N, 31° 40′ E), on the coast between Side and Korakesion, rather than the better-known city of Kibyra in northern Lykia (37° 9′ N, 29° 29′ E), *c.*100 km inland and much further W than Side. Since other evidence for Kibyra Mikra is Hl–R (e.g. Bean and Mitford 1970, 59–60), PS is the earliest evidence for its existence.   **Korakesion:** a non-*polis* in Pamphylia (Keen and Fischer-Hansen 2004, 1212; *Alanya*).

Barr. 66

102. 1. Kilikia: on the region, see Keen and Fischer-Hansen 2004, 1211–12 (see also n. on 101. 1 Pamphylia). In Hdt. 'Kilikia' refers to the much larger Persian satrapy, whereas it could also be used in a narrower sense, as here (Müller xlvi).   **Selinous:** a non-*polis* in Kilikia, Keen and Fischer-Hansen 2004, 1214 (later Traianopolis; *Kale Tepe, Gazipaşa,* f. *Selinti*).   **Charadrous:** a non-*polis*, Keen and Fischer-Hansen 2004, 1213 (*Yakacık,* f. *Kaledıran İskelesi*).   **Anemourion:** a non-*polis*, Keen and Fischer-Hansen 2004, 1213 (*Eski Anamur*); pre-Hl history unknown.   **Nagidos:** *Inv.* **1010** (*Bozyazı*).   **Setos:** a non-*polis*, Keen and Fischer-Hansen 2004, 1214 (*Softa Kalesi*), only *c.*4 km E of Nagidos.   **Poseideion:** a promontory a few km further E than Setos (*Kızıl Burun*).   **Salon:** unknown; unlocated non-*polis*, Keen and Fischer-Hansen 2004, 1214. Perhaps near *Barr.* 66 C4 Dionysophanes (E of *Kızılburun*) (Mitchell 2000, 1023).   **Myous:** a non-*polis*, Keen and Fischer-Hansen 2004, 1213 (*Yenikaş,* f. *Crionaro*). (Not the Ionian *polis* of Hdt. 1. 142.)   **Kelenderis:** *Inv.* **1008** (*Aydıncık,* f. *Gilindere*), on a promontory with a harbour.   **Aphrodisios … another harbour:** *Inv.* **1005** Aphrodisias (medieval Porto Cavaliere), on a peninsula with harbours on both sides. PS also uses ἕτερος ('the other') to refer to one of a pair of harbours at §12.   **Holmoi:** *Inv.* **1006** (*Taşucu*). Keen and Fischer-Hansen 2004, 1217, cite Hellenkemper and Hild 1986, 28 n. 12, for the suggestion that Holmoi is the E harbour of Aphrodisias. But if we add *limena* ('harbour') before *echousa* ('having'), as seems necessary, then Holmoi will be else-where—at least, PS thinks it is. *Taşucu* is *c*.8 km SW of the C4l founda-tion of Seleukeia on the Kalykadnos but lacks Greek remains (*Inv.*), so Holmoi may have been elsewhere in C4m, perhaps inland.   **Sarpe-don ... deserted city:** a non-*polis*, Keen and Fischer-Hansen 2004, 1214 (*İncekum Burnu*). It is the only town PS describes as 'deserted'; perhaps the implication, as at 103 below, is that it is not a strong naval base.   **with a river:** the Kalykadnos (*Göksü*).   **Soloi:** *Inv.* 1011 (R Pompeiopolis; *Viranşehir*).   **Zephyrion:** 'West Wind', a non-*polis*, probably non-Hellenic, Keen and Fischer-Hansen 2004, 1214 (later Hadrianopolis; *Mersin*).   **Pyramos:** the *Ceyhan Nehri*.   **Mal-los:** *Inv.* 1009, possibly a colony of Argos (later Antiochia ad Pyra-mum; near *Kızıltâhta*), today *c*.25 km up the R. Pyramos.   ***Amane:*** 'Alane', MS. Müller 77 suggests Amane the name is unattested but cf. Amanides Pylai in Strabo 14. 5. 18 (*c*.50 km ENE of Mallos), the 'gate-way' to Kilikia. The usual emendation, 'Adane' (feminine singular; i.e. *Barr.* 66 G3 Adana/Antiochia ad Sarum; *Adana*; non-*polis*, Keen and Fischer-Hansen 2004, 1213), is unviable since that site's name is usu-ally Adana (neuter plural). It is also *c*.50 km inland (PS would nor-mally say so), and on a different river that should have been named before the Pyramos and the city of Mallos. One might also consider Aigeai (on the coast *c*.24 km E of Mallos), founded as a *polis* in C4l (cf. *IG* xii. 1. 62; Samos, C4l) and later a major R port, which may well have been a Cl *emporion*—though its name, if a clone of Macedonian Aig(e)ai, should not antedate C4l.

Barr. 67

Myriandos Phoinikōn: non-*polis*, Keen and Fischer-Hansen 2004, 1213–14 (*Ada Tepe*).   **Thapsakos, a river:** mentioned in advance as the end of a region; see 104. 2 n.

102. 2. out of Sinope ... to Soloi: PS may mean to mark the end of Asia Minor with this land-based equivalent of a closing *paraplous*. The erroneous assertion that the 'waist' of Asia Minor is only a five-day journey by land is also made by Hdt. 2. 34 (cf. 89 n.). But see Mahaffy 1913, 196, suggesting that Hdt. wrote ΑΝΔΡΙΙΕΗΜΕΡΑΙ ('for a man, 15 days'), which became ΑΝΔΡΙΕΗΜΕΡΑΙ ('for a man, 5 days').

Barr. 72

103. CYPRUS

103. Kypros: PS starts in the E and keeps the coast on his l. hand (as he always does except in Sicily, 13), thus following an anti-clockwise circuit. He indicates ethnic differences between Hellenic, Phoen-ician, 'aborigines' (*autochthones*), and the barbarians of the interior.

Cyprus is the only place where PS uses 'winter harbour' and

'deserted harbour', clearly terms from a distinct source (possibly also covering nearby Sarpedon, 102. 1). In this text though not necessarily others, 'deserted harbour' means one that is vulnerable to attack, so that PS is contrasting the 'enclosed' (secure) harbour of Salamis with the rest (Counillon 1998b, 64–5).

He concentrates on areas where Athenian interests were strongest: the N and W, and Amathous in the S (C4m Athenian links: Hsch. on Ῥοίκου κριθοπομπία; Counillon 1998b, 66 n. 52). He omits Kourion (*Inv.* **1016**) and Paphos (*Inv.* **1019**) in the S, together with inland Idalion (*Inv.* **1013**) and Phoenician Kition (not in *Inv.*), also in the S, of which Idalion may have been a dependency. MS error on such a scale is unlikely; rather, PS, perhaps under the influence of sources, reflects the situation under Euagoras I of Salamis (r. 411–374/3), who built an empire with its naval centre at Salamis. PS thus downplays the Phoenician and Persian presence, also confining other barbarians to the interior (ibid. 66-7.)

Map 17. Cyprus.

Salamis: *Inv.* **1020** (later Konstantia; NW of *Ammochostos*). **Karpaseia:** *Inv.* **1014** (*Rizokarpaso*), founded from Phoenician Sidon; Greek finds begin C5. **Keryneia:** *Inv.* **1015** (*Kyrenia*). **Lepethis Phoinikōn:** *Inv.* **1017** Lapethos (N of *Karavas*); the name implies it was founded by Phoenicians, but Strabo 14. 6. 3 asserts a Spartan origin. **Soloi:** *Inv.* **1021** (SW of *Morphou*), founded from Athens. **Marion:** *Inv.* **1018** (E of *Chrysochou*). Here PS omits Paphos and Kourion (see n. on Kypros, above). **Amathous:** *Inv.* **1012** (NE of *Lemesos*), a partly non-Greek city. **they are aborigines:** the slippage from singular to plural is typical of PS and not necessarily a sign of textual damage (Allain 193); cf. 'these people are Kares', 99. 1. For 'aborigines' cf.

47. 2.   **deserted harbours:** see n. on Kypros, above.   **other cities
. . . barbarian:** see introductory n. to 103.

104–6. SYRIA–PHOENICIA TO EGYPT

Though PS does not mark a strong beginning here, he has just marked the end of Asia Minor with the land crossing to Sinope. Here begins a long passage with no Hellenic *poleis* (unless Naukratis has dropped out under Egypt) until Kyrene (108. 3). This is no accident or literary choice: only three Ar–Cl *poleis* have been positively identified from in the Levant and Africa, none of which PS names: in Syria Posideion (*Inv.* **1022**) and in Egypt Naukratis (**1023**) and Oasis (**1024**) (leaving aside the abandoned Kinyps in Libyē, 109. 4). Had PS sought to represent the world of Greek *poleis*, he would have had little to say about these regions, yet they occupy one-third of his text. Neither does he have a strong interest in trade as such (Counillon 1998b, 57, 64). Evidently his geographical aims extend to describing non-Greek parts of the *oikoumenē* and calculating their length. The new region is perhaps tacitly marked by the use of *ethnika* (Syroi, Phoinikes), rather than regional names, to introduce the passage (contrast in 93–103 Mysia, Phrygia, Troas, etc.).

For Syria, PS conveys a greater sense of the hinterland and more two-dimensionality than usual: the Phoinikes occupy a coastal strip region of variable width. He is aware that they live in city-kingdoms, but omits Byblos, even though it was shortly to be captured by Alexander (Arr. *Anab.* 2. 15. 6); also Azotos (e.g. Hdt. 2. 157, referring to the era of Psammetichos; Jos. *AJ* 13. 104, time of Ptolemy VI; *Ashdod*) and Gaza (e.g. Arr. *Anab.* 2. 26-7). He knows about the 'royal seats' in the dependent towns. His Phoenicia is a land of coastal cities with harbours, rivers, two mountains—and the location of the Andromeda myth.

At Arabia, PS again changes tack. Although the text is fragmentary, it is clear that the Arabes are characterized by a pastoral economy. PS may have said little more than that, since the remaining words concern the relationship between seas: the Mediterranean, Red Sea, and (probably) Indian Ocean. Possibly PS included some settlements of the Arabes.

Of northern Egypt we receive a narrowly topographical account. Apart from painstaking details of the distributaries of the Nile, we learn only of L. Mareia and of the overall shape of Egypt—something we did not get for Syria or, apparently, Arabia and such as we will not get for subsequent regions. We learn a surprising amount in a small space about the mythological associations of Kanopos Island, reflecting PS's occasional interest in Homeric geography. Nothing is said about Egyptians, though there are indirect mentions of king-ship. Despite Herodotean precedent (2. 9), we are told nothing in detail about the journey up the Nile, even as far as Memphis (at the southern apex of the Delta); the city is named only in passing. The great ports are conspicuous by their absence. Naukratis, *c.*70 km inland on the r. (E) bank of the Canopic channel (*Kom Gaief*), may have been mentioned in the gap on p. 94 of the MS. There is room in that gap for Alexandria too; but the *periplous* probably predates the city's foundation by a few years. If he had wanted to mention it, he had another opportunity to do so when discussing Pharos at 107. 1.

The text may thus have drawn on a separate source for each region.

104. 1. Syroi: see introductory n. above. Syria was a Persian satrapy until Alexander's expedition.   **Phoinikes:** the Phoenicians of the Levant, a city-states society (Niemeyer 2000), colonized the W Mediterranean at an early date and were believed to have founded Carthage (111. 1). See also n. on 13. 2 Phoinikes.

Barr. 67

104. 2. Thapsakos river: not in *Barr.* A river of this name at this spot is attested only here and at 102. 1; it is probably the Orontes (Müller 77). Thapsakos translates Hebrew *Tapsaḥ*, 'ford' (L. 271).   **Tripolis Phoinikōn:** not the three places named next, but three mainland towns opposite Arados (below), of which they were dependencies: Karnos, Enydra, and Marathos (all at Strabo 16. 2. 12; L. 272).

Barr. 68

Arados: *Rouad* or *Arwad*; non-Greek city on islet, with extensive *peraia* (*OCD³*). We have come over 100 km from Myriandos (102. 1), by-passing several settlements (though some are Hl foundations). **royal seat of Tyre:** i.e. Arados was a dependency of Tyre (mentioned in advance here); there is archaeological evidence for two palaces (L. 283). See next n.   **with a harbour:** some editors remove this second harbour, but there are two natural ones on the former island, one dominated by a fort that is probably PS's 'royal seat' (L. 280, 283). **8 stades:** 1.5 km. As Arados I. is *c.*2.6 km offshore, Müller cxxxviii prefers 20 st. and Lipiński (279–80) proposes 18. But as the error could have a number of causes, no particular change has a strong basis.   **a second city of Tripolis:** *Tarabulus/Tripoli*, Lebanon. **belongs to Arados and Tyros and Sidon:** i.e. was made up of settlers from these parent cities (L. 285). Sidon is mentioned in advance. **three cities:** there is no archaeological confirmation; one or two of the three ethnic communities may have lived on offshore islands (L. 285).   **Theou Prosopon:** 'God's Face', a distinctive, flat-topped mountain by the sea (*Ras Shaqqa*, SW of *Tripoli*). First recorded here (L. 287).   **Trieres:** 'Trireme'; *El Heri*, or *Batrūn* (not far N of Beirut, L. 288). Polyb. 5. 68. 8; Strabo 16. 2. 15; Steph. Byz. But Lipiński prefers 'Teros', MS. This is the earliest attestation of the place, and Trieres is probably a hellenization of a foreign word, so 'Teros' may preserve the local name.

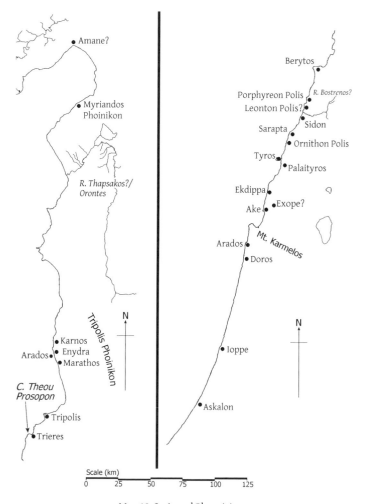

Map 18. Syria and Phoenicia.

Barr. 69

Berytos: *Beirut.* Recorded here first in Greek sources. **river Bostrenos:** Müller cxxxviii suggests this in place of 'northern (*borinos*)
harbour', MS, which has a red line indicating a place-name. **Porphyreōn:** *Khan Nebi Yulas* or *Nabe Yūnəs.* The accent on the last
syllable (proved by Polyb. 5. 68. 6) shows that this is not 'the city of
the Purple-dyers'. ⟨**Leontōn Polis**⟩: 'Lions' City'; unlocated toponym Leontopolis, Brown and Meyers 2000, 1070; tentatively *Wādī as-
Sekke* (L. 295). **Sidon:** the city-state had a hellenized dynasty in
Achaemenid times (*OCD*³). **enclosed harbour:** the port N of the
city; the absence of a 'royal seat' is consistent with a date after 346/5,
when the revolt of Tennes was put down (L. 290). On 'enclosed', see
103 n. **Ornithōn Polis:** 'Birds' City'; Roman Ad Nonum (*Adlun*; or
Tell Burāq, L. 294). **Belonging to the Sidonioi:** different punctuation would give a different sense; see Allain 194; L. 295.

104. 3. Part-way through 104. 3 we reach pp. 93–4 of the MS. This leaf
is cut off diagonally, leaving a series of increasingly short lines on
the front and back of the leaf; the lower third of each page is entirely
missing. (Undamaged text resumes at p. 95, §106. 2.) It would have
been crucial to an understanding of the *periplous* to know, for
example, whether it told us who ruled Egypt or named Alexandria.
There is a hint at 105—not noticed by earlier editors—that he may
have named the Erythraian Sea or Indian Ocean. **Sarapta:**
Sarepta/Makra Kome (*Sarefend*)—but between Sidon and Ornithōn
Polis. Sarepta, which was in revolt until 346/5, may have been a
dependency of Tyre (as PS appears to imply) only between then and
332 (L. 295). Again the punctuation is crucial. **Tyros:** Tyre (*Šur*)
was an island (Diod. 17. 40. 3–4; Arr. *Anab.* 2. 18. 2) before Alexander
built his siege-works in 332 (Pliny 5. 12/76). PS mentions only one of
its two harbours (L. 296). See n. on 'this island', below. **within a
fort:** the harbour was not within the walls, but the interior curve of
the fortifications gave this impression (L. 298). **this island:** there
is compression here; 'island' is introduced suddenly, presumably
referring to Tyre (Allain 194). Perhaps 'island' has dropped out of the
preceding words. **3 stades from the** *sea:* correct for the former
strait (L. 296), though Pliny 5. 12/76 gives a larger figure, 700 paces
or 0.7 Roman miles (*c.*1 km). But 'sea' is an error for 'land' or 'mainland' (Müller 78–9); it may be an original error by PS, though the
word order is untypical and the text may be corrupt.

The following passage is largely cut away in the MS

Palaityros: 'Old Tyre' (*Ras el-'Ain*; or *Tell ar-Rašīdīye*, L. 299); destroyed
by Alexander (Diod. 17. 40. 5). **a river:** *Wādī Uqāb* (L. 302). ⟨**Ek-**

dippa⟩: *Achziv/ez Zib* (Israel); the only significant harbour between Tyre and Akko (L. 302; already connected by Shepherd 1923). Editors have wrongly printed the definite article (τῶν) before the name. The circumflex-like mark above and r. of the tau at the cut-off edge is more consistent with Τυρίων in the form in which it occurs several times in this passage. Τ[υρίων ῞Εκδιππα] fits the gap; the rather long printed line is deceptive.   **Ake:** or Ptolemais (*Acre/Tell Acco*); Strabo 16. 2. 25 gives both Greek names.   **Exope:** L. 309 suggests that the letters in the MS, previously thought garbled, represent ʿAkšāp, the Achshaph of Egyptian Bronze Age texts (*Tell Abū Ḥawām*; or *Kafr Yasif*, Google Earth). The name may have been transferred to the dependent harbour when the city was abandoned.   ⟨**Karmelos**⟩: a major landmark.   **Arados:** ʿAtlit, with a Phoenician harbour of Cl date (L. 316–19; *Barr.* 69 A4 Boukolonpolis). (Distinct from 104. 2 Arados.)   ⟨**Magdolos, a city and**⟩ **river of the Tyrioi:** neither is in *Barr.* A place-name and the word ‘*polis*’ are clearly missing. Lipiński (320–2) supplies Magdolos (*Wādī al-Maǵāra*; cf. Maspero n.d. (1903), map), perhaps that of Hdt. 2. 159.   **Doros:** *Barr.* 69 A4 Dor(a) (*Burj et Tantura*), in decline by C4 (L. 322); a ‘little town’, Millar 1993, 267. Lipiński (329) notes the gap of *c*.70 km from here to Ioppe (next n.); finds no strong candidate for an intermediate stopover; but suggests Apollonia (*Arsūf*). We need not do PS's research for him, however, even if we think extra places stood in his sources. Gaps of over a day's sailing are frequent in the text; most or all will be original.

Barr. 70

⟨**Ioppe**⟩: *Jaffa.* The addition is certain because of the reference to Andromeda that follows.   **Androm⟨eda⟩:** her father, Kepheus, was king of the Aithiopes. On their locations in ancient thought, see Panchenko 2003; cf. 112. 5. Strabo (1. 2. 35) says some observers extended Aithiopia to here and placed the Andromeda story at ‘Iope’ (cf. 16. 2. 28).   ⟨**Aska**⟩**lon:** a small *polisma*, Strabo 16. 2. 29.   **Koile Syria:** Lipiński (333–4) notes that while Ktesias F 1b (C4e; Diod. 2. 2) uses this term in the narrow sense of inland Syria (between Mts Lebanon and Antilebanon), PS is the first to use it in the wider sense embracing the Syrian–Phoenician coast.   **2,700 stades:** *c*.500 km. ‘1,700’, MS, is much too short; plausibly emended by Müller. It might seem suspicious that, while 1,000 st. is added by emendation here, the same amount is deducted at 106. 3; yet both changes are probably correct, since the errors are large and the forms of alpha and beta used for 1,000 and 2,000, respectively, are easily confused.

105. 1. *Arabia.* A new region begins here, at least in the mind of whoever added the headings to the text, since the surviving alpha of Ἀ[ραβία] (see Greek text; omitted in the translation) is in red. The restoration is virtually certain. Arabia's Mediterranean coast was very short. Like Phoenicia, it was an area without Greek *poleis*.

About half of §105 is lost (*c*.100–150 words). Müller 79 tentatively reconstructs the lines after 'camels' as follows (I translate his Latin):

> And thi[s land is sterile and deserted, and] is for the most part w[aterless. And in its western part that inclines towards] Egypt [extends a narrow sea; and] in it [are] gul[fs, the Ailanites and the Heroöpolites; and] from the [so-called Erythraian sea or the out]side se[a] is [Arabia as far as our sea].

This will be broadly right, though whether both arms of the Red Sea were named must be uncertain (Ailanites, mod. gulf of *Aqaba*, seems to occur first in Poseidonios fr. 35 Theiler = Strabo 17. 1. 35, and elsewhere in Strabo; Heroöpolites is the gulf of *Suez*).

Er⟨ythraian sea⟩: the anc. 'Red Sea' includes the mod. Red Sea, Persian gulf, and Indian Ocean (*OCD³*). Müller's conjecture is spectacularly confirmed by the last surviving letter of p. 93 l. 15 of the MS, which M. does not record: an epsilon whose form shows it was followed by rho or xi. Xi is unlikely (the reconstruction ἐκ τῆς ἔξ[ωθεν θαλάττης], 'out of the outer sea', is ruled out as ἔξω]θεν θαλ[αττ is already at the end of the line; and PS preferred ἀπὸ in this phrase at §§17–18). Rho virtually dictates 'Erythraian'.

105. 2. Pelousion: an advance mention; see 106. 1–3, 5. **1,300 stades:** *c*.240 km.

106. 1. *Egypt.* This section is fuller than those on Syria and Arabia, but the first part is mutilated. See generally Peretti 1979, 276–89. (Region, Greek settlements: Austin 2004, 1234–5; *poleis*, 1238–40 nos 1023–4).)

Barr. 74

⟨Pelousion⟩: *Tell el-Farama.* **⟨river Neilos⟩:** from here to 108. 4 PS names no rivers. **⟨Tanitic⟩:** or 'Saitic', Hdt. 2. 17. **⟨Phatniti⟩c:** or Boukolikon Stoma, Hdt. 2. 17. **⟨Boutos⟩:** Bouto (*Kom el-Farain*). **⟨Thonis⟩:** *Abukir,* just E of the Canopic channel. Restored because it occurs at 107. 1 as if previously named. Strabo 17. 1. 16 refers to a former *polis* of Thonis where Menelaos (106. 5, 108. 1) and Helen came; Hdt. 2. 114–16 reports the version of the theft of Helen in which she is kept in Egypt until Menelaos comes for her. **⟨Mareia⟩:** L. *Mariout.* **⟨already in⟩ Libyē:** since at 107. 1 PS, consistently, begins Libyē at the Kanopic mouth, it was not necessary to mention Mareia here. Alexandria (founded soon after PS wrote) technically lay outside Egypt and was officially 'Alexandria by Egypt'.

The undamaged MS pages resume here

106. 2. **the other the Pelousiac:** 'the other' translates τὸ δὲ. In the preceding lacuna will have been a statement such as 'a little below the city of Memphis the Nile splits into two channels: the one (τὸ μὲν) is called the Kanopic …'. (Cf. similar reconstruction at Müller 80). Another form of the name, below, is translated 'Pelousian' here. PS may be using two sources, given the inconsistency just below (see n. on 106. 3 Memphis).   **split apart:** what we have of PS's account of the Nile's distributaries is accurate, whereas Hdt. 2. 17 wrongly derives the Saitic (as he calls the Tanitic) from the Sebennytic (Müller 80).

106. 3. **similar to an axe:** a double-headed axe (Müller 81), since PS says Egypt narrows as far inland as Memphis, then widens. In Hdt. 2. 7–8, slightly differently, it is wide up to Heliopolis, narrow for four days' sailing, then widens. See introductory n. to (*d*) above. **Memphis:** the 'capital' of Egypt before the foundation of Alexandria. The two different genitive forms here are probably due to inconsistent copying rather than different sources. See first n. on 106. 2. **bounds Asia and Libyē:** compare the words (partly restored) about Mareia, 106. 1. Hdt. 2. 15 (cf. Austin 2004, 1235) berates Ionian geographers (unfairly: Lloyd 1976, 82–3) for making the Nile the boundary of Asia and Libyē, for taking the Delta as the whole of Egypt (at 2. 6 his measurement of Egypt's coast is longer, 60 *schoinoi* or 3,600 st.), and for implying that the Delta is in neither continent. For him, all of Egypt is in Asia (2. 17). PS agrees with the last point, placing his *periplous* of Asia (106. 4) after that of Egypt; but he sides with the Ionians in taking the Delta as the measure of Egypt's coast (since he makes Egypt run from Pelousion to Kanopos) and thus excludes from Egypt and Asia the area W of the Delta that belongs to Egypt (107. 3).   **1,300 stades:** *c.*240 km. '2,300', MS, is much too long; several other sources agree on 1,300 (Müller 81). See n. on '2,700 stades' at 104. 3.

106. 4. Length of Asia

106. 4. On this and the other summations (part of the original text, in the present editor's view), see 69 n.

106. 5. **island:** *Barr.* 74 C2 Kanope (*Île Nelson*).   **Menelaos:** king of Homer's Sparta, husband of Helen. The *polis* of Kanobos was allegedly named after his ship-captain, who died there (Strabo 17. 17. 1). See nn. on 106. 1 Thonis; 108. 1 Menelaos.   **Pelousios … Kasion:** Pelousios is unknown (Müller 81) but apparently founded Pelousion near *Barr.* 70 C3 Casius Mons (*Ras Qasrun/Khatib el Gals*).

107–11. Libyē

The long account of Libyē (107–9) occupies one-sixth of the entire text. The first part is ruled from Egypt (107. 3). We encounter quite a detailed enumeration of ports, with a larger number of local distances than for any region since Thrace (67); often several are stated one after the other. Several Greek *poleis* are named, and there is a higher density of landmarks such as islets and anchorages. PS is the most accurate source for Cyrenaica before Ptolemy of Alexandria and the anonymous *Stadiasmos* (Müller xlvii). As with the preceding regions, he appears to have drawn upon sources specific to this region, and inserts material reflecting philosophers' interest in the natural world (Introduction, VII), such as the silphium fields and the Garden of Hesperides in Cyrenaica. At the Great Syrtis (109. 1) the density of information falls off and is only partly compensated for by information about the transhumant Makai. After a revival of the level of detail before and after Carthage (111. 1), it falls off once more along the mostly steep-to coast of Algeria.

From 111. 1, after Carthage itself, new sources again appear to have been used. PS suddenly stops using distances in stades, ceases to refer to nights' sailing, and gives no transect shorter than half a day. Confusion in the sources appears to have led him to postpone the Lesser Syrtis to the position that should be occupied by the gulf of *Hammamat*. Similarly, part of the account of the *Tangier* area is subsequently displaced to a later point (112. 4–5).

Despite Lloyd 1975, 134, this account only vaguely resembles Hdt. 4. 168–96; we cannot be sure that both authors draw upon Hekataios.

107–9. Non-Carthaginian Libyē

107. 1. Libyē begins: see n. on 106. 1 'already in Libyē'. (Region: Austin 2004, 1235–7; *poleis*, 1240–7 nos **1025–9**. Overview of Greek activity: Boardman 1999, 153–9, 275–7. Ambiguity of 'Libyē', interchangeability of ethnographic data between India and Africa: Panchenko 2003.)

Barr. 73

Adyrmachidai: *Barr.* marks them behind the coast of Egypt (31° N, 26–27° E); but PS envisages an area closer to the Delta (its W end is at 30° E). Hdt. 5. 168 makes these the first people in Libyē.   **Thonis:** see 106. 1 n.   **Pharos:** later the site of Alexandria's lighthouse. **150 stades:** as in Strabo 17. 1. 6 (measuring from the Canobic mouth). **many harbours:** in effect, repeats 'good harbours' from a few words earlier (Desanges 96–7), perhaps due to compilation. An interesting observation in the light of the foundation of Alexandria after PS

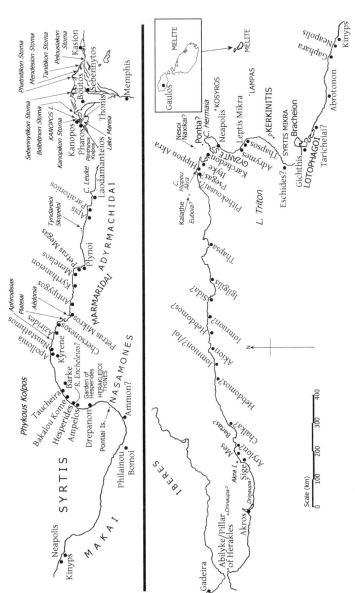

Map 19. North Africa.

wrote; Pharos was evidently seen already as a centre of maritime traffic.   **Chersonesos:** perhaps the unlocated Chersonesos Mikra (*Marabit* near Alexandria), Bernand 2000, 1122.

107. 2. Plinthinos gulf: presumably the embayment W of *Barr.* 74 B2 Plinthine (*Kom el-Nagous? c.*29° 35′ E). The W limit of Egypt (Hdt. 2. 6). **Leuke Akte:** 'White Headland'; *Barr.* 73 E2 (*Ras el-Abiad*; also *Ras el Hekma*).   **Laodamanteios:** *Barr.* 73 E2 Ladamantia (near *Ras Abu Hasafa*).   **Paraitonios:** *Barr.* 73 E2 Paraetonium/Ammonia (*Marsa Matruh*).

107. 3. Apis: *Zawiet Umm el-Rakham* (27° 3′ E). Hdt. 2. 18 puts it in the part of Egypt closest to Libyē.

108. 1. Libyes: the description as far as Carthage is based on at least two sources; that for the Cyrenaean Pentapolis evidently gave more distances (Müller xlvii). PS does not use Hdt., or not alone, since he mentions two Syrtides and the Marmaridai (not in Hdt.).   **Marmaridai . . . Hesperides:** in *Barr.* the Marmaridai are marked only W of Plynos Limen (in mod. Libya; 23–24° E). From Apis to Hesperides is in fact a vaster stretch, covering 7° of longitude and *c.*700 km. Peretti 1979, 290–302, discusses the Marmaridai and §108 generally. Hesperides is mentioned in advance.   **Tyndareioi Skopeloi:** 'Tyndareos's Rocks'; *Ishaila Rocks*, 3.4 km offshore; cf. Strabo 17. 1. 14. Tyndareōs (or -eus) was a mythical king of Sparta, father of Helen—another Spartan connection, cf. 'Menelaos' below, and n. on 106. 5 Kanopos. **Plynoi:** in *Barr.* as Catabathmus Maior/Plynos *Limen*/Tetrapyrgia (*Sollum*), just within modern Egypt.   **Petras the Great:** *Bardia/ Bardia Sliman*, Libya.   **Menelaos:** *Marsa Ahora?* See n. on Tyndareioi Skopeloi, above.   **Kyrthaneion:** *Marsa el-Afarid?*   **Antipygos:** 'Back-to-back'; *Tobruk.* Cf. 46. 1 (where *antipygos* is an adjective, not a name); Müller cxxxviii prefers Antipyrgos. (Importance of back-to-back harbours: Cary 28–9.)   **Petras the Small:** *Marsa Tarfaia.*

Barr. 38

Chersonesos: said below to be beyond Aëdonia and Plateiai, so this is *Barr.* 38 E1 Chersonesos Akra (*Ras et-Tin*; 23° 7′ E). Distinct from Azirides (below): 'these' refers to both, as a specific *paraplous* follows. **Azirides:** see n. on 47. 1 Azirides. *Barr.* 38 D1 Aziris (*Wadi el-Chalig*, 22° 55′ E); probably known to the C3 historian Menander of Ephesos (*FGrH* 783 F 3; Boardman 2010).

108. 2. Aëdonia: *Geziret el-Maracheb* (*Seal Island*).   **Plateiai:** *Bomba* promontory.   **anchorages:** *hyphormoi*, perhaps 'minor anchorages', used by PS only here (twice) and at 108. 3. For its use in other sources, see Counillon 1998b, 63, 66.   **silphium . . . as far as Hesperides:** silphium, a plant of the genus *Ferula*, produced a prized resin, a mainstay of Cyrene's export trade. Cultivation probably took place inland, in a belt S of the mountain ridge (D. J. Mattingly, pers. comm.). Hdt. 4. 169 picks out the region in similar words ('the silphium begins from this point'). Hesperides is the city (108. 5). **fields:** *gyai* (singular *gyēs*; 1. masc.), a literary word, occasionally used (sometimes metaphorically) in poetry and occasionally in documentary papyri from Egypt. It may imply a non-standard agricultural practice whereby silphium was partly wild and partly cultivated (D. J. Mattingly, pers. comm.). According to some informants (Thphr. *HP* 6. 3. 3) it required uncultivated ground, while others (6. 3. 5) prescribed digging between the plants. Silphium also appears at Ps.-Lykophron (*Alexandra*, 906), an author who appears to have consulted PS for the Daunitai (§15).   **Hesperides:** the *polis* (108. 5), mentioned in advance again.   **1,500 stades:** corrupt in the MS. **Aphrodisias:** Laia/Aphrodites Nesos (*Geziret Chersa*; or *Kirissah*). **Naustathmos:** *Marsa Hilal*. This stretch of Cyrenaica is close to Crete (*c.*280 km); unlike Strabo (e.g. 17. 3. 20) PS does not say so, though he notes the Sardinia–Libyē crossing at 7.   **harbour of Kyrene:** later Apollonia (Desanges 99) or Sozousa (*Marsa Susa*) with C4s/C3a fortifications (White and Wright 1998).

108. 3. Kyrene: *Inv.* 1028 (*Ain Shahat*, *Grennah*).   **all-weather harbours:** presumably Naustathmos and the harbour of Kyrene (above).   **refuges under islets … anchorages … headlands:** as elsewhere in this passage, PS seems to be consulting a more nautical source for local data. Cf. n. on 109. 3 Herakleioi Thines. No islets are visible, however, in Google Earth (or in US army maps on line at the Perry-Castañeda Library, University of Texas: http://lib.utexas.edu/maps/).   **the harbour by Barke:** Barke, *c.*18 km inland (*Inv.* **1025,** *el-Merg*), is thus included only indirectly. The harbour was later Ptolemais (*Tolmetta/Tulmeitia*), to which Hl Barke was subordinate (*Inv.*).   **620 stades:** accurate—actually *c.*115 km. We leap forward briefly to Hesperides.

108. 4. PS backtracks to revisit NW Cyrenaica as far as Hesperides. *divided localities:* the sense is obscure, the MS possibly corrupt. Müller 83 translates (in Latin) as 'places where the shore has remote places' (*recessus*). If *choria* means 'settlements', it may refer to the phenomenon in Cyrenaica of inland towns on the plateau, each linked to a harbour town. But of four uses of *chorion* by PS, all in Libyē (108. 4; 108. 5, twice; 109. 4), none definitely refers to a settlement (and in the last case the *chorion* is explicitly not the *polis*). The terminology presumably reflects a source, and perhaps denotes a feature of land management specific to the region.   **Phykous, a gulf:** a town (*Zaviet el-Hamama*) and cape (*Ras Aamer/Ras Sem*) not far W of Kyrene.

Cf. Strabo 17. 3. 20.   **garden of the Hesperides:** *Barr.* 38 B1 Hesperidum Horti. PS locates it inland from Phykous; but the garden, or rather gardens, have been plausibly located in natural karstic depressions near *Coefia* (Jones and Little 1971, 78–9, with 66 fig. 4 and pl. 8. 2) or *Kuwayfiyah*, *c.*10 km NE of Hesperides. Various locations were offered for the home of the Hesperid nymphs, sometimes called the daughters of Atlas and Hesperis (*OCD*³ on Hesperides), 'lady of the West'. They were usually further W, in NW Africa or Iberia (cf. Hes. *Th.* 517–20; Hdt. 4. 184. 3). (Cf. unlocated Hesperidum Horti in the 'Lixus area' of NW Morocco, Euzennat 2000, 463.) PS seems to know a version in which an originally vague location in the far west became associated with a suitably named city and a topographically plausible site. If the location is (in this sense) correct, however, PS introduces it too soon and then has to fit into the remaining geographical room too many places (Ampelos to Kaukalou Kome), which should have been distributed along the coast from Barkes Limen to Hesperides.

   It is a remarkably concentrated list of natural species, unlike anything else in the *periplous* (except perhaps the lacunose list of Arabia's animals, 105. 1). No Greek descriptions of gardens survive between Homer and Hesiod on the one hand and the late novelists on the other (Forster 1952, 63). The present exception, of course, gives no sense of cultivation taking place as opposed to a natural environmental niche. The specific range of species cannot have grown together; they include some that grow at different altitudes (L. Foxhall, pers. comm.). Still, the *Coefia* depressions, with a high water-table amid a semi-desert (D. J. Mattingly, pers. comm.), might have led them to be noted for a rich and varied flora.   **lotus ... nut-trees:** probably all regarded here as 'fruit trees', *sensu lato* (L. Foxhall, pers. comm.).

108. 5. **Ampelos:** 'Vine'; *Barr.* 38 B2 'Ampalaontes?' (*Gasr el-Arid*). **Apios:** 'Pear'; cf. Apis 'between Serapeion and Koinon' (*Barr.*); Desanges 99.   **is distant:** the Greek word is *allassei*, which it is hard to make bear this meaning; Müller 84 suspects corruption.   **Chersonesos:** unlocated toponym, *Barr.*   **Zenertis:** unlocated toponym, *Barr.*; Desanges 99.   **Taucheira:** *Inv.* 1029 (*Tocra*; 32° 32′ N, 20° 34′ E), a *polis* subordinate to Barke (Hdt. 4. 171).   ***Bakalou* Kome:** 'Bakalos's Village'; suggested by Desanges 99, cf. 'Bakales', Hdt. 4. 171. 'Kaukalou Kome', MS and *Barr.* (later Hadrianopolis; *Driana*; 20° 18′ E). **Hesperides:** *Inv.* 1026 Eu(h)esperides (near *Benghazi*); founded from Cyrene C5f but with archaeology from C6f; called Euesperides, Hdt. 4. 204, with reference to *c.*514. Both names were used from C4; Hesperides was usual later (*Inv.*). *Benghazi* is anc. Berenike, to which the

city was moved in C3. Only one most westerly Greek *polis* is known in
Africa: Kinyps, which no longer existed in C4m (109. 4).   **Encheleios:**
'Eel River'; but 'Ekkeios', MS. Unknown; not in *Barr*. It may be the
Lathon or Lethon of Strabo 17. 3. 20 (*Bu Shatin*, just S of Euesperides,
Barr.); but Desanges 100 notes that Athenaeus (2. 84/71b) refers to
eels (*encheleis*) in the Lethon near Berenike, and restores the name.
Chersonesoi of the *Azirides*: see nn. on 108. 1 and 47. 1. PS backtracks
once more, to summarize the political geography from Kyrene or
Barke to Euesperides.

109. 1. Syrtis: the Greater Syrtis, the huge bight (17°–19° E) between
Cyrenaica and Tripolitana. In PS it begins at Hesperides and its W
limit is Neapolis–Lepcis Magna. Strabo 17. 3. 20 records the treach-
erous shallows (cf. Cary 220 for lack of good harbours; *Mediterranean
Pilot* 1988, 70 no. 2.77 for reefs, coastal marshes); but the difficulties
are at least equally due to the lack of elevated landmarks such as
cliffs and capes (D. J. Mattingly, pers. comm.).   **5,000 stades:**
c.930 km. '80 st.', MS (confusion of forms of ε and π?); 5,000 in Eratosthenes (fr. 104 in Roller 2010 = fr. III B 56 Berger = Strabo 2. 5. 20). It
approximates the actual coasting from Hesperides to Lepcis Magna
(*c*.800 km); but PS's *paraploi* add up to more than this.   **to Neapolis
... days, three, and nights, three:** Neapolis/Lepcis Magna (*Lebda*).
The time is consistent only with a direct voyage; it implies *c*.3,000 st.
or *c*.560 km (actual distance *c*.480 km). Perhaps the figures are
corrupted from e.g. 5 days and 5 nights. At 109. 5 PS gives the same
or a smaller distance (3 days and 2 or 3 nights) from Hesperides to
Philainou Bomoi within the Syrtis, which will be a coastal voyage.

109. 2. Nasamones: transhumant pastoralists (Hdt. 2. 32; 4. 172) at 18–
19° E, *Barr*. Cf. Strabo 2. 5. 33; 17. 3. 20, 23. Ptol. *Geog*. 4. 5 and Pliny 5.
5/33 locate them further E, Paus. 1. 33. 5 near the Atlantic.   **Makai:**
at 15–17° E, *Barr*.; but, as with the Adyrmachidai at 107. 1, PS envisages an area further E.

109. 3. Herakleioi Thines: 'Banks of Herakles'; near *Ras Carcura*. An
area in W Cyrenaica, *c*.10 km inland from Drepanon. If it is not a
settlement but a landmark, it is another piece of nautical information in this part of the work. (Cf. n. on 108. 3 'refuges'; 110. 8
'much more dangerous'.) Having named the major tribes of the
region in advance, PS backtracks to a point just after Euesperides.
Drepanon: tentatively *Ras Carcura* (31° 28′ N, 19° 59′ E), *Barr*.; plausibly, as the low cape could be likened to a sickle (*drepanon*) in outline
(L. Foxhall, pers. comm.), though the coast may have altered since
antiquity.   **Pontiai:** Pontia, *Barr*. (*Tre Scogli*).   **Leukai:** 'White
Islands'. As there are no large ones in the Syrtis, this will be an in-

shore islet or islets (*Barr.* marks several) or a mainland feature. **Philainou Bomoi:** 'Philainos's Altars'; Arae Philaenorum (*Ras el-Aali*). See e.g. Polyb. 3. 39. 2; Strabo 3. 5. 6, 17. 3. 20. Not a *polis*. PS uses 'dependent harbour' (*epineion*) only here. Müller 86 believes PS regards this as the start of Carthaginian territory (see n. on 110. 1 'past Neapolis'). Allain 199 puts it further W, at the R. Kinyps (below). **dependent harbour;** *the grove of Ammon:* if Ammon is *Barr.* 37 E2 Ammoniou Pegai (*Maaten Bescer? Stad.* 83), *c.*60 km E of Philainou Bomoi, it is out of sequence unless the preceding words specified a relationship that is now obscure. Müller cxxxviii–cxxxix and 456 (on *Stad.* 84) revises his earlier view and suggests PS knew of an Ammonion inland from Philainou Bomoi. For the salt-hills and freshwater springs of the Ammonians, see Hdt. 4. 181.   **winter at the sea:** the Makai were ethnographically interesting to the ancients (e.g. Hdt. 4. 175, hairstyle; Diod. 3. 49. 1; Pliny 5. 5/34).

Barr. 35

109. 4. **a fine locality:** *chorion*; see n. on 108. 4 'divided localities'. **Kinyps:** *Inv.* 1027 (near *Wadi Caam* or *Ki'am*); Desanges 100. Presumably the short-lived C6l Spartan colony of Dorieus (Hdt. 5. 42; Flensted-Jensen and Hansen 2007, 233), once the most westerly Hellenic *polis* in Africa. We have jumped a long way W from Philainou Bomoi. (See also n. on 'under it', below.)   **from Neapolis . . .** *80* **stades:** Neapolis is again Lepcis Magna, the endpoint of the Syrtis at 109. 1. It is odd that (as the text stands) PS does not explicitly 'arrive' here and gives a *backwards* measurement (based on a reverse *periplous*?); all the odder since he has put Kinyps *after* the end of the Syrtis. '80 stades in every direction' (MS) does not make sense, but 80 st. (15 km) is about right for Kinyps to Neapolis.   **river Kinyps . . . island:** see n. above on Kinyps. Both are E of Neapolis–Lepcis Magna. In Hdt. 4. 175 Kinyps is in the territory of the Makai. The island is unidentified.

109. 5. **inside Hesperides towards Philainou Bomoi:** again PS backtracks, giving a *paraplous* from the start (E end) of the Syrtis to its innermost point.   **nights, ⟨2⟩:** either 2 or 3 must be right, but 3 makes the N–S width of the Syrtis too great; 3 days and 2 nights implies *c.*2,500 st. (*c.*460 km). See, however, on 109. 1 Syrtis.   **days, four, and nights, four:** implying 4,000 st.; Müller 85 reckons *c.*3,000. Another backwards measurement; longer than 109. 1 Hesperides–Neapolis. Possibly two sources are being combined.

110–11. CARTHAGINIAN TERRITORY

Even more than in Spain and Libyē, Greek trade and settlement were very restricted here, perhaps by the will of the Carthaginians. But Morocco's main connections were with the N shore of the Mediterranean rather than the rest of North Africa, because of the mountainous coast of Algeria to its E (Cary 227). If PS was not using Carthaginian sources he may well have used, directly or indirectly, Massaliote information, conceivably from Pytheas.

110. 1. Lotophagoi: marked at 10° E in *Barr.* though their literary location varies; cf. 22. 2 above; Hom. *Od.* 9. 82–104; Hdt. 4. 177–8; Strabo 1. 2. 17, etc. (Lotophagoi, §110 generally: see Peretti 1979, 303–44.) **the other Syrtis:** Hdt. knows only one (Müller xlvii; cf. 2. 32, 150; 4. 169, 173).   **past Neapolis:** Neapolis is again Lepcis Magna (14° 17′ E). PS has not specified where Carthaginian territory begins (Allain 200); while Müller puts it at Philainou Bomoi (see 109. 3 n.), Allain prefers the Kinyps (109. 4). The MS implies the latter, the river being named before the *paraplous* at 109. 5. 'In the territory of the Karchedonioi' may be a way of marking the start of that area. *Gaphara:* either *Marset ed-Dzeira* (13° 51′ E; *Barr.*; Desanges 100), or *Rās al-Ḡefara c.*15 km E of it, which may preserve the name (L. 348).

110. 2. Abrotonon: *Sabrata, Zuaga,* Libya (12° 28′ E). See Peretti 1961, 31–3. The city existed from at least C5 (L. 352).

110. 3. Taricheiai: 'Salteries', referring to fish processing. Perhaps *Barr.* 35 D1 Taricheiai/Zouchis (*Henchir el-Mdeina*, Tunisia; 11° 26′ E; Strabo 17. 3. 18; Slim *et al.* 2004, 91–3, no. 1); also called Zeocharis, 600 st. W of Sabratha, *Stad.* 101–2. Alternatively Lokros (probably *Zawara*), 300 st. W of Sabratha (*Stad.* 100; L. 353–4). (Factories: Trousset 2004, 19–21. Black Sea origin (early Cl) of preparation techniques, introduction to the West by Greeks and Phoenicians: Counillon and Étienne 1997.) Another Taricheiai in Libyē (*Barr.* 35 H3; *Tocra*; *c.*15° 20′ E) is not included. But Strabo puts Abrotonon W of Zouchis (Allain 200), and such factories were common in North Africa (Müller 86), so there may have been a Taricheiai W of Abrotonon. (L. 353–4 retains 'Tarilia', MS, doubting that a scribe failed to recognize a Greek noun; but the MS garbles many names, and the retrospective mention of Taricheiai below requires an earlier one.)

110. 4. Bracheion: *Barr.* 35 C1 Meninx/Lotophagitis/Girba (*Gerba*; 10° 53′ E). (Ancient sites: Slim *et al.* 2004, 99–102, nos 16–21.)   **Taricheiai:** as at 110. 3, this rests on an emendation.   **300 stades:** the only other island whose length and width PS compares is 21. 2 Istris. Pliny's 25 miles (5. 7/41), i.e. 200 st. (*c.*37 km), is more accurate (Müller 87). The width varies from *c.*16 to *c.*26 km.   **lotus … wine:**

as at Hdt. 4. 177, though there from one variety.   **wild olive-trees:** usually grown as root-stock for the domesticated olive. Elsewhere in Cl prose, *kotinos* occurs only in PS's contemporaries Arist. (*Gen. an.* 755b11; *Hist. an.* 596a25) and Thphr. (often in *HP*, e.g. 1. 4. 1; also *CP* 1. 3. 3, 1. 6. 10). On the uses of 'wild' olives in olive cultivation, see Foxhall 2007, esp. 5, 10–13, 109–10.   **Taricheiai:** Lipiński (354) retains only this third mention, locating it at the lagoon of *Baḥirat al-Bibān* (Strabo's Zouchis; 11° 18′ E).

110. 5. *Gichthis:* 'Epichos' twice in MS, then at 110. 6 'Eschides'. Epichos probably conceals Gigthis (*Barr.* 35 C1, *Bou Grara*; Slim *et al.* 2004, 105–6, no. 25), in the bay behind *Gerba* I. (see n. on 110. 4 Bracheion). Müller 87 and Desanges 101 see Eschides, too, as a corruption of Gigthis. But if ΓΙΧΘΙΣ to ΕΠΙΧΟΣ is a small step, ΓΙΧΘΙΣ to ΕΣΧΙΔΕΣ is not so easy. (The derivation by L. 358–60 of Epichos from the verb *epicheō*, 'overflow', seems far-fetched, but he may be right to relate Gigthis to a Hebrew word for trampling, in an allusion to the oil produced on *Djerba*).

Here PS should have described the Lesser Syrtis, if Eschides (next n.) is correctly placed at *La Skhirra*; he returns to it after 110. 8 Adrymes.

Barr. 33

110. 6. *Eschides:* see previous n. Not in *Barr.*; perhaps *As-Ṣhira* (L. 361; *As-Suhayrah*, Google Earth, 34° 17′ N, 10° 4′ E; *La Skhirra* (Slim *et al.* 2004, 113–14) near the end of the Lesser Syrtis (gulf of *Gabès*). I have supplied the first mention in the text.   ⟨**to Neapolis**⟩: either Makomades (Phoenician-Punic for 'New City') or Neapolis (the same in Greek) stood here (Müller 87); this makes sense of the distances. See *Barr.* 33 F4 Macomades Minores/Iunci (*Bordj Younga*; *Onga*, Slim *et al.* 2004, 121–2, no. 54; 34° 29′ N, 10° 26′ E). (Distinct from Neapolis–Lepcis Magna, 109. 1 and 4, 110. 1; and Neapolis–*Nabeul*, 110. 8.)

110. 7. **Kerkinitis:** *Gharbi*, the westernmost and second largest of a group of islands, the largest being Cercina (*Grand Kerkenna*). See Strabo 17. 3. 16. (Sites: Slim *et al.* 2004, 125–30, nos 57–67.)   **from this:** probably the Neapolis–Makomades added at 110. 6.   **Thapsos:** *Ras-Dimas* (*c.*35° 5′ N, *c.*11° 3′ E). See n. on 110. 8 Adrymes.

110. 8. ⟨**Leptis**⟩ **the Small:** Leptis Mikra (*Lamta*; Lat. Lepti Minus). See D. J. Mattingly *et al.* 2001, and next n.   **Adrymes:** Hadrumetum/ Iustinianopolis (*Sousse*). In Steph. Byz. and Herodian (*De prosodia catholica*, ed. Lentz 1867–70, iii. 1. 1–547, at 70. 8–10) it is Adrymes, Adrymetos, or Adrymeton. The preceding three places—Thapsos, Leptis Mikra (restored), and Adrymes—are in their correct S–N order.   **a great gulf inside:** probably the start of an account of the gulf of *Hammamet*, N of Adrymes. This is then interrupted by text ('in

which is the Small Syrtis ... very beautiful'), perhaps from another source, about the Lesser Syrtis (gulf of *Gabès*). This should have come earlier (Desanges 97; L. 365), after 110. 5, where the text already seems corrupt. The confusion may be due to the fact that both gulfs end with a Neapolis (Desanges 101; Peyras and Trousset 1988, 164–5; L. 370), namely 110. 6 Neapolis–Makomades and 110. 8 Neapolis–*Nabeul*. It may be compounded by the similarity of 'Leptis the Small' to 'Syrtis the Small'. (Müller 88 and Peretti 1979, 312–14, 321, however, take the latter to be a mistaken reference to the gulf of *Hammamet*.) The confusion may also be the reason for uncertainty in later writers as to the location of L. Triton(itis), which should be in the Lesser Syrtis (Peyras and Trousset 1988, 164–5). PS now jumps back to the Lesser Syrtis and L. Triton.

The following passage refers to places between 100. 5 Gichthis and 110. 6 Eschides

the Small Syrtis, called Kerkinitis: the gulf of *Gabès*. On its coastscape and resources see Trousset 2004, 15–17.   **much more dangerous:** another piece of nautical information (cf. nn. on 108. 3 'refuges'; 109. 3 Herakleioi Thines).   **2,000 stades:** too long. Strabo 2. 5. 20 gives 1,600 st., the entrance being framed by Meninx (110. 4 Bracheion) and Kerkina; Pliny 5. 4/26 cites Polybios for 300 miles (2,400 st.). Syrtis Minor is a nearly semicircular bay *c.*90 km (*c.*720 st.) across; from the end of Bracheion to the point opposite Kerkina, its circumference is only *c.*190 km (*c.*1,100 st.). These longer distances should refer to the voyage from Bracheion to 110. 7 Thapsos.   **island of the Triton ⟨with a lake⟩ ... Athena Tritonis:** *Chott el Jérid* (Salinarum Lacus, *Barr.*); extensive inland lake with narrowing E arm (cf. PS's words 'the lake has a small mouth'). The island will be one in this lake rather than (as L. 370) *Gerba*. For the lake cf. Hdt. 4. 178–80. **about 1,000 stades:** today much larger, *c.*430 km or *c.*2,350 st., even taking no account of its extremely dissected outline.

110. 9. live around it: Lipiński (370–1) follows the MS, implausibly translates *periepousi* as 'honour' (rather than 'treat', 'handle'), and applies it to Athena; but her mention is now a long way back. *Gyzantes: pantes* ('all'), MS. It is hard to see how 'all' the Libyans could be the subject of the verb; a specific *ethnikon* makes more sense. Emended in the light of Hdt. 4. 194. Zygantes, Hekat. F 337; Zygeis (or Gyzeis), Ptol. *Geog.* 4. 5. 22. All these names may be related to Byssatis (Polyb. 3. 23. 2), Byzakis (Polyb. 12 ap. Steph. Byz.), Lat. Byzacium (Trousset 2004, 39, 43–4), extending from the gulf of *Hammamet* to that of *Gabès*. The name given by Hdt., though dismissed by Steph. Byz., is likeliest for a non-travelling C4 author. Hdt.'s Gyzantes are not around L. Triton (Allain 202–3). Desanges 99 (favouring 'Byzantes') notes that, as well as misplacing the Lesser Syrtis to the area of the gulf of *Hammamet*, PS has left in it features of the Byzacium: fertility, and the length of 2,000 st. (see n. on 110. 8).   **fair-haired:** an alternative restoration (Vossius, also Allain 203) gives 'All these Libyans are said to be naturally golden'. It seems unlikely that a Cl writer would distinguish natural blond(e)s from fake. The frequency of blond hair and blue eyes among Berbers has been exaggerated (L. 370). PS twice says they are beautiful; a sign of compilation?

Barr. 32

The 'flashback' ends; the account of the coast after Adrymes continues

110. 10. Neapolis: *Nabeul* (Slim *et al.* 2004, 169, no. 135), at the root of C. *Bon* (next n.).   **Hermaia, a cape:** *Cap Bon* or *Ras Addar* (from Punic 'cape of the almighty', L. 371–2). (Distinct from the Hermaia at 112. 1.) Since the city follows the cape, it have been suggested that it is not *Kerkouane* on the E side of C. *Bon*, but *El-Haouaria*, where Agathokles landed in 310 (Slim *et al.* 2004, 183, no. 158). Desanges 102 suggests the city may be *Ras ed Drek* (SE of C. *Bon*), a Punic town destroyed together with Carthage.   **Karchedon:** advance mention; see 111. 1.   **the river:** as none has been mentioned, some words must have dropped out earlier. Müller rejects Gail's suggestion of Katada (Ptolemy 4. 3. 7) and notes an unnamed river near the isthmus. Lipiński (373) posits a stopover at *Henchir Mraïssa* (Carpis) between C. *Bon* and Carthage. A kind of *saut du même au même* (West 1973, 24–5) between Katada (or Karpis) and Karchedon may have played a part.

111. 1. Karchedon: founded trad. 814/3. On Carthage and §111 see Peretti 1979, 345–72 (also 101–3).   **a half of a day:** implying *c*.250 st. (*c*.46 km). The direct voyage is *c*.64 km, a long half-day; the coasting is *c*.97 km, a full day.

111. 2. Pontia: not in *Barr.* Allain 203 suggests Aigimouros (Strabo 2. 5. 19, 6. 2. 11), *Barr.* 32 G2 Aegimoeroe (*Zembra* Is., Tunisia). The largest of these is the only notable island off this coast. Desanges 102 thinks this possible.

Barr. 47 inset

Kosyros … a day: the substantial islet (14 by 8 km) of *Pantelleria* (Italy), between Carthage and Sicily. It is *c*.71 km (*c*.350 st.) E of C. *Bon*, a short day's sail. Strabo 17. 3. 16 gives 400 st. from C. Taphitis near Neapolis.

111. 3. upcoming sun: see 47. 3 n.   *a long way:* 'a little way', MS; clearly untrue of the Maltese Is. We could repunctuate 111. 2–3, but 'a little way' is also untrue of *Pantelleria*. The emendation adopted is only one possibility, given the potential for confusion with μικραί below (cf. perhaps ἡμέρας μακρᾶς, 22. 3; ἄκρα μακρά, 66. 3). Saying a place is 'a long way' from another may be a way of saying that the distance is unknown; or PS may know that Malta is much closer to Sicily but wants to treat Carthaginian islands together.   **Melite . . . Gaulos:** *c.*300 km ESE of C. *Bon*, though from there it is more natural to say they are *c.*200 km beyond *Pantelleria*.   **Lampas:** *Lampedusa* (Italy; Lat. Lopadusa), between Tunisia and Malta. See e.g. Strabo 17. 3. 16.   **two or three towers:** suggesting more than one source, perhaps oral.   **Lilybaion:** the W cape of Sicily; see 13. 3. At 7 PS gave the distance from Sardinia to Libyē.

Barr. 32

111. 4. after Karchedon: PS does not use his usual formula about 'returning to the mainland'.   **Ityke:** Utica (*Henchir-bou-Chateur*, Tunisia); coastal in anc. times but now over 10 km inland (Slim *et al.* 2004, 195–6, no. 174). It was known to the Romans at the time of their treaty with Carthage (Polyb. 3. 24. 2).   **1 day:** only 200 st. in Ps.-Arist. *Mir. ausc.* 134. 844a8–9.

111. 5. Of all the cities named in the following lines, only Iol (MS) and Sige are firmly identified (Peretti 1979, 356); and even Iol is uncertain (see n. on Iomnion, below). Peretti sees the passage as a 'survival' (he uses the English word) from the *periplous* of Skylax. More likely it is from a source other than that used in the previous paragraphs. After Ityke PS gives no distances between staging-posts. His material hardly overlaps with what we know of Hekataios, but he may preserve Ar material that he could not check, characterized by islands as stopovers (Desanges 103, 108–10) rather than towns. Cf. n. on 'Naxian islands', below.   **Hippou Akra:** 'Horse's Cape'; either C. *Bizerta*, which terminates Ǧebel Ḥara *c.*6 km N of the city, or C. *Blanc* *c.*1.5 km further N (Promunturium Candidum; Pliny 5. 2/23; Mela 1. 34; Desanges 103; L. 383–4).   **Hippou ⟨Akra⟩, a city:** later Hippo Diarrhytus (*Bizerte*, *Banzart*; 9° 52′ E; Peretti 1979, 348–9; Desanges 103; L. 383). Cf. Polyb. 1. 77. 1. (Distinct from Hippo Regius; *Annaba*, f. *Bône*, Algeria; 7° 45′ E.)   **a lake . . . islands:** the later Hipponensis L. (*Lac de Bizerte*). At its W edge a low islet is shown in Google Earth and on US 1:250,000 military map NJ 32-11 (on line at University of Texas, see 108. 3 n.). Alternatively, PS's source took the isthmus between this lake and its W neighbour, and/or two prominent hills, to be islands (L. 386; cf. no. 112. 5 Kerne).   **Psegas:** *Ras Ben-Sekka* (17 km NW of *Bizerta*), the N point of Africa (37° 20′ N), may preserve the name (L. 386; not in *Barr.*; unidentified, Desanges 103).   **Naxian**

islands: probably the *Cani* group (not labelled in *Barr.*), ENE of Hippo Diarrhytos. The name, referring to Sicilian Naxos (founded from Chalkis in Euboia), may be evidence of an early source (Desanges 103–4; L. 387) or of links with central Greece or Euboia; homonyms of places there point to exploration, perhaps from Sicily, before the battle of Alalia (see n. on 6 Kyrnos; Desanges 105), which seems to have deterred further Greek settlement in the West.   **Pithekousai:** not in *Barr.*; though purportedly on an island, it can be linked to Steph. Byz. on Pithekōn Kolpos ('Monkeys' Gulf') near Carthage. Juvenal (10. 194–5) alludes to monkeys in the forests around Thabraca (*Tabarka*), midway between Hippo Diarrhytus and Hippo Regius (Desanges 104–5; L. 387–9). Pithekoussai shares its name with the Euboian colony in the bay of Naples; see n. below for a Euboia. **over against it:** the MS reads 'and opposite them'; perhaps a copyist misunderstood Pithekoussai as a group of islands rather than a single mainland place.   **Kalathe island:** an easy emendation for the uncharacteristic 'both an island and' of the MS. Müller 90 identifies the island as Kalathe or Galata (*La Galite* or *Zalita*; 37° 31′ N, 8° 55′ E; Slim *et al.* 2004, 220–1, no. 210), though without seeing the possibility for emendation. It may have been a stepping-stone between Africa and Sardinia, *c*.150 km to the N.   **Euboia:** not in *Barr.* Boardman 2006 discusses Euboian colonies in the Carthage area. The restoration of Kalathe (previous n.) makes Euboia a city on that island rather than the island itself (as in Desanges 105). (Peretti 1979, 351–2 nn. 385–6, prefers *Tabarka*.)

Barr. 31

Thapsa: Rusicade or Thapsus (*Ras Skikda*, Algeria; 6° 53′ E), Strabo 17. 3. 16. PS appears to omit Hippo Regius, but archaeology points to a Hl date for it (L. 389–92 notes that). The Algerian section contains some of the most intractable problems of identification. Generally Lipiński puts place-names further E than other scholars.   *Igilgilis:* or Igilgili (*Jijel* or *Ǧiǧel*; 5° 45′ E). 'Kaukakis', MS, otherwise unknown; plausibly emended by Peretti 1979, 357 and n. 389. Lipiński (394) concurs, though pre-C3 archaeology is lacking.   **Sida:** not in *Barr.* Perhaps Salda (Strabo 17. 3. 12; *Béjaia*; 5° 5′ E), though Phoenician–Punic remains may not antedate 225–200 (Desanges 106; L. 396–7, following Gsell 1920, 158). Alternatively, Phoenician Rusuccuru (3° 55′ E; Peretti 1979, 358); but then restoring Iomnion (4° 7′ E; below) involves an inversion.

   Between Thapsa (*c*.7° E) and Iol (*c*.2° E) the coast is steep-to as far as *c*.4° E (*Mediterranean Pilot* 1978, 131, para. 6.1), but with many rivers, small harbours, and ancient towns. Around and behind *Algiers* (*c*.3° E) there is a substantial cultivable plain, with ancient coastal towns and with Iol (next n.) at its W end.

Barr. 30

Iomnion: 'Cape Iouliou', MS, is usually identified (e.g. at Desanges 106) with Iol Caesarea (*Cherchel*; 2° 11′ E). Lipiński (397–8), however, suggests Roman Iomnium (*Tigzirt*; 4° 7′ E), with the cape 3 km E at anc. Rusippisir (C. *Tedless*; or *Taksebt*, Culican 1991, 496). The coast here is again generally steep-to with a few narrow coastal plains and alluvial valleys. Notable ancient towns are fewer.   **Hebdomos:** not in *Barr*. Lit. 'Seventh' (masculine); perhaps the seventh stage on a Phoenician itinerary. Müller 90, who suspects MS corruption, locates it at Kounouki (Kanouk(k)is, Ptol. *Geog*. 4. 2. 5) or Gunugu (*Sidi-Brahim*; 1° 51′ E). Lipiński 1992–3, 303, suggested *Wad Damous* (15 km W of Gunugu/*Gouraya*), but now prefers *Wad Sebaou* at *Dellys* (3° 55′ E), though Punic archaeology is lacking before C3 (L. 399–400). (Peretti 1979, 359: iron resources in hinterland.)   **Akion island:** not in *Barr*. Müller 90 suggests *Ashak*, which has shrunk in modern times (Desanges 107). Others (Culican 1991, 496; L. 403) link the name to Ikosion, *Algiers* (3° 3′ E), which takes its modern name from 'the islets' (Arabic *al-Ǧazā'ir* or *El-Jazair*) in the bay.   **Psamathos island:** 'Sandy Island'; not in *Barr*. Müller 90 (citing Lapie) suggests *Colombi* (*Hadjra*, GE), *c*.36 km W of *Ténès* (Chalka, below). It is rocky, whereas the Greek name implies a sandy place (Peretti 1979, 359–60); at only *c*.100 m long it scarcely has room for a settlement; but like *Ashak* it was once larger (Desanges 106–7). Lipiński (405) proposes *Joinville* near Iol, with C5 and earlier Punic material. Peretti 1979, 359–62, and Desanges 107 prefer to keep Psamathos with the next group of places in the gulf of *Arzew*, much further W (see next n.).   **gulf . . . Bartas:** not in *Barr*. Either Error I. (*sic*; *Île Plane*; Müller 90, following Lapie) or the gulf of *Arzew* (Portus Magnus; *Bettioua/Saint-Leu*; *c*.0° 15′ W; Desanges 106–7, L. 409–10). If the latter, PS has inverted Bartas and Chalka (L. 409).   **Chalka:** near Cartenna (*Ténès*; 1° 18′ E), *Barr*. Desanges 107–8 thinks two of Chalka, Arylon, and Mes will be at *Les Andalouses* (see n. on Mes, below) and *Mersa Madakh* (1° 4′ W; cove with Punic finds, C6 on). Lipiński (408), however, suggests anc. Kouiza or Quiza Cenitana (*Sidi Bel-Aḏar* or *el Bénian*; *c*.0° 15′ E) on the R. Chylimath (*Shelif*), a R site incompletely explored. The resources of the interior suit the bronzeworking implied by the name Chalka (Peretti 1979, 362).   **Arylon:** not in *Barr*. Peretti and Lipiński place it in the bay of *Oran*; L. 411–13 specifically at *Oran* or *Mers al-Kébir*, Strabo's Theōn Limen or 'harbour of the gods' (17. 3. 9), later Portus Divinus. See previous n.   **Mes:** not in *Barr*., but L. 413–15 links it to Castra Puer(or)um (0° 53′ W; *Les Andalouses*) in *Itin. Ant*. See n. on Chalka, above.

Sige . . . in the river: *Barr.* 29 D1 Siga (*Takembrit*; 1° 28′ W). The river is the *Tafna*; *Takembrit* is on the l. (W) bank, 3 km upstream from *Rach-goun* on the r. bank. If Akra (below) is near Siga, PS names only Akros and Drinaupa in a space of *c.*350 km, so his source for Algeria was less complete than for Libya and Tunisia.   **Akra:** *Rachgoun* I. (Algeria), only *c.*725 by 240 m, 1.8 km off Siga (Desanges 108; Culican 1991, 496; L. 417–18); domestic and funerary remains, mainly Ar; appears unused after C5e. 'Great' is surprising.   **Akros, the city:** not in *Barr.* Probably the anc. town on the E side of 16 km long C. Rus-addir or Akra Megale (*Cap des Trois Fourches*; *Melilla*, Spanish enclave within mod. Morocco; Desanges 108; L. 419–20), though secure archaeology for the city does not precede C3 (Lipiński). Distinct from Akra I., above (Müller 90; Allain 205; L. 419.)   **the gulf in it:** this odd phrase may refer to the 23 km long lagoon (*Bhar Amezzyan* or *Mar Chica*; Morocco) SE of *Melilla*, separated from the sea by a natural sandbar.   **Drinaupa:** not in *Barr.* Müller 90 suggests either one of the *Djafarin, Zaffarines*, or *Chafarinas* Is. (Spain; Tres Insulae, *Barr.*); or the midsea *Alborán* (Spain), *c.*57 km N of C. Rusaddir (Akros, above) and *c.*90 km from the Spanish mainland. Müller and Desanges 108 prefer *Alborán*. If Akros is *Melilla*, Drinaupa should be further W, ruling out the *Chafarinas*; but PS does not say whether Drinaupa is inshore or midsea. A better candidate, since PS is *en route* for the Straits, not Iberia, may be the three *Alhucemas* Is. (Spain; 35° 12′ N, 3° 53′ W; not marked in *Barr.*), *c.*300 m off the coast S of the town of *Al Hoceïma* (Morocco); specifically the largest, *Ḥaǧrat Nkur* (*Peñon de Alhucema*; L. 420).

111. 6. Pillar of Herakles: see n. at §1.   **Abilyke:** 'Apinilyë', MS. The sense seems to require the cape to be distinct from the pillar in Libyē. At 111. 7 this pillar is low, that in Europe high, surely a comparison between the peaks framing the narrows rather than between a feature near *Cádiz* and another in Africa far to the S. Since *Gibraltar* (anc. Kalpe, not named by PS) attains only 426 m, the Libyan pillar cannot be the highest point on the Libyan side, *Ǧebel Mūsā* (839 m) W of *Ceuta*. The pillar will rather be *Monte Acho* (181 m), the promontory E of *Ceuta* marking the entry to the straits (*Barr.*; Desanges 108; L. 421–5). Abilyke—if it is a mountain as well as a cape—will then be *Ǧebel Mūsā*. Lipiński (423) divides the name into Apini, which he posits as an unattested earlier form of 'Abilyke', and Lyë, an equally unknown settlement further W, which he puts (425–6) at *Ksar as-Seǧir* or *Ksar es-Srir* (see next n.). To do this is to multiply entities unnecessarily; and the latter site may not be pre-Hl. The form 'Abilyke' is confirmed by Strabo 3. 5. 5 (from Eratosthenes), so 'Apinilyë' is probably a corruption of it. (Lipiński inserts here the Krabis–Soloëis passage from 112. 4, which probably refers to the area between Abilyke and *Tangier*; but see introductory n. to part D.)   **city in a river:** Peretti 1979, 365–6 n. 400 believes this is Exilissa by the R. Oualōn (Ptol. *Geog.* 4. 1. 5). Desanges 108 (following Gsell 1920, 168) suggests *Ksar es-Srir* (5° 33′ W), a Punic site on the R. *el-Ksar*, between *Ceuta* (anc. Septem) and *Tangier*. Perhaps *Ksar* preserves the ancient name. **opposite it the Gadeira islands:** see n. on §2 Gadeira. Müller xli–xlii regards this as a gloss, since they are in Europe, not Libyē; but more likely PS is using more than one source; see n. on §1 Pillars.   **given the finest sailing:** *plous* is usually 'voyage', but here the conditions of travel (Allain 205, following Bunbury 1883, i. 391). In giving distances, ancient geographers assume a favourable wind, see Arnaud 1993, 227.   **days, seven, and nights, seven:** actually *c*.1,450 km in a straight line (*c*.7,200 st.), which matches the duration; but the coasting is *c*.1,600 km (*c*.8,600 st.), or *c*.9 days and 8 nights.

111. 7. These islands: if Gadeira did not stand in the original text here (in the MS it precedes these words as a heading which, like others, is presumably an addition), the author may have inserted the preceding *paraplous* into his notes on Gadeira, expecting the reader to remember the name from a few lines above. On Gadeira and the straits, see 1–2 nn.   **beside Europe:** only here does PS use 'towards' (*pros*) with a case other than the accusative (unless at 26. 2, emended in this edition). This tends to confirm the use of a specific source. **in Libyē low … in Europe high:** see n. on 111. 6 Abilyke.   **a voyage of a day:** this repeats, with slight alteration, what is said at 1.

111. 8. Length of Libyē

111. 8. days, *50* and 4: '70 and 4', MS. The figure probably represents a sailing season (L. 431–2).

111. 9. townships or trading-towns … all of the Karchedonioi: on their harbours, see Lipiński 1993. To be consistent with his implicit placing of the start of Carthaginian territory at or before Neapolis–Lepcis Magna (see n. on 110. 1 'past Neapolis'), PS should not mean all towns from Hesperides westwards, but those that follow the Syrtis beside Hesperides. This is not quite contradictory, despite Desanges 97.

112. Beyond the Pillars of Herakles

Although he has completed his tour of the inner coasts of Europe, Asia, and Libyē, PS has still to fulfil his undertaking (§1) to go beyond the Straits. This he now does. The tenor of his account, however, changes once more, probably reflecting a change of source. At least two are used. The first part of 112, like parts of the preceding passage, reflects nautical experience (Peretti 1979, 391, 393 n. 425); yet there are no local distances, only three long ones and a summation. The second part is dominated by ethnographic detail, more so than any other passage in the work, but lacks the fascination with the outlandish that we see in Herodotos and other authors (Peretti 1979, 415). On the other hand, the sketch of Ethiopian customs draws on conventional tropes. (Peretti 1979, 373–417, discusses §112 generally.)

At 112. 1–5 PS names the following African places: (i) the gulf of Kotes, running from the Pillars via a city at Pontiōn on L. Kephisias (with Meleagrid birds) to a second C. Hermaia; (ii) the R. Anides with a lake, R. Lixos, city of Lixos, *R. Krabis, Thymiateria, C. Soloësa (with altar of Poseidon), and C. Soloëis (same as Soloësa?);* then (iii) the R. Xion and Kerne I. He gives the lengths of these three stretches as 2, 3, and 7 days.

The passage has provoked intense debate and many geographical reconstructions (see e.g. Peretti 1979, 373–417; Roller 2006, 22–43; L. 337–434). Müller 91 and Lipiński (not citing M.) offer the elegant solution, followed here, that the part of the list *italicized* above has been displaced from 111. 6 and refers to an area between the *Gibraltar–Ceuta* strait and *Tangier*—essentially a 'flashback'. This allows PS to agree with the firm evidence (e.g. Hdt. 2. 32, cf. 4. 43) that Soloëis is C. *Spartel* (the NW tip of Africa), not a cape further S (e.g. C. *Cantin*). As a methodological caution, we should remember the propensity of place-names to migrate (Peretti 1979, 373 n. 406; Roller 2006, 36 n. 105); but this is less likely to happen to outstanding geographical features such as C. *Spartel*. (Lipiński moves the relevant words back to stand after 111. 6 Abilyke—unnecessarily since the dislocation, like that at 110, may be original.) A *prima facie* difficulty with this view is that PS's sailing times are then too large. Lipiński, however, suggests that they have been inflated to take account of the insertion of the misplaced passage. Alternatively, we could invoke the usually adverse (eastward) current through the Straits as making journeys longer (B. Lowe, pers. comm.).

In the view of Müller and Lipiński, PS combines and confuses at least two earlier sources; in Roller's view, three. One may be Euthymenes of Massalia (*c.*500). Some information may be from Carthaginians in Athens (M. Woolmer, pers. comm.). The most controversial possible source is Hanno (Introduction, VII). Roller 2006, 19, believes that PS does use Hanno, but indirectly since he covers the latter's voyage only as far as Kerne (Hanno goes 26 days further) and contradicts Hanno in several respects. To the present editor, however (as to Peretti 1979, 473), the two writers seem independent. The only places they both name are Thymiateria/Thymiaterion, Soloëis/Soloësa, and Kerne (though PS's Lixos and Xion may be related to Hanno's Lixitai). Another difficulty is that PS's Lixos precedes Thymiateria and Soloëis, with Xion later, just before Kerne, where Hanno puts his Lixitai.

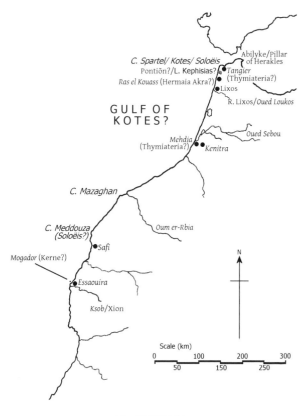

Map 20. NW Africa

So, whatever Hanno's date, PS is drawing on sources that have little in common with him. The key point for present purposes is that PS places Kerne 12 days from the Pillars and 7 from C. Soloëis (probably *Spartel*), while Hanno (if we assume that the distances he leaves unstated are short) puts Kerne *c*.8½ days from Soloëis. The implied position of Kerne is thus in effect the same—a warning to those who implausibly stretch PS's narrative as far as the *Rio de Ouro* bay (23¾° N; Cary 230) and Hanno's to the R. *Sénégal*, the gulf of *Guinea*, or even Cameroon (doubted by Casson 2007; Cary 229). In reality, Kerne should be no further S than northern Morocco, probably *Mogador* (31½° N; so Lipiński).

112. 1. holding Libyē on the left: the same words occur in a different order at Strabo 17. 3. 2—a possible echo of PS, whom he probably read (see n. on 93 Olbia).   **great gulf:** that of Kotes, named belatedly just below. If Hermaia is S of *Spartel* (see next n.), it is odd to call this straight coast a gulf. Perhaps it includes all the waters from the point where the strait of *Gibraltar* widens out with C. *Trafalgar* to the N and *Spartel* *c*.40 km away to the S. Seeing Europe fall away on his r. hand, a sailor might perceive himself to be in a gulf that was opening ever wider. See n. on Kotes, below. On the sandy, exposed Atlantic coast, see *Africa Pilot* 1953, 172.   **Hermaia:** perhaps *c*.30 km S of C. *Spartel*, at or near *Ras el Kouass/Akouass* (35° 31′ N) in the marshy *Tahadart* basin (*Barr.*; Tissot 1877, 54–60 and pl. 3; L. 452), perhaps specifically N of *Oued Garifa*, a C5 or earlier Punic site (Desanges 112–13, also locating Pontiōn here). There is no prominent cape now, but on a straight, low coast any sandy spit at a river mouth may serve as a landmark, especially if it has an altar of Hermes. (Peretti 1979, 384–9 esp. 387–8, also 394 n. 426, believes Hermaia is at *Sidi Haj Derbala* I., S of *Rabat*, but has been misplaced to C. *Spartel*, which he believes is also a C. Hermaia. Lipiński (449) identifies Hermaia with Kotes, but Kotes may rather be another name for *Spartel*; see n. below.)   **here, too:** a reference back to Hermaia E of Carthage (110. 10).   **Pontiōn:** perhaps between *Spartel* and *Akouass* (Desanges 112–13; Euzennat 2000, 464). Müller 91 suggests that Pontiōn is Sicyon (see n. on 112. 4 Krabis), which he places further S (see n. on Kephisias below), though he does not propose to emend here. There is a cluster of central Greek, perhaps Boiotian, toponyms (Kephisias, Kotes, Pontiōn), evidence of early exploration (Roller 2006, 14–15). Kottes, a monster in Boiotian Hesiod (*Theogony*, 149), was the brother of Briareos, after whom the Pillars of Herakles were once named (Aelian, *VH* 5. 3; Antonelli 1995, 78–80).   **galingale:** probably *Cyperus longus*, a European medicinal plant (rather than the Asian *Alpinia galangal*).   **Meleagrid birds:** perhaps guinea fowl (*Numida meleagris*; LSJ; Cappelletto 2003, 302). There is a Moroccan variety, but since many genetic changes can occur in 2,400 years it would be rash to opt for a particular one. They could equally be migratory water-birds. Mnaseas, too, puts them in NW Africa (see n. on 112. 4 Krabis). They are recorded elsewhere, including in East Africa (Agatharchides frs 82a, 83a Burstein; but his description evokes NW Africa, Panchenko 2003, 283). The claim that they occur only here may be a story told by bird-catchers to deter trade elsewhere, as at 1 and 112. 6. Meleagrids may have been a *topos* of continental theory; Panchenko 2003, 278 and 283, plausibly relates their several locations to theories of a circular (not necessarily spherical) earth and a land bridge between India and West (*sic*) Africa.   **Kephisias:** probably the Cephisis of Asrubas, a Punic or Phoenician contemporary of Pliny, who cites him (37. 11/37) for *electrum* (amber) in this lake by the Atlantic coast in the land of the Mauri (i.e. Mauretania Tingitana). (See n. on 112. 4 Krabis for further ramifications.) Its location will follow that of Pontión (see n. above; Euzennat 2000, 459), which we have placed close to *Spartel*; accordingly, Lipiński (448–9) proposes *Sidi Kaṣem* (35° 43′ N). The only other suitable locale is *Merdja Zerga* (34° 50′ N), 108 km SSW of *Spartel* (now a nature reserve), where Müller places Kephisias and Pontión–Sicyon.   **Kotes:** PS does not specify whether it is also a settlement (as in *Barr*.; e.g. Pliny 5. 1/2; 37. 6/15; two places?) or just a cape (Strabo 17. 3. 2, using the plural Koteis; cf. Ptol. *Geog*. 4. 1. 2). Desanges 111–12 takes the natural line that the cape is *Spartel*, the Ampelousia (Greek name) of Roman sources (Mela 1. 25; Pliny 5. 1/2), and links the name Kotes to Gytte (Hanno 5). PS may reflect the extension of the name from a cape, and possibly an early town, to the 'gulf'. The Roman garum factory at Cotta near *Ras Ashakar* (35° 45′ N), 5 km S of C. *Spartel*, may take its name from one of these.

112. 2. great reefs: there are dangerous shoals off Spain (*African Pilot* 1856, 1) and rocks off C. *Spartel* (*Africa Pilot* 1953, 172–3). PS, perhaps unintentionally, gives the impression that they extended all the way across. See Avienus, *OM* 319–26, and Suda's third entry on 'Herma' (ε 3022), for the story that the rocks were part of a road or fortification made by Herakles. (Alternatively, cf. sandbanks beyond *Rabat*: Peretti 1979, 387–8 and fig. 25.)   **washes over them:** cf. Ps.-Arist. *Mir. ausc.* 136. 844a27–8 for Phoenicians from Gades encountering rocks only covered at high tide.   **Hieron:** 'Sacred Promontory'; either C. *St Vincent* (Portugal; Lat. Sacrum Promuntorium; Roller 2006, 77) or C. *Trafalgar* (Sacrum Iugum, Knapp and Stanley 2000, 437), closer to the Straits; both were called Hieron (Peretti 1979, 394 n. 426). Strabo 3. 2. 11 (Artemidoros) puts it 5 days or 'not more than 1,700 st.' from Gadeira, whereas the statement that Hieron is 'opposite' C. Hermaia (*Ras el-Akouass*, above; or *Spartel*) suits Trafalgar better. Peretti detects confusion caused by an interpolator who had *Trafalgar* in mind; but the mistake could be original. Peretti 1979, 397, regards this brief detour to Europe as violating the 'one-dimensional principle' of the *periplous*, and thus as an interpolation; but PS gives lateral distances over major bodies of water elsewhere, and it does not negate the idea of a single author.

112. 3. Anides: perhaps the *al-Ġarifa*, near Hermaia (112. 1; L. 452). Often, however, it is equated with Pliny's Anatis, supposedly 496 Roman miles (734 km) from the Straits (5. 1/9). Desanges 113 puts it at the *Oum er-Rbia* or *Tensift* (33° 19′ N, near *Azemmour* and C. *Mazaghan*), though this is only *c*.260 Roman miles from *Spartel* and *c*.310 from the Straits (cf. *Barr.*; L. 464). It is unclear, however, whether Pliny is citing Polybios or Agrippa; if Polybios, one wonders whether he specified 496 *stades* (this, like a number of the figures in this passage, is a multiple of 8), i.e. 62 Roman miles. See also next n. (Peretti 1979, 399 n. 431, doubts that the river can be identified.) **Lixos, and a city:** R. *Loukos* and *Tchemmisch* (spellings vary), an excavated site (Roman Lixus) near *Larache* (35° 12′ N; Desanges 113–14; L. 455–6; *Barr.*; Cañete and Vives-Ferrándiz 2011 on the nature of culture contact at Lixus). These and/or the Xion (112. 5) may be linked to the Lixitai (Hanno 6–8, 11). Peretti 1979, 373, emphasizes that Polybios (in Pliny 5. 1/9) places the Lixus 205 miles (303 km) beyond the Anatis (but see previous n.: it may be Agrippa he is citing), and follows Müller (*FHG* iii, map 1, and others in positing a second R. Lixos at or near the R. *Dra* (28° 40′ N; *Barr.* 1a B3 Darat), opposite the Canary Is. (Spain). Alternatively, the name Lixos may have migrated S as exploration opened up NW Africa.   **second city ... harbour:** local pottery occurs at Lixus and along the river, including its l. (S) bank; the harbour may be *Larache* (previous n.), though there has been no excavation (L. 456).

This passage probably refers to the area E of Tangier *already described (111. 6)*

112. 4. See n. on 111. 6 Abilyke.   Krabis river: I retain this spelling (with Müller; Allain 206–7), since—even if we identify Krabis and Crathis (below), a view not taken here—the spelling in Pliny's MS may have been influenced by the well-known Krathis in South Italy (13. 5). After citing Asrubas for amber in L. Cephisis (see n. on 112. 1 Kephisias), Pliny immediately (37. 11/38) cites a Hl geographer, Mnaseas of Patara (fr. 44 Cappelletto), for amber at a 'place' (*locus*) in Africa called Sicyon beside the R. Crathis that flows from the lake with the Meleagrid birds. The equation of Krabis and Crathis is made by, among others, Müller 91 and Desanges 114, who (with Tissot

1877; Gsell 1920, 176) locates it at the *Sebou* (34° 15′ N, near *Kenitra*), well S of the (first) R. Lixos. This 'common-sense' view has unwelcome consequences, chiefly (*a*) the need to find two capes with a name like Soloëis; (*b*) the difficulty of finding a spot more sacred, or more suited to a sanctuary of Poseidon, than the extremity of Africa where one leaves Europe behind. But if we accept that Soloëis = Soloësa = *Spartel* and that some of this passage refers to the area E of *Spartel* and *Tangier*, we cannot equate Krabis and Crathis without (*a*) relocating the Meleagrid lake to the *Tangier* area, where there is no suitable body of water, or (*b*) leaving it on the Atlantic coast while connecting parts of 112. 4 to two different contexts, or (*c*) positing two rivers called Lixos. The present editor favours (*b*) and follows L. 426 in locating the Krabis at one of the streams not far E of *Tangier*. (L. 459 relates the Crathis to Hanno's Chretes, part of the *Sebou* basin; I prefer to leave the nexus of places including Crathis close to C. *Spartel*.) We should therefore (with Lipiński) resist the temptation to identify the Krabis with the Crathis.   **Thymiateria:** 'Incense-burner', 'Censer' (Desanges 114). Lipiński (426) suggests that the name refers (jocosely?) to a lighthouse. Steph. Byz. simply says 'city in Libyē'. Hanno locates it 2 days from the Pillars, the same distance PS gives to C. Hermaia; but the location is probably Tingi (*Tangier*; Euzennat 1994, 563–4; L. 426–7). Alternatively, it is further S at *Mehedia* or *Mamoura* (34° 18′ N) by the *Sebou* (*GGM* iii, map 1; Desanges 114, tentatively).   **Soloësa:** apparently the same as Soloëis, below. Probably C. *Spartel* (35° 47′ N), the 'promontory' (*akrotērion*) of Libyē at Hdt. 4. 43; cf. Hanno 3. (*GGM* iii, map 1, and Peretti 1979, 382–4, prefer C. *Cantin*, now *Meddouza* (32° 32′ N). I retain the two spellings, which may be from different sources.   **inner-sea:** *pontos*, used as a common noun only here in PS. It tends to support the placing of Soloëis at *Spartel* rather than further S, *Spartel* being imagined as projecting into the Mediterranean.   **altar of Poseidon:** the location will follow that of Soloëis—here taken to be *Spartel*. Hanno 4–5 builds a temple to Poseidon at Soloëis.

Barr. 1a

The 'flashback' ends, and the narration of NW Morocco resumes

112. 5. river . . . Xion: in view of phonetic similarity, this might be the Lixos (n. at 112. 3 above) or a different river. Since it is linked with Kerne I., which PS and Hanno place a similar distance from the Pillars (see 112 n.), it is better to separate the Xion from Lixos and accept a long gap, from the R. Anides to here, with no named settlements—perhaps the result of PS's having used multiple sources. The Xion will then be the *Oued Ksob* (31° 29′ N). Similarly, Lipiński (459;

like Müller) distinguishes the Xion from PS's Lixos, the presumed home of Hanno's Lixitai. Having regard to Hanno's sailing times, however, he puts the Xion and Kerne at the *Sebou* (34° 15′ N, near *Kenitra*). (He also identifies the Xion with Mnaseas's Sicyon. This is incompatible with his placing of the bird lake much further N, pp. 448–9. Sicyon is not a water feature but a *locus*, 'place'—unless we read *lacus*, 'lake'. His identification of the Crathis with the Chretes of Hanno 9 is open to the same objection.)   **Sacred Aithiopes:** the adjective is *hieroi*. at *Odyssey* 1. 22–4 the Aithiopes live in two places, 'some where Hyperion' (i.e. the sun) 'sinks, some where he rises'. Editors of PS have suggested 'western (*hesperioi*)', but this is too literal-minded and the MS makes sense as it stands. Allain 207 retains *hieroi*, invoking the benefits granted to the Aithiopes by the gods; e.g. Hom. *Il.* 1. 423, 'the splendid (*amymones*) Aithiopes'. Lipiński (459) implausibly takes 'sacred' to mean 'huge'; in fact PS referred to 'great' Aithiopes at §1, using the adjective *megaloi*, which would hardly be confused with *hieroi*. He is probably, as so often, drawing on different sources. His Aithiopes extend across Africa (112. 12), and he is probably drawing on a stock of stereotypes about them (Lonis 1979), some taken directly or indirectly from Hdt.'s account (3. 17–24) of the Long-lived Aithiopes of the Upper Nile (Desanges 96). Greek geographers argued over whether there was a land link between India and East Africa (Romm 1992, 82 n. 1) or even West Africa, and the same ethnographic observations are reported about all three areas (Panchenko 2003).   **Kerne:** one of the most uncertain locations in Greek geography; but it should go with the R. Xion (see n. above). Given its distance from the Pillars (on which PS and Hanno agree closely: see introductory n. to 112), the likeliest location is *Mogador* I. in the bay of *Essaouira* (31° 30′ N; Euzennat 2000, 457; *Barr.* 1a C2; Desanges 118–19). This is one of the few notable islets along this coast, if not the only one. Perhaps coincidentally, its length (900 m) matches its circumference in Hanno 8 (5 st.). Phoenician and Greek pottery, however, is Ar and Hl rather than Cl (Roller 2006, 42 n. 138; Jodin 1966). (There is no island at the *Sebou*, where Lipiński puts Kerne; see n. on Xion, above; Google Earth, 4 May 2010; US 1 : 10,000 map of *Port Lyautey* on line at University of Texas, see 108. 3 n. above). The only possible 'islands' are the *c.*50 m high sandridge behind the shore and the 56 m high acropolis at *Kenitra*, 4 km inland; cf. 111. 5 for a similar case.) Other locations proposed for Kerne include *Herne* (near *Dakhla*, Western Sahara; 23° 43′ N), *Arguin* (Mauritania; 20° 36′ N), and the *Sénégal* delta (Mauritania–Senegal border; 16° 3′ N; Roller 2006, 37). Amiotti 1987, 47, prefers the first and unconvincingly links it to the gold trade.   **to Hermaia Cape:**

days, two: a reasonable time from *Ceuta* to *Rās al-Akouass* (see n. on 112. 1). See n. on 'days, twelve', below.   **to Cape Soloëis ... days, three:** but on the view taken here Soloëis (*Spartel*) precedes Hermaia (*Ras el-Kouass*); nor can they be more than half a day apart. Lipiński (462–3) suggests that this is an adjustment to take account of the (mis)placing of the Krabis–Soloëis passage (see 112. 4 nn.). Three days is reasonable from *Monte del Hacho* to *Ras el-Kouass*. See next n. **days, twelve:** 'ten two', MS. Lipiński (462–3) attributes 12 days to an adjustment (see previous n.) and supposes that PS's source gave 10 days. The removal of 3 would, however, reduce the total to 9. 'Ten two' may simply reflect scribal error. Twelve days (*c*.6,000 st. or *c*.1,100 km) is the largest distance in PS except for the continental summations (69, 106. 4, 111. 8) and that of Thrace (67. 8). On this triple *paraplous* see Peretti 1979, 376–90 (with different locations).

112. 6. sailable no further: owing to an outflow of desert sand (Roller 2006, 19, citing *Africa Pilot* 1953–4, i. 202)? Or were such claims concocted or exaggerated by authors to conceal their ignorance (Plut. *Thes.* 1; Allain 207; Desanges 115–16) or locals seeking to monopolize trade (L. 459–60)? This would not mean PS invented the claim; it may be from his source, which was not Hanno (Allain 207). Desanges 115–16, while believing that Phoenician trade really took place in NW (not West) Africa, thinks we should not try to identify specific areas of mud and seaweed. Panchenko 2003, esp. 280–2, sees this passage, and similar assertions in other authors (e.g. Hdt. 4. 43), as traces of the notion that one could not sail around Libyē and return to the Red Sea because it was joined to India. But, if so, PS would contradict himself at 112. 12; so it probably comes from nautical talk, not continental theory.   **sharp above:** i.e. at the tip (L. 463).

112. 7. the traders ... are Phoinikes: from Gadeira or Lixos rather than Carthage (Desanges 116). PS writes as if he has already mentioned traders, but he has not; he may be drawing information from a specific source. The specifics of 112. 7–11 may be purely conventional tropes about Aithiopes.   **having made tents:** Müller 94 deduces that there was no permanent settlement on Kerne, but it is hard to separate fact from fiction here. Hdt. 4. 196 describes similar Carthaginian 'silent bargaining' in NW Africa, though PS uses a source independent of Hdt. giving, for example, more detail of the goods traded.

112. 8. deer: or gazelles, L. 463.   **teeth:** i.e. tusks.   **(skins) of domestic animals:** or carcases, L. 463.

112. 9. pricked with decoration: 'skins' or a similar word may be missing.   **largest of all ... whoever is tallest:** like the Fish-eating

Aithiopes of the Upper Nile (Hdt. 3. 20) and the Aithiopes in PS's contemporary Aristotle (*Pol*. 4. 4. 1290b4–5).   **fire-hardened:** Hdt. 7. 71
(in different words) mentions Libyan Aithiopes in the Persian army
using fire-treated javelins; cf. Strabo 3. 5. 1 on the pre-Phoenician
people of the Balearic Is.

112. 10. **perfumed oil:** vegetable oil was the normal base for ancient
perfumes. Pliny 13. 2/6 and other sources attest to Phoenician un-
guent.   **Aigyptian stone:** the *Periplus maris Erythraei* (Roman
period), 6. 4, mentions the trade in Egyptian 'glass stones' (trans.
Casson 1989, 53; the text depends on a likely restoration, λιθίας
ὑ⟨α⟩λῆς). Allain compares Hdt. 2. 69 (crocodiles' earrings 'of molten
stone'); Strabo 16. 2. 25 ('glass-sand' or 'glassy earth' in Egypt).
other mined (**ones**): Lipiński (463 and n. 116) is unduly dismissive of
all proposed emendations.   **artefacts:** PS uses the odd word *plas-
mata*, 'shapings', 'things formed'. I have chosen a formal word to
translate it.   **Choës:** the Ionian festival of Anthesteria is chiefly
known from Athens, where it was central to the calendar; on its
second day, named Choës (Χόες), participants drank a *chous* of wine,
roughly a gallon (*OCD*[3] on Anthesteria). The fact that PS refers to it
without further specification supports the case that he is resident in
Athens. For Attic pottery in Iberia, cf. n. on 'trading-towns', §1. Gill
1988, 6–9, examines Ar–Cl trade in the western Mediterranean by
Phoenicians, including Greek goods; for finds at *Mogador*, see n. on
112. 5 Kerne.

112. 11. **much wine:** Desanges 117 notes that wine production (attested in late medieval Morocco and implied by the ancient name of C.
Spartel, Ampelousia or 'vine cape', see n. on 112. 1 'the gulf . . . Kotes')
is not surprising, assuming Kerne was N of the tropics.   **a great
city:** Lipiński (464) plausibly regards this as another reference to
Lixos. Alternatively the city is Mēnē, a city of the Fish-eating Aithiopes (Diod. 3. 53. 6), and/or Magium (Pliny 5. 8/44), a city of the Aethi-
opes. 'Great' (*Megale*) could conceal such a name.

112. 12. **these Aithiopes . . . to Aigyptos:** along the S coast of a
truncated Africa; see n. on 112. 4 Soloësa. Cf. Hdt. 4. 197 (Libyē's two
aboriginal peoples, Libyes in the N and Aithiopes in the S).   **Libyē
is a headland:** cf. 12 on Lucania, 93 on Mysia, and 110. 10 on Carthage; but here PS engages with the philosophical debate about the
relationship between the continents. Hdt. 4. 42, too, makes Libyē cir-
cumnavigable except where it joins Asia, a view implicitly accepted
by PS's contemporary and probable associate Aristotle (*Mete*. 2. 1.
354a1–6).

So our *periplous* concludes—and so it probably did in its original form, since the summative characterization of Libyē gives closure.

113–14. Endmatter

These two sections, containing two *diaphragmata* and a list of the twenty largest islands, are clearly unrelated (or badly related) to the rest of the text, and are probably a later addition though still possibly late Cl/early Hl in origin.

113. 1. The *diaphragmata* relate only to the Aegean, while the list of islands is heavily biased towards the same sea. The *diaphragmata*, however, are not necessarily much later than the *periplous*, since both Aristotle and Dikaiarchos in C4l computed long sea distances by adding up short ones (Introduction, VII), and nothing in the language of 113 requires a late date. Their geographical rather than navigational character may be judged by comparing them with *Stad.* 282–3, from a Roman-period portulan: 'If you wish to sail through (the) islands . . .'.   **the sea:** the Aegean (see previous n.).   **fairly . . . fashion:** on ἐπιεικῶς, see n. on 65. 2 'probably'. The phrase recalls Dikaiarchos's division of the *oikoumenē* into a northern and a southern half 'by a straight, proportioned cut' (τομῇ εὐθείᾳ εὐκράτῳ; fr. 123, trans. Mirhady). Here, however, only the Aegean is bisected. **Paionion:** unknown elsewhere (Müller 95), though restored at *Stad.* 283. It will refer to Apollo, of whom Paion was one title.   **the Aulon:** the channel between Andros and Tenos (Müller 95). **Rhenaia:** the main text uses the form Rhene (58. 1).   **Melantioi Skopeloi** ('Rocks'): 9.3 km (*c.*50 st.) ESE of Mykonos (*Barr.* 61 B3). **to Ikaros:** *c.*36 km (190 st.).   **300 stades:** actually *c.*40 km or *c.*200 st., not allowing for indentations. Agathemeros 26 Müller gives 300; Strabo 14. 1. 19 makes this the circumference, a patent error.   **200 stades:** end-to-end Samos is *c.*43 km (*c.*215 st.); more by sea. Perhaps the distance given is to the harbour of Samos (see next n.) rather than the jumping-off point to Mykale.   **7 stades:** actually *c.*1.6 km (8 st.) at the closest.   **The whole:** it is probably futile to try to reconstruct the arithmetic.   **reckoning in addition:** the verb προσλογίζομαι is rare in Cl sources; apart from Hdt. 2. 16, 5. 54, and 7. 185 (προσλογιστέα), and Lysias 19. 44, it is used only by PS's contemporary Aristotle (*De caelo*, 294a4).

113. 2. **Aigilia:** not in the *periplous*; *Barr.* 57 B6 Aigilia/Ogilos, *Antikythira/Lious*; a non-*polis*, Shipley 2004a, 573, though the *ethnikon* Aigilios survives on sling-bullets (Cl?) found there. Fortified in C5, it was a stopover between Laconia and Crete.

114. A different author here ranks what are claimed as the twenty largest islands; the heading above the MS, surely added later, promised only seven. The order broadly matches their actual ranking (as measured today) by area or length, with two glaring anomalies: (1) Aigina is much smaller than many Greek islands that are absent (many of them are in PS's text); (2) on Kasos, see below. The list is also heavily biased towards Greece, omitting e.g. the larger Balearic and Dalmatian islands.

The list may fit the context of late Cl/early Hl geographical debate. Similar lists appear in Hl authors (e.g. Timaios ap. Strabo 14. 2. 10; Ps.-Arist. *De mundo*, 3. 393a12–15; Strabo 2. 5. 19), but usually contain seven items (like the list alluded to at Ps.-Arist. *Mir. ausc.* 88. 837a31–2). Ptolemy's (7. 5. 11) is quite different and includes the Atlantic and Indian Ocean as well; since Markianos repeats it (*Periplous of the Outer Sea*, 1. 9), he probably did not write §114.

Sardo: besides PS, only Hdt. 5. 106 (cf. 6. 2) and Timaios (Strabo 14. 2. 10) rank Sardinia first (Allain 110). It is so similar to Sicily in area and length that ancient geographers found them hard to separate. **Kasos:** cf. 99. 3, and 114 n. It is only 69 sq km and 17 km long, but ranked absurdly high. As the list contains almost exclusively Greek islands, we should probably substitute Ikaros (§58. 2; 260 sq km, 39 km) or Karpathos (§99. 3; 320 sq km, 57 km)—the second involves a greater alteration to the text but fits this ranking.

After §114 stands a closing title in the MS, Σκύλακος Καρυανδέως περίπλους τῆς οἰκουμένης ('Voyage round the inhabited earth, by Skylax of Karyanda'). Like the title and introductory note before §1, this can be assumed not to be part of the original work.

SELECT *APPARATUS CRITICUS*

THIS includes erasures newly identified during inspection of D in 2007. Variant readings are noted selectively. A reading may be noted because an editor reads D differently or does not note that his text differs from D. The secondary MSS have not been inspected, but *m* was checked in the file downloadable from the Bayerische Staatsbibliothek. Most corrections to names are not problematic and are therefore not noted, though when an editor misreports D it may be noted. Readings in D and modern suggestions may be abbreviated. Sometimes a reading is attributed to D and to an editor; in such cases, capitalization (the absence thereof) follows D. Unnecessary iota subscripts are usually ignored.

1. Ἡράκλειαι D: -εῖαι G.: -ειοι M. | ἐμπόρια πολλὰ κ written over erasure of μέχρι Ἡρακλείων στηλῶν τῶν | τενάγη Gail: πελάγη D

2. ἴβηρ D: Iberus M.ᵗ. See Comm. | καὶ νῆσοι ... στηλῶν del. P.: after §1 ἡμέρας M. | ⟨καὶ⟩ C. (pers. comm.) | πόλις Ἑλληνίς F.: πόλιν ἑλληνίδα D (π. Ἑλ. ἢ ὅ. Ἐμ. deleted as gloss by M.)

4. ἀντίου D: Ἀλπίου G.: Ἀντιπόλεως F. | ⟨καὶ ... λιμήν⟩ S. (inferring *saut du même au meme*): ⟨Ταυροέντιον, Ὀλβία, Ἀντίπολις⟩ Cluv.: ⟨κ. Ταυροεις κ. Ὀ.⟩ M.ᶜ (also adding 'Antium' in M.ᵗʳ): ⟨κ. Τ. κ. Ὀ. κ. Ἀντίπολις⟩ F. | δύο ... δύο M.ᶜ: δ΄ ... τεσσάρων D

12. Ϝ΄ ... Ϝ΄ D: γ΄ ... γ΄ M.ᶜ | καὶ (after Ποσειδωνία) D: om. M. | Ἐλέα, ⟨Λᾶος⟩ K. O. Müller 1828, 159 n. 95, K. O. Müller 1832, 2023: ἐλᵃὰ D ‖ Κλαμπέτεια M.ᶜ: πλατεεῖς D

13. 1. ἐπὶ M.ᶜ: ἐ D: εἰς M.ᵗ | ἀπὸ Ῥηγίου del. M.; see Comm. ‖ 4. ἔστι δὲ ἡ ... ͵αφ΄ after ἥμισυ M. | ͵αφ΄ M.: μφ D (not βφ as in M.ᶜ) | μετὰ ... νῆσός ἐστι M.: κατ περαν (*sic*) πόλιν λιπαρὰ ν. ἐ. D: κατ᾽ ἀντιπέραν ταύτης Λ. ν. F.: καὶ τὰ Θέρμα πόλις. ἔστι P.

14. Ὑρίωνος S.: ἀριονος D, α corrected probably from δὲ: δρίονος G.: Δρίου Garzón Díaz 2008, 283 n. 110: Ὠρίωνος M. | ἢ τῷ D: ἤτοι Bursian: is ἤτοι τοῦ Ἰονίου a gloss?

15. δαυνῖται D, Musti, Marcotte 2000, cxxvi–cxxvii: Σαυν- K. (and elsewhere in 15–16) | ἐν δὲ τούτῳ ... Πευκετιεῖς del. M.: ἐν δὲ τούτῳ ... Ἀδρίαν by P.: ἤτοι στόματα and δὲ by S. | αἵδε P.: τάδε D | Ὑρίωνος S.: ἀριονος D | Ἀλφατέρνιοι P.: λατ- D: Κλιτ- Bursian: Ἀτ- M.ᶜ | Καρακῶνες P.: κραμόνες D

16. αὐτοῖς S. (cf. 17): αὐτη D: αὐτῷ F.

17. τὸ ὀμβρικὸν D: τὴν Ὀμβρικὴν Gail | ἔξωθεν del. P.: M. moves sentence to 18 | κόλπων[1] S.: διήκοντες D | αὐτοῖς F.: αὐτη (sic) D | ⟨Σπῖνα⟩ M. | καὶ τυρρηνία ... κόλπον[2] D: M. moves to 18 and adapts | ⟨Τυρρηνῶν ... μιᾶς⟩ P. | πόλεων obelized by P.: ἀπὸ π. πόλεως del. M. | after καί ἐστιν M. adds ἐπ' αὐτῆς and brings ἀπὸ Πίσης πόλεως from 19 (but see Peretti 1979, 208–12)

18. ⟨διήκοντες ... κόλπον⟩ P., adapted from 17: ⟨διήκοντες⟩ M.

19. Ἑνετῶν P.: ἐντεῦθεν D | εὐθείας P.: αὐτῆς D | ἀπὸ ... πόλεως del. M.: other solutions have been proposed

20. ἔθνος ἴστροι D: Ἴ. ἔ. editors | ἐν διεσκεδασμένῃ (or διασκεδαν-νυμένῃ) εὐνῇ, ὡς ⟨ὁ Νεῖλος⟩ εἰς S. (εὐνῇ Müller; ⟨ὁ Νεῖλος⟩ R. Hansen): ἐνδιασκευνῶς εἰς D: ἐν διασκευῇ ὡς εἰς K.: ἐν δισσῇ or δι-σκελεῖ εὐνῇ M.[c]: ἐν διασκευῇ ὡς ⟨ὁ Νεῖλος εἰς τὸν Ὠκέανον ῥεῖ καὶ⟩ εἰς R. Hansen; ἐν διασκοπῇ ὡς εἰς A. | Ἴστρων Suić: ἰστριανῶν D

21. 1. Ἀρσίας S.: λιὰς D: Ἄλως M.[c, tr]: αἴδε F.: Ἄλβον Garzón Díaz 2008, 288 n. 129 | Δασσάτικα, Σενίτης Holsten: ἴδασσα· ἀττιενίτης D: Ἰαδερατῖνοι Suić | Ἀψύρτα S. (-αι Suić): δυύρτα D | Λουψοί M.: ἀλ- D: Ἀλ- F. | Ὀρτοπελῆται M.: ὀλσοί· πεδήται (sic) D: Ὀλσοὶ, Νεδήται (sic) Suić | Ἡγῖνοι M.: ἡμίονοι D: Αἴνωνοι Suić ‖ 2. Ἠλεκτρίδες K.: κλείτρει λιτρία D: Κασσιτερίδες Suić | Καταιβά-της Rendić-Miočević: καταρβάτης D

22. 2. Ἰαδασ(τ)ινοί P.: ἱεραστάμναι D: Ἰαδερατῆναι M.[c] | Ὕλλοι Gail: ὑλλινοί D: del. M.: perhaps ⟨ἢ⟩ Ὑλλινοί? | αὐτοὺς κατοικίσαι M.: αὐτοὺς τοῦ κατοικῆσαι D: αὐτοὺς αὐτοῦ κ. K.: τοῦ del. C.: perhaps υἱὸν αὐτοὺς κατοικίσαι? ‖ 3. lacuna S. | ⟨νῆσός ἐστι⟩ P.: ⟨Σίσσα ν.⟩ M. | παρὰ στόμιον ὀρθόν S.: παραστόνιον ὀ. D, m: παρα⟨τείνει⟩ ὡς ταινίον ὀ. M.: παρὰ στόμιον ⟨πλοῦς⟩ ὀρθός Suić: παρὰ στενὸν (στενὰ A.) ὀρθόν P.: ⟨παραλία ἀνήκει⟩ ὀρθόν C. | ποταμόν Gail: κόλπον D

23. 1. after Νέστοι P. adds ἀπὸ δὲ Βουλινῶν Νεσταῖοί εἰσιν ἔθνος Ἰλ-λυρικὸν ἐπὶ Νέστον ποταμόν: perhaps e.g. ἀπὸ δὲ Β. ἐστιν ἔ. Ἰ. Νεσ-ταῖοι | perhaps ⟨ὁ⟩ πλοῦς? ‖ 2. Τραγυρὰς M.[c]: προτεράς D: πρό-τεραι Suić | Βραττία S.: Βράττια Suić: κρατειαὶ D: Κρατειαὶ, ⟨Βραττία⟩ M.[c, tr] | νῆσος Φάρος ⟨καὶ⟩ πόλις S.: νέος φάρος μέσος D (not φ. ν. μ. as in M.[c]): νέος Φ., νῆσος M. ‖ 3. ἐξέχει P.: ἐρρέχ- D: ἐκτρέχ- Hoeschel: ἀπέχ- Salm.: ἐντρέχ- Suić: ἐπέχ- C. | τῷ ἑνὶ τῶν ἀκρωτηρίων M.: περὶ τὸ ἀκρωτήριον D | κ΄ D: π΄ M.: ρκ΄ P.

24. 1. Νάρωνά eds: ἄρωνα D | Ἰλλυρίων F.: -ριοι (-ρροι?) D | Νά-ρων[2] D: Δρίλων Suić ‖ 2. ἀρίωνα D: Δρίλωνα Suić (but see Lučić 1959): Ῥίζωνα P. | Ἀρίωνος ⟨ἐπὶ τὸν Ῥιζοῦντα⟩ ποταμὸν S.: ἀ. ποταμοῦ D: Ἀ. π. ⟨ἐ. τ. Ῥ. ποταμὸν⟩ M.: Δρίλωνος ποταμοῦ Suić:

Ῥίζωνος π. P. (cf. Polyb. 2. 11) | after ἥμισυ P. adds εἰς τὸ ἄνω ἐμπόριον | before ἄπωθεν M. adds οὐκ: P. rejects | Ῥιζοῦντος (twice) M.: ἀρίωνος (twice) D: Δρίλωνος … Νάρωνος Suić: Ῥίζωνος (twice) P. | Βουθόην ὁ πλοὺς καὶ τὸ ἐμπόριον D: B. ⟨πόλιν Ἑλληνίδα ἴσος⟩ ὁ πλ. κ. ⟨εἰς⟩ τὸ ἐ. P.: B. ὁ πλ. ⟨ἡμέρας ἥμισυ, ὅσος⟩ κ. ⟨εἰς⟩ τὸ ἐ. M.ᶜ: B. ὁ πλ. ⟨ἡμ. ἥμ.⟩ F. (deleting κ. τὸ ἐ.)

26. 1. Ταυλαντίων δέ ἐστι M.: κατ᾽ ἄντιον (ἀντίον K., Suić) δέ ἐστιν D || **2.** πρὸς Ὠρικὸν Suić, Hammond (with lacuna before): προσωρίκου D: πρὸς Ὠρίκου C.: πρὸς δ᾽ Ἀμαντίας M.; before it M. inserts 1st sentence of 27. 1 | εἴσω μᾶλλον D: ἐκβάλλει Suić | κόλπον Hammond: ἰώνιον D: Ἰόν- M., Suić | before τῆς Ὠρικίας M. adds Ὠρικός || **3.** Ἄμασιν Bursian: ἄπ- D | μεσογείᾳ Ἀτιντᾶνες M.: -γείας ἀγ- D | καρίας D, Hammond: Χαονίας V.: Δεξαρίας K. (comm.): Ἀμαντίας C. | ἰδονίας D: Δωδωνίας Palmer: Χαονίας P. | ἐν τῇ … βουκολεῖν del. M. | Κάστιδι D, Hammond: Κέστριδι Holsten | οἰκεῖν Bursian: ἥκειν D | ⟨ᾧ⟩ S. (cf. 26. 1 and ᾗ ὄνομα below)

27. 1. οἱ δὲ … χώρας put before 26. 2 by M.: after κατοικοῦσι P. adds τὴν παραλίαν | οἵδε D: perhaps οὗτοι? | Ἀμαντιεῖς del. M. || ⟨ὅ⟩ M.

30. Ἐλαία V., Hammond: ἔλεδ (sic) D

34. 1. καὶ ἔξω … αἵδε after Ἀνακτόριον καὶ λιμήν M. | Εὔριπος … κοινῷ Marcotte: εὔ. καὶ οὐριτὸν ἐν τῷ ἰκονίῳ D (οὐριτὸν accented despite Marcotte 1985, 255): Εὔ. κ. Θύριον ἐ. τ. κόλπῳ V.: Εὔ. Διόρυκτος ἐ. τ. ἰσθμῷ M. (as gloss after ἀποτεταφρευμένη): om. F. | Ἀμβρακικοῦ Marcotte: ἀνακτορ- D | ⟨πόλεις⟩ S. | ⟨ἐν⟩ G. | ⟨ὁρατόν⟩ F.: ⟨ἄποπτον⟩ or ⟨ἐκφαινόμενον⟩ M.: perhaps προέχον? | ὠνομάζετο F.: -οντο M. | τούτους M.ᶜ: τοῦτον D: τούτων M.ᵗ | φαρά D: Πάλαιρος Wirbelauer || **2.** Ἐχινάδες Höschel: αἰχινάδες or αἱ Χινάδες D (lenis corrected to asper or vice versa)

35. Αἰτωλία¹: A om. rubricator | τούτου D: omitted, M. (oversight?)

36. ⟨οἱ⟩ S.

37. ἔθνος φωκεῖς D: Φ. ἔ. eds

38. λιμήν, Εὔτρησις M.ᶜ·ᵗʳ: λ. εὔτριτος D: λ. Κρεῦσις τρίτος Roesch | τεῖχος Βοιωτῶν Salm.: τ. ὁ βοηθῶν D: τ. τῶν Θεσπιέων F.: τ. Θ. Roesch | ⟨ἢ⟩ S.; or ἡμισείας ἡμέρας ἔλαττον?

39. Αἴγειρος G.: ἄρις D

40. Λέχαιον M.: αἴγνον D: ἄγιον V.: Αἰγαῖον K.: ⟨Ἥρας⟩, Λέχαιον F.

41. στάδια D: -ίων M.

43. Ἀχαιοὺς M.: -εῖς D | ⟨ὅρους⟩ K.

44. Λέπρεον M.: -έων D | ⟨ἡ Μεγάλη Πόλις⟩ S.

45. Κυπάρισσος ... ἑπτά, Πρωτὴ ... λιμήν F.: πρώτη μεσσήνη· καὶ λ. κυπ. ... ζ′ D

46. 1. ⟨μετὰ δὲ Μεσσήνην⟩ Gail | ἀσίνη, μοθώνη D: M.ᶜ reverses order | ἀχίλλειος ... ψαμαθοῦς D: F. reverses order ‖ 2. Ἀνθάνα Gail: μέθανα D

47. 1. ἄνεμον: ἀνέμου D | Ἀζίριδας Bursian: ἁλιάδας D: Ἀχιλ(ιτ)ίδες M.ᶜ·ᵗʳ: Ἁλιάδας K.; cf. 108. 1, 5 ‖ 3. ⟨ἐπὶ Κωρύκ⟩ῳ ἀκρωτηρίῳ ἐστὶ M.ᶜ: ὡς ἀ. D: ὡς ἀκρωτηρίων. ἐστὶ K.: ἐπὶ ἀκρωτηρίῳ P.: ὡς ἀκρωτήριον (sc. ἀκρωτήριόν) ἐστὶ C. | δὲ Λίσσα M.: μέλισσα D (not μὲν Λίσσα as F.) | πρὸς βορέαν δὲ ... πᾶν put before 47. 4 Πρασός by M. | ἄνεμον ἡ Ἀπτεραία V.: ἄνηα πτερέα D | λαμπαία D: Λαππ- C. | μεσάπος D (corrected from μεσάπις?): Μεσάπιος M.: Μεσσάπιος P. | after ἐν αὐτῇ ἐστί P. adds Ῥήθυμνα πόλις καὶ λιμὴν πρὸς βορέαν, πρὸς νότον δὲ Φοῖνιξ καὶ λιμήν ‖ 4. ταύτην ὄρος Ἴδα C.: ὁσμίδαν D: Φοίνικα P. | after Σύβριτα M.ᶜ·ᵗʳ adds πρὸς βορέαν δὲ Πάνορμος: P. adds π. β. Ἀστάλη instead | Φαιστός: Φ. δὲ P. | Ὀαξὸς K.: παξὸς D | Κνωσσός M.: κνῶσις D | Ῥαῦκος Holsten: βαῦ- D | ⟨ἐν μεσογείᾳ⟩ C.: ⟨ἐν μ.. Χερσόνησος καὶ λιμήν πρὸς βορέαν⟩ P. | ⟨πρὸς ... †πᾶν ...⟩ M. from 47. 3 | Κάδιστος C.: κάλλιστον D: Κάδιστον M. | καὶ πᾶν D: om. C.: Καμάρα M.ᶜ (cf. Ptol. 3. 17; Stad. 361): καὶ †πᾶν P. | Πρασός S., M.ᶜ (misprint?): πρασίς D: Πραισός Meursius, M.ᵗ: also Πρᾶσος M.ᶜ: perhaps Πρασία? cf. Thphr. HP 3. 3. 4 (τιρασίαν in MSS) and fr. 113 Wimmer (Strabo 10. 2. 14) | Ἴτανος V.: γρᾶνος D: Γράμ(μ)ιον M.ᶜ: Ἴ. or Δραγμὸς C.: perhaps e.g. Ἴ. ⟨πόλις καὶ⟩?

48. Φολέγανδρος M.ᶜ: νοχίορος D (corrected in MS from νω-): Ὠλίαρος Salm. | Σίκινος Salm.: κίνες D | νῆσος καὶ πόλις S.: αὕτη ἡ π. D: αὕτη κ. π. V.

50. 1. Ἐπιδαυρία S.: ἐπίδαυρος D

51. 2. Σούνιον corrected in MS from σούριον

52. 1. Τροιζὴν S.: -νία D ‖ 2. Καλαυρία M.: -ουρία D | τ′ D: τριάκοντα (i.e. λ′) F.

54. Ἐπιδαυρίας S.: ἐπίδαυρον D (ί corrected from, or possibly to, ὶ): -δαύρου eds; see n. on 50. 1 | ⟨ρ⟩λ′ Lapie: λ′ D: ⟨σ⟩λ′ M.ᶜ

55. κεγχρεία D: Κορινθία M. | ⟨ἡ⟩ Gail

57. 1. καὶ νῆσος Σαλαμίς del. M.ᶜ, noting that without καὶ it could be a heading (hence καὶ bracketed by S.) ‖ 2. υϙ′ Gail: ξ′ D | Βοιωτῶν Gail: -ίων D

58. 1. ⟨Ποιήεσσα πόλις⟩ V.

59. οὗτοι καὶ S., tentatively: καὶ οὗτοι D

61. καὶ οὗτοι D: perhaps οὗτοι καὶ? | θρόνιον D: Τιθρώνιον Nielsen 2000, 108 (Nielsen 2004b, 665); or Τειθρ-, Oulhen 2004, 426

62. 1. ἐν τούτῳ … Κυτίνιον del. M. | τῷ clear in D: marked as supplement by M. || 2. Μηλιεῖς M.: μιλιεῖς | ⟨Μαλιεῖς⟩ M. | Μαλιεῦσιν: -εὺς D | πόλις D: πόλεις M. (misprint) | ἐσχάτη M.: ἔσχατον D | ἐχῖνος D, corrected in MS from ἐσχῖνος

63. εἰσὶν M.: εἰσὶ δὲ D | μαλιαίου D (cf. Suda on λιμὸς Μηλιαῖος): Μαλιέων eds | Παγασητικῷ M.: παγαγιτικῷ (sic) D

64. 1. Θετταλία: Θ om. rubricator | ἐκ M.: ἐν D | Ἀμφῆναι M.: ἀμφῆναὶ D (not ἀμφαναῖον) | Κιέριον F.: ἱερὸν D: Κίερον M. || 2. Παγασητικοῦ M.: παγσιτικοῦ (sic) D | Παγασητικῷ M.: πα^{γα}σιτικη (γα above πασ) D

65. 1. ⟨μετὰ δὲ Θετταλίαν⟩ M.^c | Μάγνητες S.: -ήτων D | Τίσαι M.^{c, tr}: ἴσαι D: καὶ Salm. | Ἄμυρος Decourt: μύραι D || 2. ⟨τὰ⟩ … ὁμοίως S.: καὶ ἐπιθαλ^α~ πᾶσα ἑλλάδι ὅμοιόν (sic) D: ἐπιθάλασσα ⟨ἐν⟩ Ἑ. ὁμοίως Marcotte 1990, 77 n. 6: ⟨ἡ⟩ ἐπὶ θαλάττῃ πᾶσα ⟨ἐν⟩ Ἑ. ὁμοίως M.

66. 2. Λουδίας F.: λυδ- D || 3. Θραμβηῒς M.: ὁρ- D (not noted by M.) || 4. Θυσσὸς M.: θῦος D (not Θῦον as in M.) | Ἀκρόθωοι Ἑλληνίς M.: ἀκροθῶται ἕλληνες D (not V. as in M.) | δύο ἡμερῶν D: δ´ ἡμερῶν καὶ (sc. δ´) νυκτῶν M.

67. 1. Φάγρης V.: φάγρη D (not φήγρη as in M., F.; correct in K.) | Θασίων Slothouwer: σαγίων D || 2. καὶ πόλεις F.¹: αἵδε πόλεις D: αἱ δὲ π. K. || 3. ταῦτα … τεῖχος M., F. (but with Δουρίσκος after τεῖχος): ταῦτα (sic) ἐν τηι (sic) ἠπείρῳ· ἐμπόρια δρυζώνη· σαμοθράκη· κατατ (sic) καὶ λιμήν. ποταμὸς δουσρισκός (sic)· αάβαρος· καὶ ἐπ᾽ αὐτῷ τεῖχος D | ⟨νῆσος⟩ M. | κόλπος M.: κόεπος D || 4. Μέλανα M.: μέλαινα D || 5. ⟨ὅ⟩ K. || 8. ἔλθῃς Gail: -η D | τὸ στόμα S.: τοῦ στόματος D || 9. Ὀδησὸς πόλις C.: ὀδήσοπος D | ⟨Ἴστρος⟩ S.: ⟨Ἴ. πόλις⟩ C.

68. 1. Τύρας S.: τρίσσης D: Τύρις ποταμός M. | Νικώνιον πόλις: νεονείων πόλεις D (πόλεις written over erasure of λιμήν) | ὀφιοῦσα D: -σσα C. || 2. ἠπείρου M.: ἡ πέτρου D | ⟨καὶ πόλεις ἐν αὐτοῖς⟩ S. (cf. 68. 1): ⟨καὶ πόλεις αὐτῶν⟩ M. || 3. Νύμφαιον C.: -α D | Μυρμήκιον M.^c: -ηκον D: -ήκειον M.^t | παράπλους D: perhaps πλοῦς? || 4. κ´ D: ⟨ρ⟩κ´ Müller || 5. εἰς del. M. | συρμάται ἔθνος D: ΣΥΡΜΑΤΑΙ. ⟨μετὰ δὲ Σκύθας Συρμάται⟩ ἔθνος M.

69. εὐρώπης … στηλῶν written over erasure of ταυρικῆς εἰς τὴν μαιώτην λίμνην, S. (partially read by C.), repeated from 68. 5 | λογιζομένῳ S.: -μένοις D: λ. δὲ M. | ὅσαι Salm.: σῶσαι D (not σωσαι as in M.): perhaps ὁπόσαι? | ἡμέραν τοῦ πλέοντος S.: ἡμεραίου τοῦ πλεόνους (sic) D: ἡμεραῖον τὸν πλοῦν Salm.: ἡμεραίου τοῦ πλέοντος C. | τοῦ πόντου . . . ἴσου (sic) . . . λίμνης del. S. (perhaps e.g. μέχρι τῆς Μαιώτιδος λ. stood here or after Εὐρώπῃ): τοῦ ἡμ. μέρ. τοῦ Π. ὄντος ἴσου τῆς Μαι. λ. M.

70. Σαυρομάται[1] M.: -βάται D (here; put before ἀπὸ Ταναΐδος by M.) | γυναικοκρατούμενοι D: -μενον M.

71. τῶν Γυναικοκρατουμένων: rather Γ. δὲ (cf. 9–12) or τῶν δὲ Γ.?

73. ⟨ἤτοι Τορέται⟩ C.

74. before καὶ πόλις M. and F. add ΤΟΡΕΤΑΙ. μετὰ δέ Κερκέτας Τορέται ἔθνος

77. μετὰ . . . (78) ἔθνος added in ν

78. Κορική added in ν: Κωλική V. | κορικὴ D: Κωλικὴ V.

79. Μελάγχλαινοι (twice) M.: μελαγχνάνοι (sic) D (not μελαγχλᾶναι as in M.) | Κορικὴν C.: κωρ- D: Κωλ- M.

80. γέλων D: Γελωνοὶ Κ.: Γέλωνες M.

81. Διοσκουρίας C.: -κουρὶς D | Χιρόβος C.: χιρόβιος D: Χερόβιος M. | Χόρσος C.: χόρσο (sic) D | ἄριος D: Χαρίεις M.ᶜ | πόλιν Αἶαν (Αἰαίην G.) μεγάλην C.: π. μάλην μεγάλην D: π. μεγ. M. | Μήδεια M.: μιδία D (not μιδιὰ as in C.)

82. βούσηρες (twice) D: Βύζ- V. | δαραανῶν D: Ἀρχαβῶν M.ᶜ

83. βούσηρας D, C.: Βύζ- Κ. | πορδανὶς D, C.: Πρύτανις M. (comm. 82) | ὠδεινιὸς D, C.: Ὠδείνιος M, Inv.: Ἀδιηνὸς F.

84. δ' C.: δὲ D: om. M. | Βέχειρες C.: -ος D (not noted by M.): -οι Κ. | βεχειρὰς D: -ιὰς Salm.

87. Μοσσυνοίκους F.: μοσσινοὺς D: -υνοὺς Κ.: -ύνους M.

88. γενέσιντις D: Γενήτης Κ. | Ἀμένεια D, C.: Σταμένεια Κ. | Ἰασονία V.: ἀσινεία D: Ἰασώνιον Κ. | ἄκρα καὶ πόλις C.: ἀκρόπολις D: ἄκρα, ⟨Σίδη⟩ πόλις M.ᶜ

89. θεμίσκυρα D (above ἑλληνὶς) | ἀρμένη D, M.: Ἀ- C.

90. λιμὴν ⟨καὶ . . . Ἕλλην⟩ίς S.: λϊμ^{ην}ίης D | Κολοῦσσα C.: κολού- D: Κόλου-M. | Κίνωλις M.: κορωνὶς D: Κιμωλὶς V. | Κάραμβις eds: -μως D | Τίειον eds: τίθιον D | καλλίχωρος D: -χορος M.

92. ἀρτώνης D: -άνης V. | Θυνίας F.: θηνιάς D (not noted by M.): Θυνιὰς V. | εὐθὺς Πόρος D: εὐ. ⟨ὁ⟩ π. M.ᵗ: εὐ. ⟨ὁ Βόσ⟩πορος M.ᶜ: perhaps also delete εὐθὺς? | Καλχηδὼν S. (-ῶν C.): καλχιδων D: Χαλκηδὼν M. | ⟨τῆς⟩ S.: ⟨τοῦ πόρου τῆς⟩ M.ᶜ | Μαριανδύνων

M.: μαρσαν- D: Μαριανδυνῶν F.; see 91 ‖ 2. ἕως D: ἕως ⟨ἐπὶ or εἰς⟩ Gail: ἕως ⟨ἐπὶ⟩ M.

96. ⟨Ἄσσος ... ἐν δὲ μεσογείᾳ (μ. δὲ S.) αἵδε⟩ M.$^{c, tr}$; see Comm.

97. Μυτιλήνην S.: μιτυ- D | ταύτῃ D: -ης M. | before Πορδο-σελήνη Wade-Gery 1938, 473, adds Νῆσος, καὶ

98. 1. Αἰολίδος S.: ἰνδίσης D: Αἰολικῆς M. (there are other sugges-tions) | τὸ κάτω D: τὰ κ. M.^{c} | καὶ αὕτη S., tentatively: καὶ αὐτὸ ἦν (ἦν added from above) M.^{c}: δι᾽ αὐτὴν M.^{t}: δι᾽ αὐτὴν D ‖ 2. ⟨Ἀρ-τέμιδος, καὶ⟩ V.: οι\ (i.e. οἱ or οιον) D | ⟨μετὰ⟩ δὲ ⟨Ἀδραμύττιον⟩ ἡ S.: ἡ δὲ D: εἶτα ἡ M.^{c}; εἶτα δὲ (*sic*) ἡ F. | ⟨πόλις καὶ⟩ M.^{c} | ἐν ᾗ D: ἐξ ἧς M.^{c} ‖ 3. Αἰραὶ S.: ἄγρᾳ D: Γέραι M. | ἠπείρῳ D: μεσογείᾳ M.^{c} ‖ 4. Ἀστύρων M.: ἀσσυρίων D: Ἀστυρίων V.

99. 2. τῆς Κνίδου from margin, S.; see Comm. | κράγος D: Κρυασσὸς M. ‖ 3. ⟨Ῥόδος⟩ S. | νῆσος ⟨καὶ πόλις᾽ καὶ⟩ ... αὐτῇ M.: ν. τρίπο-λις. ἀρχαία πόλις καὶ ἐν αὐτῇ D: ν. τ.᾽ Ἀχαΐα π. ἐν αὐτῇ καὶ Pugliese Carratelli | Κάσος V.: κρασός D | Κράγον K.: -σον D: Κρυασσὸν M.

100. 1. Τελμισσὸς V.: θεανισσὸς D (not -αὶ as in Miller, M.) | ⟨Ξάνθον πόλιν⟩ M., cf. Strabo 14. 3. 6, where next place, Patara, is coastal | πόλις S.: πόλιν D: πόλις ⟨ἢ⟩ M. ‖ 2. φασιλὶς πόλις D: Φασελὶς (*sic*) ⟨ὅρος καὶ ἐπὶ θαλάσσῃ Φασελὶς⟩ π. M.^{c} | ἔστι δὲ τοῦτο D: μετὰ δ. τ. Gail: ἔστιν ἐνταῦθα F. | νῆσος D: καὶ ν. Bursian | ἐπ᾽ εὐθείας δὲ M. (cf. 19): ἐντεῦθεν D: εὐθὺς δὲ F. | παράπλους D: perhaps πλοῦς? | Λυκίας ἀπὸ [—] ἡμέρας M.: ἀπὸ λ. ἡμ. D | ἔστι ... κολπώδης after τούτου M.

102. 1. Νάγιδος K.: ναβαὸς D (noted by Miller, not M.): em. V. | σητὸν D: Κητ(ι)ὸν M.: Συκήν G. | λιμένες S.: λιμένος (?) D: λιμένα eds | ⟨λιμένα⟩ ἔχουσα M.^{c}: ἀπέχουσα D | Ἀμάνη M.: ἀλάνη D: Ἀδάνη Salm.: perhaps Αἰγέαι? | μυριανδὸς D: Μυρί- M.: Μυριανδ-ρὸς K.: Μυρί- F. (manuscript *m* ends here)

103. ἔχουσι (after λιμένας) F. (ν added by S.): -σαι D

104. 2. Θαψάκου ποταμοῦ: θαμψάκου ποταμὸς D | τρίπολις φοινί-κων del. M.$^{c, tr}$ | καὶ λιμὴν ὅσον η᾽ στάδια V.: ὅσ. η᾽ στ. καὶ λ. D: κ. λ. del. F.^{1} | ἑτέρα πόλις D; del. M.^{c}; πόλις F. | ἑκάστη F.: -ῃ D | ἔχει M.: ἐˣ D: ἔχον K. | Τριήρης G.: τῆρος D | ⟨πόλις⟩ V. | Βοστρηνὸς ⟨ποταμός⟩ M. (p. cxxxviii): βορινὸς D): Λεόντων πόλις F. | Πορφυ-ρεῶν Salm.: -έων D | ⟨Λεόντων πόλις⟩ S. (here), cf. L. 295; before Πορφυρεῶν M.$^{c, tr}$ | Σιδωνίων ... Ὀρνίθων πόλεως: L. punctuates thus; after Σ. add δὲ or ἔστι? ‖ 3. ἄλλη del. M.^{c} (but see his ad-denda): καὶ αὐτὴ ἡ F. | θαλάττης D: obelized by S.: γῆς or ἠπείρου M.^{c}: ἠπείρου F.: ἀπὸ τοῦ παρὰ θάλατταν or ἀπὸ τῆς γῆς L. (comm.) | ποταμὸς D: π. ⟨ὅς⟩ M. | τ[υρίων D (rather than τ[ῶν M., L.) |

Ἔκδιππα S.: -ων V. | Ἐξώπη (misprinted Ἔ-) L.: ἔξω πή (sic) D: ἐξῆς
Βῆλος V. | Μάγδωλος πόλις L.: Συκαμινῶν π. V. | κ[αὶ S.: [καὶ] F.
| Ἰόππη πόλις M. | ‚βψ′ M.: αψ D

105. 1. ἐρ[υθρᾶς (or ἔξ[ωθεν) S. (ligature dictates one or other): [Ἐ-
ρυθρᾶς λεγομένης θαλάττης ἢ τῆς ἔξω]θεν M. ‖ 2. τῆς S. in view of
line length | αὐτῆς D: τῆς M.

106. 1. Πηλουσιακόν M.: Πελυσ- F. | Τανιτικὸν F. (but not at 106. 2;
by oversight?): Τανικὸν M. | after Τανιτικὸν S. omits M.'s ἐφ᾽ ᾧ |
Μενδήσιον … πόλις F.: Με. καὶ π. M. | Βοῦτος λίμνη M.: λ. Β. F. |
Βολβιτινὸν F.: -ικὸν M. | Κανωπικὸν F.: Κανωβ- M. | Μάρεια …
ἐν τ]ῇ M.: Μαρεῶτις ἢ τῆς Μαρείας. ἡ δὲ λίμνη ὅμορός ἐστι τ]ῇ F. ‖
2. Τανιτικὸν S. (cf. 106. 1): τανικὸν D | κανώπου D (not κανώβου as
in M.): -πικοῦ M. | ἕλη M.: ἔλη D ‖ 3. τὸ μέρος … μέμφιδος D: Αἰ-
γύπτου del. M.ᶜ: τὸ μ. τὸ ἄν. Μέμ. Αἰγ. Gail: τὸ μ. Αἰγ. τὸ ἄν. Μέμφεώς
(sic) F.; given variation between Μέμφεως (above) and Μέμφιδος,
perhaps τὸ μ. τὸ ἄν. Αἰ. μεῖζόν | τὸ πλεῖστον D: τριπλάσιον F. |
‚ατ′ Miller: βτ D ‖ 5. τὸ μνῆμα del. Letronne | πρόσχωροι S.:
-χώριοι D | ἥκειν[1] K.: ἔξειν (sic) D: ἐλθεῖν V. | ἥκειν[2] K.: ἥξειν
(sic) D: ἐλθεῖν V.

107. 1. πλοῦς D: π. ⟨ἐστὶν⟩ F. | εὐλίμενος … ἄνυδρος del. Gail: -ον
… -ον V. | ἐν δὲ φάρῳ D: εἰσὶν (sic) δ᾽ ἐν αὐτῇ F.

108. 1. μέχρι D: -ις M. | πλύνους D: -ὸν F. | πλύνων D: -οῦ F. |
Πέτραντα τὸν μέγαν Letronne: πέτράντατον (sic) μ[υ] D | ἀντίπυγος
D: Ἀντίπυργος M. (addenda) | ⟨τοῦ⟩ M. | Χερρόνησος S., cf.
Desanges (tr.): -οι D | Ἀζίριδες Bursian: ἀχιτίδ- D: Ἀλιάδ- K.:
Ἀχιλ(ιτ)ίδ- M.: Ἀζίλιδ- Desanges; cf. 47. 1 ‖ 2. ἐν γύαις M.ᶜ: γῦης D:
γῆς P.: perhaps ἐκ γῆς? | παρήκει M.: -άγει D | ‚αφ′ M.ᵗ: μφ D:
‚αψ′ M.ᶜ ‖ 3. οἱ D: om. M. ‖ 4. τάδε K.: ψάδε D (not ὑψάδε as in
M.) | βαθὺς Salm.: ξαθὸς D: βάθος K. | μεμαίκυλα S. (cf. Thphr.
HP 3. 16. 4): μεμή- D (not μιμή- as in Peretti 1979, 298 n. 328): μιμαί-
Salm. | συκάμινα: σύμνα D, em. Salm. ‖ 5. δὲ (after ἐστὶ) del. M.:
γὲ K. | ἄπιος D: Ἄπις M.ᶜ | Βακαλοῦ Desanges 99: καυκάλου D |
ἐγχέλειος Desanges (Ἐ- S.): ἐκκειός D: ἐκχεῖται Gail: Ἔκκειος K. |
κατὰ D: καὶ Gail | Χερρονήσου S.: -ων D | Ἀζιρίδων Bursian:
ἀντίδων D: Ἀχιλιδῶν (Achilidibus) M.ᵗʳ: Ἀλιάδων K.; cf. 47. 1, 108. 1

109. 1. ‚ε M.: π′ D ‖ 2. Λιβύων ἔθνος Νασαμῶνες K.: λυβίων ἔ.
νασ[αι]μώνες D: Ν., Λ. ἔθ. F. | νασ[αι]μώνες μέχρι τοῦ written over
erasure of παρὰ τὴν σύρτιν μέχρι τοῦ (S.), μ. τ. rewritten in exactly
the same place | ἔχονται: F. moves Μάκαι here ‖ 3. πρῶτοι D:
om. M.: perhaps πρῶτον? | εἶτα M.: κατὰ D: καὶ F. | αἱ Λευκαὶ κα-
λούμεναι S.: Λ. καλοῦνται D: αἱ Λ. κ. Miller: Λ. ⟨αἳ⟩ κ. M.: Λ. καλού-
μεναι F. | ἐν τῷ μυχῷ del. M. | Φιλαίνου βωμοὶ M.: φιλαιοῦ

βωμός D: Φιλαίνων βωμοί F. | Ἄμμωνος M.: ἄμμουνες D | ἄλσος
M.ᶜ: ἀλοῦς D: ἁλίς Fiaccadori (but cf. only Eust. ad Il. 3. 398. 6) |
lacuna M. (not A.) | τῆς Σύρτιδος del. F. || 4. ἔξω τῆς Σύρτιδος
del. Gail | π′ πάντη D: π′ M.ᴸ: π′ πέντε M.ᶜ: π′ καὶ ἑκατόν (deleting
ὑπ᾽ αὐτὸν) Müller 461: perhaps e.g. ὀγδοήκοντα? | αὐτῷ S.: -ὸν D:
-ῶν K. || 5. ⟨β′⟩ S.: or γ′

110. 1. Γάφαρα M.ᶜ: γράφαρα D | ταύτης M.: -ῃ D || 2. Γαφάρων
M.ᶜ: γρ- D || 3. Ταριχεῖαι M.: ταριλία D || 4. κατὰ¹ D: μετὰ M. |
βραχείων D: Ταριχειῶν F. | μετὰ Λωτοφάγους κατὰ Ταριχείας V.: μ.
λ. καταριχίας D: μ. Λ. ⟨καὶ⟩ κατὰ Τ. Gail: all del. F.: μ. Τ. Peretti: μ. Λ.
κατὰ ριχίας (sic; sc. ῥηχίας?) L.: ἤτοι Λωτοφάγων (alone) M.ᶜ | με-
μαίκυλον S. (cf. 108. 4): μιμαίηνκλον (sic) D || 5. ἔπιχος D: Γιχθίς
M.ᶜ: Ἔσχιδες A. | Γιχθὶν F.: ἔπιχον D, L. | ἡμέρας K.: -ᾳ D: -α F. |
ἡμισείας M.: -ᾳ D: -α K. || 6. ⟨... Ἐσχίδες ...⟩ S.: ⟨μετὰ δὲ Γιχθίν
ἐστι Νέα πόλις⟩ P. | ἐσχίδων D: Ἐπίχων or Ἐπιχίων Gail: Ἐπιχίδος
K.: Γιχθέως F. | ⟨εἰς Νέαν πολιν⟩ P.: ⟨εἰς Μακομάδα⟩ F.: ⟨εἰς Μ. ἢ
Νεάπολιν⟩ M. || 7. Κερκινῖτις V.: ἀκακινίτης D: Κερκενῖτις P. |
ἀπὸ δὲ Θάψου ⟨εἰς Λέπτιν ... ἀπὸ δὲ Λέπτεως⟩ τῆς μικρᾶς
supplemented from F.¹, M. (omitting Θάψου καὶ before Λέπτεως²):
ἀπὸ δὲ θάψου τῆς μικρᾶς D: ἀπὸ δὲ Θ. ⟨καὶ Λέπτεως⟩ τῆς μ. P. || 8.
καὶ Ἀδρύμητός M.: κ. δρονίτις D: κ. Τριτωνίτης V.: εἰς Ἀδρύμητα
⟨πλοῦς ἡμέρας⟩ P. | Κερκινῖτις V.: καρκινίτης D: Κερκενῖτις P. |
δυσπλωτοτέρα S.: -πλοτοτέρα D: -πλοωτέρα M. | τρίτωνος D, K.:
-νὶς M. | ⟨καὶ λίμνη⟩ here S.: after νῆσος M. | ὅταν D (not ὁ τῆς
as in M., P.) | οὐκ ἔχει εἴσπλουν ⟨ναυ⟩σὶν, ὡ⟨ς⟩ φαίνεται S.
(ναυσὶν Salm., ὡ⟨ς⟩ S., φαίνεται P.): οὐκ ἔˣ εἴσπ. συνϋφαίνουσᾳ D:
οὐκ ἔχειν εἴσπ. ἐστὶ φαίνουσα M. || 9. περιοικοῦσι M.: -έπουσι D
Λίβυες V.: λίβυοι (not λίβιοι as in M.) D: Λιβύων P. | Γύζαντες M.ᶜ᾿
ᵗʳ: πάντες D: Βύζ- Desanges: Ζύγ- K. (nn.) | τὸ ἐπέκεινα F.: τὸ ὑπέ- D:
τὰ ἐ. M. | Γύζαντες M.ᵗʳ: ἄπ- D | ἅπαντες (after ξανθοὶ) M.ᵗʳ:
ἄπαστοι D: ἄριστοι K. (comm.): ἄπλαστοι A.: ἀγαστοὶ Gail | καὶ
κάλλιστοι² del. M. || 10. ἡμέρας ἐστί(ν) M.: ἡμερῶν στ′ D (not ἡμ.
οτ′ as in M., F., L.): ἡμερῶν γ′ K. | ⟨πόλεώς⟩ V. | ⟨... ποταμὸς
...⟩ S.

111. 2. ἐπὶ (first) S.: ἐν D || 3. μακρὰν ἀπὸ Ἑρμαίας S.: μικρὸν ἀπὸ
ἑρμαίας (sic) D, del. M. || 5. εἰς ... ⟨ἄκρα⟩ πόλις P. (Ἄκρα S.): εἰς
ἵππου ἄκρα ἵππου πόλις D: Ἴ. Ἄ. ⟨ἢ⟩ Ἱππῶν π. M.: Ἴ. ἄ. ⟨καὶ⟩ Ἵπ. π. F.:
εἰς Ἴ. Ἄ. [—] Ἱππῶν π. A. | ἐν ταῖς νήσοις del. M. | Καλάθη S.: καὶ
D | Ἰγίλγιλις P.: καύκακις D (there are other suggestions) | σίδα
D: Σάλδα Gsell | Ἰόμνιον L. (comm.): ἰουλίου D: Ἰῶλ M.ᶜ |
μεγάλη D: Μεταγώνιον G. | ⟨καὶ⟩ after μεγάλη G. || 6. Ἡράκ-
λειος M.: ἡράκλεια D | ⟨ἡ⟩ M. | Ἀβιλυκὴ G.: ἄπινιλύη D: Ἀπανι-
λύη K.: Ἄπινι, Λύη L. | ⟨καὶ⟩ M. | after ποταμῷ L. inserts Κράβις

... Σολόεντος ἄκρας from 112. 4–5 | νῆσοι M.: νῆσος D | should ἀπὸ Καρχηδόνος ... ἑπτά precede ἄκρα Ἀβιλυκή? ‖ 7. Ἡράκλειοι M.: -ειαι D | ὑψηλή K.: ἡψηλή D (not noted by M.) | αὗται² del. F. ‖ 8. Κανωπικοῦ M.: κανώβου D | ν´ καὶ δ´ S.: ο´ καὶ δ´ D: νδ´ Müller xl, Desanges ‖ 9. ⟨τῶν⟩ S.

112. 1. Ἡρακλείους M.: ἡρακλείας D | κύπειρος ... θρυόν Salm.: κύπρος καὶ φλοιόν· καὶ ὀρύον D | (αἱ K.) Μελεαγρίδες Salm.: λιμελελίφιδες D: αἱ λιμενῆτιδες (sic) L. ‖ 2. ἀπὸ δὲ τῆς D: ἀπὸ δὴ τῆς M.: τῆς om. P. ‖ 3. ἀνίδης D: Ἄνιδος K. | Ἀνίδην [εἶτά] ἐστὶν M.: ἀνιδίευτα ἔστιν (sic) D: Ἄνιδον εἶτα ἐστὶν K.: Ἀνίδ⟨ην [—] Σολόεις ἄκρα⟩, εἶτά ἐστιν P. ‖ 4. κράβις D: Κράθις F. | ⟨πλοῦς⟩ M.ᶜ | σολόεσαν D: -εντα M. | πάσης Bursian: πᵃγ (?) D: πᾶσα K. | μεγαλοπρεπὴς M. (there are other suggestions): μεγ· ποινής D | γεγραμμένοι D: γεγλυμ- F. | ἀνδριάντες D: ἄνδρες, γυναῖκες F. ‖ 5. ξιῶν D: Λίξος M.ᶜˑᵗʳ | ἱεροί D: ἑσπέριοι Slothouwer | δύο D: δ´ P. | δώδεκα: δέκα δύο D (a post-Cl form) ‖ 6. δοχμῆς K.: λόγμης D (not λοχμῆς as in M.) ‖ 8. οὗτοι del. F.¹: οὗτοι ⟨οἱ⟩ P. | πρὸς ... Αἰθίοπες del. P. | οἱ M.: δὲ D | καὶ ὀδόντας M.: κ. ὀδόντων D: μετ᾽ ὀδόντων V. ‖ 9. κόσμῳ [—] στίκτοις S.: κοσμοστίκτοις D: κοσμοστ. ⟨ἐσθήμασι⟩ Salm., P: κόσμῳ στ. δοραῖς (or δέρμασι) M.ᶜ: κόσμῳ ⟨κατα⟩στίκτοις ⟨δέρμασι⟩ F.: perhaps καὶ τῶν ἡμέρων βοσκημάτων ⟨τοῖς δέρμασιν⟩ οἱ Αἰ. χρῶνται κόσμῳ στ.? ‖ 10. οἱ δὲ Φοίνικες ... τῇ ἑορτῇ put before πωλοῦσι by P. | ἄλλους ἐξορύκτους M.: ἄπρους ἐξαράκτους D | τῇ ἑορτῇ D: gloss? ‖ 11. αὐτοὶ D: -ὸν M. ‖ 12. ⟨τὴν⟩ M.

113. 1. ⟨ἀπὸ⟩¹ Gail | Γεραιστὸν G.: γεραισὸν D (not noted by M.) | ψ´ καὶ ν´ M.: ζ´ κοινή D: ρ´ κοινῇ K. | αὐτῆς τῆς Ἄνδρου Gail: ἀπὸ τῆς ἄνδρου D: ἀπὸ ⟨Παιωνίου⟩ τῆς Ἄ. M. | Τήνου S.: νήσου D | διάπλου: διάπλους D (not noted by M.) | μ (twice) D: ἑξήκοντα (i.e. ξ´) F. (twice) | μ³ D: ρμ´ M. | ἐπὶ (before μῆκος) D: ἐστι V. | σ´ D: σν´ ⟨ἔστι τὸ μῆκος⟩ F. | ζ´ D: ιζ´ M. | πλῷ ἀρίστῳ M.ᶜˑᵗʳ: πρὸ ἀρίστου D | ⟨τοῦ ... Σάμον⟩ M. ‖ 2. ⟨ἀπὸ Μαλέας⟩ M. | ρλ´ M.: λ´ D | ρ´ D: σ´ M. | Αἰγιλίαν K.: αἴγιναν D: Αἴγιλαν F. (then Αἰγίλας twice) | ⟨αὐτῆς ... προαριστίδιος⟩ M. | βφ D: ͵αφ´ M.: ͵αχ´ F. (expanded) | ρ (after κάρπ. στ.) D: φ´ M.: υ´ K. (nn.) | ρ (after μῆκ. στ.) D: ρμ´ and lacuna K. (nn.): τ´ M. | ρ´ (after πλ. στ.) D: τ´ M. | χ´ D: φ´ F. | δσο D: δυο´ K.: τετρακισχίλια καὶ ἑκατόν (i.e. ͵δρ´) F.

114. κάσος obelized by S.: see Comm. | ἐννεακαιδεκάτη K.: ἐννα- D

WORKS CITED

Abbreviations follow *OCD³* or *L'Année philologique*.

Africa Pilot (1953), *Africa Pilot*, 11th edn, i. London.

—— (1953–4), *Africa Pilot*, 11th edn. London.

African Pilot (1856), *The African Pilot*, i. London.

Agbunov, M. V. (1979), 'Le Niconium grec antique', *Arkheolohia* 32: 13–19.

—— (1981), 'Материалы по античной географии северо-западного причерноморья', *VDI* 155: 124–43.

Allain, M. L. (1977), 'The Periplous of Skylax of Karyanda', Ph.D. thesis. Ohio State University.

Amiotti, G. (1987), 'Cerne: "ultima terra"', in M. Sordi (ed.), *Il confine nel mondo antico* (Milano), 43–9.

Antonelli, L. (1995), 'Aviénus et colonnes d'Hercule', *MCV* 31: 77–83.

—— (2002), 'Piceni e Peucezi: un'identità contesa', *PP* 57: 196–215.

Archibald, Z. H. (2004), 'Inland Thrace', *Inv.* 885–99.

Arnaud, P. (1989), 'Pouvoir des mots et limites de la cartographie dans la géographie grecque et romaine', *DHA* 15: 9–29.

—— (1992), 'Les relations maritimes dans le Pont-Euxin d'après les données numériques des géographes anciens', *REA* 94: 57–77.

—— (1993), 'De la durée à la distance: l'évaluation des distances maritimes dans le monde gréco-romain', *Histoire et mesure* 8: 225–47.

—— (2001), 'Les Ligures: la construction d'un concept géographique et ses étapes de l'époque archaïque à l'empire romain', in V. Fromentin and S. Gotteland (eds), *Origines gentium* (Bordeaux), 327–46.

—— (2005), *Les Routes de la navigation antique*. Paris.

Austin, M. M. (2004), 'From Syria to the Pillars of Herakles', *Inv.* 1233–49.

—— (2006), *The Hellenistic World from Alexander to the Roman Conquest*, 2nd edn. Cambridge.

Avram, A. (2004), 'The Propontic coast of Asia Minor', *Inv.* 974–99.

——, Hind, J., and Tsetskhladze, G. (2004), 'The Black Sea areas', *Inv.* 924–73.

Baladié, R. (1980), *Le Péloponnèse de Strabon*. Paris.

Baschmakoff, A. A. (1948), *La Synthèse des périples pontiques*. Paris.

Bean, G. E. (1968), *Turkey's Southern Shore*, 1st edn. London.

—— (1979), *Turkey's Southern Shore*, 2nd edn. London.

—— and Mitford, T. B. (1970), *Journeys in Rough Cilicia 1964-1968*. Wien.

Beaumont, R. L. (1936), 'Greek influence in the Adriatic sea before the fourth century BC', *JHS* 56: 159–204.

—— (1939), 'The date of the first treaty between Rome and Carthage', *JRS* 29: 74–86.

Bennet, J., and Reger, G. (2000), 'Map 60 Creta', *Barr. Dir.* ii. 919–36.

Bernand, A. (2000), 'Map 74 Delta', *Barr. Dir.* ii. 1117–24.

Boardman, J. (1999), *The Greeks Overseas*, 4th edn. London.

—— (2006), 'Early Euboean settlements in the Carthage area', *OJA* 25: 195–200.

—— (2010), 'Where is Aüza?', *OJA* 29: 319–21.

Borza, E. N. (2000), 'Map 51 Thracia', *Barr. Dir.* ii. 772–84.

Bosworth, A. B. (1994), 'Alexander the Great part 1: the events of the reign', in *CAH*, 2nd edn, vi. *The Fourth Century BC*, 791–845.

Bousquet, J. (1989), *Les Comptes du quatrième et du troisième siècle*. Paris.

Braudel, F. (1972), *The Mediterranean and the Mediterranean World in the Age of Philip II*. 2 vols. London.

Braund, D. C. (2000a), 'Map 85 Oudon–Rha', *Barr. Dir.* ii. 1213–16.

—— (2000b), 'Map 87 inset Cimmerius Bosphorus', *Barr. Dir.* ii. 1243–54.

—— and Sinclair, T. (2000), 'Map 87 Pontus–Phasis', *Barr. Dir.* ii. 1226–42.

Brown, J. P., and Meyers, E. M. (2000), 'Map 69 Damascus–Caesarea', *Barr. Dir.* ii. 1056–73.

Bryer, A., and Winfield, D. (1985) with R. Anderson and J. Winfield, *The Byzantine Monuments and Topography of the Pontos*. Washington D.C.

Bunbury, E. H. (1883), *A History of Ancient Geography*, 2nd edn. 2 vols. London.

Burstein, S. M. (1976), *Outpost of Hellenism*. Berkeley–Los Angeles.

—— (ed. 1989), *Agatharchides of Cnidus, On the Erythraean Sea*. London.

Cahill, N. D. (2002), *Household and City Organization at Olynthus*. New Haven–London.

Cañete, C., and Vives-Ferrándiz, J. (2011), '"Almost the same": dynamic domination and hybrid contexts in Iron Age Lixus, Larache, Morocco', *WA* 43

Cappelletto, P. (ed. 2003), *I frammenti di Mnasea*. Milano.

Cary, M. (1949), *The Geographic Background of Greek and Roman History*. Oxford.

Casson, L. B. (1989), *The Periplus Maris Erythraei*. Princeton.

—— (2007), review of D. W. Roller, *Through the Pillars of Herakles*, *IJNA* 36 (1): 204–5.

Castiglioni, M. P. (2008), 'The cult of Diomedes in the Adriatic:

complementary contributions from literary sources and archae-ology', in J. Carvalho (ed.), *Bridging the Gaps* (Pisa),

Cataudella, M. R. (1989–90), 'Quante erano le colonne di Ercole?', *AFLM* 22–3: 315–37.

Caven, B. M. (1990), *Dionysius I*. New Haven–London.

Chandler, L. (1926), 'The north-west frontier of Attica', *JHS* 46: 1–21.

Cherry, J. F., Davis, J. L., and Mantzourani, E. (1991), *Landscape Archae-ology as Long-term History*. Los Angeles.

Clarke, K. (1999), *Between Geography and History*. Oxford.

Cluverius, P. (1624), *Italia antiqua*. Leiden.

Colonna, G. (2003), 'Il medio Adriatico: tradizioni storiografiche e in-formazione storica', *SE* 69: 3–12.

Constantakopoulou, C. (2007), *The Dance of the Islands*. Oxford.

Cooper, F. A. (1972), 'Topographical notes from southwest Arcadia', *AAA* 3: 359–67.

Coppola, A. (1993), 'I due templi Greci di Ancona: per l'iconografia della Colonna Traiana', in L. Braccesi (ed.), *Hesperìa*, 3 (Venezia), 189–91.

Cornell, T. J. (1995), *The Beginnings of Rome*. London–New York.

Counillon, P. (1998a), 'Datos en Thrace et le périple du Pseudo-Skylax', *REA* 100: 115–24.

—— (1998b), 'Λιμὴν ἔρημος', in P. Arnaud and P. Counillon (eds), *Geographica historica* (Bordeaux–Nice), 55–67.

—— (2001a), 'La description de la Crète dans le Périple du Ps.-Skylax', *REA* 103: 381–94.

—— (2001b), 'Les Cyclades chez les géographes grecs', *REA* 103: 11–23.

—— (2004), *Pseudo-Skylax, Le Périple du Pont-Euxin*. Bordeaux.

—— (2007a), 'L'ethnographie dans le Périple du Ps.-Skylax entre Tanaïs et Colchide', in A. Bresson, A. Ivantchik, and J.-L. Ferrary (eds), *Une koinè pontique* (Bordeaux), 37–45.

—— (2007b), 'Le Périple du Pseudo-Skylax et l'Adriatique (§17–24)', in S. Čače, A. Kurilič, and F. Tassaux (eds), *Les Routes de l'Adriatique antique—Putovi antičkog Jadrana* (Bordeaux), 19–29.

—— (2007c), 'Pseudo-Skylax et la Carie', in P. Brun (ed.), *Scripta Anatolica* (Bordeaux), 33–42.

Counillon, P., and Étienne, R. (1997), 'Les Taricheiai d'après les sources grecques', in R. Étienne and F. Mayet (eds), *Itinéraires lusi-taniens* (Paris), 181–93.

Craik, E. M. (1980), *The Dorian Aegean*. London, etc.

Culican, W. (1991), 'Phoenicia and Phoenician colonization', in *CAH*, 2nd edn, iii. 2. *The Assyrian and Babylonian Empires and Other States of the Near East, from the Eighth to the Sixth Centuries BC*, 461–546.

D'Andria, F. (1990), 'Greek influence in the Adriatic: fifty years after

Beaumont', in J.-P. Descoeudres (ed.), *Greek Colonists and Native Populations* (Oxford), 281–90.

d'Ercole, M. C. (2000), 'La légende de Diomède dans l'Adriatique préromaine', in C. Delplace and F. Tassaux (eds), *Les Cultes polythéistes dans l'Adriatique romaine* (Bordeaux),

Davies, M. (1991), *Poetarum melicorum Graecorum fragmenta*, i. Oxford.

Dawson, R. (ed. 1993), *Confucius, The Analects*. Oxford.

Decourt, J.-C., Nielsen, T. H., and Helly, B. (2004), 'Thessalia and adjacent regions', *Inv.* 676–731.

Dench, E. (1995), *From Barbarians to New Men*. Oxford.

Desanges, J. (1978), *Recherches sur l'activité des Méditerranéens aux confins de l'Afrique*. Rome.

Diller, A. (1952), *The Tradition of the Minor Greek Geographers*. Lancaster, Pa.–Oxford.

Dimakis, P. (1984), ''Η Πρώτη: ἡ μικρὴ ἱστορία ἑνὸς ἐρήμου νησιοῦ', in *2nd Messenian Congress*, 44–54.

Dittenberger, W. (1915–24), *Sylloge inscriptionum Graecarum*, 3rd edn. 4 vols. Leipzig.

Dittrich, H. T.: *see* Fabricius, B.

Drews, R. (1963), 'Ephorus and history written κατὰ γένος', *AJPh* 84: 244–55.

Dueck, D. (2005), 'The parallelogram and the pinecone: definition of geographical shapes in Greek and Roman geography on the evidence of Strabo', *AncSoc* 35: 19–57.

Edlund-Berry, I. E. M., and Small, A. M. (2000), 'Map 46 Bruttii', *Barr. Dir.* i. 695–708.

Eser, E. (2004), 'Kinolis (Ginolu) Kalesi', *Hacettepe Üniversitesi Edebiyat Fakültesi Dergisi* 21: 171–94.

Euzennat, M. (1994), 'Le périple d'Hannon', *CRAI* 1994: 559–79.

—— (2000), 'Map 28 Mauretania Tingitana', *Barr. Dir.* i. 457–66.

Fabre, P. (1965), 'La date de rédaction du périple de Scylax', *LEC* 33: 353–66.

Fabricius, B. (1841), 'Ueber den Periplus des Skylax', *Zeitschrift für die Alterthumswissenschaft* 8: 1105–20.

—— (1844), 'Ueber den Periplus des Skylax (Fortsetzung)', *Zeitschrift für die Alterthumswissenschaft* 11 (²2): 1081–103.

—— (1846), 'Ueber den Periplus des Skylax: zweiter Abschnitt', *Archiv für Philologie und Paedagogik* 12: 5–85.

—— (1878), *Anonymi vulgo Scylacis Caryandensis periplum maris interni*, 2nd edn. Leipzig.

—— (ed. 1848), *Scylacis Periplus*. Dresdae.

Falkner, C. L. (1994), 'A note on Sparta and Gytheum in the fifth century', *Historia* 43: 495–501.

Figueira, T. J. (1981), *Aegina*. New York.

—— (1991), *Athens and Aigina in the Age of Imperial Colonization*. Baltimore.

—— (2004), 'The Saronic gulf', *Inv.* 620–3.

Fischer-Hansen, T., Nielsen, T. H., and Ampolo, C. (2004a), 'Italia and Kampania', *Inv.* 249–320.

——, ——, and —— (2004b), 'Sikelia', *Inv.* 172–248.

Flensted-Jensen, P. (1995), 'Hvorfor læse Ps.-Skylax' Periplous?', in *Studier et alia til ære for Mogens Herman Hansen* (København), 13–16.

—— (2004a), 'Karia', *Inv.* 1108–37.

—— (2004b), 'Thrace from Axios to Strymon', *Inv.* 810–53.

—— and Hansen, M. H. (1996), 'Pseudo-Skylax' use of the term polis', in M. H. Hansen and K. Raaflaub (eds), *More Studies in the Ancient Greek Polis* (Stuttgart), 137–67.

—— and —— (2007), 'Pseudo-Skylax', in M. H. Hansen (ed.), *The Return of the Polis* (Stuttgart), 204–42.

Forster, E. S. (1952), 'Trees and plants in the Greek tragic writers', *G&R* 21: 57–63.

Fortenbaugh, W. W., Huby, P. M., Sharples, R. W., and Gutas, D. (eds) (1992), *Theophrastus of Eresus: Sources for his Life, Writings, Thought and Influence*. 2 vols. Leiden–New York–Köln.

Foss, C. (2000), 'Map 86 Paphlagonia', *Barr. Dir.* ii. 1217–25.

——, Mitchell, S., and Reger, G. (2000), 'Map 56 Pergamum', *Barr. Dir.* ii. 841–61.

Fossey, J. M. (1990), *The Ancient Topography of Opountian Lokris*. Amsterdam.

—— and Morin, J. (2000), 'Map 55 Thessalia–Boeotia', *Barr. Dir.* ii. 818–40.

Fotheringham, J. K. (1919), 'Cleostratus', *JHS* 39: 164–84.

—— (1920), 'Cleostratus: a postscript', *JHS* 40: 208–9.

—— (1925), 'Cleostratus (III)', *JHS* 45: 78–83.

Foxhall, L. (2007), *Olive Cultivation in Ancient Greece*. Oxford.

Fraser, P. M. (1994), 'The world of Theophrastus', in S. Hornblower (ed.), *Greek Historiography* (Oxford), 167–91.

—— and Bean, G. E. (1954), *The Rhodian Peraea and Islands*. London.

Freitag, K., Funke, P., and Moustakis, N. (2004), 'Aitolia', *Inv.* 379–90.

Funke, P., Moustakis, N., and Hochschultz, B. (2004), 'Epeiros', *Inv.* 338–50.

Gabrielsen, V. (2000), 'The Rhodian peraia in the third and second centuries BC', *C&M* 51: 129–83.

Gail, J. F. (1825), *Dissertation sur le Périple de Scylax*. Paris.

—— (1826), *Geographi Graeci minores*, i. Parisiis.

Gardiner-Garden, J. (1988), 'Eudoxos, Skylax and the Syrmatai', *Eranos* 86: 31–42.

Garzón Díaz, J. (2008), *Geógrafos griegos*. Oviedo.

Gehrke, H.-J., and Wirbelauer, E. (2004), 'Akarnania and adjacent areas', *Inv.* 351–78.

Geographical Handbooks (1944–5a), *Greece*. 3 vols. [London].

—— (1944–5b), *Jugoslavia*. 3 vols. [London].

—— (1945), *Albania*. [London].

Gill, D. W. J. (1988), 'Silver anchors and cargoes of oil: some observations on Phoenician trade in the western Mediterranean', *PBSR* 56: 1–12.

González Ponce, F. J. (1991), 'Revisión de la opinión de A. Peretti sobre el origen cartográfico del Periplo del Ps.-Escílax', *Habis* 22: 151–5.

—— (1994), 'Ps.-Escílax §20, la descripción del Danubio y el problema de las fuentes del Periplo', *Emerita* 62: 153–65.

—— (1997), 'Suda s.v. Σκύλαξ: sobre el título, el contenido y la unidad de FGrHist III C 709', *GeogrAnt* 6: 37–51.

—— (2011a), '2038 Phileas von Athen', in H.-J. Gehrke (ed.), *Die Fragmente der griechischen Historiker*, v. 1. (Leiden).

—— (2011b), '2208 Hanno von Karthago', in H.-J. Gehrke (ed.), *Die Fragmente der griechischen Historiker*, v. 1. (Leiden).

Gronovius, J. (ed. 1697), *Geographica antiqua*. Lugduni Batavorum.

—— (ed. 1700), *Geographica antiqua*. Lugduni Batavorum.

Gsell, S. (1920), *Histoire ancienne de l'Afrique du Nord*, ii. Paris.

Hammond, N. G. L. (1954), 'The main road from Boeotia to the Peloponnese through the northern Megarid', *ABSA* 49: 103–22.

—— (1967), *Epirus*. Oxford.

Hansen, M. H. (1995), 'Kome: a study in how the Greeks designated and classified settlements which were not poleis', in M. H. Hansen and K. Raaflaub (eds), *Studies in the Ancient Greek Polis* (Stuttgart), 45–81.

—— (1996), 'Πολλαχῶς πόλις λέγεται (Arist. Pol. 1276a23): the Copenhagen inventory of poleis and the lex Hafniensis de civitate', in M. H. Hansen (ed.), *Introduction to an Inventory of Poleis* (Copenhagen), 7–72.

—— (1997a), 'Emporion: a study of the use and meaning of the term in the archaic and classical periods', in T. H. Nielsen (ed.), *Yet More Studies in the Ancient Greek Polis* (Stuttgart), 83–105.

—— (1997b), 'The polis as an urban centre: the literary and epigraphical evidence', in M. H. Hansen (ed.), *The Polis as an Urban Centre and as a Political Community* (Copenhagen), 9–86.

—— (2004a), 'Attika', *Inv.* 624–42.

—— (2004b), 'Boiotia', *Inv.* 431–61.

—— (2004c), 'Introduction', *Inv.* 3–154.

—— (2006a), 'Emporion: a study of the use and meaning of the term in the archaic and classical periods', in G. Tsetskhladze (ed.), *Greek Colonisation*, i. (Leiden), 1–39.

—— (2006b), *Polis*. Oxford.

—— and Nielsen, T. H. (2004), *An Inventory of Archaic and Classical Poleis*. Oxford.

——, Spencer, N., and Williams, H. (2004), 'Lesbos', *Inv.* 1018–32.

Hansen, R. (1879), *Beiträge zu alten Geographen*. Sondershausen.

Hatzopoulos, M. B. (1996), *Macedonian Institutions under the Kings*, i. Athens.

Hellenkemper, H., and Hild, F. (1986), *Neue Forschungen in Kilikien*. Wien.

Hiller von Gaertringen, F., Freiherr (1906), *Inschriften von Priene*. Berlin.

Hoeschelius, D. (ed. 1600), *Geographica Marciani Heracleotae, Scylacis Caryandensis, Artemidori Ephesii, Dicaearchi Messenii, Isidori Characeni*. Augustae Vindelicorum.

Horden, P., and Purcell, N. (2000), *The Corrupting Sea*. Oxford–Malden, Mass.

Hornblower, S. (1982), *Mausolus*. Oxford.

Hosgormez, H., Etiope, G., and Yalçin, N. (2008), 'New evidence for a mixed inorganic and organic origin of the Olympic Chimaera fire (Turkey): a large onshore seepage of abiogenic gas', *Geofluids* 4: 263–73.

Hudson, J. (1698), *Geographiae veteris scriptores Graeci minores*, i. Oxoniae.

Jacoby, F. (1923–58), *Die Fragmente der griechischen Historiker*. 3 in 16 vols. Berlin–Leiden.

Jameson, M. H., Runnels, C. N., and van Andel, T. H. (1994a), *A Greek Countryside*. Stanford, Calif.

——, ——, and —— (1994b), 'Pseudo-Scylax on the coast of the Akte', in M. H. Jameson, C. N. Runnels, and T. H. van Andel, *A Greek Countryside* (Stanford, Calif.), 568–72.

Janni, P. (1982), review of A. Peretti, *Il periplo di Scilace*, *Athenaeum* 66: 602–7.

—— (1984), *La mappa e il periplo*. Roma.

—— (1998), 'Cartographie et art nautique dans le monde ancien', in P. Arnaud and P. Counillon (eds), *Geographica historica* (Bordeaux-Nice), 41–53.

Jodin, A. (1966), *Mogador*. Rabat/Tanger.

Jones, G. D. B., and Little, J. H. (1971), 'Coastal settlement in Cyrenaica', *JRS* 61: 64–79.

Katsonopoulou, D. (1990), 'Studies of the eastern cities of Opuntian
Lokris: Halai, Kyrtones, Korseia, Bumelitaia', Ph.D. thesis. Cornell
University.

Keen, A. G. (1998), *Dynastic Lycia*. Leiden.

—— and Fischer-Hansen, T. (2004), 'The south coast of Asia Minor
(Pamphylia, Kilikia)', *Inv*. 1211–22.

—— and Hansen, M. H. (2004), 'Lykia', *Inv*. 1138–43.

Keyser, P. T. (2000), 'The geographical work of Dikaiarchos', in W. W.
Fortenbaugh and E. Schütrumpf (eds), *Dicaearchus of Messana* (New
Brunswick–London), 353–72.

Kirigin, B. (1990), 'The Greeks in central Dalmatia: some new evidence', in J.-P. Descoeudres (ed.), *Greek Colonists and Native Populations* (Oxford), 291–321.

Klausen, R. H. (ed. 1831), *Hecataei Milesii fragmenta; Scylacis Caryandensis Periplus*. Berolini.

Knapp, R. C., and Stanley, F. H., Jr. (2000), 'Map 26 Lusitania–Baetica',
Barr. Dir. i. 415–39.

Legon, R. P. (2004), 'Megaris, Korinthia, Sikyonia', *Inv*. 462–71.

Lentz, A. (1867–70), *Grammatici Graeci*, iii. 1–2. Leipzig.

Letronne, A.-J. (ed. 1840), *Fragments des poèmes géographiques de Scym-
nus de Chio et du faux Dicéarque*. Paris.

Leue, G. (1884), 'Dionysios Kalliphontos 31–38', *Philologus* 42: 178–81.

Leutsch, E. L., and Schneidewin, F. G. (eds 1839), *Corpus paroemiogra-
phorum Graecorum*, i. Gottingae.

Liddell, H. G., and Scott, R. (1968), *A Greek–English Lexicon*, 9th edn.
Oxford.

Liddle, A. (ed. 2003), *Arrian, Periplus Ponti Euxini*. London.

Lipiński, É. (1992–3), 'Sites "phénico-puniques" de la côte algéri-
enne', *REPPAL* 7–8: 287–324.

—— (1993), 'La Méditerranée centrale d'après le Pseudo-Skylax', *JMS*
3: 175–97.

—— (2003), *Itineraria Phoenicia*. Leuven.

Lloyd, A. B. (1975), *Herodotus Book II: Introduction*. Leiden.

—— (1976), *Herodotus Book II: Commentary 1-98*. Leiden.

Lonis, R. (1979), 'Les éthiopiens du Pseudo-Scylax: mythe ou réalité
géographique?', *Revue française d'histoire d'Outre-Mer* 66: 101–10.

Lordkipanidze, O. (2000), *Phasis*. Stuttgart.

Loukopoulou, L. (2004a), 'Thrace from Nestos to Hebros', *Inv*. 870–84.

—— (2004b), 'Thrace from Strymon to Nestos', *Inv*. 854–69.

—— (2004c), 'Thracian Chersonesos', *Inv*. 900–11.

—— and Łaitar, A. (2004), 'Propontic Thrace', *Inv.* 912–23.

Lučić, J. (1959), 'Pseudo-Skilakov Arion i Rijeka Dubrovačka', *Anali Historijskog Instituta Jugoslavenske Akademije Znanosti i Umjetnosti u Dubrovniku* 6–7: 117–20.

McInerney, J. J. (1999), *The Folds of Parnassos.* Austin.

Mahaffy, J. P. (1913), 'The arithmetical figures used by Greek writers during the classical period', in E. C. Quiggin (ed.), *Essays and Studies presented to William Ridgeway* (Cambridge), 195–7.

Malkin, I., Constantakopoulou, C., and Panagopoulou, K. (eds 2007), *Networks in the Ancient Mediterranean.*

——, ——, and —— (eds 2009), *Greek and Roman Networks in the Mediterranean.* London.

Marcotte, D. (1985), 'Le premier κοινόν acarnanien et la fin de la seconde ligue délienne: note critique', *AC* 54: 254–8.

—— (1986), 'Le périple dit de Scylax: esquisse d'un commentaire épigraphique et archéologique', *BollClass* 7: 166–82.

—— (1990), *Le Poème géographique de Dionysios, fils de Calliphon.* Lovanii.

—— (2000), *Introduction générale; Ps.-Scymnos, Circuit de la terre.* Paris.

Martinovic, J. (1966), 'Nouveaux moments dans l'interprétation des chap. 24 et 25 du périple de Pseudo-Scylax', *Starinar* 17: 116–17.

Maspero, G. (n.d. (1903)) with A. H. Sayce, *History of Egypt, Chaldaea, Syria, Babylonia, and Assyria*, iv. London.

Mattingly, D. J., Stone, D., Stirling, L., and Ben Lazreg, N. (2001), 'Leptiminus (Tunisia): a "producer" city?', in D. J. Mattingly and J. Salmon (eds), *Economies beyond Agriculture in the Classical World* (London–New York), 66–89.

Mattingly, H. B. (1996), 'Athens and the Black Sea in the fifth century BC', in P. Lévêque and O. Lordkipanidze (eds), *Sur les traces des Argonautes*, 151–7.

Mediterranean Pilot (1978), *Mediterranean Pilot*, 10th edn, i. Taunton.

—— (1987), *Mediterranean Pilot*, 10th edn, iv. Taunton.

—— (1988), *Mediterranean Pilot*, 6th revised edn, v. Taunton.

Mee, C. B., and Forbes, H. A. (eds 1997), *A Rough and Rocky Place.* Liverpool.

Merker, I. L. (1989), 'The Achaians in Naupaktos and Kalydon in the fourth century', *Hesperia* 58: 303–11.

Metcalfe, M. J. (2005), 'Reaffirming regional identity: cohesive institutions and local interactions in Ionia 386–129 BC', Ph.D. thesis. University College London.

Millar, F. G. B. (1993), *The Roman Near East.* Cambridge, Mass.–London.

Miller, E. (1839), *Périple de Marcien d'Héraclée, épitomé d'Artémidore, Isidore de Charax, etc.* Paris.

Miller, S. G. (1982), 'Kleonai, the Nemean games, and the Lamian war', in A. L. Boegehold and others, *Studies in Athenian Architecture Sculpture and Topography presented to Homer A. Thompson* (Princeton, NJ), 100–8.

—— (1988), 'The theorodokoi of the Nemean games', *Hesperia* 57: 147–63.

—— (ed. 1990), *Nemea*. Berkeley.

Mirhady, D. C. (2000), 'Dicaearchus of Messana: the sources, text and translation', in W. W. Fortenbaugh and E. Schütrumpf (eds), *Dicaearchus of Messana: Text, Translation, and Discussion*, 1–142.

Mitchell, S. (2000), 'Map 66 Taurus', *Barr. Dir.* ii. 1013–24.

—— (2004), 'Troas', *Inv.* 1000–17.

Moreno, A. (2009), 'Hieron: the ancient sanctuary at the mouth of the Black Sea', *Hesperia* 77: 655–709.

Morgan, C. A., and Hall, J. M. (2004), 'Achaia', *Inv.* 472–88.

Müller, C. W. L. (1855–61), *Geographi Graeci minores*. 3 vols. Paris.

—— (ed. 1841–70), *Fragmenta historicorum Graecorum*. 5 vols. Paris.

Müller, K. O. (1828), *Die Etrusker*. 2 vols. Breslau.

—— (1832), review of R. H. Klausen, *Hecataei Milesii fragmenta; Scylacis Caryandensis Periplus*, *GGA* 1832 (202–3): 2019–24.

Muller, A. (1982), 'Mégarika', *BCH* 106: 379–407.

Nagle, D. B. (2006), *The Household as the Foundation of Aristotle's Polis*. Cambridge.

Nenci, G. (1977), 'Καταρβάτης ποταμός (Ps. Scylax 21)', *RFIC* 105: 164–5.

Nicolet, C. (1991), *Space, Geography, and Politics in the Early Roman Empire*. Ann Arbor.

Nielsen, T. H. (1997), 'Triphylia: an experiment in ethnic construction and political organisation', in T. H. Nielsen (ed.), *Yet More Studies in the Ancient Greek Polis* (Stuttgart), 129–62.

—— (2000), 'Epiknemidian, Hypoknemidian, and Opountian Lokrians: reflections on the political organisation of east Lokris in the classical period', in P. Flensted-Jensen (ed.), *Further Studies in the Ancient Greek Polis* (Stuttgart), 91–120.

—— (2002), *Arkadia and its Poleis in the Archaic and Classical Periods*. Göttingen.

—— (2004a), 'Arkadia', *Inv.* 505–39.

—— (2004b), 'East Lokris', *Inv.* 664–73.

—— (2005), 'A polis as a part of a larger identity group: glimpses from the history of Lepreon', *C&M* 56: 57–89.

—— and Gabrielsen, V. (2004), 'Rhodos', *Inv.* 1196–210.

Niemeyer, H. G. (2000), 'The early Phoenician city-states on the Mediterranean: archaeological elements for their description', in M. H. Hansen (ed.), *A Comparative Study of Thirty City-state Cultures* (Copenhagen), 89–115.

Nixon, L., and Price, S. (1990), 'The size and resources of Greek cities', in O. Murray and S. Price (eds), *The Greek City* (Oxford), 137–70.

Oikonomides, A. N., and Miller, M. C. J. (eds 1995), *Hanno the Carthaginian, Periplus or Circumnavigation [of Africa]*, 3rd edn. Chicago.

Oulhen, J. (2004), 'Phokis', *Inv.* 399–430.

Panchenko, D. V. (1998), 'Scylax' circumnavigation of India and its interpretation in early Greek geography, ethnography and cosmography, I', *Hyperboreus* 4: 211–42.

—— (2002), 'Scylax in Philostratus' Life of Apollonius of Tyana', *Hyperboreus* 8: 5–12.

—— (2003), 'Scylax' circumnavigation of India and its interpretation in early Greek geography, ethnography and cosmography, II', *Hyperboreus* 9: 274–94.

—— (2005), 'Scylax of Caryanda on the Bosporus and the strait at the Pillars', *Hyperboreus* 11: 173–80.

Pariente, A., and Touchais, G. (eds 1998), Ἄργος και Ἀργολίδα—*Argos et l'Argolide*. Paris/Nafplio/Athènes.

Pelling, C. B. R. (2007), 'Ion's Epidemiai and Plutarch's Ion', in V. Jennings and A. Katsaros (eds), *The World of Ion of Chios* (Leiden), 75–109.

Peretti, A. (1961), 'Eforo e Pseudo-Scilace', *SCO* 10: 5–43.

—— (1963), 'Teopompo e Pseudo-Scilace', *SCO* 12: 16–80.

—— (1979), *Il periplo di Scilace*. Pisa.

Perlman, P. J. (2000), *City and Sanctuary in Ancient Greece*. Göttingen.

—— (2004), 'Crete', *Inv.* 1144–95.

Petronotis, A. (1973), Ἡ Μεγάλη Πόλις τῆς Ἀρκαδίας. Athens.

Peyras, J., and Trousset, P. (1988), 'Le lac Tritonis et les noms anciens du Chott el Jérid', *AntAfr* 24: 149–204.

Pfeiffer, R. (1949–53), *Callimachus*. 2 vols. Oxonii.

Phaklaris, P. V. (1990), Ἀρχαία Κυνουρία. Athina.

Pharaklas, N. (1972a), Ἐπιδαυρία. Athens.

—— (1972b), Τροιζηνία, Καλαύρεια, Μέθανα. Athens.

—— (1973), Ἑρμιονίς-Ἁλιάς. Athens.

Piérart, M. (2004), 'Argolis', *Inv.* 599–619.

Pikoulas, G. A. (1988), Ἡ νότια μεγαλοπολίτικη χώρα. Athina.

Poulain de Bossay, P. A. (1864), 'Recherches sur Tyr et Palaetyr', *Recueil de voyages et de mémoires* 7: 455–680.

Pritchett, W. K. (1989), *Studies in Ancient Greek Topography*, vi. Berkeley–Los Angeles–London.

Radke, G. (1964a), 'Brundisium', *KP* i. 952–3.

—— (1964b), 'Daunia', *KP* i. 1399.

Reber, K., Hansen, M. H., and Ducrey, P. (2004), 'Euboia', *Inv.* 643–63.

Reger, G. (2001), 'The Mykonian synoikismos', *REA* 103: 157–81.

—— (2004), 'The Aegean', *Inv.* 732–93.

Rendić-Miočević, D. (1950), 'Prilozi etnografiji i topografiji naše obale u staro doba, II: Pseudo Skylakov Καταρβάτης ποταμός i južna granica Liburnije', *Historijski zbornik* 3: 221–32.

Richardson, A. (2009), 'Redressing the "Samnites": adornment and identity in central Italy between 750 and 350 BC', Ph.D. University of Reading.

Roesch, P. (1980), 'Le géographe Skylax et la côte méridionale de Béotie', *Mémoires du Centre Jean Palerne* 2: 123–30.

Roller, D. W. (2006), *Through the Pillars of Herakles*. London–New York.

—— (2010), *Eratosthenes, Geography*. Princeton.

Romm, J. S. (1992), *The Edges of the Earth in Ancient Thought*. Princeton.

Rose, V. (1886), *Aristotelis qui ferebantur librorum fragmenta*. Lipsiae.

Roseman, C. H. (1994), *Pytheas of Massalia, On the Ocean*. Chicago.

Rousset, D. (2004a), 'Doris', *Inv.* 674–5.

—— (2004b), 'West Lokris', *Inv.* 391–8.

Roy, J. (1997), 'The perioikoi of Elis', in M. H. Hansen (ed.), *The Polis as an Urban Centre and as a Political Community* (Copenhagen), 282–320.

—— (2002a), 'The pattern of settlement in Pisatis: the "eight poleis" ', in T. H. Nielsen (ed.), *Even More Studies in the Ancient Greek Polis* (Stuttgart), 229–47.

—— (2002b), 'The synoikism of Elis', in T. H. Nielsen (ed.), *Even More Studies in the Ancient Greek Polis* (Stuttgart), 249–64.

Rubinstein, L. (2004a), 'Aiolis and south-western Mysia', *Inv.* 1033–52.

—— (2004b), 'Ionia', *Inv.* 1053–107.

Sakellariou, M., and Faraklas, N. (1971), *Corinthia and Cleonaea*. Athens.

Schepens, G. (1998), '1000 (= 709). Skylax of Karyanda', in J. Bollansée, G. Schepens, J. Engels, and E. Theys (eds), *Felix Jacoby, Die Fragmente der griechischen Historiker Continued*, iv A 1 (Leiden–Boston–Köln), 2–24.

Shepherd, W. R. (1923), *The Historical Atlas*. New York.

Shipley, D. G. J. (1987), *A History of Samos 800–188 BC*. Oxford.

—— (2000), 'The extent of Spartan territory in the late classical and hellenistic periods', *ABSA* 95: 367–90.

—— (2004a), 'Lakedaimon', *Inv.* 569–98.

—— (2004b), 'Messenia', *Inv.* 547–68.

—— (2006), 'Sparta and its perioikic neighbours: a century of re-assessment', *Hermathena* 181: 51–82.

—— (2007), review of P. Counillon, *Pseudo-Skylax, Périple du Pont-Euxin*, *CR* n.s. 57 (2): 346–7.

—— (2008), 'Pseudo-Skylax on the Peloponnese', in C. Gallou, M.

Georgiadis, and G. M. Muskett (eds), *Dioskouroi* (Oxford), 281–91.

—— (2010), 'Pseudo-Skylax on Attica', in N. V. Sekunda (ed.), *Ergasteria: Works presented to John Ellis Jones* (Gdańsk), 100–14.

—— (forthcoming), '2046 [Skylax]', in H.-J. Gehrke (ed.), *Die Fragmente der griechischen Historiker*, v. 2. (Leiden).

—— (under review), 'Pseudo-Skylax the Peripatetic'.

Slim, H., Trousset, P., Paskoff, R., and Oueslati, A. (2004), 'Catalogue des sites', in H. Slim, P. Trousset, R. Paskoff, and A. Oueslati, *Le Littoral de la Tunisie* (Paris), 89–226.

Suić, M. (1953), 'Gdje se nalazilo jezero iz 24. pogl. Pseudo Skilakova Peripla?', *GZMBH* n.s. 8: 111–29.

—— (1955a), 'Granice Liburnije kroz stoljeća', *Radovi Zadar* 2: 273–96.

—— (1955b), 'Istočna jadranska obala u Pseudo Skilakovu Periplu', *Radovi Zadar* 306: 121–85.

Sundwall, G. A. (1996), 'Ammianus geographicus', *AJPh* 117: 619–43.

Talbert, R. J. A. (1974), *Timoleon and the Revival of Greek Sicily 344-317 BC*. Cambridge.

—— (1987), review of O. A. W. Dilke, *Greek and Roman Maps*, *JRS* 77: 210–12.

—— (1989), review of J. B. Harley and D. Woodward, *The History of Cartography*, *AHR* 94 (2): 407–8.

—— (ed. 2000), *Barrington Atlas of the Greek and Roman World*. Princeton–Oxford.

Theiler, W. (ed. (1982), *Posidonios, die Fragmente*, i. Berlin.

Thomas, R. (2000), *Herodotus in Context*. Cambridge.

Tissot, C. (1877), *Recherches sur la géographie comparée de la Maurétanie Tingitane*. Paris.

Tomlinson, R. A. (1972), *Argos and the Argolid*. London.

Trousset, P. (2004), 'Le milieu littoral et les hommes dans l'Antiquité: aspects régionaux', in H. Slim, P. Trousset, R. Paskoff, and A. Oueslati, *Le Littoral de la Tunisie* (Paris), 13–88.

Tuan, Y.-F. (1974), 'Space and place: humanistic perspective', in C. Board, R. J. Chorley, P. Haggett, and D. R. Stoddart (eds), *Progress in Geography*, vi. (London), 211–52.

—— (1977), *Space and Place*. London/Minneapolis.

van Bremen, R. (2003), 'Family structures', in A. Erskine (ed.), *A Companion to the Hellenistic World* (Malden, Mass.), 313–30.

Vandermersch, C. (1994), 'Les îles de Crotone: légende ou réalité de la navigation grecque sur le littoral ionien du Bruttium?', *PP* 49: 241–67.

Vetter, E. (1953), *Handbuch der italischen Dialekte*. Heidelberg.

Vossius, I. (1639), *Periplus Scylacis Caryandensis*. Amstelodami.

Wade-Gery, H. T. (1938), 'The islands of Peisistratos', *AJPh* 59: 470–5.

Walbank, F. W. (1957), *A Historical Commentary on Polybius*, i. Oxford.

—— (1957–79), *A Historical Commentary on Polybius*. 3 vols. Oxford.

Warmington, E. H. (1934), *Greek Geography*. London/Toronto/New York.

Webb, E. J. (1921), 'Cleostratus redivivus', *JHS* 41: 70–85.

—— (1928), 'Cleostratus and his work', *JHS* 48: 54–63.

Wehrli, F. (1967), *Dikaiarchos*, 2nd edn. Basel–Stuttgart.

—— (1969), *Herakleides Pontikos*, 2nd edn. Basel–Stuttgart.

Weitemeyer, C., and Döhler, H. (2009), 'Traces of Roman offshore navigation on Skerki Bank (Strait of Sicily)', *IJNA* 38: 254–80.

Welles, C. B. (1934), *Royal Correspondence in the Hellenistic Period*. New Haven/London/Prague.

West, M. L. (1973), *Textual Criticism and Editorial Technique*.

—— (1989), *Iambi et elegi Graeci ante Alexandrum cantati*, 2nd edn, i: *Archilochus, Hipponax, Theognidea*. Oxford.

White, D., and Wright, G. R. H. (1998), 'Apollonia's east fort and the strategic deployment of cut-down bedrock for defensive walls', *Libyan Studies* 29: 3–33.

Whitelaw, T. M. (1991), 'The polis center of Koresos', in J. F. Cherry, J. L. Davis, and E. Mantzourani, *Landscape Archaeology as Long-term History* (Los Angeles), 265–81.

Wilkes, J. J. (1969), *Dalmatia*. London.

—— (1992), *The Illyrians*. Oxford–Cambridge, Mass.

—— and Fischer-Hansen, T. (2004), 'The Adriatic', *Inv*. 321–37.

Wimmer, F. (ed. 1862), *Theophrasti Eresii opera quae supersunt omnia*, iii. Leipzig.

Wirbelauer, E. (1998), 'Kephallenia und Ithaka: historisch-geographische und quellenkritische Untersuchungen zu zwei Inseln im ionischen Meer', Habilitationsschrift. Universität Freiburg.

Wiseman, J. (1978), *The Land of the Ancient Corinthians*. Göteborg.

Zaninović, M. (1991–2), 'Heraclea Pharia', *VAMZ* 34–5: 35–48.

Zhmud, L. (2006), *The Origin of the History of Science in Classical Antiquity*. Berlin–New York.

SELECT INDEX

This covers (1) names in the Greek text (section numbers also indicate relevant passages of Translation and Commentary; main reference in **bold**); (2) topics in the Introduction (section I, II, etc.; these topics in **bold**). Forms of names vary. '*Polis*' is not indexed; *chora* selectively. Mythical and historical names (non-literary) are in SMALL CAPITALS. Some entries cover a place and its cognates (e.g. *ethnikon*). *Bis, ter, quater* = 2–4 occurrences; for more, '(5)', etc., are used. Where a name is emended or excised in the Greek text, the locator is in [ ]. *s.a. = see also.*

Abdera, §67. 2
Abilyke, §111. 6
Abrotonon, §110. 2, 3 *bis*
Abydos, §94
Academy (Athens), VII
Achaioi: (*a*) Black Sea, **§75,** §76; (*b*) Peloponnese, **§42,** §43; *chora*, §42; (*c*) A. Phthiotai, **§63** *ter*, §64. 1 *bis*
Achaiōn Limen, §98. 2
Acheloös, R., §34. 2 *bis*, 3
Acheron, R., §30 *bis*
Acherousia, §30
Achilleion, §95
Achilleios Limen, §46. 1
ACHILLES, §68. 4
Adramyttion, §98. 2 *bis*
Adrias (Kolpos), §14 *bis*, §15, §17 *bis*, §18 *ter*, §27. 2 *bis*
Adrymes, §110. 7, 8, 10
Adyrmachidai, **§107. 1**
Aëdonia, §108. 2
Agora (city), §67. 6
agriculture (*s.a.* wheat; fruit-trees), §24. 1, §94
Aia, §81
Aias, R., §26. 1 *bis*
Aigai: (*a*) Achaia, §42; (*b*) Mysia, §98. 2
Aigaion Pelagos, §58. 4
Aigeira, §42
Aigeiros, §39
Aigilia, §113. 2 *ter*
Aigina, §53, §114
Aigion, §42
Aigipios, R., §79
Aigos Potamos, §67. 5

Aigosthena, §39
Aigyptos, §20, §105. 1, 2, **§106. 1,** 2, 3 *ter*, §111. 8, §112. 12; Aigyptioi, §105. 2, §106. 5, §107. 3; *Aigyptia lithos*, §112. 10; Aigypt—, §105. 2
aims, ðf PS, V
Aineia, §66. 2
Ainianes, §35, §62. 2, §64. 1
Ainos, §67. 3
Ainioi, §67. 3
Aiolides poleis, §96
Aiolis, **§96,** §98. 1; *A. nesos,* §97
Airai, §98. 3
Aithalia, §6
AITHIOPES: Great, §1; Sacred, §112. 5, 8 *bis*, 9 *bis*, 11, 12
Aitolia, **§35** *ter*; Aitoloi, §35, §36
Akadamis, §98. 3
Akanthos, §66. 4
Akarnanes, §34. 1, 2; Akarnania, **§34. 1,** 2, 3, §35
Ake, §104. 3
Akion, §111. 5
Akra (*polis*), §111. 5
Akragas, §13. 3
Akros, §111. 5
Akrothoöi, §66. 4
Akte (Akarnania), §34. 1
Alapta, §66. 4
Alfaterni, §15
ALKINOÖS, §22. 1
alluvation, §34. 3
Alope, §60

Alopekonnesos, §67. 5
Aloros, §66. 2
Alphaternioi, §15
Alpheios, R., §43
altars, §109. 3, §112. 4
Alyzia, §34. 2
Amane, §102. 1
Amantes, §26. 3; Amantia, §26. 1, §26. 2; *chora*, §27. 1; Amantieis, [§27. 1]
Amathous, §103
Ambrakia, **§33. 1,** 2, §34. 1, §65. 2
Ambrakikos Kolpos, §34. 1
Ameneia, §88
Ammonos Alsos, §109. 3
Amorgos, §58. 2
Ampelos, §108. 5
Amphenai, §64. 1
Amphilochian Argos, §34. 1
Amphipolis, §67. 1
Amphissa, §36
Amyros, §65. 1
Anaia, §98. 3
Anaktorikos Kolpos §31 *bis*
Anaktorion, §34. 1
Anaphe, §48
Anaphlystos, §57. 2
Anaplous, §67. 8
anchorages, §108. 2 *bis*, 3, cf. §112. 7
ANDROMEDA, §104. 3
Andros, §58. 1, 3, §113. 1 *bis*
Anemourion, §102. 1
Anides, R., §112. 3 *bis*
animals (*s.a.* pastoral

238   INDEX

Daunitai, §15, §16; *chora* of, §15

days, of sailing, IV, VI; half-days (W. Europe), §6, §11, §13. 4, §24. 2, §28, §30, §31; (continuous Hellas) §36, §37, §38, §40; (Asia) §101. 1; (Libyē) §107. 2 *bis*, §108. 1 *ter*, §110. 5, 7, 10 *bis*, §111. 1; mornings, §64. 2, §13. 1 *ter*, 2 *bis*; onethird, §7

Delion, §59 *bis*

Delos, §58. 1

Delphikos Kolpos, §35

Delphoi, §37

DEMETER, §57. 1

Demetrion, §63

Deris, §67. 3

deserted places: cities, §102. 1, §109. 4; harbours, §103; islands, §6, §7, §34. 3, §68. 4, §106. 5, §107. 1, §110. 7, §111. 5

diaphragmata, VI

Dikaia, §67. 2

Dikaiarchos, VI, VII

Diktynnaion, §47. 3

DIOMEDES, hero, §16

Dion, §66. 2, 4

Dionysias, §100. 1

Dioskourias, §81

distances, IV, VI

Dolopes, §64. 1

Dorieis, §62. 1

Doros, §104. 3

Douriskos, §67. 3

Drepanon, §109. 3

Drinaupa, §111. 5

Drys, §67. 3

Dyme, §42

Echedoros, R., §66. 2

Echinades, Is., §34. 3

Echinos, §62. 2

Ekdippa, §104. 3

Ekecheirieis, §83, §84

Elaia: (a) Mysia), §98. 2; (b) Thesprotia, §30

Elaious, §67. 5, 6

Elaphonnesos, §94

Elateia, §61

Elea, §12

Eleioi (of Elis), §43

Elektrides, Is., §21. 2

Eleusis, §57. 1

Eleuthernai, §47. 4

Elis: *ethnos*, §43, §44; *polis*, §43; Eleioi, §43

ELPENOR, hero, §8

Elymoi, §13. 2

Elyros, §47. 3

emporia, see trading-towns

Emporion, §2, §3

Encheleios, R.? §108. 5

Encheleis, §25

enclosed harbours, §29, §33. 1, §47. 3 *bis*, §58. 1, §67. 1, §88, §98. 3, 4, §99. 1 *bis*, 2, §103, §104. 2

Enetoi, §19 *bis*, §20

Epeiros, §26. 3; introductory n. to §§28–33. 1

Ephesos, §98. 3

Ephoros, VII

Epidamnos, §25, §26. 1 *bis*

Epidauros: (a) Argolis, §54, §55; *chora*, §50. 1, 2, §54; (b) Laconia, §46. 2

Epileukadioi, §34. 1

Erasistratios, §98. 3

Eresos, §97

Eretria, §58. 3, 4

Eridanos, R. (Italy), §19

Erineos, §62. 1

Erytheia (Illyria), §26. 3

Erythra Thalassa, §105. 1

Erythrai, §98. 2

Eschides, §110. 6 *bis*

ethnē, V, VI

ethnography, VII

Euanthis, §36

Euboia: (a) Greece, §58. 3 *ter*, §60, §114; (b) Libyē, §111. 5

Euripos: (a) Akarnania, §34. 1; (b) Boiotia, §59, §113. 1

Europe: boundaries, §68. 5, §106. 3; cape of, §112. 2; distance from other land masses, §13. 1, §47. 1, §111. 7, §112. 2, §113. 1; first people in, §2; Pillars, §1 *bis*, §69, §111. 7; rivers, §69; sailing length, §69, §92. 2,

§111. 8

Eurotas, R., §46. 1

Eurymedon, R., §101. 1

Eurymenai, §65. 1

Eutresis, §38

Euxeinos Pontos (s.a. Pontos), §67. 1

Exope, §104. 3

fire, §100. 1, §112. 9

forts (s.a. Teichos): Ambrakia, §33. 1; continuous Hellas, §38, §39, §46. 1, §55 *ter*, §56, §57. 1, 2 *quater*, §59 *bis*; Sicily, §13. 3; Syria, §104. 3; Thrake, §67. 3, 7

founders (s.a. colonies), §22. 2, §67. 2

Frentani, §15

fruit-trees (s.a. olivetrees), §108. 4, §110. 4

Gadeira, §2, §111. 6, [7]

Gagaia, §100. 1

Galepsos, §67. 1

Ganiai, §67. 7

Ganos, §67. 7

Gaphara, §110. 1, 2

Garden of Hesperides, §108. 4

Gargara, §96

Gaulos, §111. 3

Gela, §13. 3

Gelon, §80

Genesintis, §88

genre, periplographic, VIII

geography: in Academy and Peripatos, VI, VII; in PS, V, VI; PS's contribution, I.9

geology, VII

Geraistos, §58. 3, §113. 1 *bis*

Geraneia, §39

GERYONES, §26. 3

Gichthis, §110. 5 *bis*

Gortyna, §47. 4

Gryneion, §98. 2

Gyenos: *polis*, §81; river, §81

Gynaikokratoumenoi, §70, §71

Gytheion, §46. 1

Gyzantes, §110. 9 *bis*

---

sources, of PS, VII
Spalauthra, §65. 1
Sparta, §46. 2
Spercheios, R., §62. 1, 2
Spina, §17
stades (stadia), IV, VI
Stephane, §90
Strymon, R., §66. 5, §67. 1, 10 bis
Stymphalos, §44
Suda, on PS, II
Sybaris, §13. 5
Sybrita, §47. 4
Sylleion, §101. 1
Symaithos, R., §13. 3
Syrakousai, §13. 3
Syria (s.a. Koile S.; Syroi), §104. 1, §105. 1, 2
Syrmatai, §68. 5
Syroi, §104. 1
Syros I., §58. 1
Syrtis: (a) Greater, §109. 1, 2 bis, 3 quater, 4 bis, 5, §110. 1, 8 ('other'), 9; (b) Lesser, §110. 1 ('other'), 8 bis ('Kerkinitis'), 10
Tainaros, §46. 1
Tanaïs, R., §68. 5, §69, §70
Tanitikon Stoma, §106. 1, 2
Taras, §14
Taricheiai, §110. 3, 4 bis
Taucheira, §108. 5
Taulantioi, §26. 1
Taurike, §68. 2 bis, 5
Tauroëis, [§4]
Tauroi, §68. 2
Tauromenion, §13. 3
Tegea, §44
Teichos (s.a. forts), §67. 7 bis; T. Boiotōn, see §38 comm.
Teiristasis, §67. 7
TELEPHOS, §98. 2
Telmissos, §100. 1
Telos, §99. 3
Tempe, §64. 1
Tenedos, §95
Tenos, §58. 1, §113. 1 bis
Teos, §98. 3
Terias, R., §13. 3
Terina, §12
Tetrakis, §89
Teuthrania, §98. 1
text, of PS, I

Thapsa, §111. 5
Thapsakos, R. (Kilikia), §102. 1 bis, §104. 2, 3
Thapsos, §110. 7 ter
Thasos, §67. 1, §114; Thasioi, §67. 1
Thebai: (a) Boiotia, §59; (b) Phthiotic, §63
Themiskyra, §89
Theophrastos, VII
Theopompos, VII
Theou Prosopon, Mt, §104. 2
Thera, §48
Thermai Himeraiai, §13. 3 comm.
Thermaios Kolpos, §66. 1
Therme, §66. 2
Thermodon, R., §89
Thermopylai, §62. 1
Thespiai, §59
Thesprotia, §29, §30, §31; Thesprotoi, §30
Thettalia, §64. 1 ter, §65. 1; Thettaloi, §64. 1
Theudosia, §68. 3
Thines, Herakleioi, §109. 3
Thonis, §106. 1, §107. 1
Thorikos, §57. 2
Thouria, §12, §13. 5; Thourioi (people), §12
Thrake, §66. 5, §67. 1 bis, 3, 9, 10 bis, §68. 1, §92. 1 bis; (Bithynian), §93; Thrakes Bithynoi, §92. 1; Thrakia Chersonesos, §67. 5, 6 bis; Thrakian forts, §66. 7
Thrambeïs, §66. 3
Thronion, §61
Thymiateria, §112. 4 bis
Thynias, §92. 1
Thyrrheion, §34. 1
Thyssos, §66. 4
Tibarenoi, §87, §88
tides, §1, §110. 9, cf. §112. 2
Tieion, §90
Tiryns, §49
Tisai, §65. 1
Toretai, §73, §75
Torikos, §74
Torone, §66. 4
Trachis (= Herakleia),

§62. 1
traders, V, §112. 7, 10, 11
trading-towns: Europe, §1, §2, §24. 1 bis, 2, §67. 1, 3 ter, §68. 2; Asia, §102. 1; Libyē, §111. 9
Tragyras, §23. 2
translation, of PS, I
Trapezous, §85
trees (s.a. fruit-t.; olive-t.), §110. 4
Trieres, §104. 2
Triopion, C., §99. 2
Tripolis: (a) Tripoli, Lebanon, §104. 2; (b) T. Phoinikōn, §104. 2
triremes (s.a. ships; Trieres), §24. 1
Triton, R., §110. 8
TRITONIS ATHENA, §110. 8
Tritonos Nesos, §110. 8
Troas, §95; Troes, §13. 2
Troia, §106. 5
Troizen, §52. 1; Troizenia, §51. 2, §54
Tyndareioi Skopeloi, §108. 1 bis
Tyras, R., §68. 1
Tyros, §104. 2 bis, 3; Tyrioi, §104. 3 (6)
Tyrrhen-ia, §6 bis, §8, [§17]; -oi, §5, §17 bis, §18; -ikon Pelagos, §15, §17
variatio, VIII
verbal maps, V
vines, §108. 4, 5, §112. 11
wheat, §110. 4
wine (s.a. vines), §110. 4, §112. 11
women, §21. 1, §70, §112. 9
world measurement, VI
Xanthos: polis, §100. 1; river, §100. 1
Xion, R., §112. 5
Xiphoneios, §13. 3
Zakynthos, §43, §114
Zenertis, §108. 5
Zephyrion, §102. 1
Zephyrios Limen, §86
ZEUS, §104. 3; Kenaios, §58. 3
Zone, §67. 3